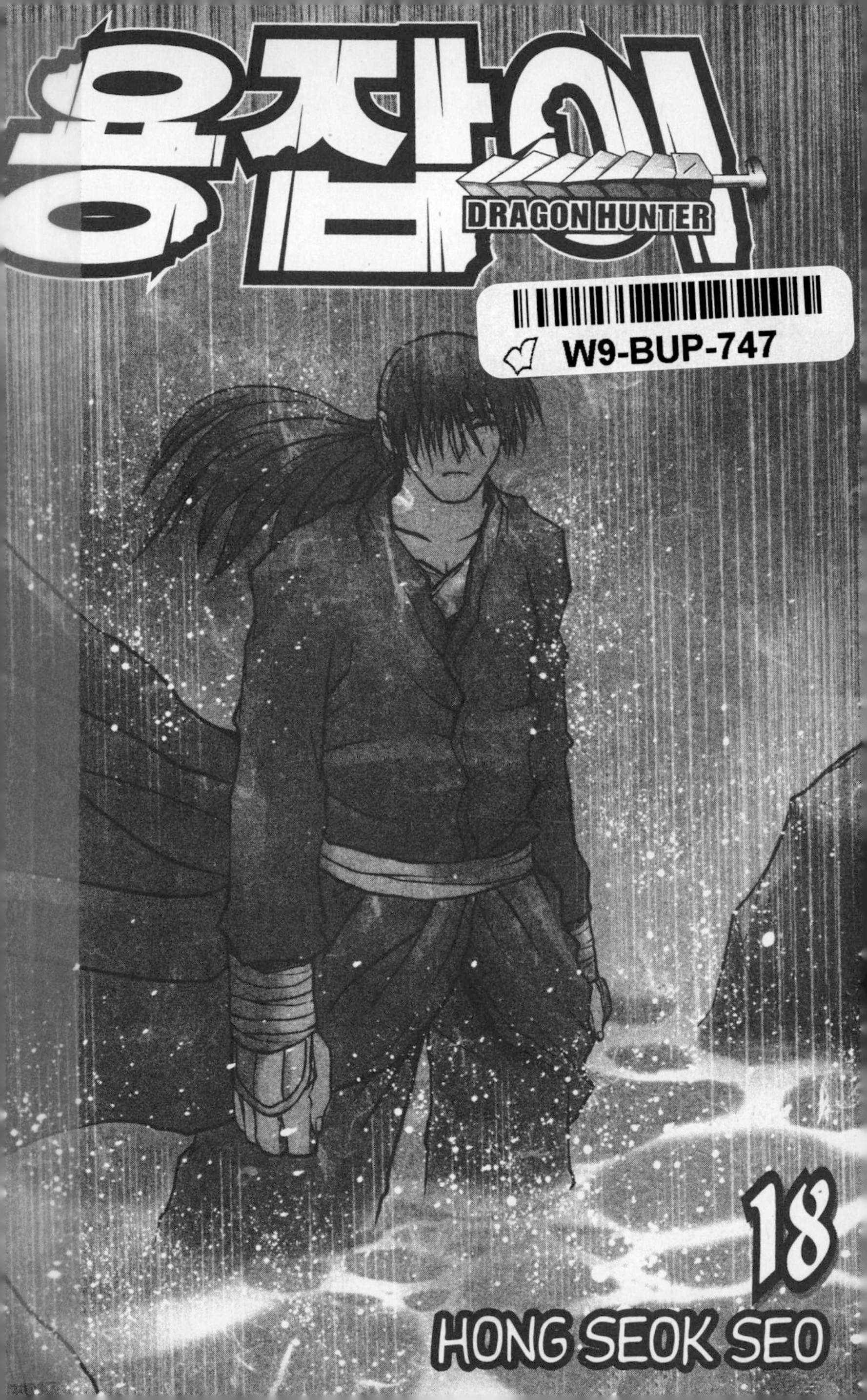
용잡이
DRAGON HUNTER
W9-BUP-747
18
HONG SEOK SEO

Dragon Hunter Volume 18
Created by Hong Seock Seo

Translation - Hye Young Im
English Adaptation - Magdalena Sniegocki
Copy Editor - Shannon Watters
Retouch and Lettering - Star Print Brokers
Production Artist - Vicente Rivera, Jr.
Graphic Designer - James Lee

Editor - Nikhil Burman
Digital Imaging Manager - Chris Buford
Pre-Production Supervisor - Lucas Rivera
Production Manager - Elisabeth Brizzi
Managing Editor - Vy Nguyen
Creative Director - Anne Marie Horne
Editor-in-Chief - Rob Tokar
Publisher - Mike Kiley
President and C.O.O. - John Parker
C.E.O. and Chief Creative Officer - Stu Levy

A 🐢 TOKYOPOP® Manga

TOKYOPOP and 🐢 are trademarks or registered trademarks of TOKYOPOP Inc.

TOKYOPOP Inc.
5900 Wilshire Blvd. Suite 2000
Los Angeles, CA 90036

E-mail: info@TOKYOPOP.com
Come visit us online at www.TOKYOPOP.com

ISBN: 978-1-59532-654-6

First TOKYOPOP printing: June 2008
10 9 8 7 6 5 4 3 2 1
Printed in the USA

Dragon Hunter™

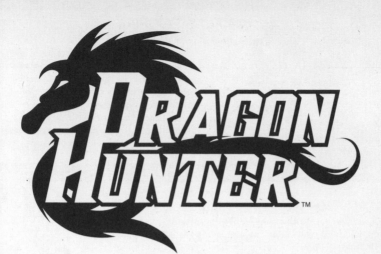

Volume 18

By

Hong Seock Seo

with

Studio Redstone

TOKYOPOP®

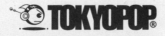

HAMBURG // LONDON // LOS ANGELES // TOKYO

WHO'S WHO IN DRAGON HUNTER

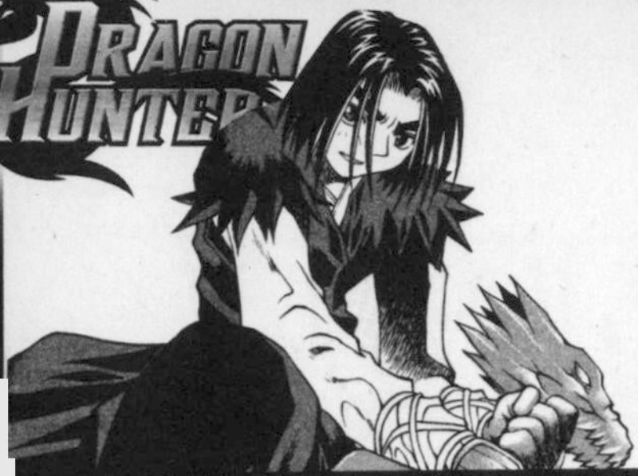

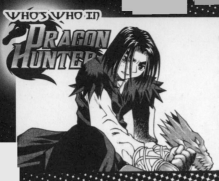

SEUR-CHONG:

There's only on thing Seur-Chong loves more than hunting dragons, and that's getting paid for doing it. He's infected with the Dragon's Curse, a condition that gives him incredible strength and stamina but is slowly killing him. Despite his greedy nature,he has a heart almost as big as his enormous sword.

MYUNG-HO:

A shaman born with exceptional gifts, Myung-Ho can control the minds of most lesser dragons, and assists Seur-Chong with his slaying. After one particular fierce battle left Myung-Ho mortally wounded, Seur-Chong purposely infected Myun-Ho with the Dragon's Curse in order to save the shaman's life. As a result, Myun-Ho's mystical powers increased, and he gained precognitive and clairvoyant abilities that manifest themselves in the third form of a third eye that appears on his forhead.

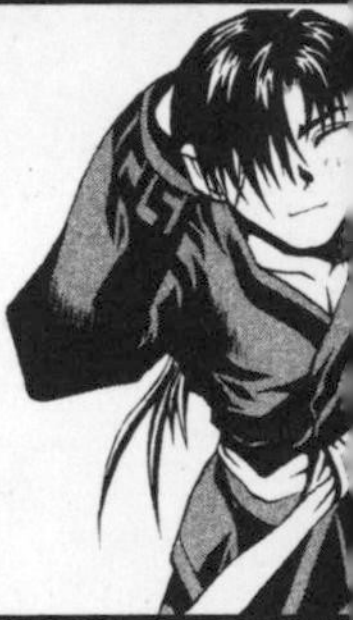

MONG-YEUN:

A shaman with a soft spot for dragons, she was in So-Chun's service until she stole a dragon from her master. Now she works with Seur-Chong and Myung-Ho, but she finds the mercenary lifestyle--and the frequent empty stomachs that come with it--not to her liking. It appears Myung-Ho has a secret crush on Mong-Yeun, though Mong-Yeun seems to be attracted to Seur-Chong.

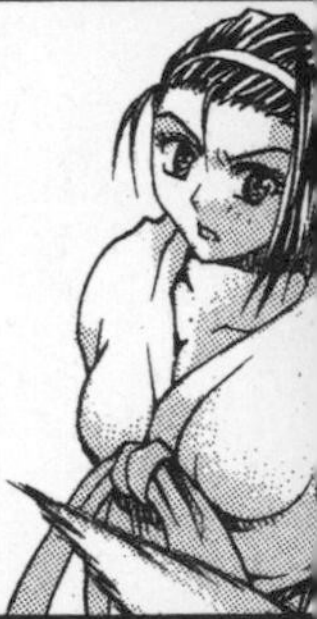

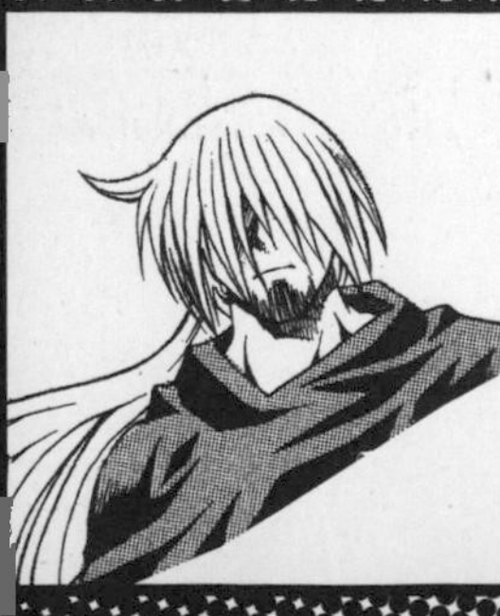

DAECHANG-NIM / SEUR-CHUN

A former leader of the Invisible Shadow Killer Clan of the Chunjoo. Like Seur-Chong, Seur-Chun has the Dragon's Curse. He recently revealed that Yeun-Wha (Seur-Chong's mother) is his wife, and that Seur-Chong is his son.

Fruits Basket
By Natsuki Takaya
Volume 20

Can Tohru deal with the truth?

After running away from his feelings and everyone he knows, Kyo is back with the truth about his role in the death of Tohru's mother. But how will he react when Tohru says that she still loves him?

Winner of the American Anime Award for Best Manga!

The #1 selling shojo manga in America!

© 1998 Natsuki Takaya / HAKUSENSHA, Inc.

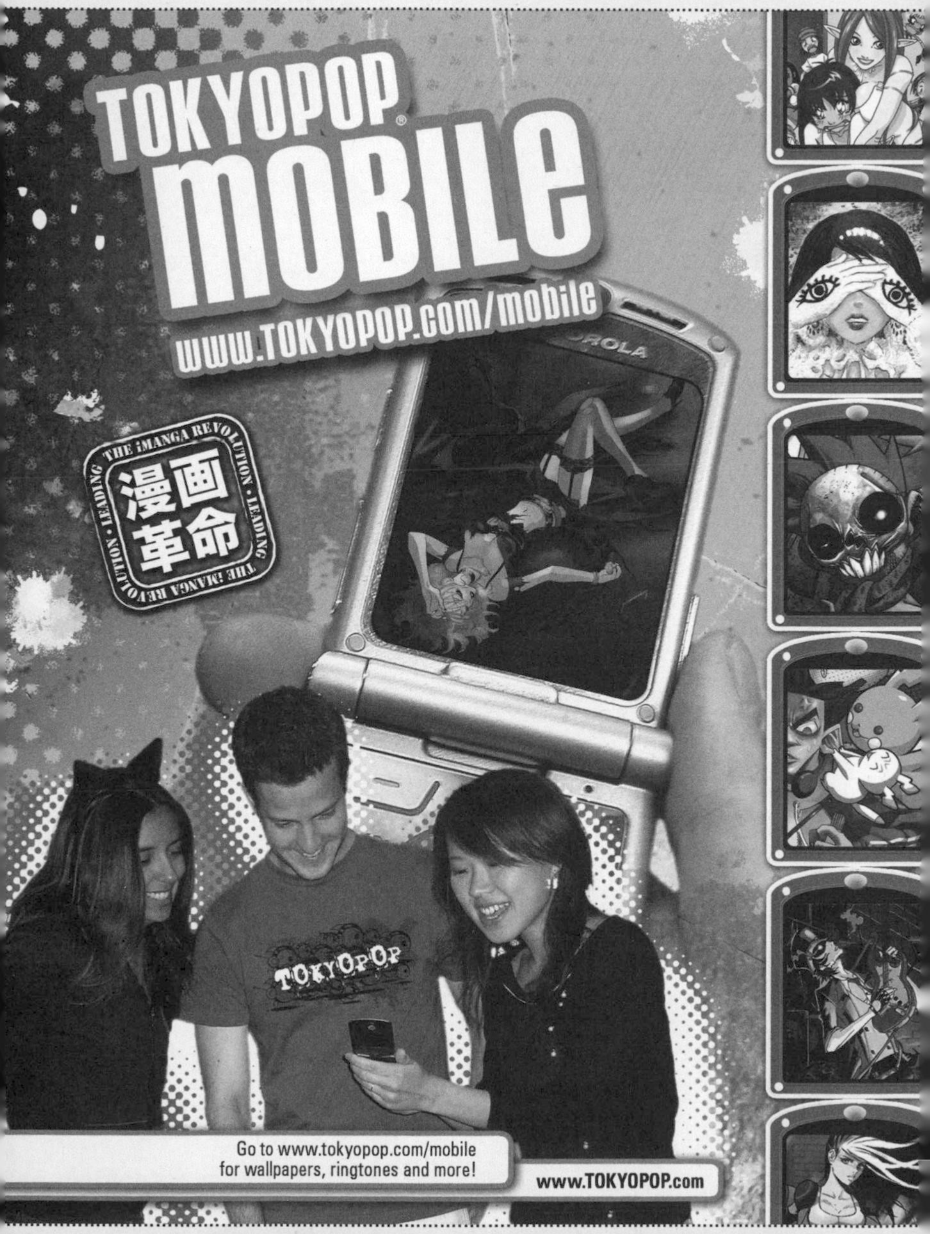
TOKYOPOP®
MOBILE
www.TOKYOPOP.com/mobile
THE iMANGA REVOLUTION · LEADING
漫画革命
LEADING · THE iMANGA REVOLUTION
TOKYOPOP
Go to www.tokyopop.com/mobile
for wallpapers, ringtones and more!
www.TOKYOPOP.com

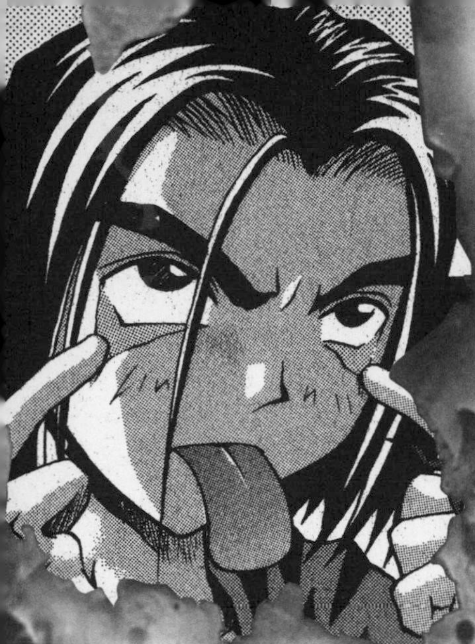

DRAGON HUNTER

IN THE NEXT VOLUME OF

DRAGON HUNTER

The climax is building...
Who will live? Who will die? What outrageous action is yet to be seen? What spine-tingling secrets are yet to be revealed?!

The only way to find out for sure is by reserving your volume of DRAGON HUNTER volume 19 today!

The fight continues in DRAGON HUNTER volume 19!

THE STUDIO REDSTONE STORY (CHAPTER 18)

HELLO, THIS IS HONG-SEOK.
THIS IS VOLUME 18.

THE WEATHER IS...
...REALLY VERY NICE!
TREES ARE GETTING GREENER.

HERE'S SOME NEWS FROM GLOOMY STUDIO REDSTONE. ^^;;

I'VE GIVEN UP GAMES FOR A WHILE. T.T
I HAVEN'T BEEN PLAYING MY XBX, PS2 OR GC. SOB!
I THOUGHT I WOULDN'T BE ABLE TO WORK IF I BROUGHT THEM INTO THE STUDIO.
SO THEY ARE DISPLAYED IN MY HOUSE.
AT LEAST I'M HAPPY ABOUT PLAYING GAMEBOY ADVANCE SP.
I HEARD SO MANY NEW AWESOME GAMES ARE COMING THIS YEAR...SOB...
AND PSP IS COMING, TOO... THIS IS THE SEASON OF TEMPTATION.

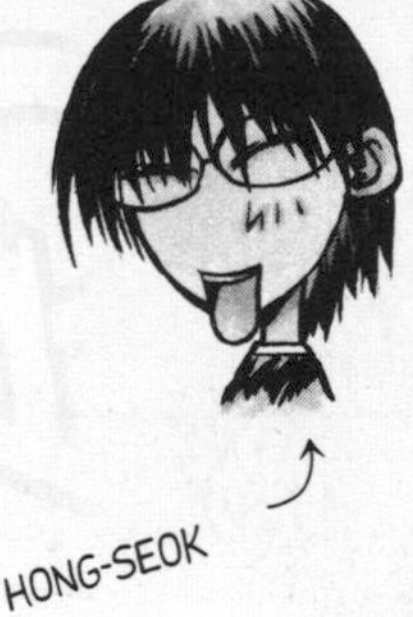
HONG-SEOK

MAY IS A HARD MONTH FOR EVERYONE SINCE THERE ARE SO MANY FAMILY EVENTS.
BUT IT'S HARDER FOR ME BECAUSE I'M LEARNING TO DRIVE AT THIS LATE STAGE IN MY LIFE.
I HOPE TO GET MY DRIVER'S LICENSE BEFORE VOLUME 19 COMES OUT.
I THOUGHT I WOULDN'T EVER NEED A CAR, BUT I REALIZED HOW MUCH I NEED ONE NOW THAT I'M MARRIED.
SO I'M TRYING HARD TO LEARN. (AT THIS POINT, I ONLY HAVE THE ROAD TEST LEFT.)

IF YOU ARE SOMEONE WHO BUYS DRAGON HUNTER, THIS ISN'T DIRECTED AT YOU,
BUT I FEEL I HAVE TO SAY THIS HERE. A FEW DAYS AGO, I SAW A SCANLATION OF DH.
I FELT WEIRD ABOUT IT. (HAPPY CUZ PEOPLE WERE READING IT, SAD BECAUSE IT'S SO WRONG!)
I KNOW MANY PEOPLE LIKE FREE THINGS, BUT...THIS IS A COPYRIGHT VIOLATION.
I FEEL REALLY SAD ABOUT THE WHOLE SITUATION... T.T

I KNOW IT'S NOT EASY TO RESIST DOWNLOADING FREE STUFF FROM THE INTERNET.
BUT--THIS IS MY LITTLE WISH--PLEASE REMEMBER:
IT'S NOT RIGHT TO DOWNLOAD SCANNED COMICS.

OK, ENOUGH OF THE HEAVY STUFF.
NEXT TIME I TALK TO YOU, I'LL BE DRIVER HONG.

SEE YOU IN VOLUME 19!

HONG-SEOK SEO
MAY 23, 2004

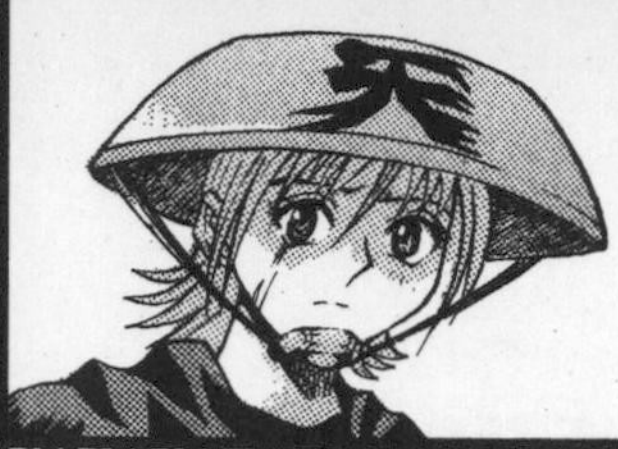

RU-AHN

The general's right-hand woman. Daechang-Nim assassinated her father, and it seemed she was biding her time as his assistant until she could avenge her father's death. However, though she recently had the perfect opportunity, she mysteriously did not take her revenge.

TAE-RANG / KOK-JUNG

A former colleague turned rival of Seur-Chong, formerly known as Kok-Jung (which means "worry" in Korean).

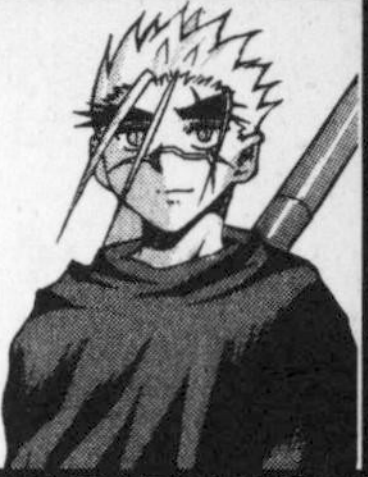

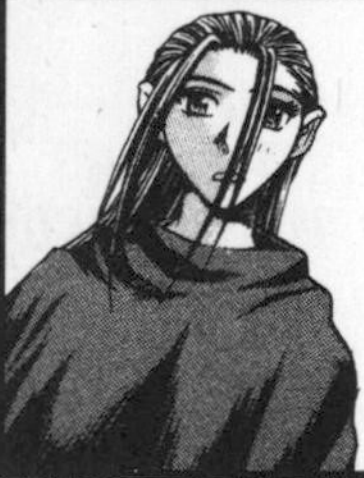

BEUL-HEE

A sometimes mean and stuck-up shaman, Beul-Hee trained at the same time and place as Mong-Yeun...though Mong-Yeun's abilities far outshined Beul-Hee's. When her training had been completed, Beul-Hee's first assignment was to a rough, unglamorous area near the Chinese border.

SO-CHUN

A powerful shaman, she's also the feudal lord of the Kaya Province. She served as a shaman's apprentice under Yeun-Wha, and she was Mong-Yeun's superior. Though a basically good person, So-Chun does have her petty side... which she shows to Mong-Yeun more often than not.

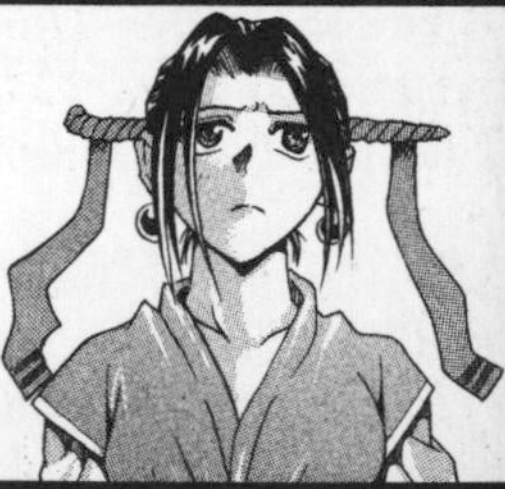

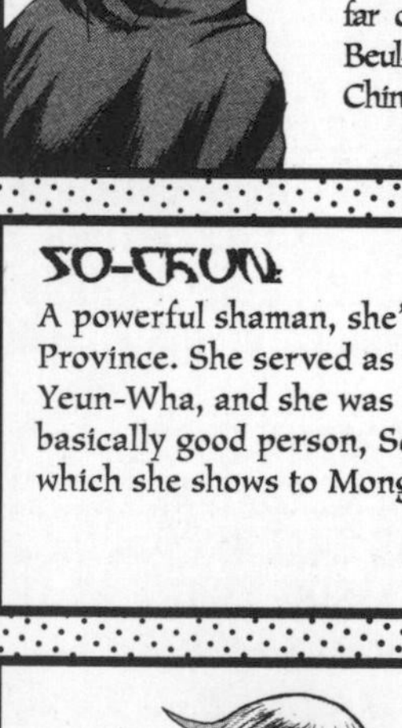

RIAH

The illegitimate daughter of the legendary King Arthur, she wields the spirit sword Excalibur, which is an astral version of the original sword.

THE STORY THUS FAR

SEUR-CHONG IS AN ELITE (AND CASH-OBSESSED) DRAGON HUNTER WHO, DUE TO AN INVOLUNTARY INFUSION OF DRAGON'S BLOOD, POSSESSES INCREDIBLE STRENGTH AND DURABILITY...ALONG WITH A SUBSTANTIALLY SHORTENED LIFESPAN. SEUR-CHONG'S PARTNER, MYUNG-HO, IS A SHAMAN WHO CAN USE MAGIC TO CONTROL DRAGONS--AND THUS MAKE THEM EASIER TO KILL.

DURING A PARTICULARLY DIFFICULT DRAGON HUNT, THE CHUNJOO--A MYSTERIOUS AND POWERFUL DRAGON-HUNTING GANG THAT DOESN'T TOLERATE COMPETITION--INTERFERED AND MORTALLY WOUNDED MYUNG-HO.

SEEING ONLY ONE WAY TO SAVE MYUNG-HO'S LIFE, SEUR-CHONG GAVE HIS DYING FRIEND A DRINK OF DRAGON'S BLOOD. THE YOUNG SHAMAN'S STRENGTH WAS RESTORED, BUT NOW MYUNG-HO MUST ENDURE THE DREADED DRAGON'S CURSE: POWER THAT WILL EVENTUALLY COST HIM HIS LIFE. MYUNG-HO HAS ALREADY MANIFESTED AN INCREDIBLE "SECOND SIGHT"...SEEN THROUGH A MONSTROUS THIRD EYE THAT APPEARS IN THE MIDDLE OF HIS FOREHEAD!

LATER, AN ATTEMPT BY THE DUO TO END THE DRAGON'S CURSE BY SLAYING THE DRAGON GOD, SEVERAL LIVES WERE LOST, AND REVELATIONS WERE FOUND--ONE OF THEM BEING THAT THE DAECHANG-NIM (LEADER OF THE GROUP OF ASSASSINS KNOWN AS THE CHUNJOO) WAS ACTUALLY SEUR-CHUN, SEUR-CHONG'S FATHER.

SOON AFTER, SEUR-CHUN LEARNED THAT ASSISTING SEUR-CHONG IN HIS HUNT FOR THE DRAGON GOD PUT BOTH OF THEM AND ALL OF THEIR ASSOCIATES ON THE CHUNJOO'S MOST-WANTED LIST.

BELIEVING THE BEST DEFENSE TO BE A GOOD OFFENSE, SEUR-CHONG AND MYUNG-HO VENTURE TO SHI-LA TO DESTROY THE CHUNJOO ONCE AND FOR ALL...BUT FOR EACH ENEMY THEY FIGHT, THEY'VE FOUND AS MANY SHOCKING AND UNFORSEEN TRUTHS!

HYUN-JONG REVEALS THAT HE IS A SUCCESSOR OF THE SHAMANIC COUNCIL. MEANWHILE, MONG-YEUN DISCOVERS TWO SHOCKING THINGS ABOUT HER PAST: THAT SA-MI IS HER SISTER AND CHONG-KWAN-JANG IS HER FATHER. FURTHERMORE, CHONG-KWAN-JANG ALSO REVEALS THAT HE HAD A HAND IN CREATING THE WORLD OF DRAGON HUNTERS. AND LATER, DURING A FACE-OFF AGAINST CHONG-KWAN-JANG, GOON-CHUN DISCOVERS A SHOCKING SECRET: SA-MI AND MONG-YEUN ARE CHONG-KWAN-JANG'S DAUGHTERS.

AS CHONG-KWAN-JANG'S SECRETS ARE REVEALED, SEUR-CHONG AND HIS GANG TRY TO STOP HIM BUT DISCOVER HIS POWER IS GREATER THAN THEY THOUGHT. MEANWHILE, GOONG-CHUN AND MYUNG-HO ATTEMPT TO RESCUE MONG-YEUN AND SA-MI WHO ARE UNDER CHONG-KWAN-JANG'S SPELL.

DRAGON HUNTER

ABOUT DRAGON HUNTER, PART 18

HELLO, READERS OF DRAGON HUNTER.
THIS IS HONG SEOCK.

IT'S ALREADY VOLUME 18. I STARTED THE
STORY OF THE WOOSAN KINGDOM IN VOLUME 17,
AND IT CONTINUES IN THIS VOLUME. I WOULD
LIKE TO TALK ABOUT YOH-E-JU THIS TIME.

A YOH-E-JU IS A CRYSTAL BALL THAT A DRAGON
MUST HAVE TO ASCEND TO HEAVEN. ACCORDING
TO LEGEND, A YOH-E-JU CAN TRANSFORM
HUMANS, READ PEOPLE'S MINDS, MAKE THEM
FLY AND DO OTHER FANTASTIC THINGS.

IN THIS BOOK, DRAGONS HAVE LOTS OF POWER.
THEY CULTIVATE IT FROM WHEN THEY'RE
HATCHLINGS, AND WHEN THEY FINALLY GROW
INTO FULL-BLOWN DRAGONS, THEY USE ALL
THE POWER THEY CAN MUSTER TO GO TO
HEAVEN WITH A YOH-E-JU IN THEIR MOUTHS.

I INTEND TO HAVE MORE DRAGONS COME YOUR WAY.
THIS BOOK IS CALLED DRAGON HUNTER, YOU KNOW...

PLEASE ENJOY THE BOOK!

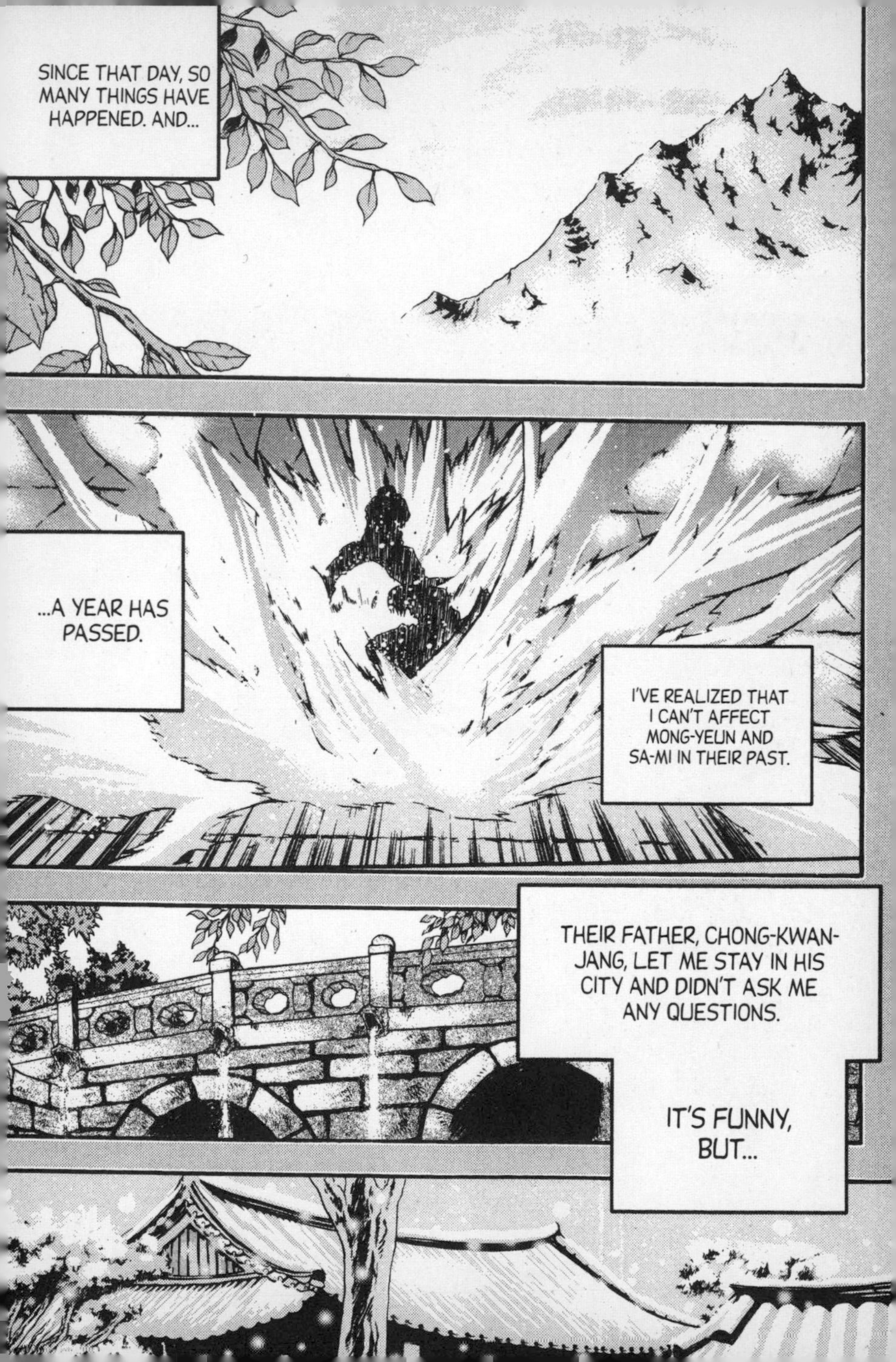
SINCE THAT DAY, SO MANY THINGS HAVE HAPPENED. AND...
...A YEAR HAS PASSED.
I'VE REALIZED THAT I CAN'T AFFECT MONG-YEUN AND SA-MI IN THEIR PAST.
THEIR FATHER, CHONG-KWAN-JANG, LET ME STAY IN HIS CITY AND DIDN'T ASK ME ANY QUESTIONS.
IT'S FUNNY, BUT...

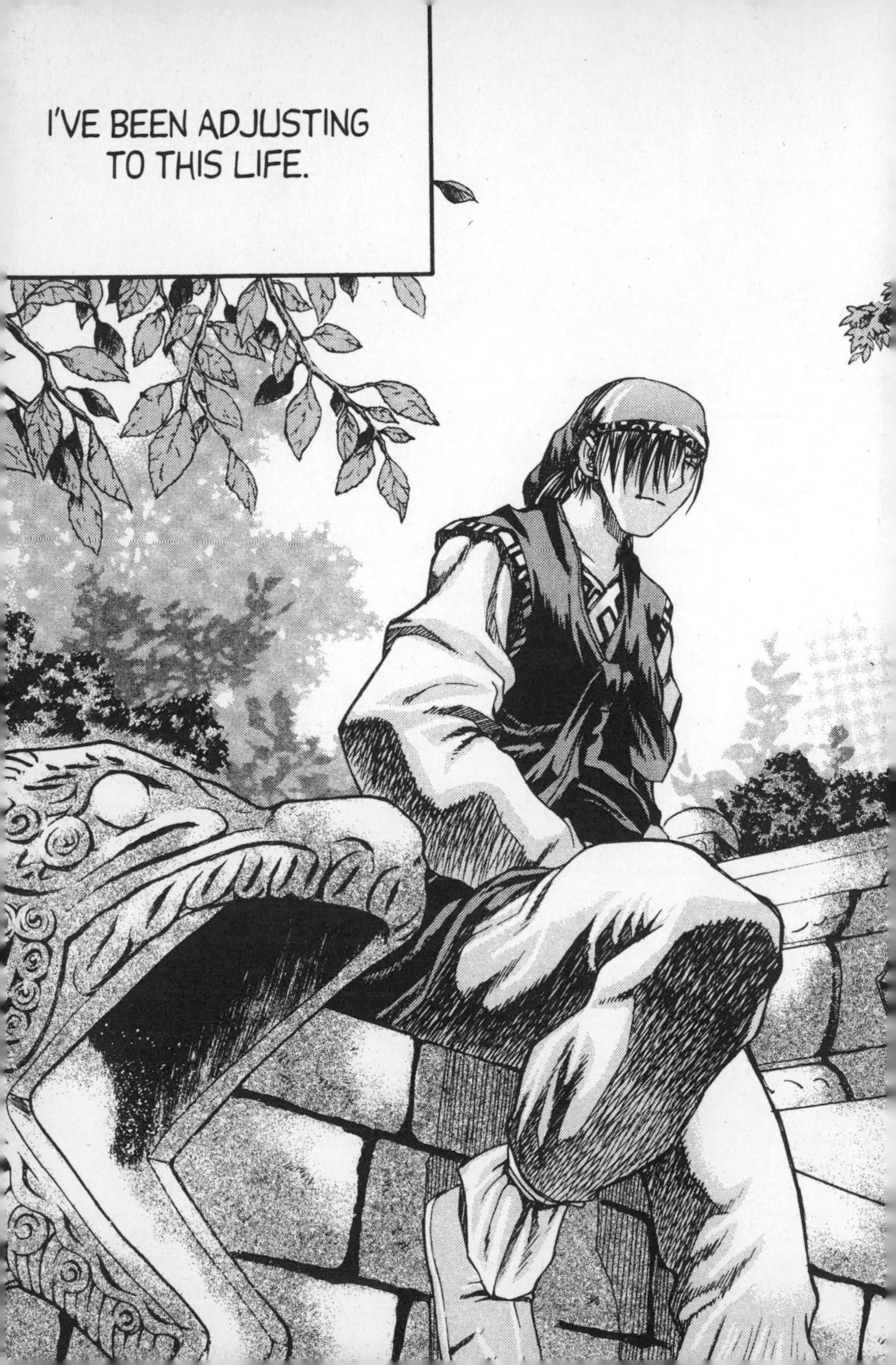
I'VE BEEN ADJUSTING TO THIS LIFE.

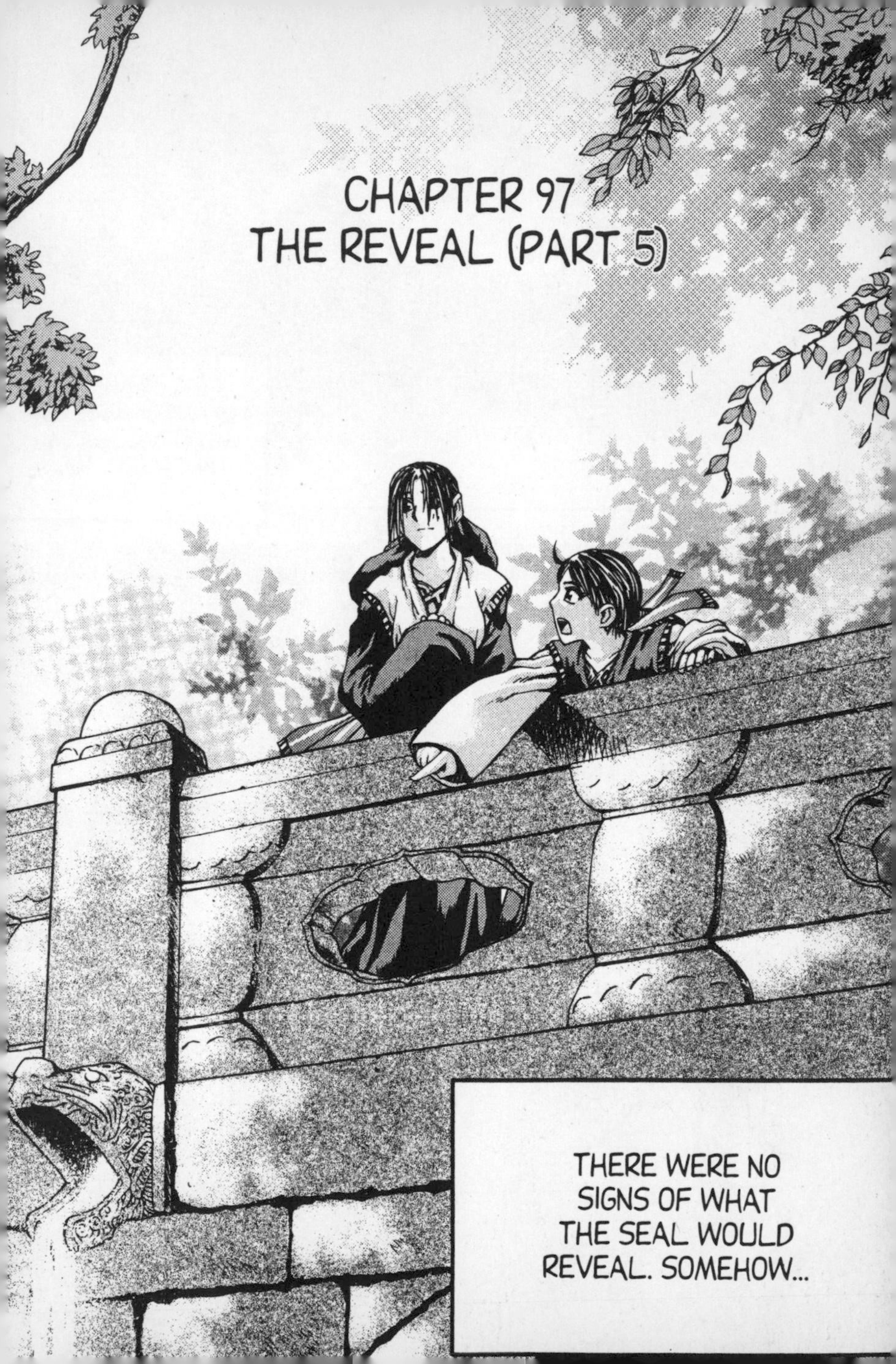
CHAPTER 97
THE REVEAL (PART 5)
THERE WERE NO SIGNS OF WHAT THE SEAL WOULD REVEAL. SOMEHOW...

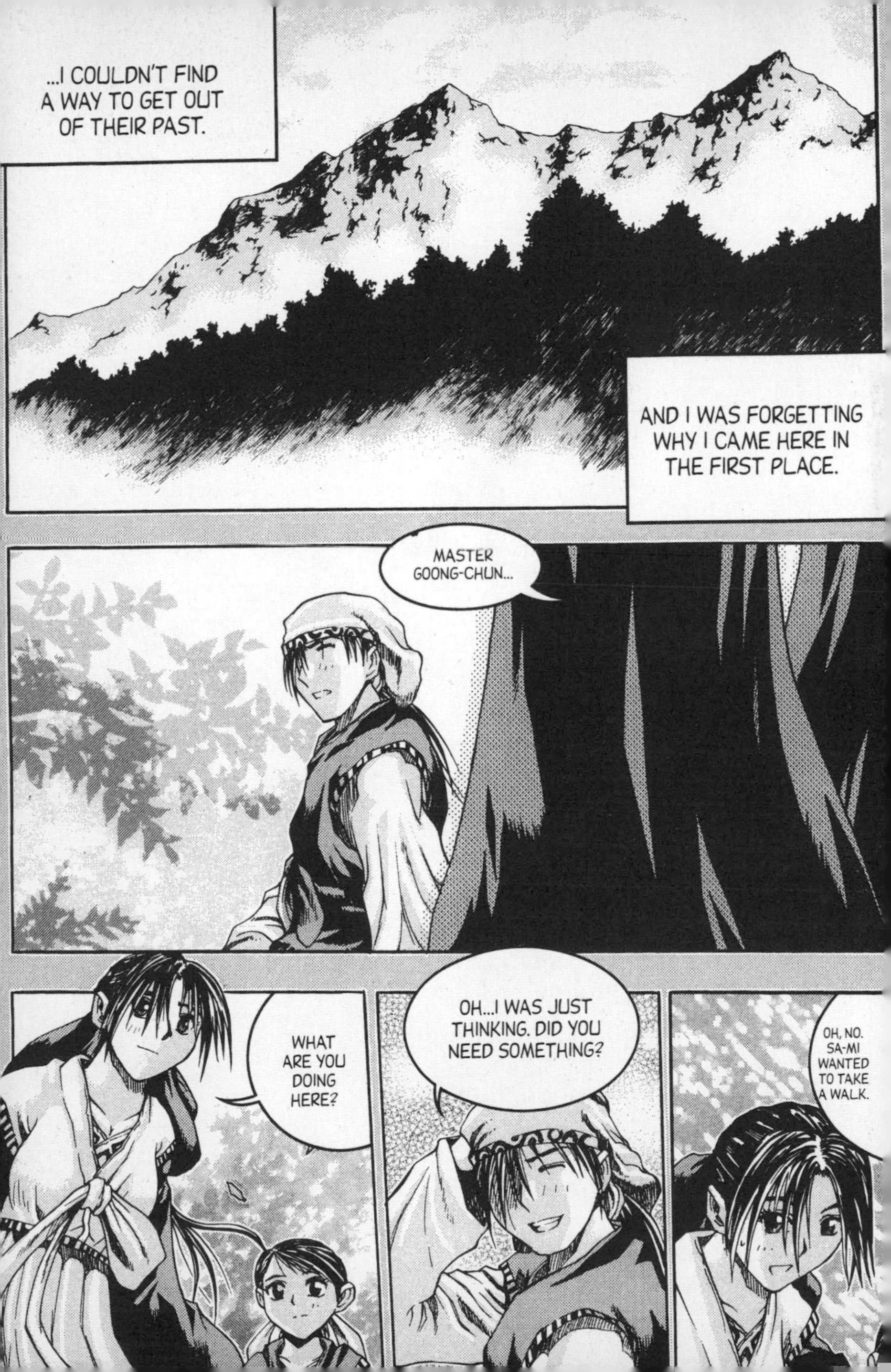
...I COULDN'T FIND A WAY TO GET OUT OF THEIR PAST.
AND I WAS FORGETTING WHY I CAME HERE IN THE FIRST PLACE.
MASTER GOONG-CHUN...
WHAT ARE YOU DOING HERE?
OH...I WAS JUST THINKING. DID YOU NEED SOMETHING?
OH, NO. SA-MI WANTED TO TAKE A WALK.

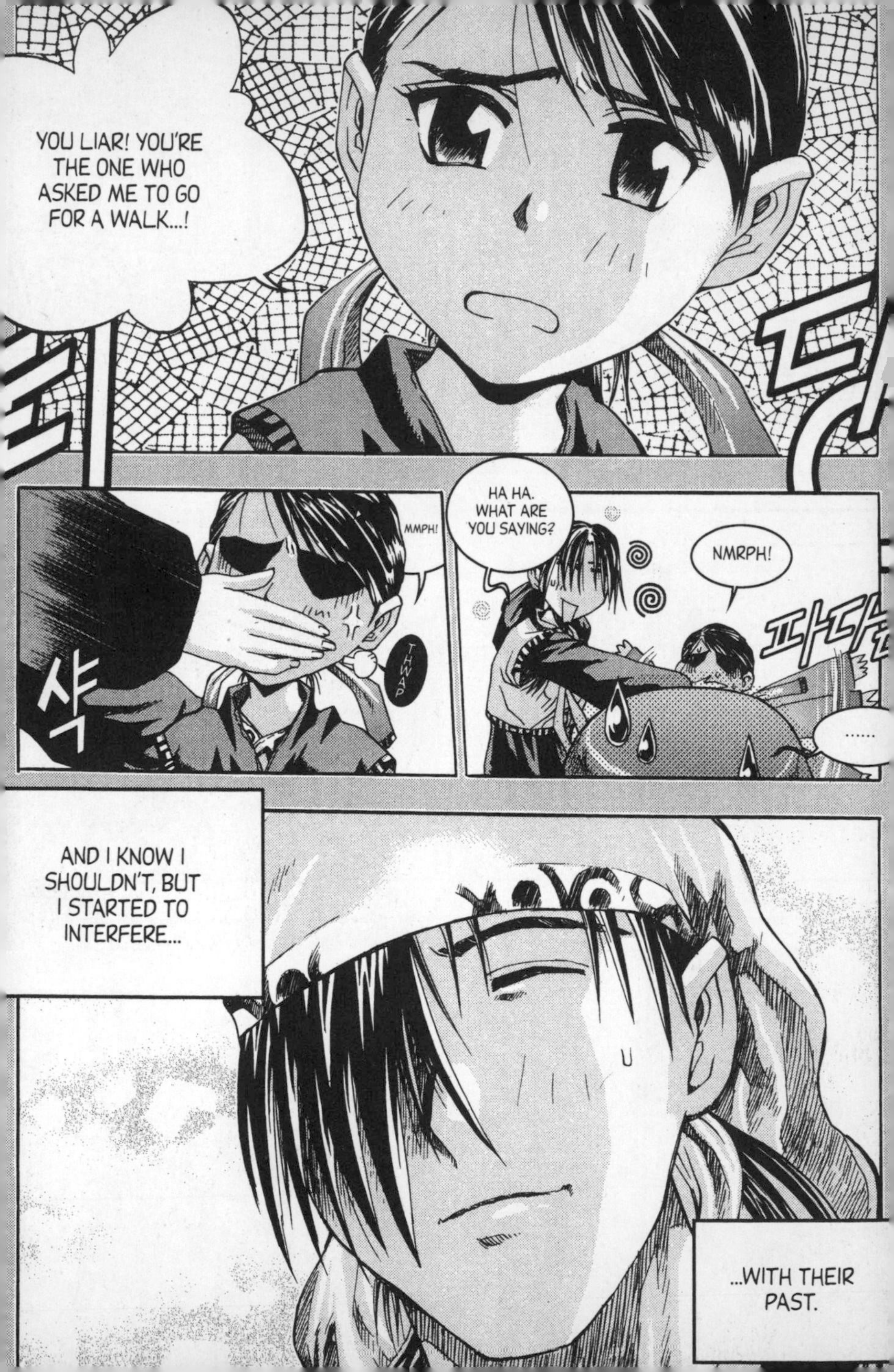
YOU LIAR! YOU'RE THE ONE WHO ASKED ME TO GO FOR A WALK...!
MMPH!
THWAP
HA HA. WHAT ARE YOU SAYING?
NMRPH!
......
AND I KNOW I SHOULDN'T, BUT I STARTED TO INTERFERE...
...WITH THEIR PAST.

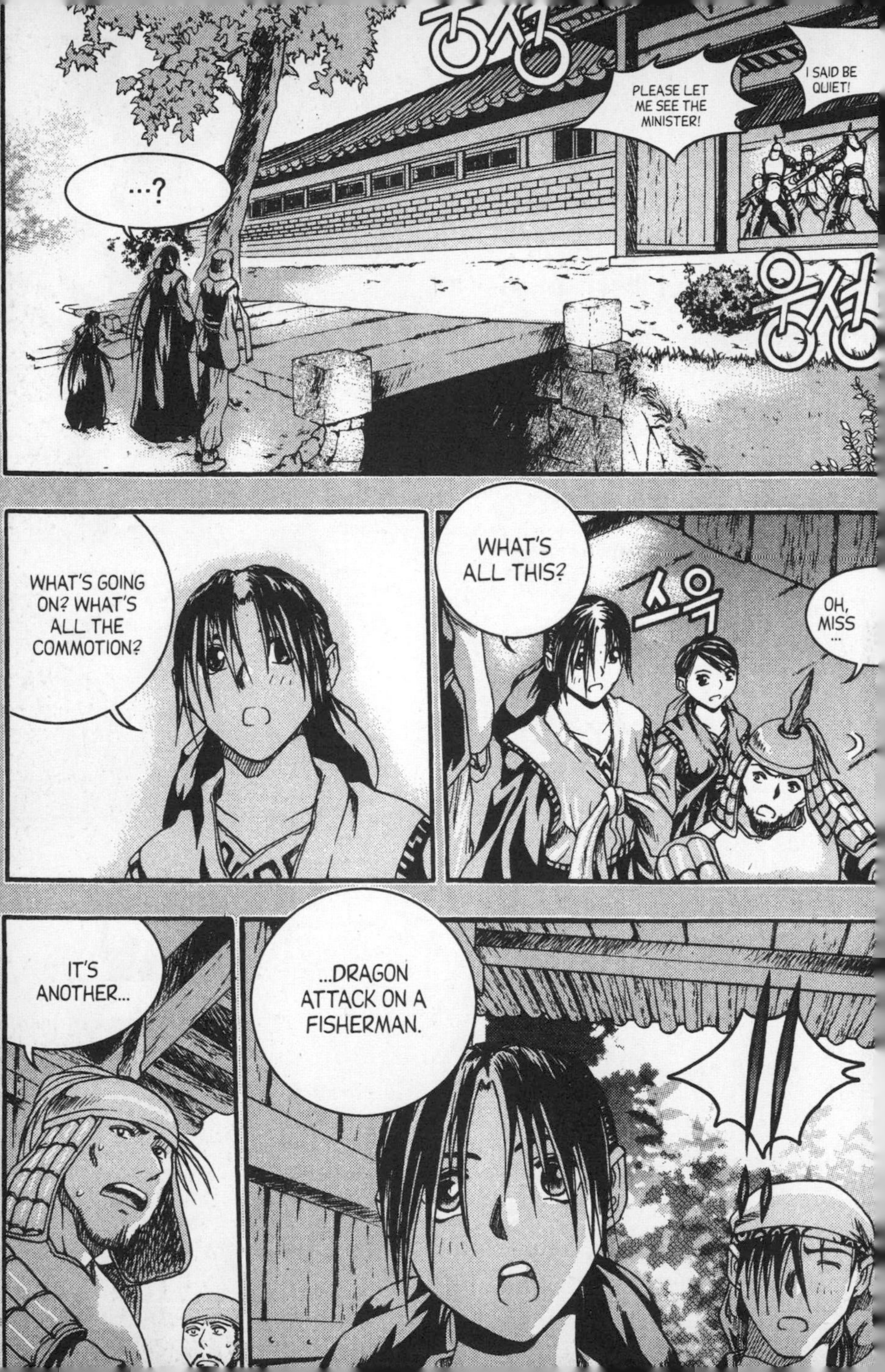
PLEASE LET ME SEE THE MINISTER!
I SAID BE QUIET!
...?
WHAT'S GOING ON? WHAT'S ALL THE COMMOTION?
WHAT'S ALL THIS?
OH, MISS ...
IT'S ANOTHER...
...DRAGON ATTACK ON A FISHERMAN.

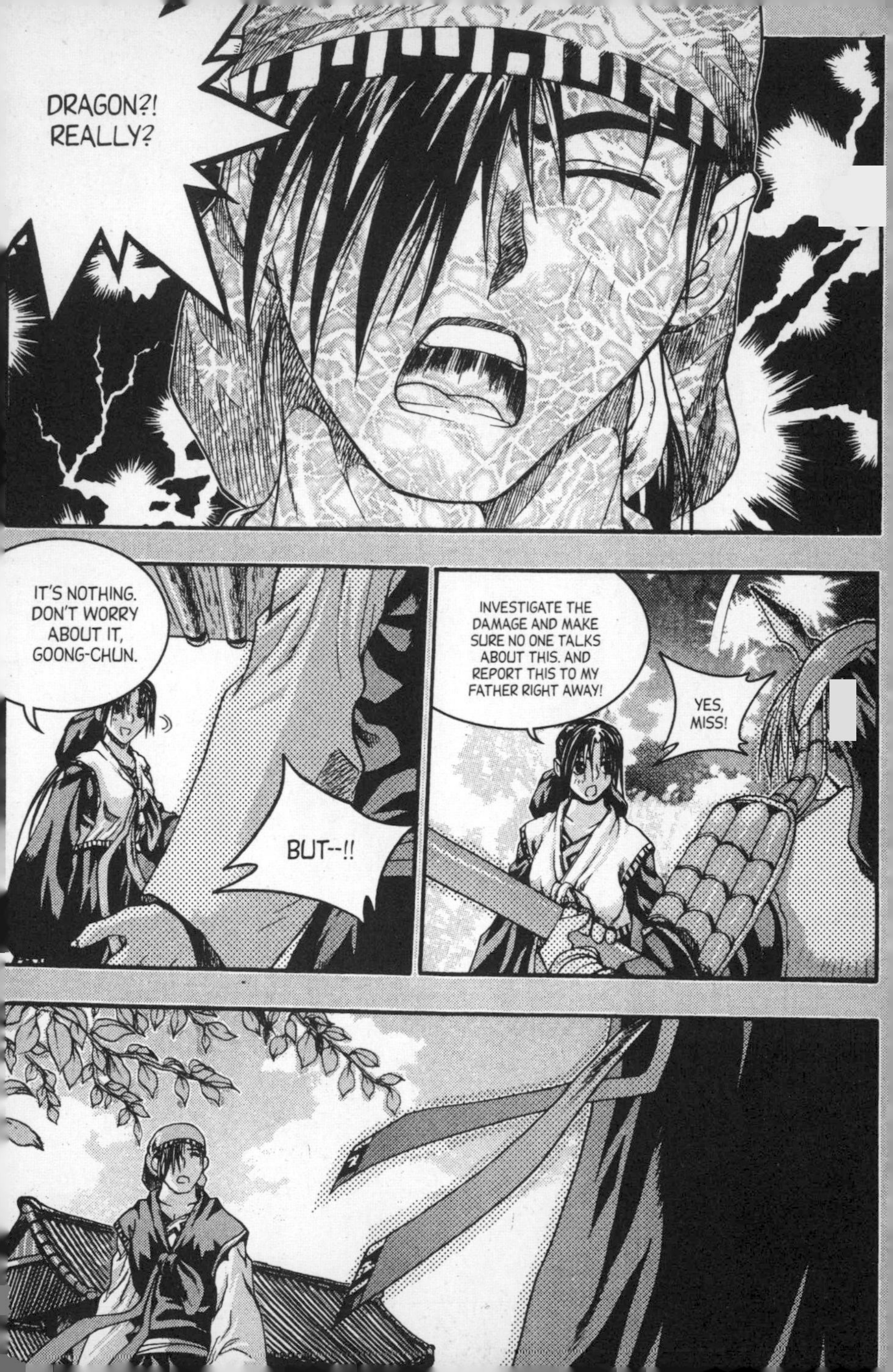
DRAGON?! REALLY?
IT'S NOTHING. DON'T WORRY ABOUT IT, GOONG-CHUN.
BUT--!!
INVESTIGATE THE DAMAGE AND MAKE SURE NO ONE TALKS ABOUT THIS. AND REPORT THIS TO MY FATHER RIGHT AWAY!
YES, MISS!

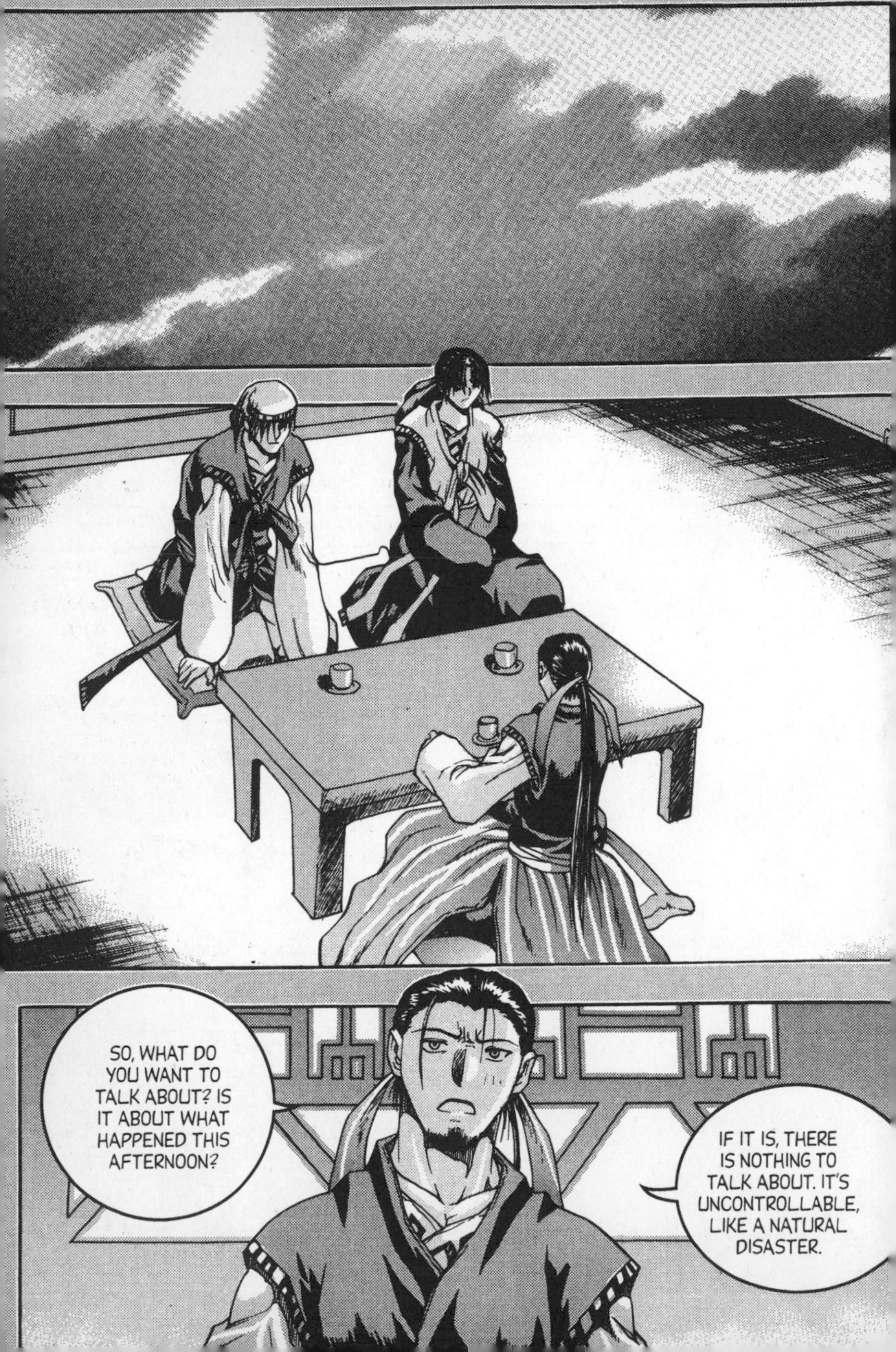
SO, WHAT DO YOU WANT TO TALK ABOUT? IS IT ABOUT WHAT HAPPENED THIS AFTERNOON?
IF IT IS, THERE IS NOTHING TO TALK ABOUT. IT'S UNCONTROLLABLE, LIKE A NATURAL DISASTER.

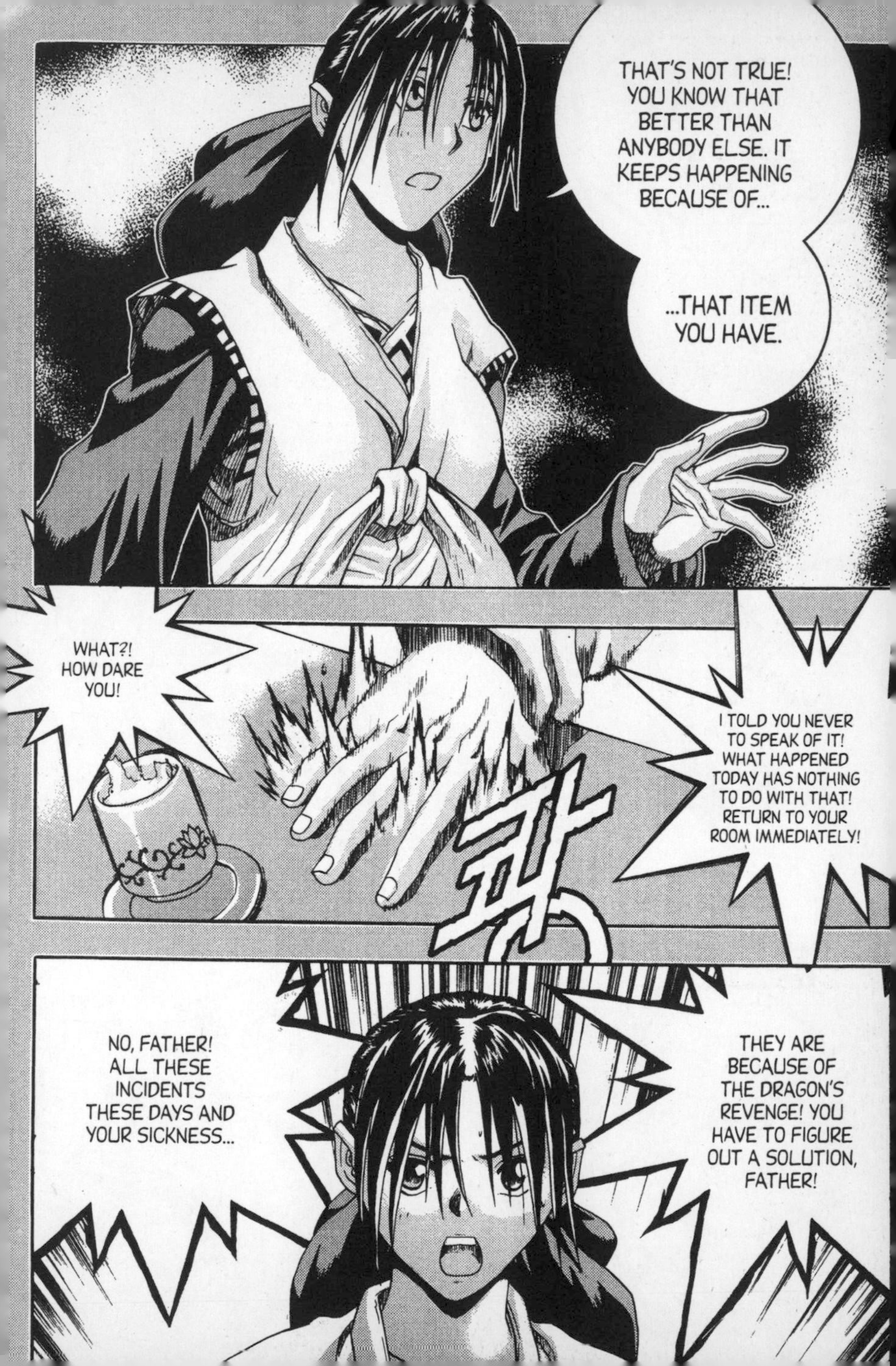
THAT'S NOT TRUE! YOU KNOW THAT BETTER THAN ANYBODY ELSE. IT KEEPS HAPPENING BECAUSE OF...
...THAT ITEM YOU HAVE.
WHAT?! HOW DARE YOU!
I TOLD YOU NEVER TO SPEAK OF IT! WHAT HAPPENED TODAY HAS NOTHING TO DO WITH THAT! RETURN TO YOUR ROOM IMMEDIATELY!
쾅
NO, FATHER! ALL THESE INCIDENTS THESE DAYS AND YOUR SICKNESS...
THEY ARE BECAUSE OF THE DRAGON'S REVENGE! YOU HAVE TO FIGURE OUT A SOLUTION, FATHER!

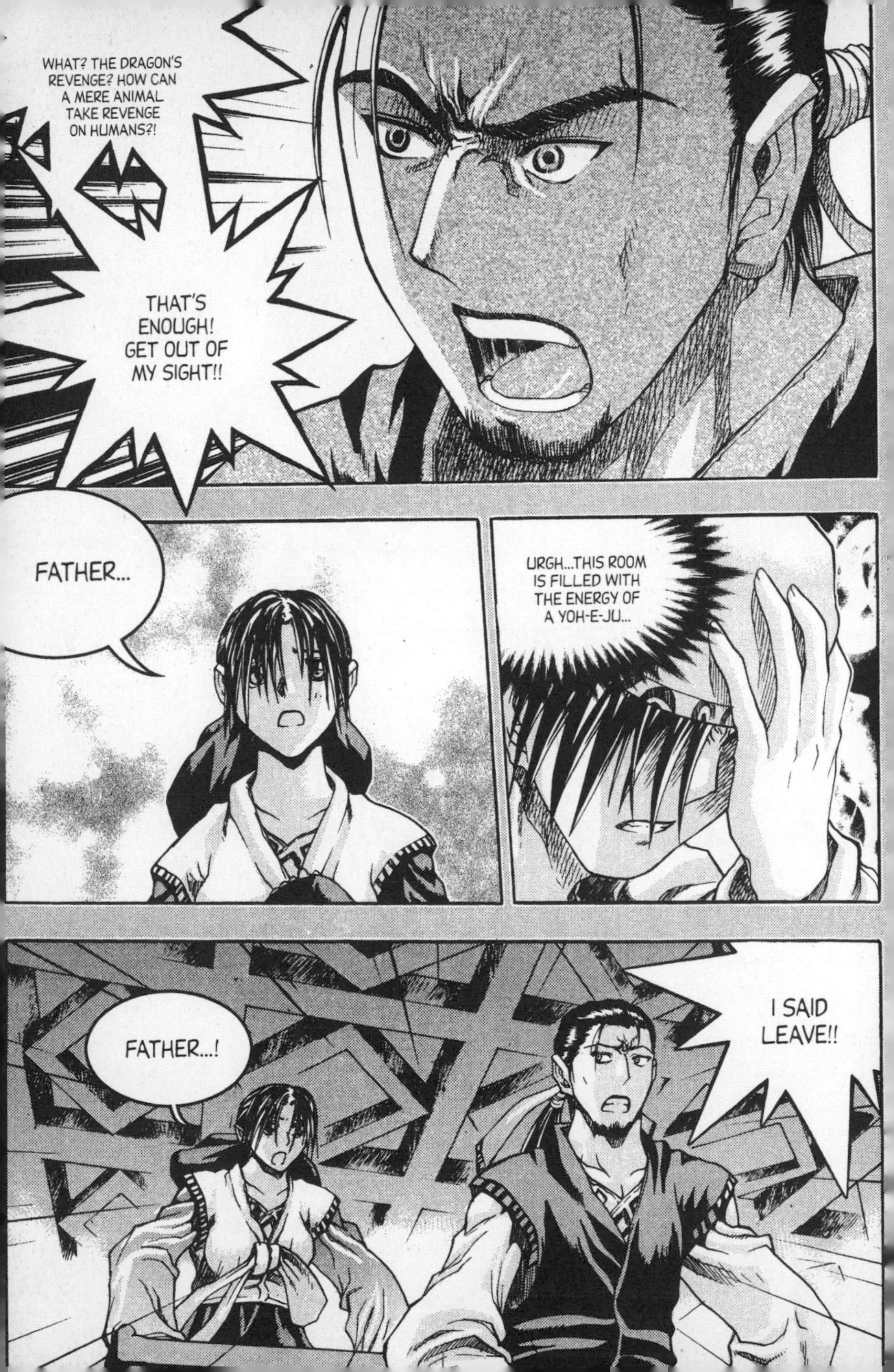
WHAT? THE DRAGON'S REVENGE? HOW CAN A MERE ANIMAL TAKE REVENGE ON HUMANS?!
THAT'S ENOUGH! GET OUT OF MY SIGHT!!
FATHER...
URGH...THIS ROOM IS FILLED WITH THE ENERGY OF A YOH-E-JU...
FATHER...!
I SAID LEAVE!!

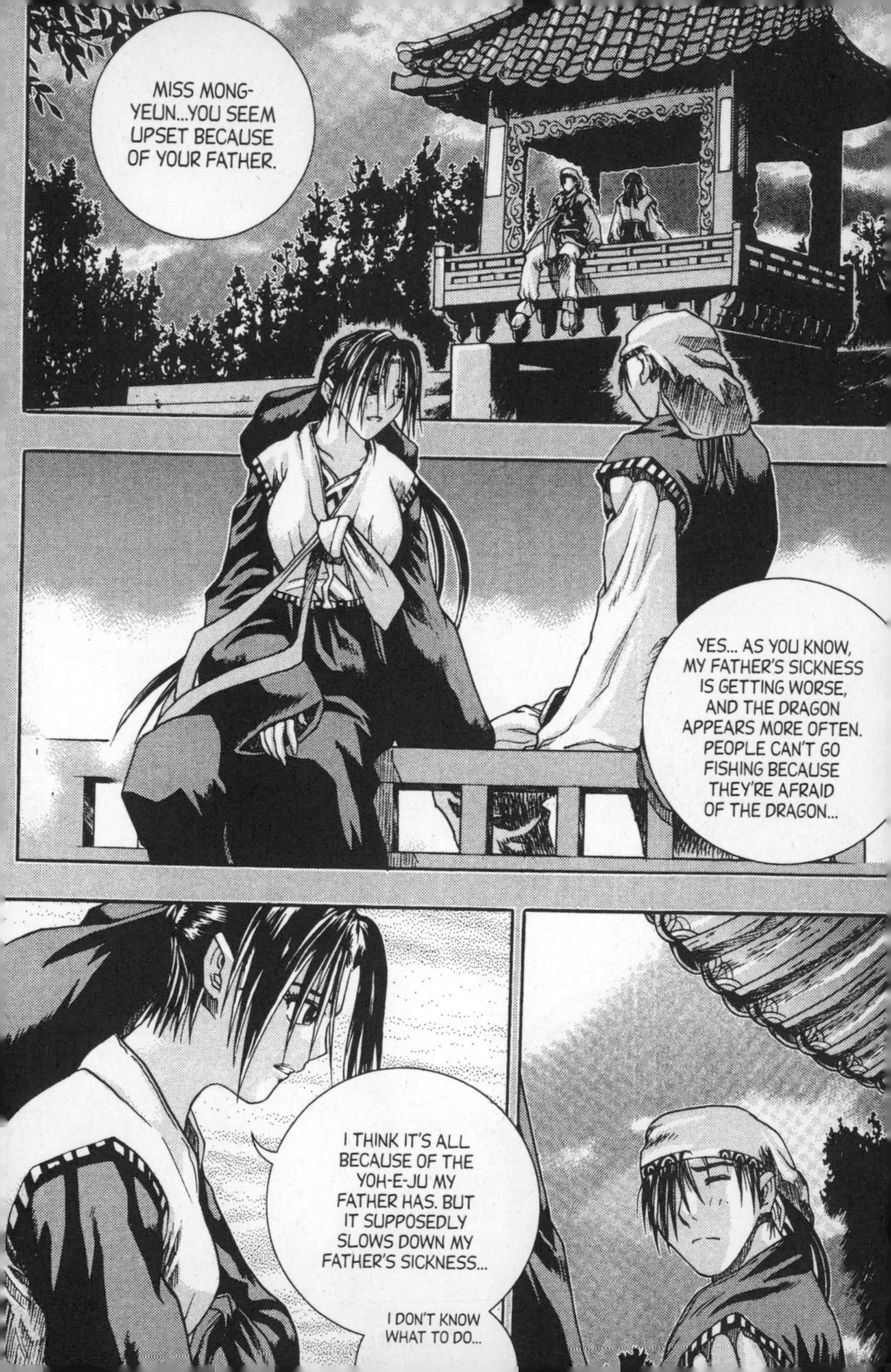
MISS MONG-YEUN...YOU SEEM UPSET BECAUSE OF YOUR FATHER.
YES... AS YOU KNOW, MY FATHER'S SICKNESS IS GETTING WORSE, AND THE DRAGON APPEARS MORE OFTEN. PEOPLE CAN'T GO FISHING BECAUSE THEY'RE AFRAID OF THE DRAGON...
I THINK IT'S ALL BECAUSE OF THE YOH-E-JU MY FATHER HAS. BUT IT SUPPOSEDLY SLOWS DOWN MY FATHER'S SICKNESS...
I DON'T KNOW WHAT TO DO...

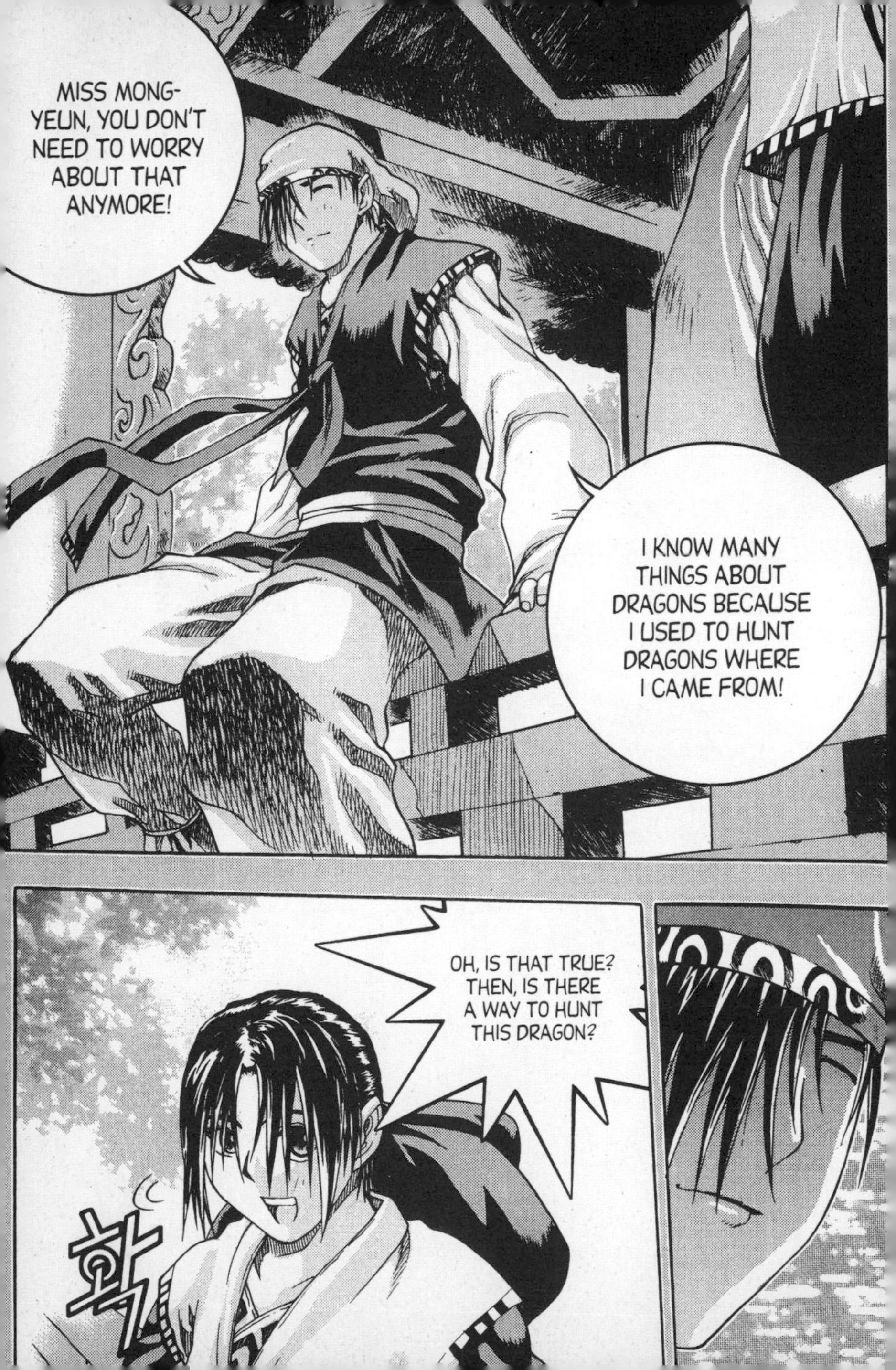
MISS MONG-YEUN, YOU DON'T NEED TO WORRY ABOUT THAT ANYMORE!
I KNOW MANY THINGS ABOUT DRAGONS BECAUSE I USED TO HUNT DRAGONS WHERE I CAME FROM!
OH, IS THAT TRUE? THEN, IS THERE A WAY TO HUNT THIS DRAGON?

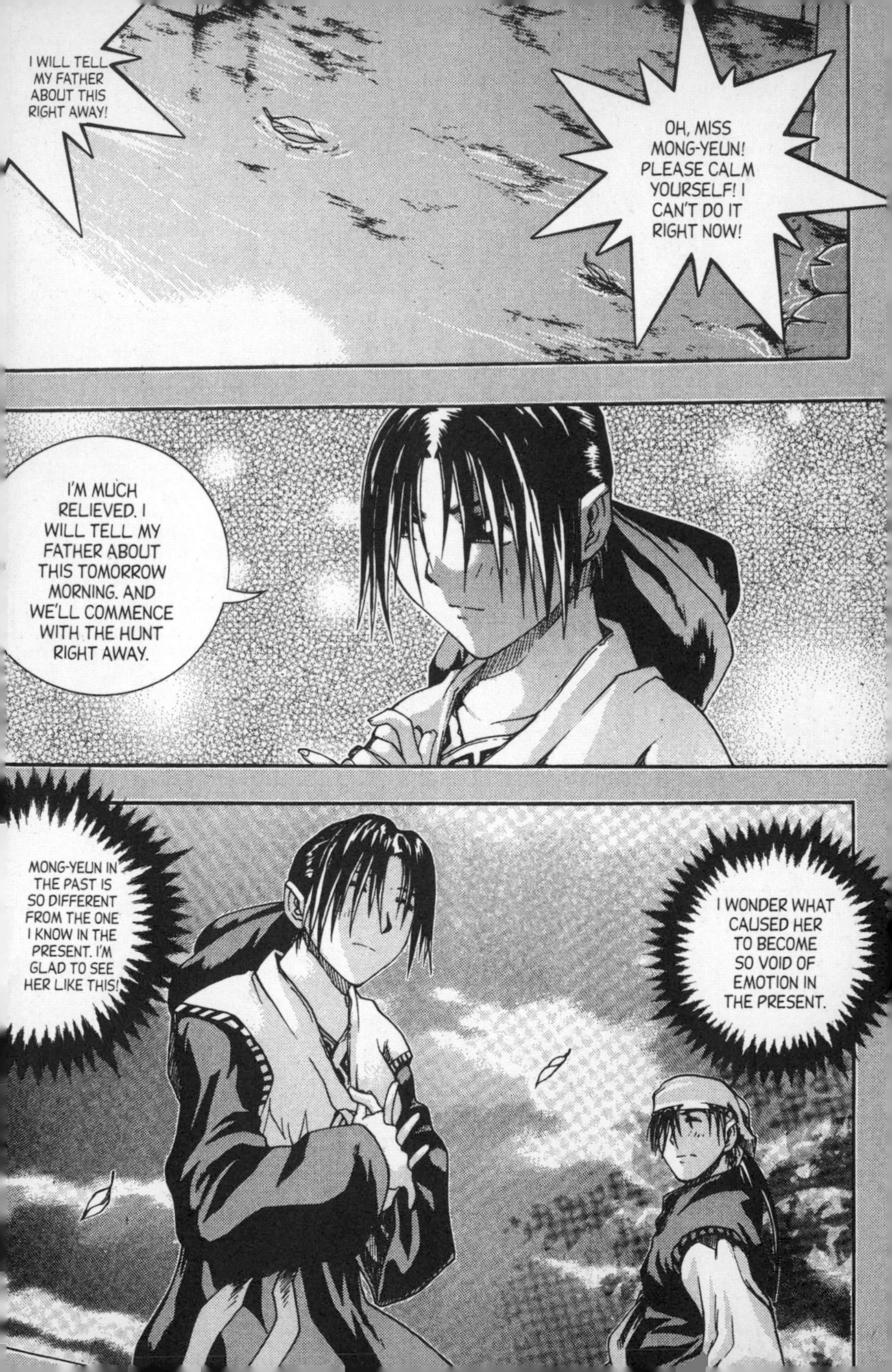
I WILL TELL MY FATHER ABOUT THIS RIGHT AWAY!
OH, MISS MONG-YEUN! PLEASE CALM YOURSELF! I CAN'T DO IT RIGHT NOW!
I'M MUCH RELIEVED. I WILL TELL MY FATHER ABOUT THIS TOMORROW MORNING. AND WE'LL COMMENCE WITH THE HUNT RIGHT AWAY.
MONG-YEUN IN THE PAST IS SO DIFFERENT FROM THE ONE I KNOW IN THE PRESENT. I'M GLAD TO SEE HER LIKE THIS!
I WONDER WHAT CAUSED HER TO BECOME SO VOID OF EMOTION IN THE PRESENT.

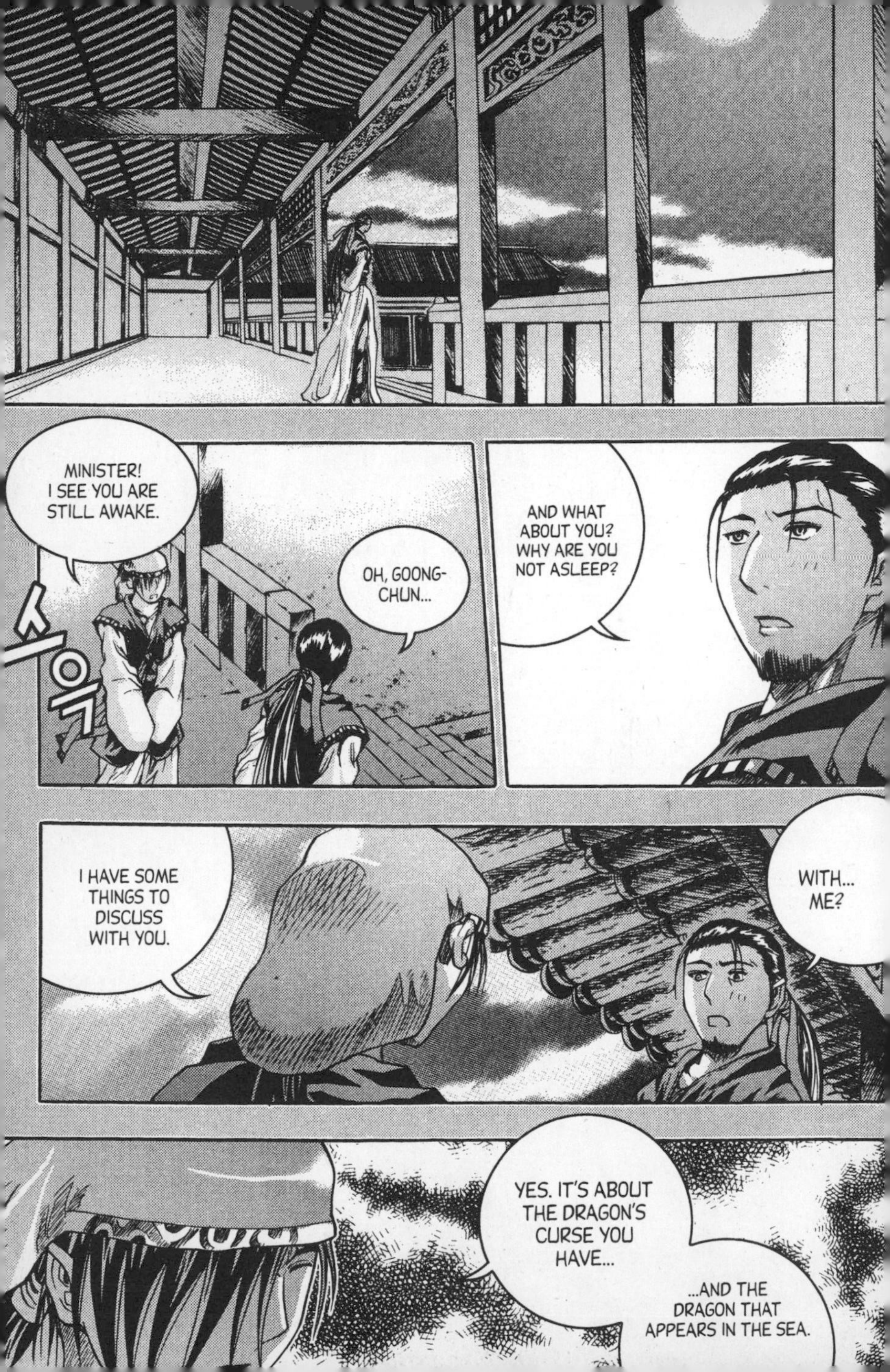
MINISTER! I SEE YOU ARE STILL AWAKE.
OH, GOONG-CHUN...
AND WHAT ABOUT YOU? WHY ARE YOU NOT ASLEEP?
I HAVE SOME THINGS TO DISCUSS WITH YOU.
WITH... ME?
YES. IT'S ABOUT THE DRAGON'S CURSE YOU HAVE...
...AND THE DRAGON THAT APPEARS IN THE SEA.

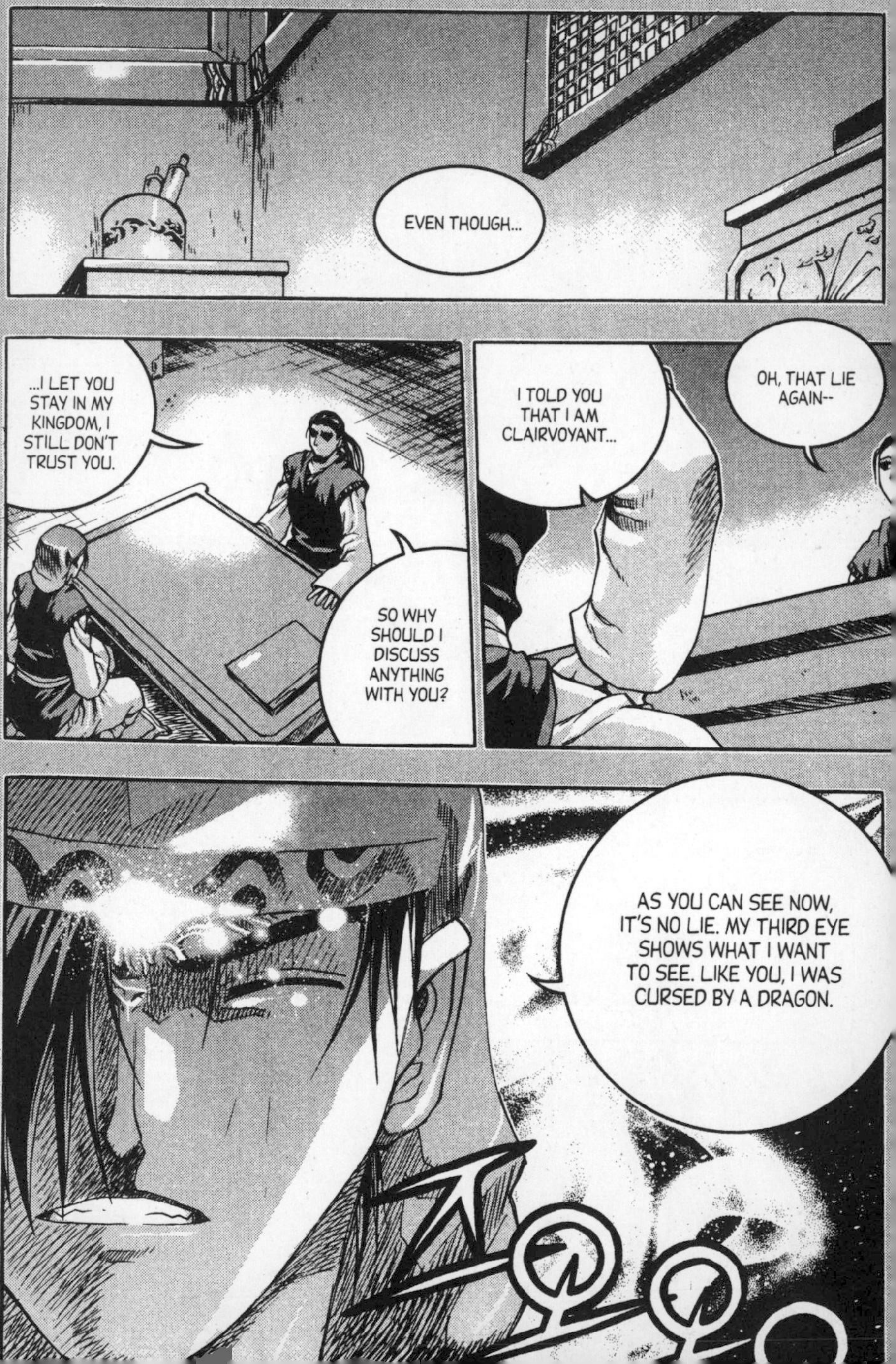
EVEN THOUGH...
...I LET YOU STAY IN MY KINGDOM, I STILL DON'T TRUST YOU.
SO WHY SHOULD I DISCUSS ANYTHING WITH YOU?
I TOLD YOU THAT I AM CLAIRVOYANT...
OH, THAT LIE AGAIN--
AS YOU CAN SEE NOW, IT'S NO LIE. MY THIRD EYE SHOWS WHAT I WANT TO SEE. LIKE YOU, I WAS CURSED BY A DRAGON.

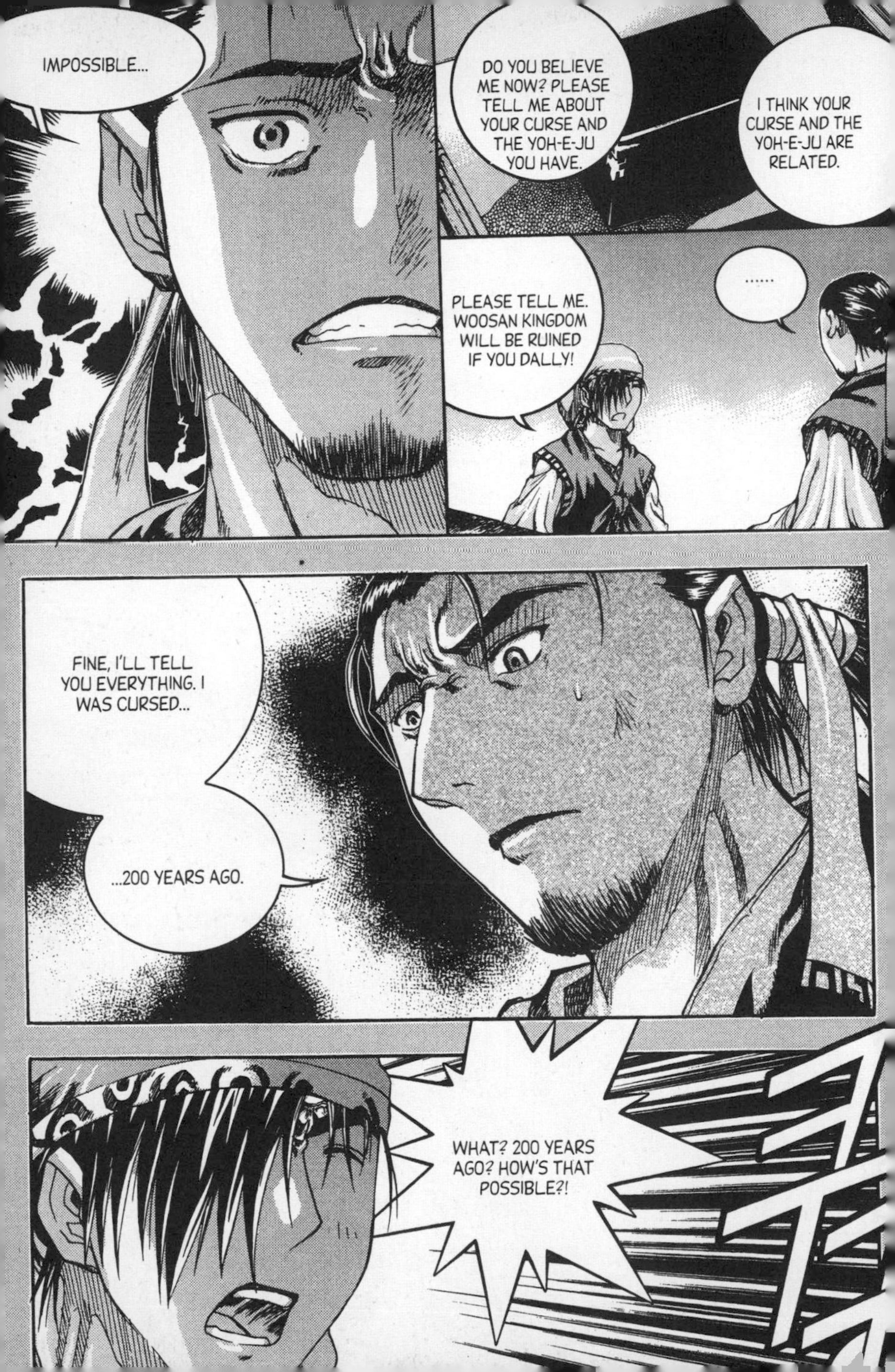
IMPOSSIBLE...
DO YOU BELIEVE ME NOW? PLEASE TELL ME ABOUT YOUR CURSE AND THE YOH-E-JU YOU HAVE.
I THINK YOUR CURSE AND THE YOH-E-JU ARE RELATED.
PLEASE TELL ME. WOOSAN KINGDOM WILL BE RUINED IF YOU DALLY!
......
FINE, I'LL TELL YOU EVERYTHING. I WAS CURSED...
...200 YEARS AGO.
WHAT? 200 YEARS AGO? HOW'S THAT POSSIBLE?!

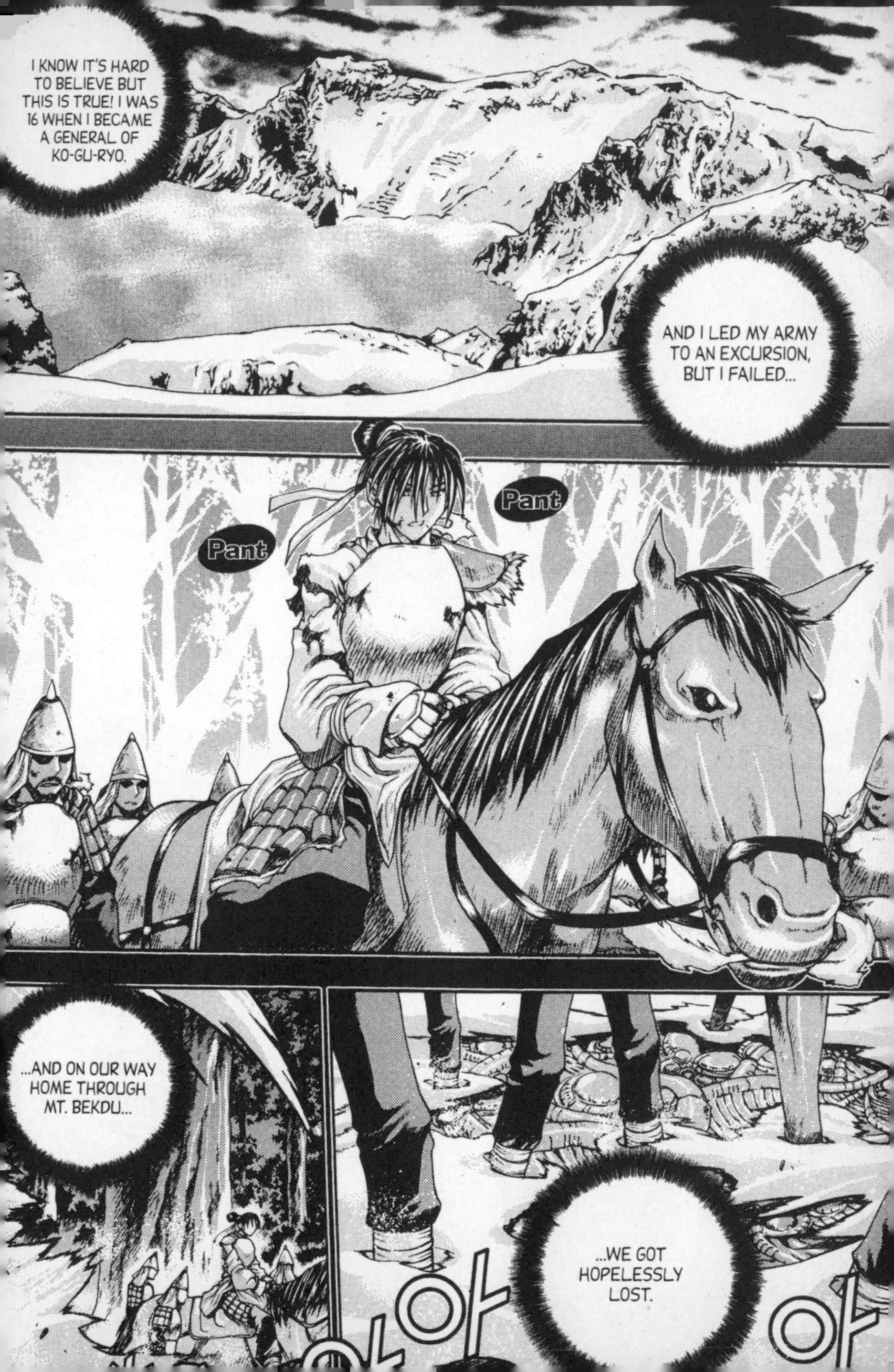
I KNOW IT'S HARD TO BELIEVE BUT THIS IS TRUE! I WAS 16 WHEN I BECAME A GENERAL OF KO-GU-RYO.
AND I LED MY ARMY TO AN EXCURSION, BUT I FAILED...
Pant
Pant
...AND ON OUR WAY HOME THROUGH MT. BEKDU...
...WE GOT HOPELESSLY LOST.

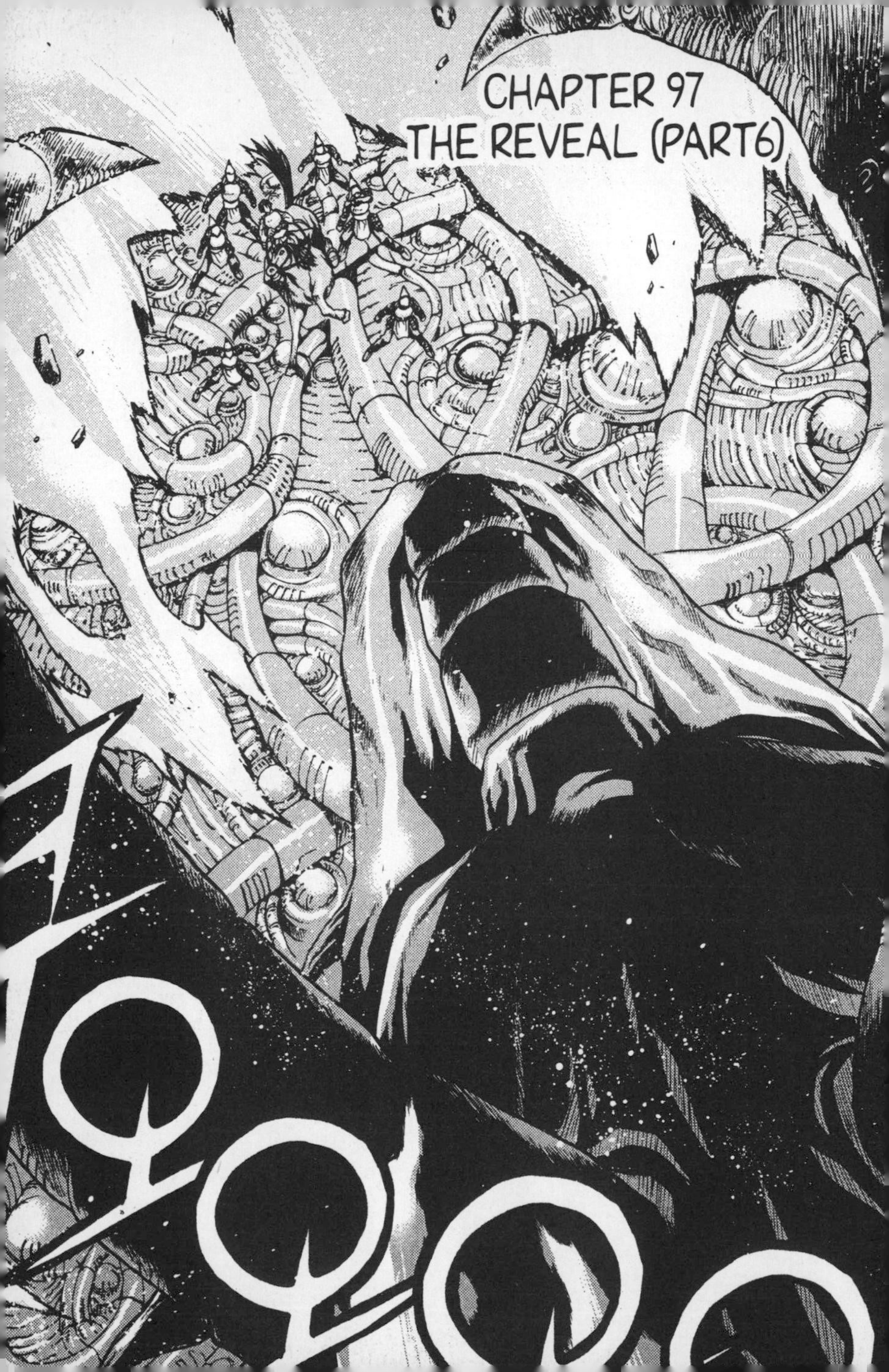
CHAPTER 97
THE REVEAL (PART6)

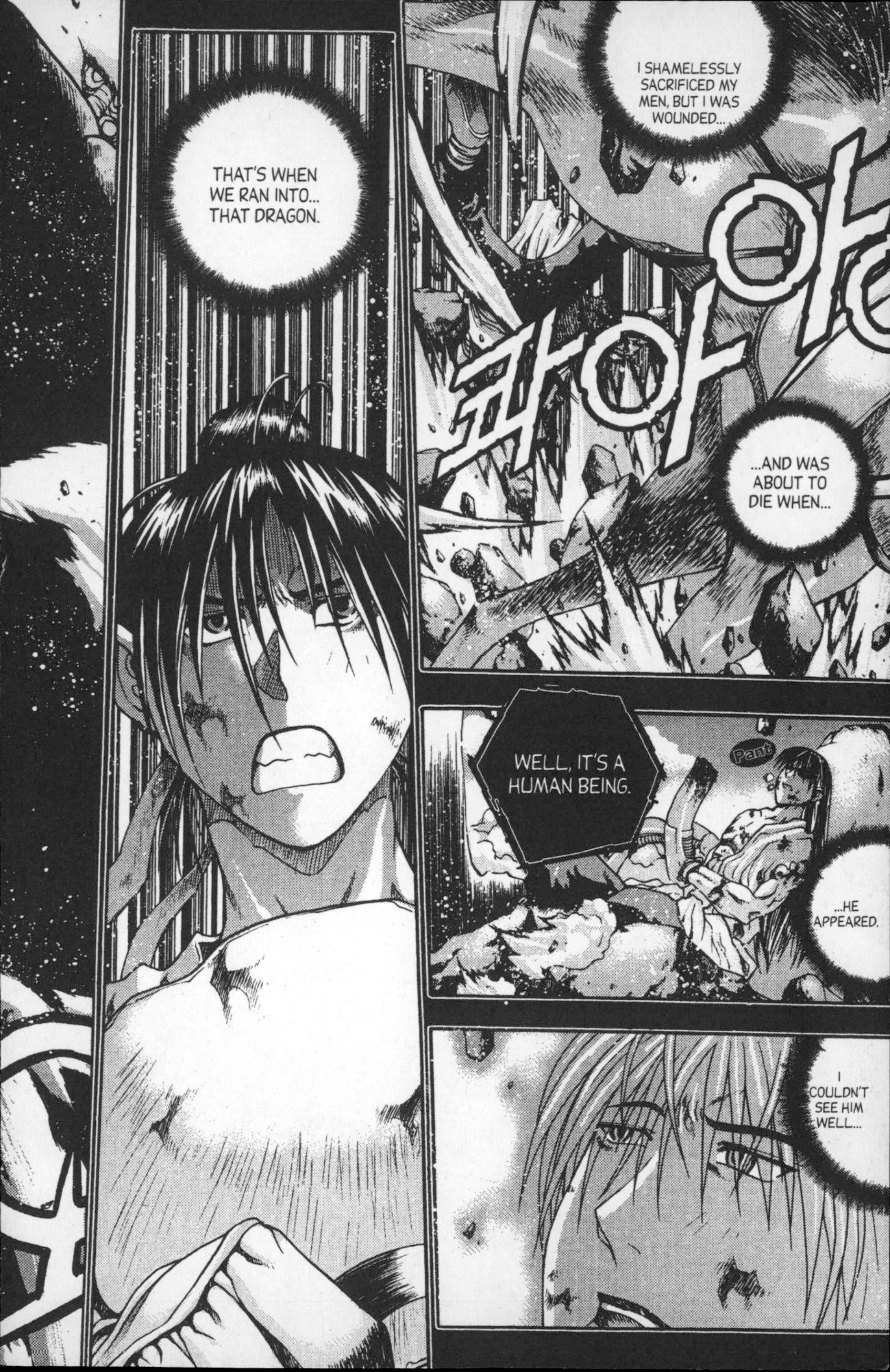
THAT'S WHEN WE RAN INTO... THAT DRAGON.
I SHAMELESSLY SACRIFICED MY MEN, BUT I WAS WOUNDED...
...AND WAS ABOUT TO DIE WHEN...
WELL, IT'S A HUMAN BEING.
Pant
...HE APPEARED.
I COULDN'T SEE HIM WELL...

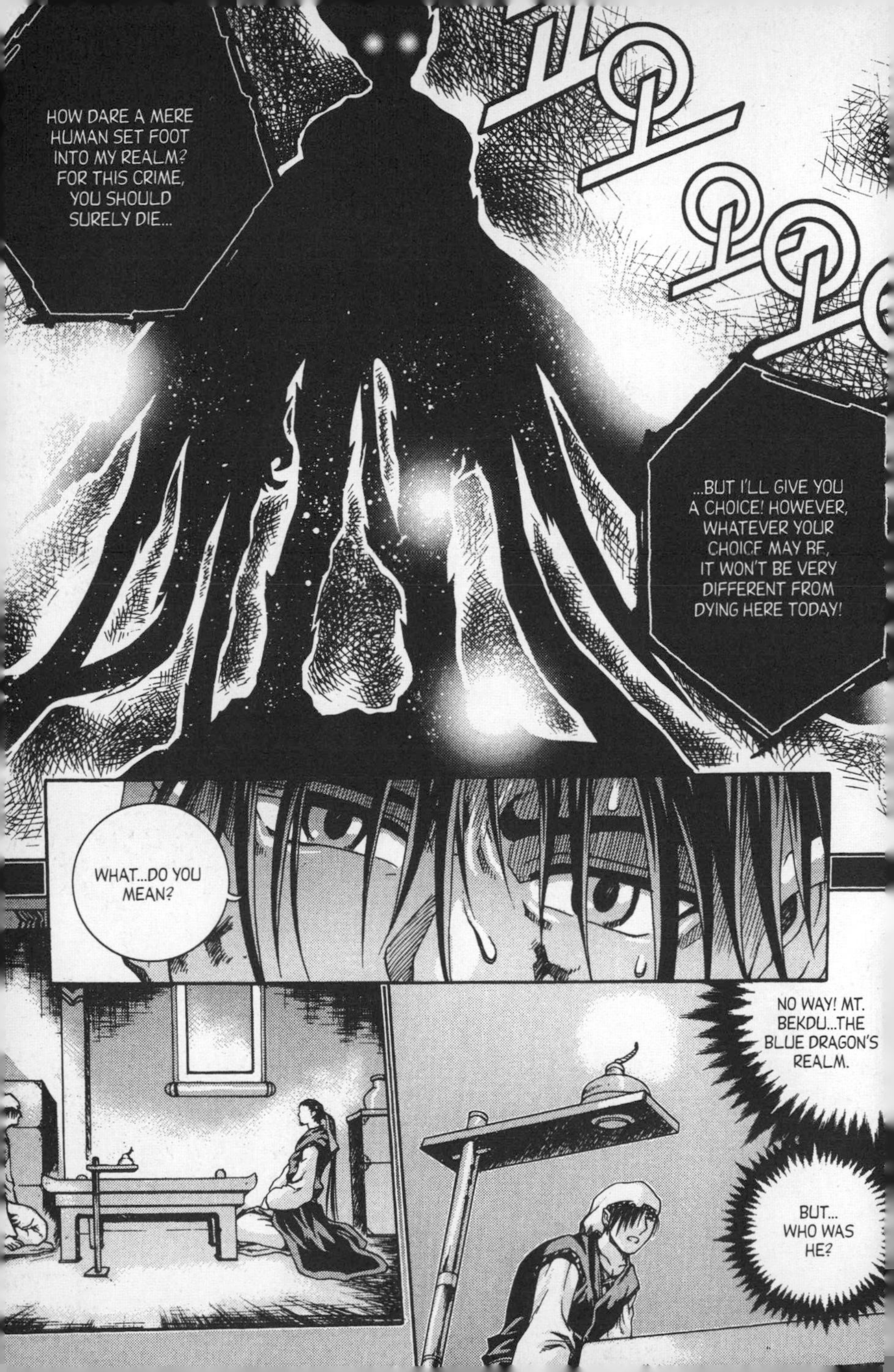
HOW DARE A MERE HUMAN SET FOOT INTO MY REALM? FOR THIS CRIME, YOU SHOULD SURELY DIE...
...BUT I'LL GIVE YOU A CHOICE! HOWEVER, WHATEVER YOUR CHOICE MAY BE, IT WON'T BE VERY DIFFERENT FROM DYING HERE TODAY!
WHAT...DO YOU MEAN?
NO WAY! MT. BEKDU...THE BLUE DRAGON'S REALM.
BUT... WHO WAS HE?

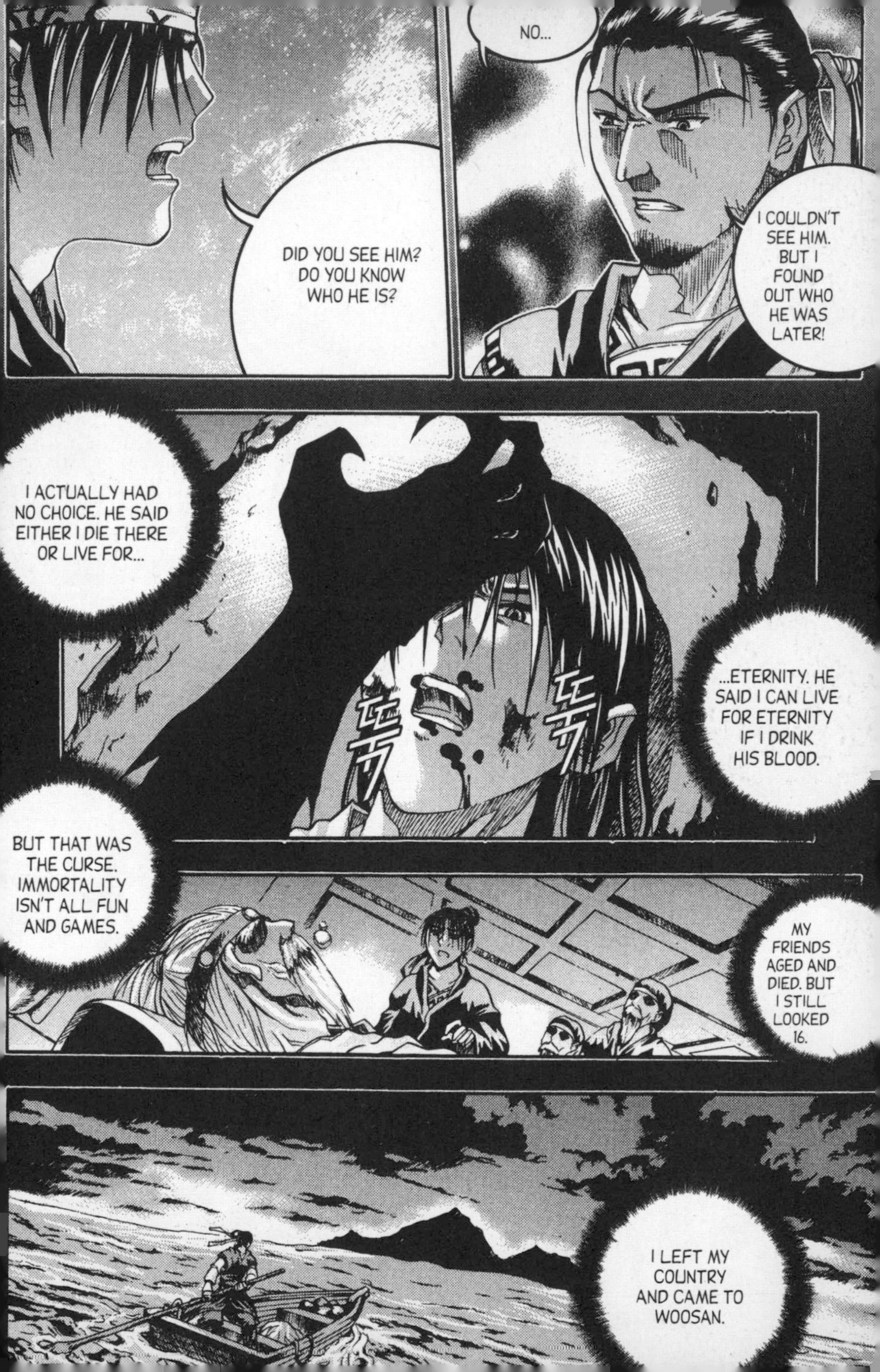

DID YOU SEE HIM? DO YOU KNOW WHO HE IS?
NO...
I COULDN'T SEE HIM. BUT I FOUND OUT WHO HE WAS LATER!
I ACTUALLY HAD NO CHOICE. HE SAID EITHER I DIE THERE OR LIVE FOR...
...ETERNITY. HE SAID I CAN LIVE FOR ETERNITY IF I DRINK HIS BLOOD.
BUT THAT WAS THE CURSE. IMMORTALITY ISN'T ALL FUN AND GAMES.
MY FRIENDS AGED AND DIED. BUT I STILL LOOKED 16.
I LEFT MY COUNTRY AND CAME TO WOOSAN.

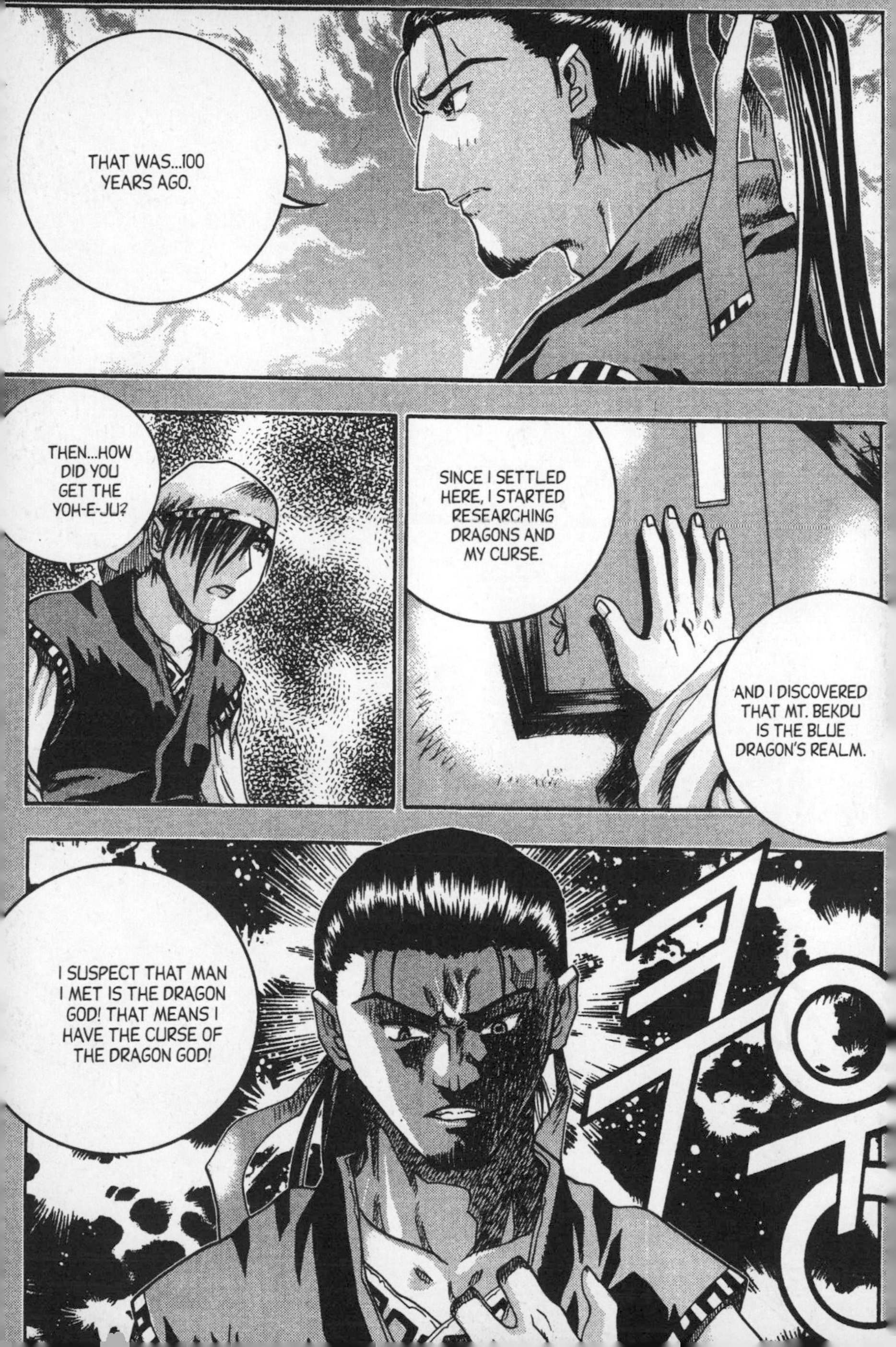
THAT WAS...100 YEARS AGO.
THEN...HOW DID YOU GET THE YOH-E-JU?
SINCE I SETTLED HERE, I STARTED RESEARCHING DRAGONS AND MY CURSE.
AND I DISCOVERED THAT MT. BEKDU IS THE BLUE DRAGON'S REALM.
I SUSPECT THAT MAN I MET IS THE DRAGON GOD! THAT MEANS I HAVE THE CURSE OF THE DRAGON GOD!

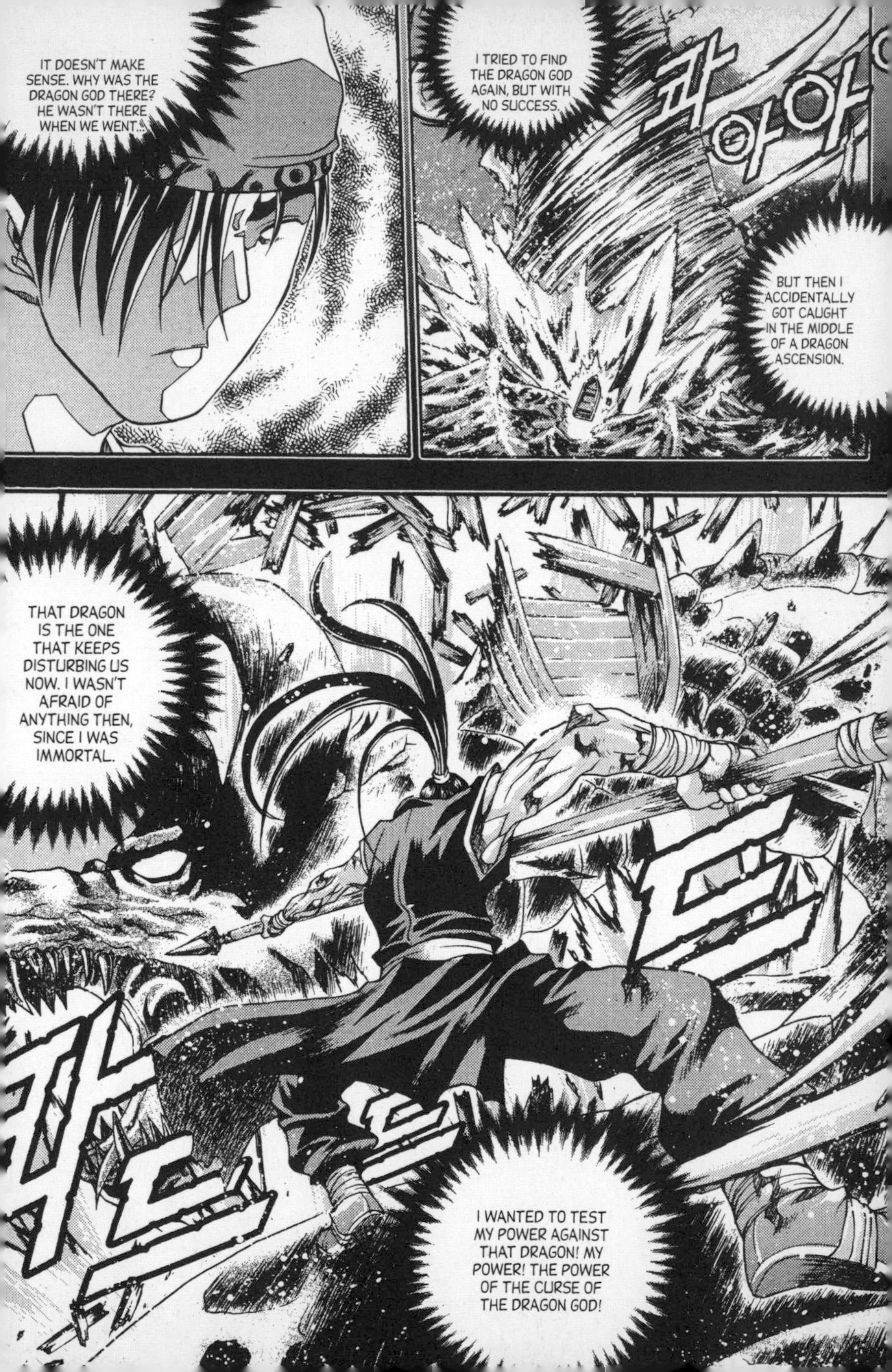
IT DOESN'T MAKE SENSE. WHY WAS THE DRAGON GOD THERE? HE WASN'T THERE WHEN WE WENT...
I TRIED TO FIND THE DRAGON GOD AGAIN, BUT WITH NO SUCCESS.
BUT THEN I ACCIDENTALLY GOT CAUGHT IN THE MIDDLE OF A DRAGON ASCENSION.
THAT DRAGON IS THE ONE THAT KEEPS DISTURBING US NOW. I WASN'T AFRAID OF ANYTHING THEN, SINCE I WAS IMMORTAL.
I WANTED TO TEST MY POWER AGAINST THAT DRAGON! MY POWER! THE POWER OF THE CURSE OF THE DRAGON GOD!

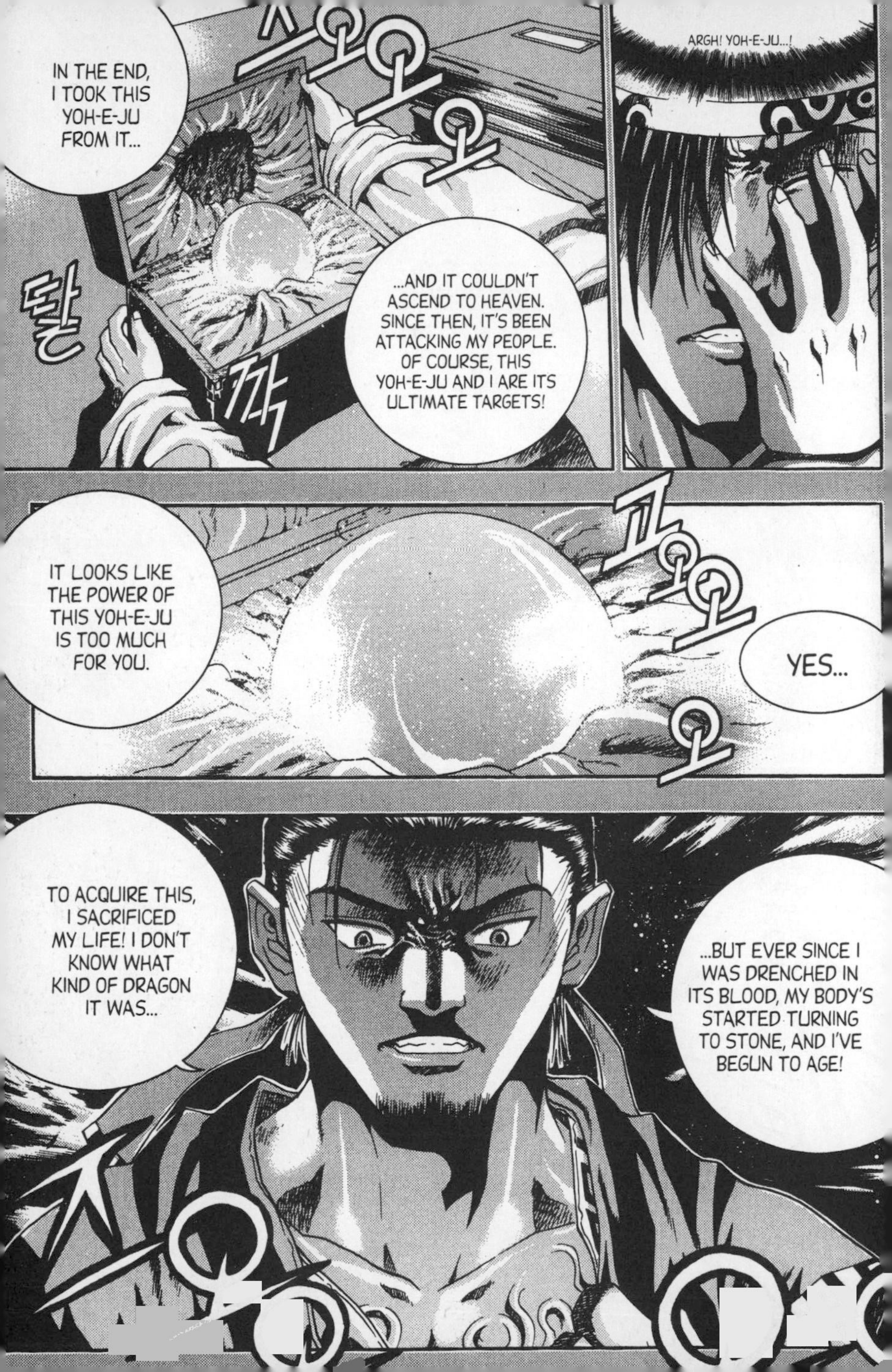
IN THE END, I TOOK THIS YOH-E-JU FROM IT...
...AND IT COULDN'T ASCEND TO HEAVEN. SINCE THEN, IT'S BEEN ATTACKING MY PEOPLE. OF COURSE, THIS YOH-E-JU AND I ARE ITS ULTIMATE TARGETS!
ARGH! YOH-E-JU...!
IT LOOKS LIKE THE POWER OF THIS YOH-E-JU IS TOO MUCH FOR YOU.
YES...
TO ACQUIRE THIS, I SACRIFICED MY LIFE! I DON'T KNOW WHAT KIND OF DRAGON IT WAS...
...BUT EVER SINCE I WAS DRENCHED IN ITS BLOOD, MY BODY'S STARTED TURNING TO STONE, AND I'VE BEGUN TO AGE!

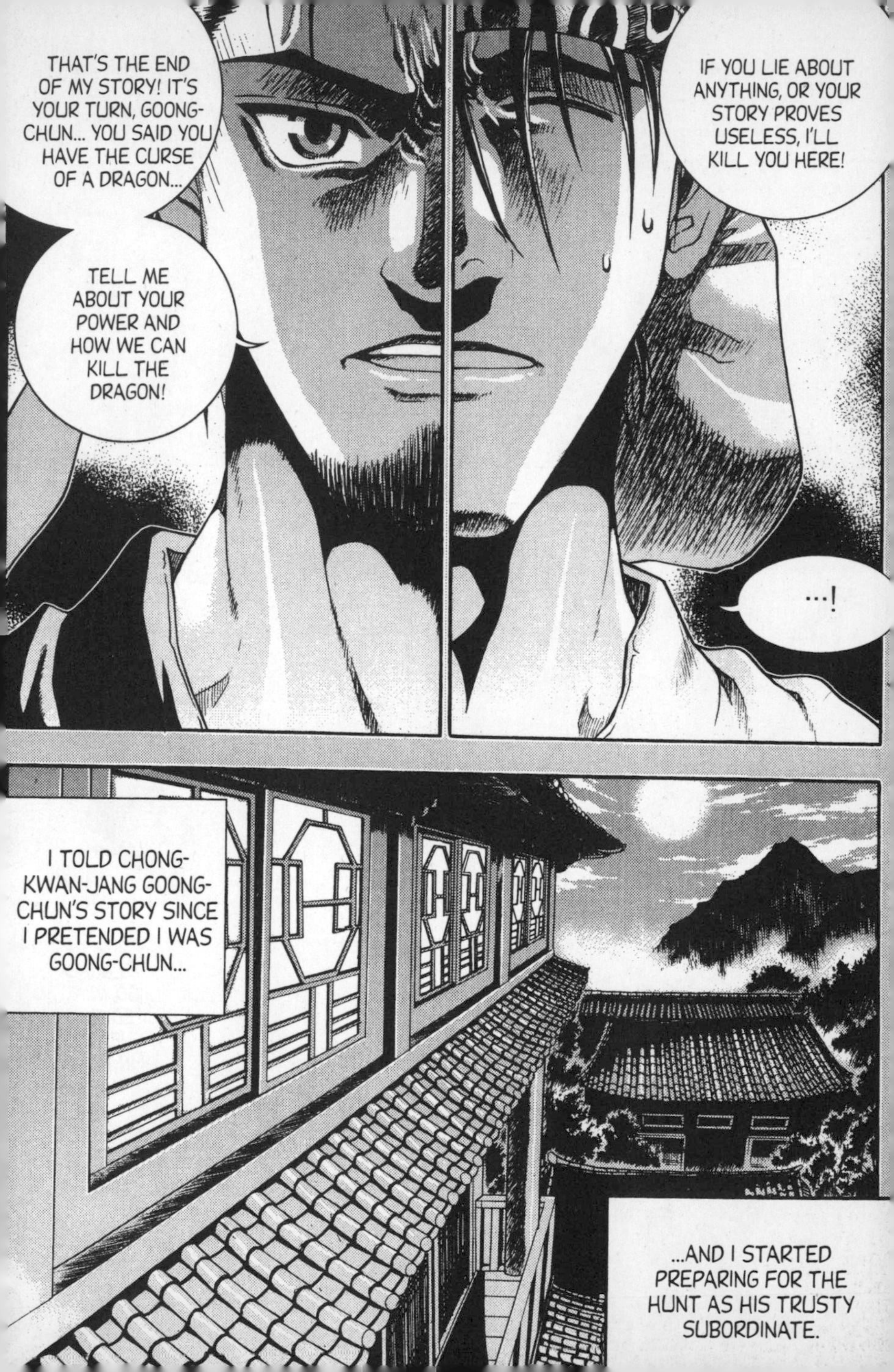
THAT'S THE END OF MY STORY! IT'S YOUR TURN, GOONG-CHUN... YOU SAID YOU HAVE THE CURSE OF A DRAGON...
TELL ME ABOUT YOUR POWER AND HOW WE CAN KILL THE DRAGON!
IF YOU LIE ABOUT ANYTHING, OR YOUR STORY PROVES USELESS, I'LL KILL YOU HERE!
...!
I TOLD CHONG-KWAN-JANG GOONG-CHUN'S STORY SINCE I PRETENDED I WAS GOONG-CHUN...
...AND I STARTED PREPARING FOR THE HUNT AS HIS TRUSTY SUBORDINATE.

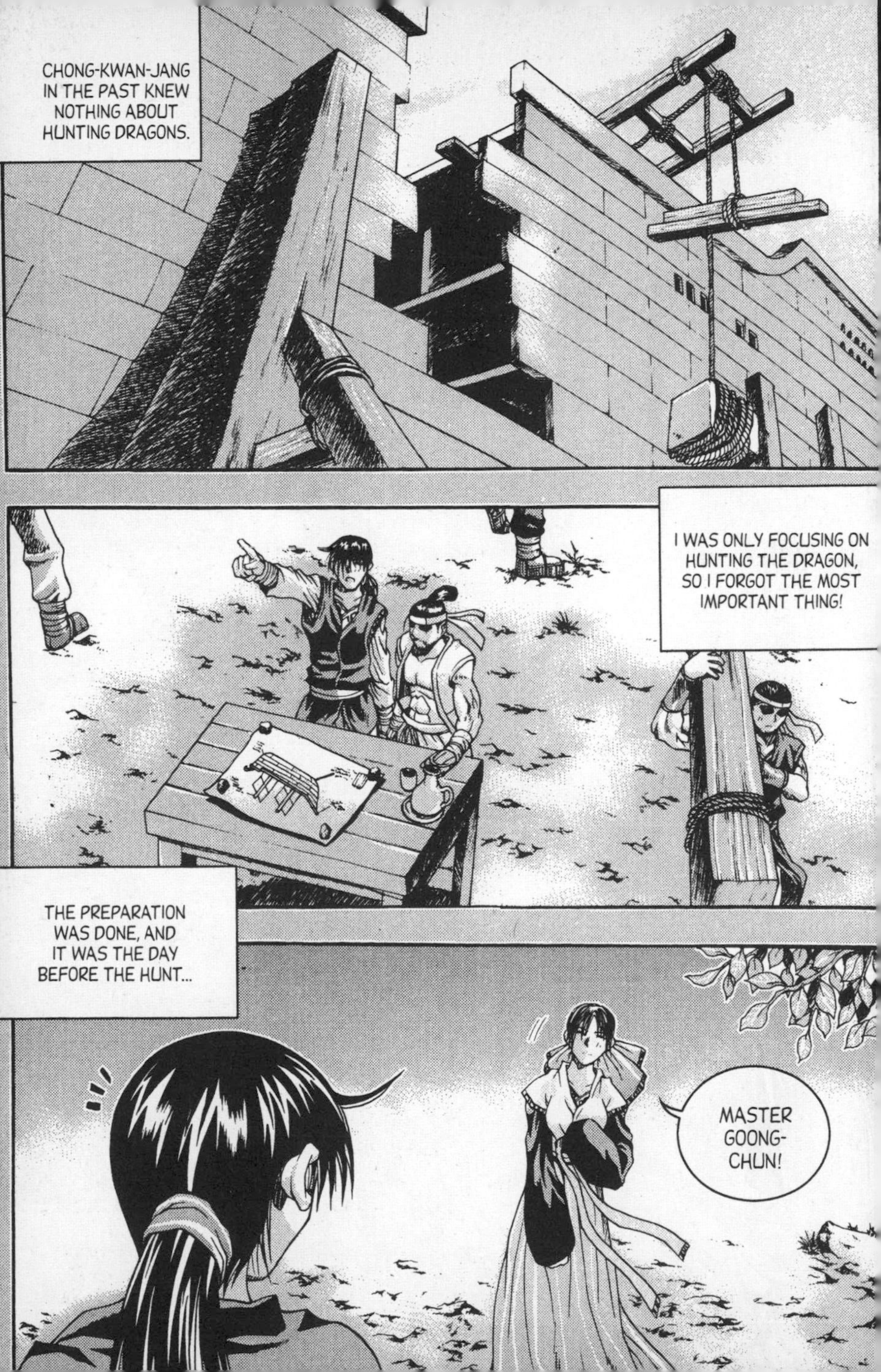
CHONG-KWAN-JANG IN THE PAST KNEW NOTHING ABOUT HUNTING DRAGONS.
I WAS ONLY FOCUSING ON HUNTING THE DRAGON, SO I FORGOT THE MOST IMPORTANT THING!
THE PREPARATION WAS DONE, AND IT WAS THE DAY BEFORE THE HUNT...
MASTER GOONG-CHUN!

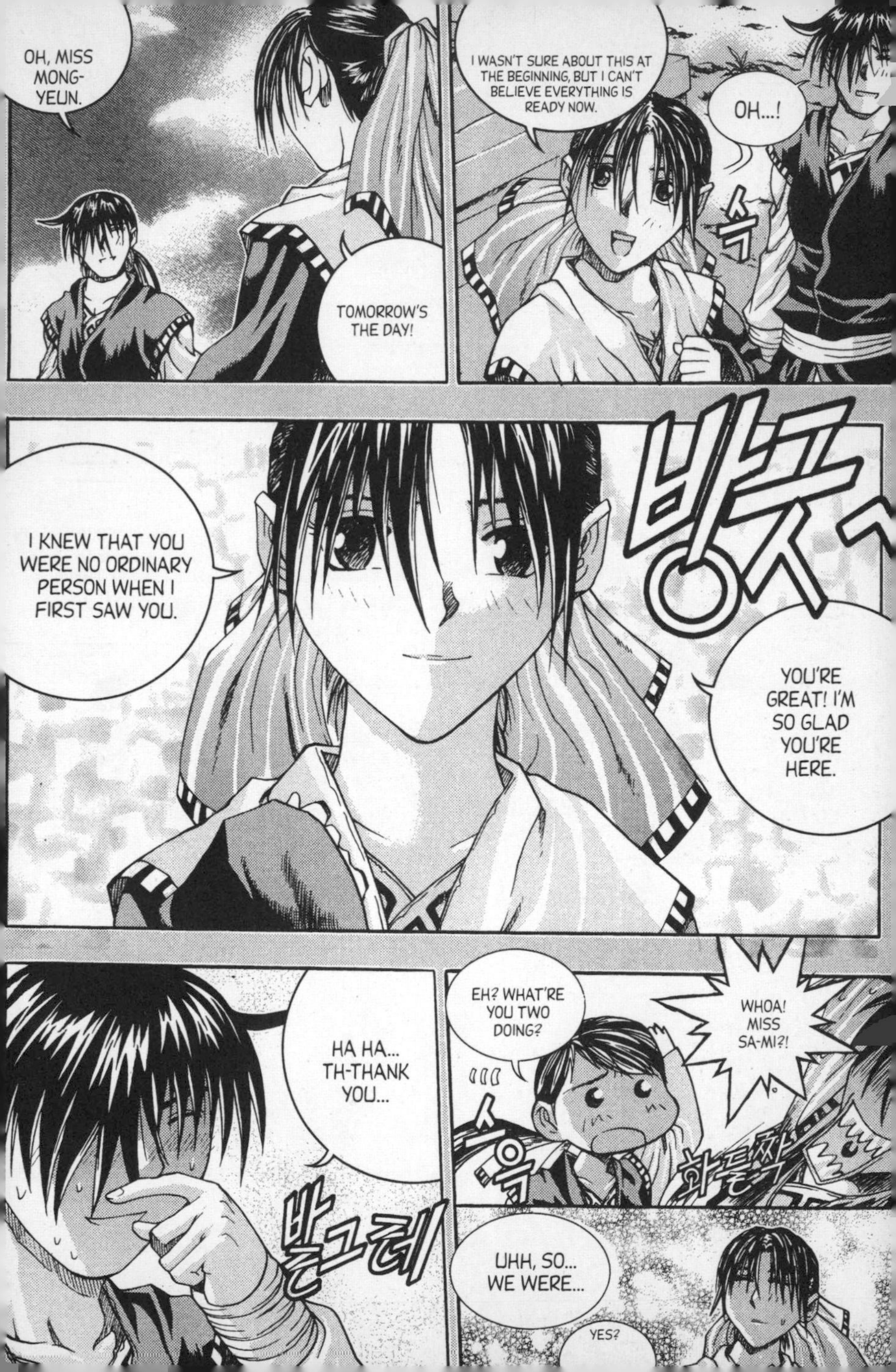
OH, MISS MONG-YEUN.
TOMORROW'S THE DAY!
I WASN'T SURE ABOUT THIS AT THE BEGINNING, BUT I CAN'T BELIEVE EVERYTHING IS READY NOW.
OH...!
I KNEW THAT YOU WERE NO ORDINARY PERSON WHEN I FIRST SAW YOU.
방긋
YOU'RE GREAT! I'M SO GLAD YOU'RE HERE.
HA HA... TH-THANK YOU...
발그레
EH? WHAT'RE YOU TWO DOING?
WHOA! MISS SA-MI?!
화들짝
UHH, SO... WE WERE...
YES?

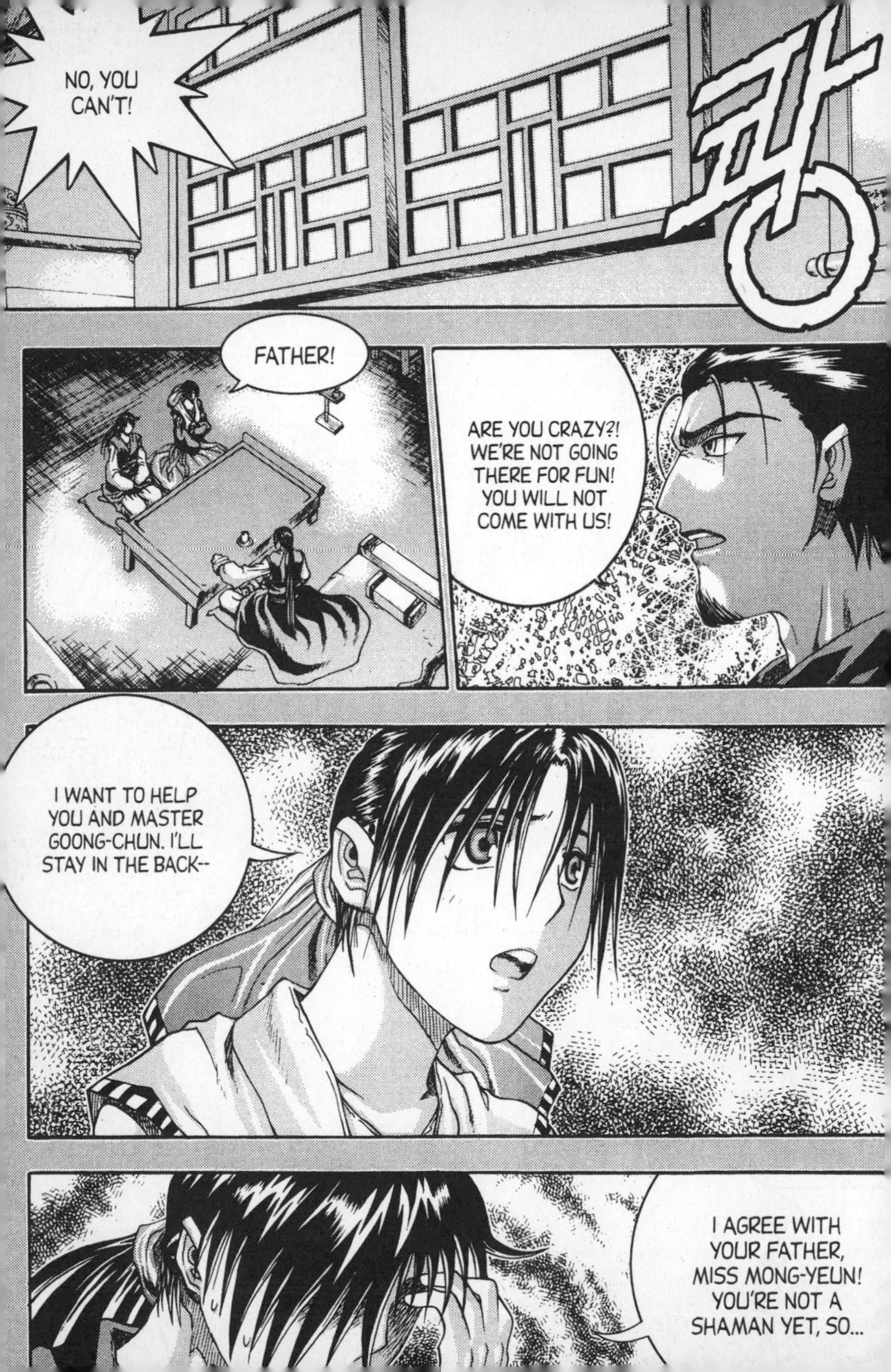
NO, YOU CAN'T!
FATHER!
ARE YOU CRAZY?! WE'RE NOT GOING THERE FOR FUN! YOU WILL NOT COME WITH US!
I WANT TO HELP YOU AND MASTER GOONG-CHUN. I'LL STAY IN THE BACK--
I AGREE WITH YOUR FATHER, MISS MONG-YEUN! YOU'RE NOT A SHAMAN YET, SO...

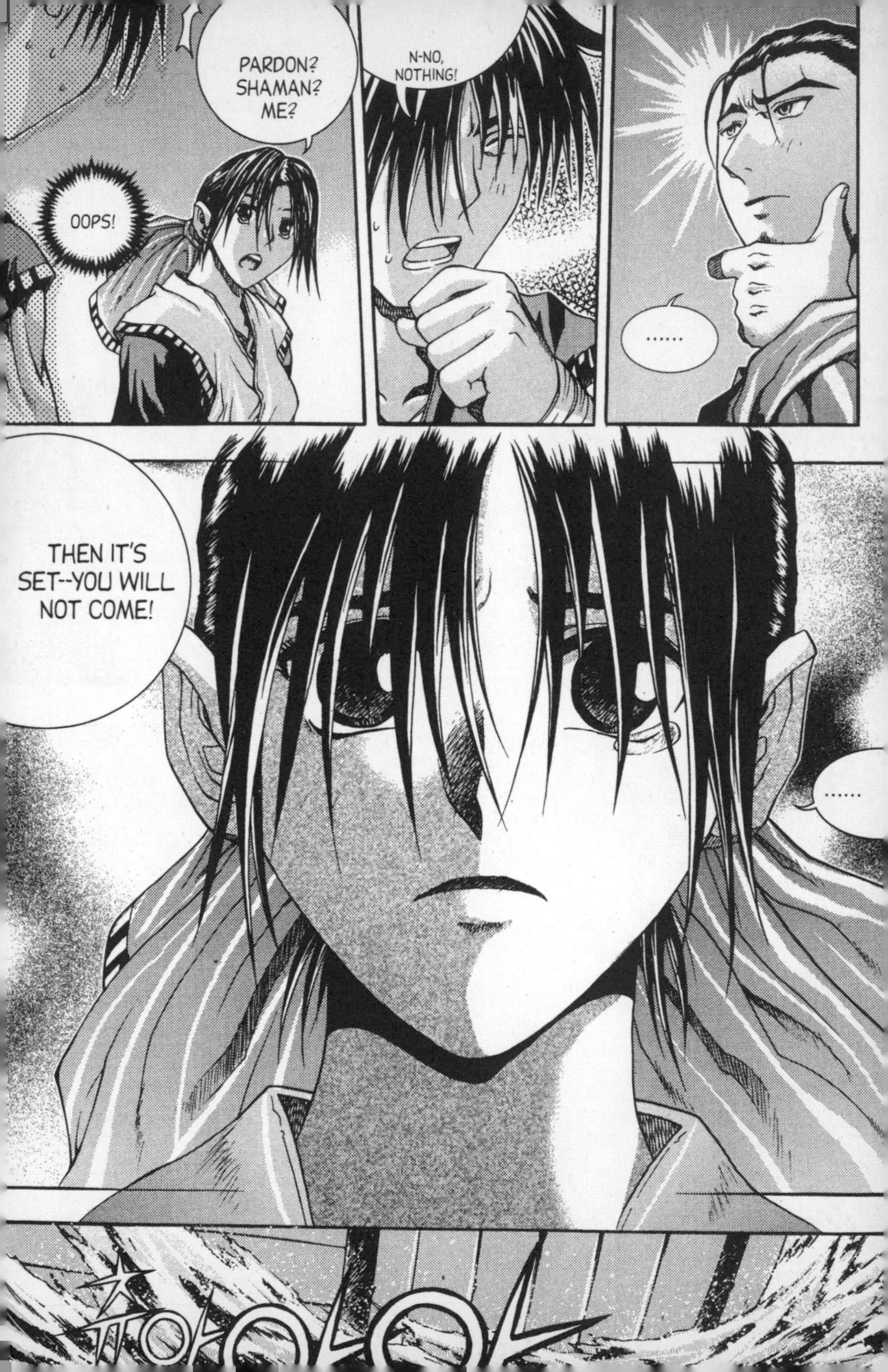
PARDON? SHAMAN? ME?
OOPS!
N-NO, NOTHING!
......
THEN IT'S SET--YOU WILL NOT COME!
......

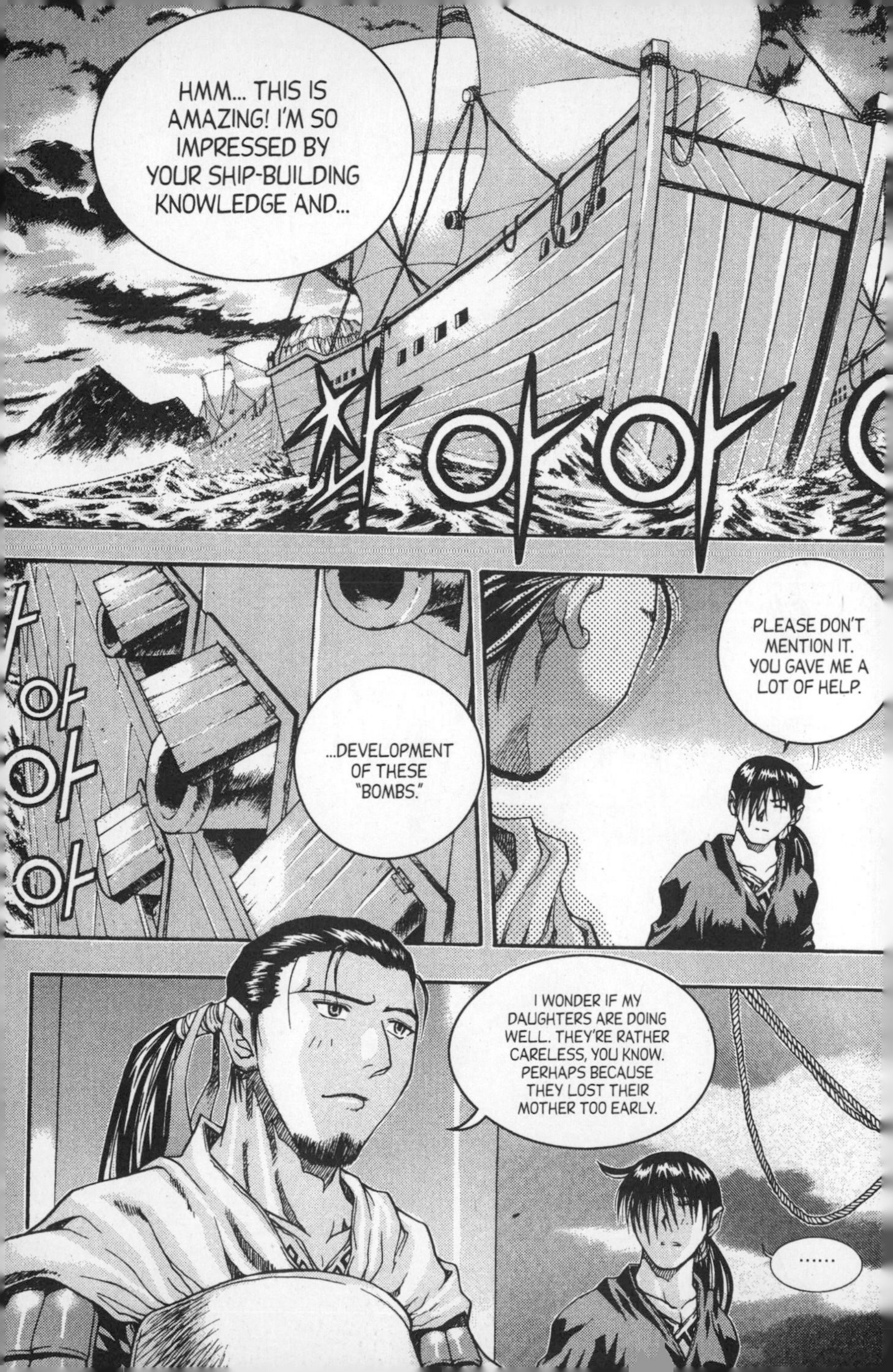

HMM... THIS IS AMAZING! I'M SO IMPRESSED BY YOUR SHIP-BUILDING KNOWLEDGE AND...
아아아
...DEVELOPMENT OF THESE "BOMBS."
PLEASE DON'T MENTION IT. YOU GAVE ME A LOT OF HELP.
I WONDER IF MY DAUGHTERS ARE DOING WELL. THEY'RE RATHER CARELESS, YOU KNOW. PERHAPS BECAUSE THEY LOST THEIR MOTHER TOO EARLY.
......

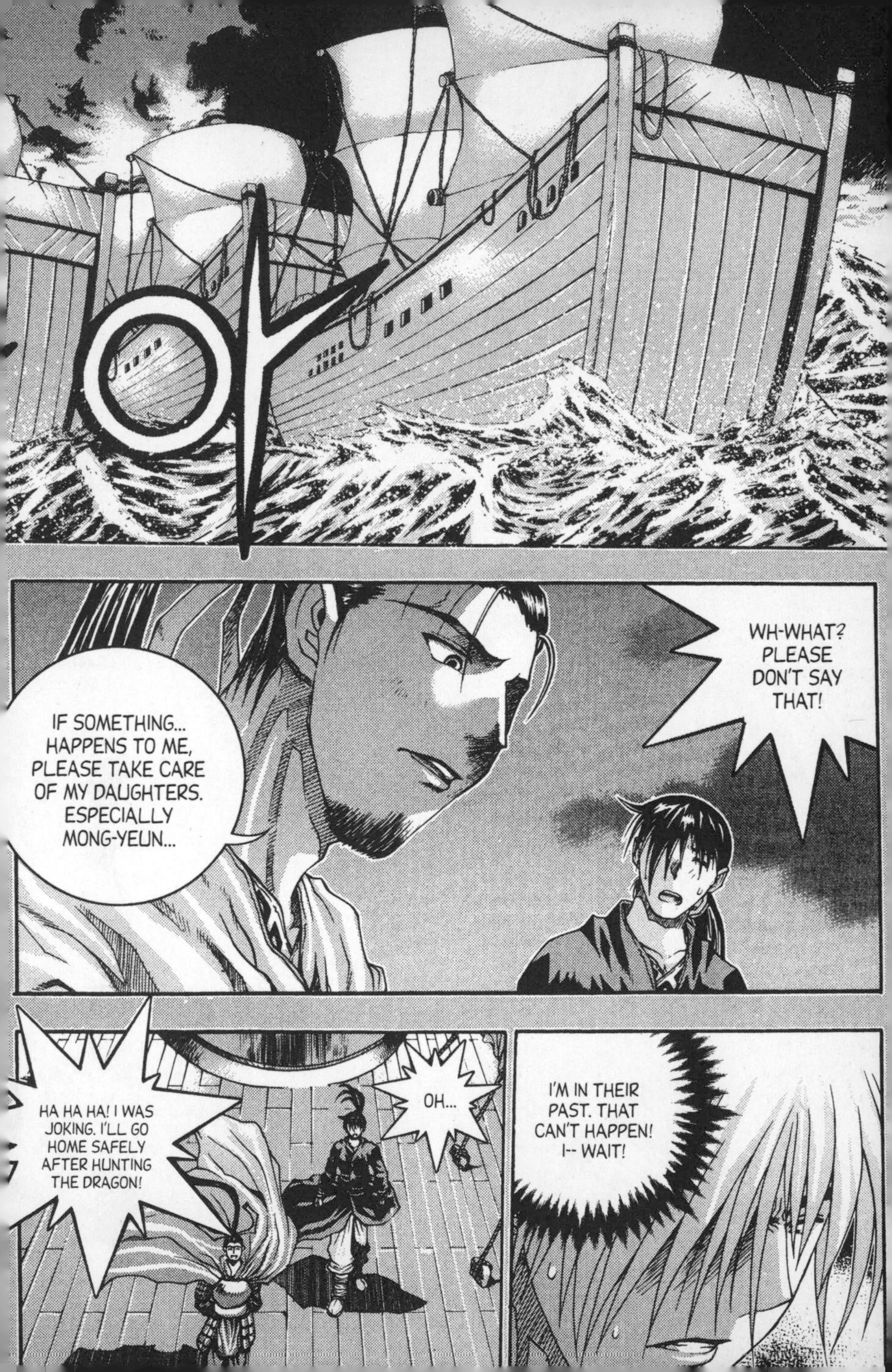
IF SOMETHING... HAPPENS TO ME, PLEASE TAKE CARE OF MY DAUGHTERS. ESPECIALLY MONG-YEUN...
WH-WHAT? PLEASE DON'T SAY THAT!
HA HA HA! I WAS JOKING. I'LL GO HOME SAFELY AFTER HUNTING THE DRAGON!
OH...
I'M IN THEIR PAST. THAT CAN'T HAPPEN! I-- WAIT!

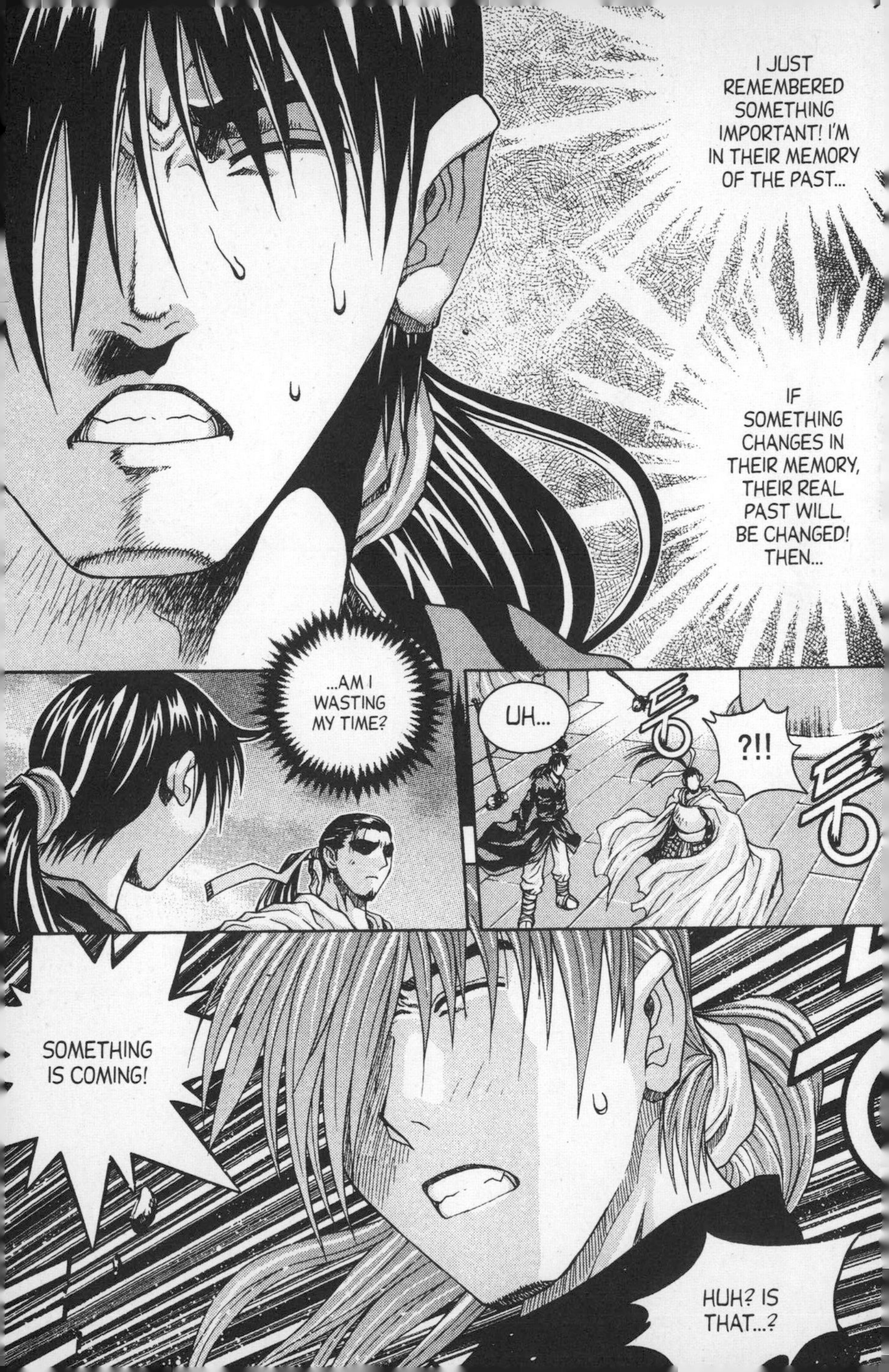
I JUST REMEMBERED SOMETHING IMPORTANT! I'M IN THEIR MEMORY OF THE PAST...
IF SOMETHING CHANGES IN THEIR MEMORY, THEIR REAL PAST WILL BE CHANGED! THEN...
...AM I WASTING MY TIME?
UH...
?!!
SOMETHING IS COMING!
HUH? IS THAT...?

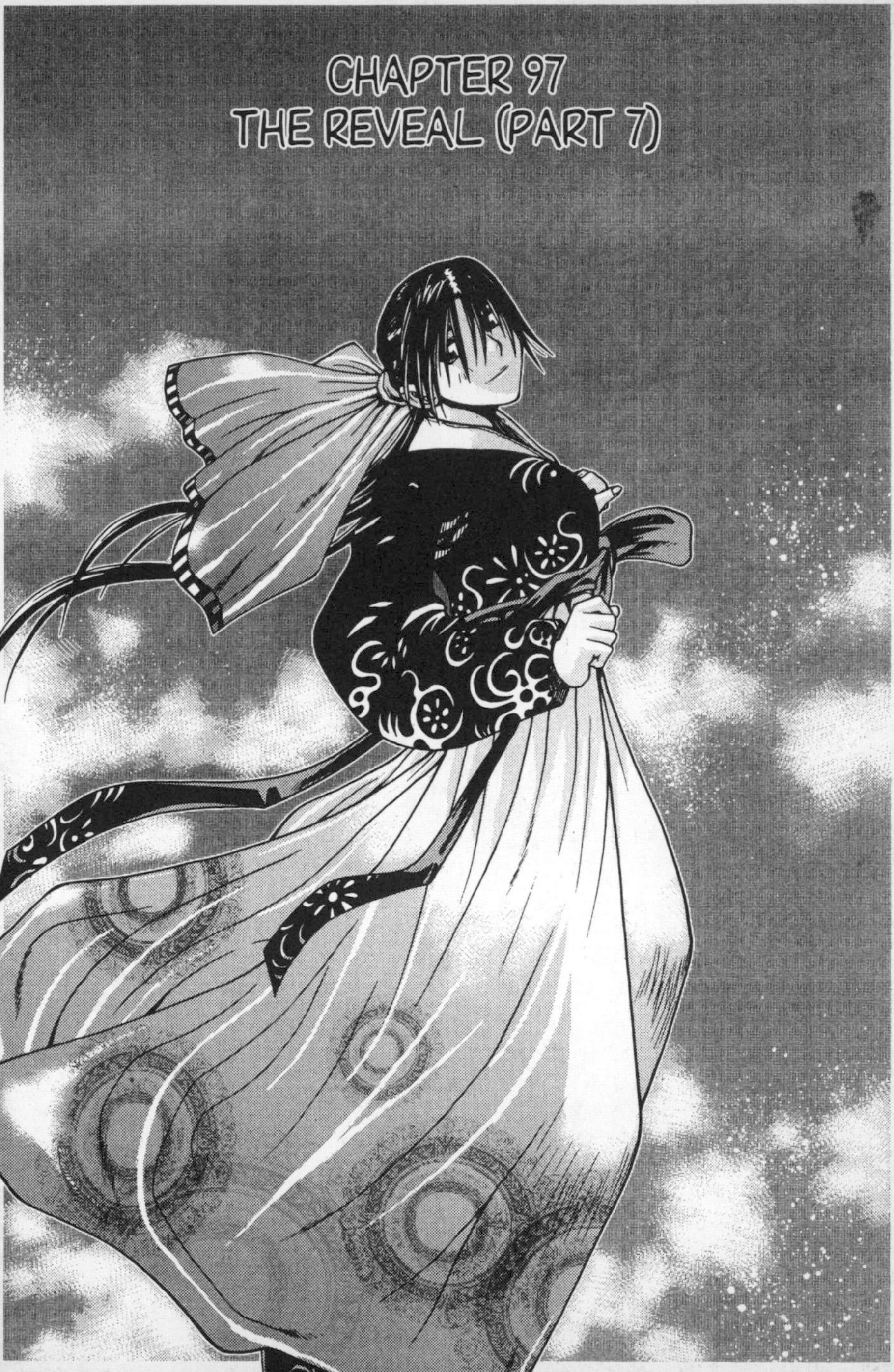
CHAPTER 97
THE REVEAL (PART 7)

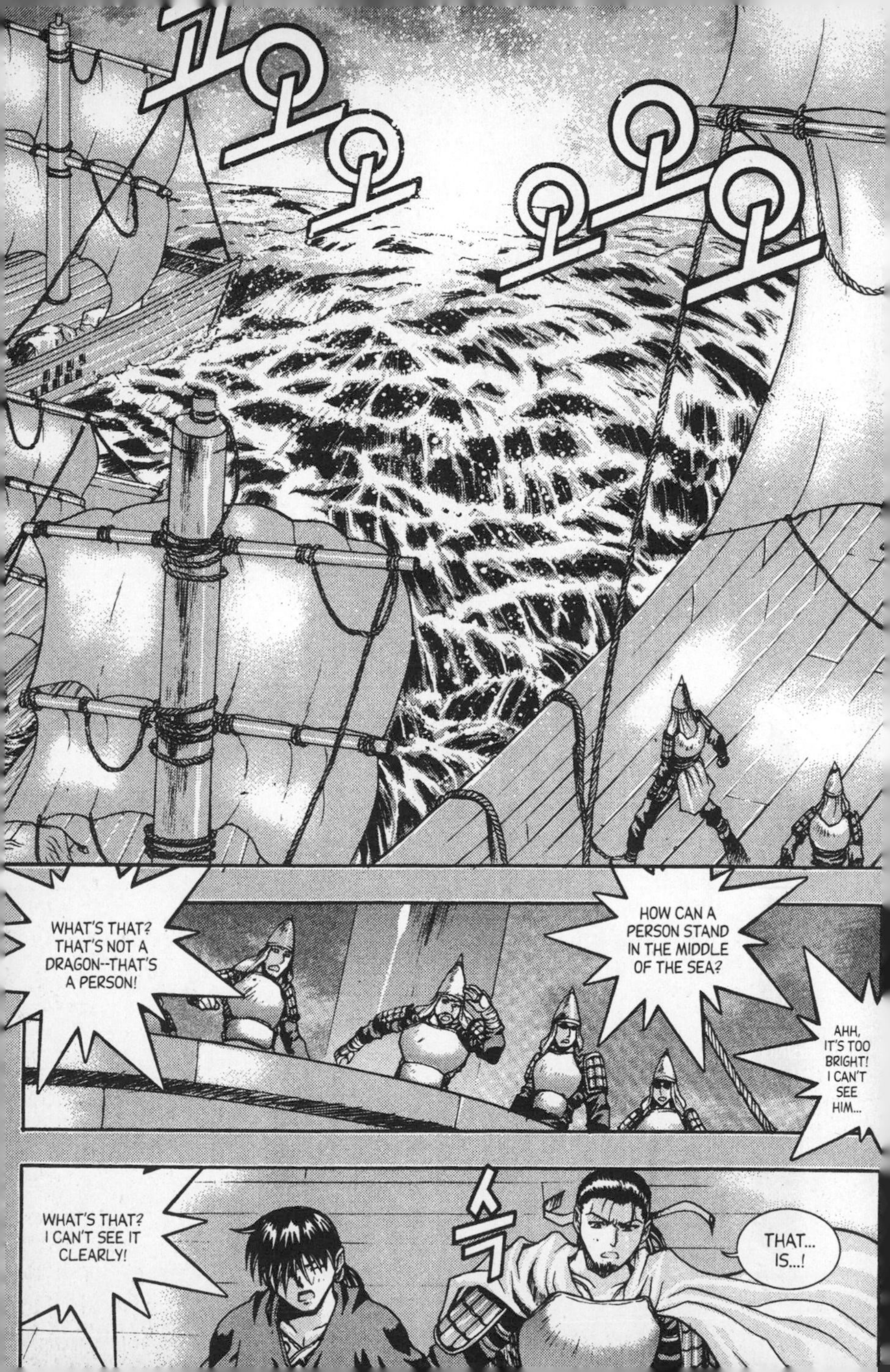
WHAT'S THAT? THAT'S NOT A DRAGON--THAT'S A PERSON!
HOW CAN A PERSON STAND IN THE MIDDLE OF THE SEA?
AHH, IT'S TOO BRIGHT! I CAN'T SEE HIM...
WHAT'S THAT? I CAN'T SEE IT CLEARLY!
THAT... IS...!

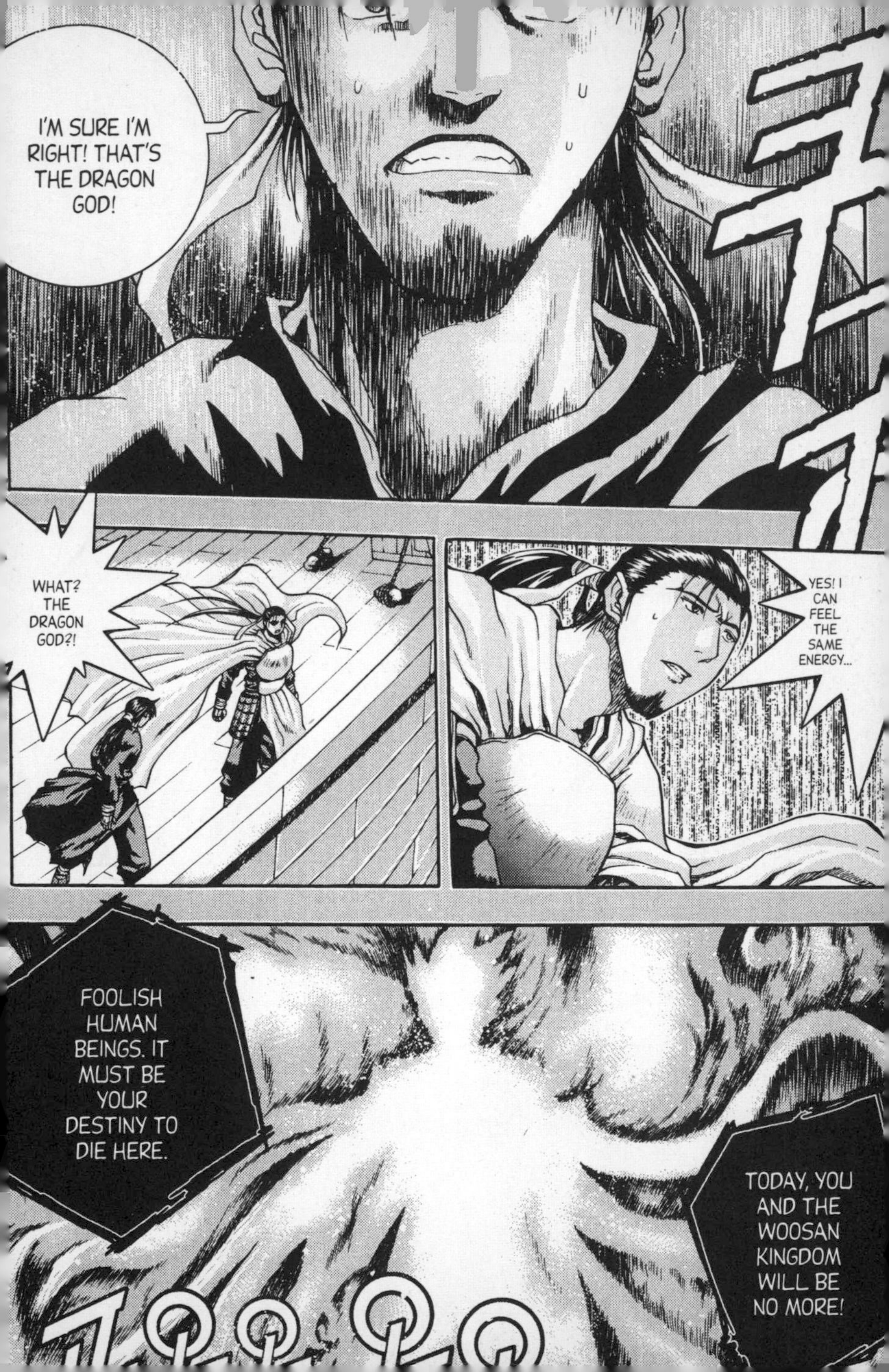
I'M SURE I'M RIGHT! THAT'S THE DRAGON GOD!
WHAT? THE DRAGON GOD?!
YES! I CAN FEEL THE SAME ENERGY...
FOOLISH HUMAN BEINGS. IT MUST BE YOUR DESTINY TO DIE HERE.
TODAY, YOU AND THE WOOSAN KINGDOM WILL BE NO MORE!

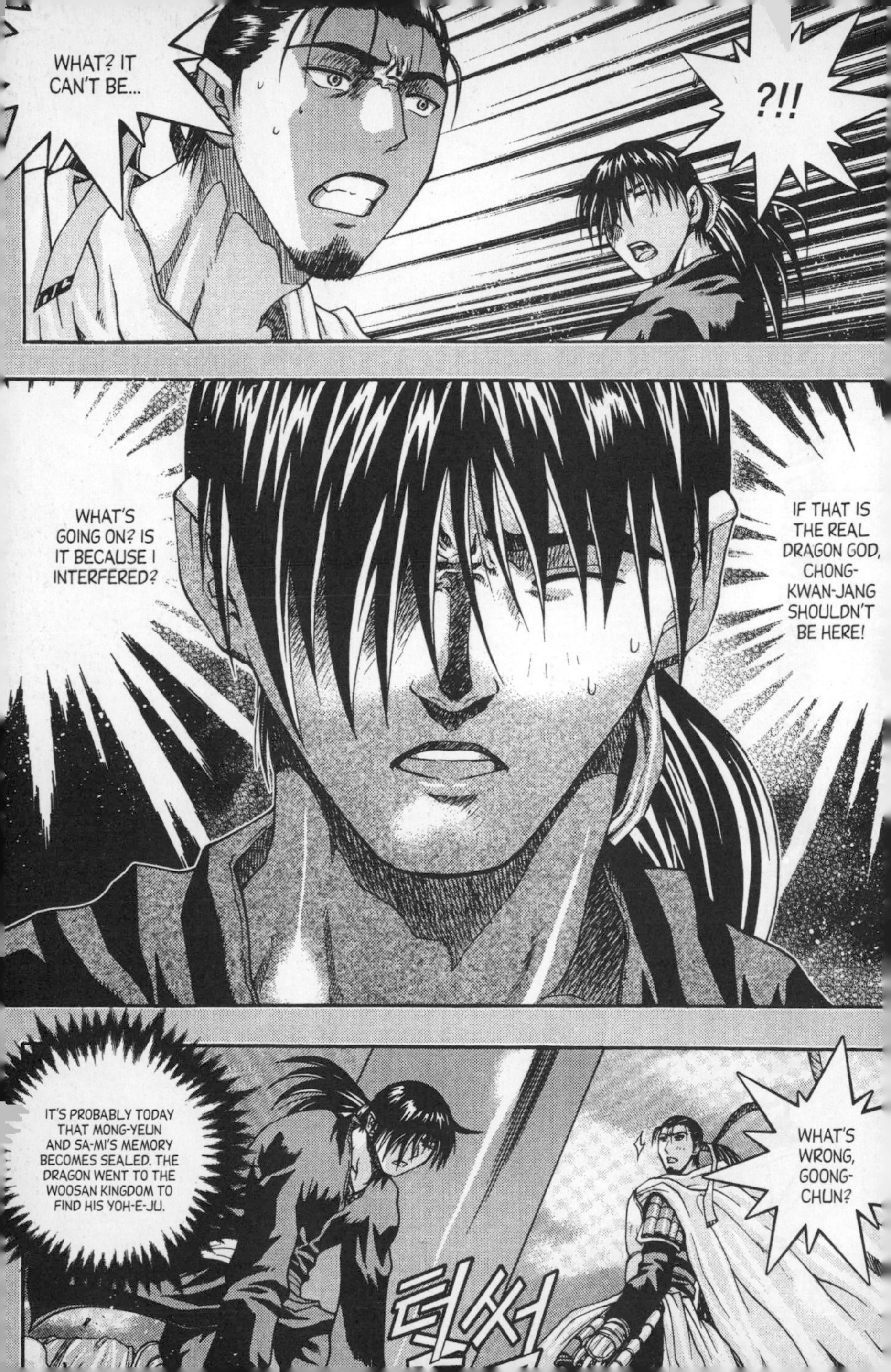

WHAT? IT CAN'T BE...
?!!
WHAT'S GOING ON? IS IT BECAUSE I INTERFERED?
IF THAT IS THE REAL DRAGON GOD, CHONG-KWAN-JANG SHOULDN'T BE HERE!
IT'S PROBABLY TODAY THAT MONG-YEUN AND SA-MI'S MEMORY BECOMES SEALED. THE DRAGON WENT TO THE WOOSAN KINGDOM TO FIND HIS YOH-E-JU.
WHAT'S WRONG, GOONG-CHUN?

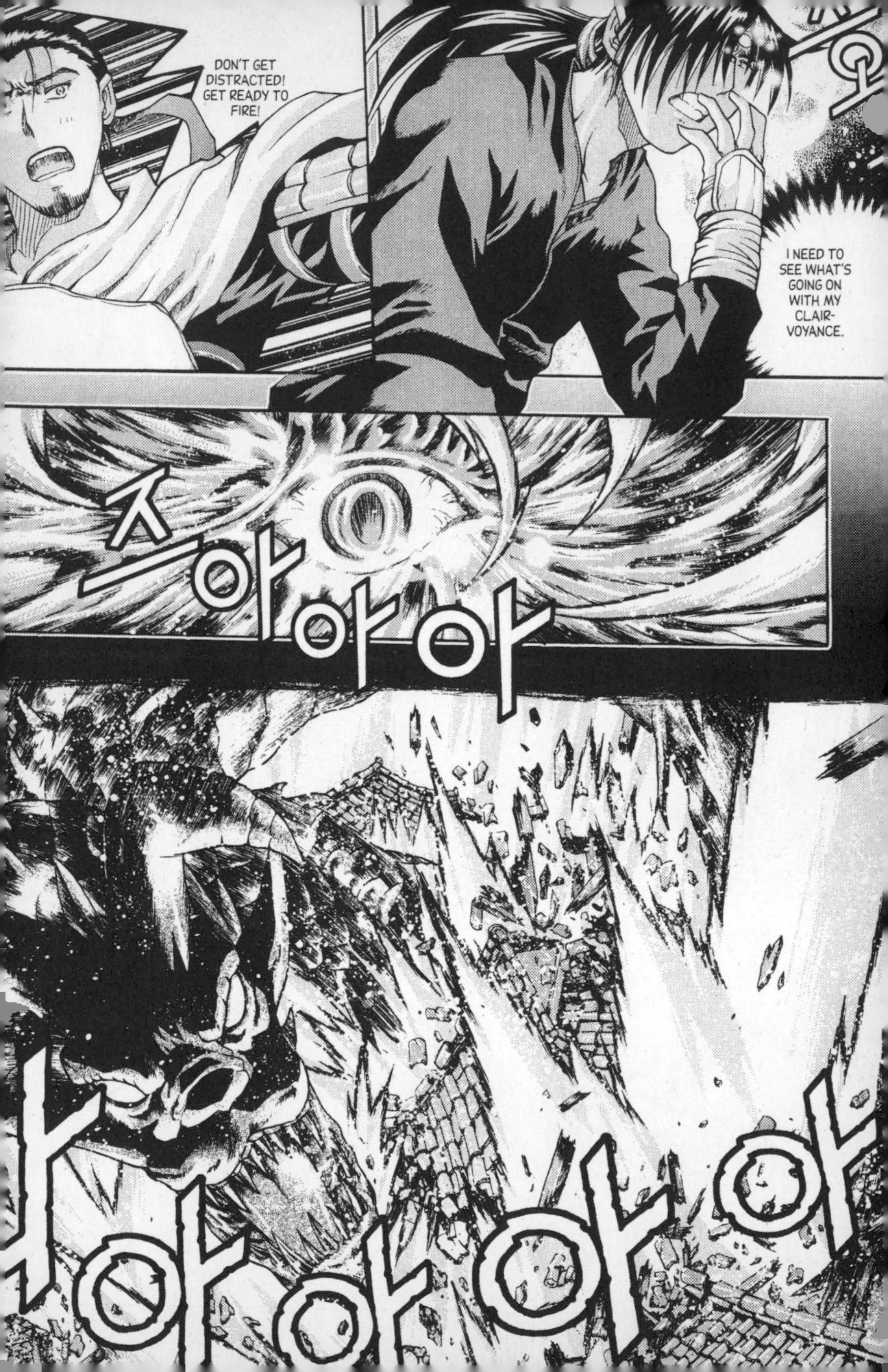
DON'T GET DISTRACTED! GET READY TO FIRE!
I NEED TO SEE WHAT'S GOING ON WITH MY CLAIR-VOYANCE.

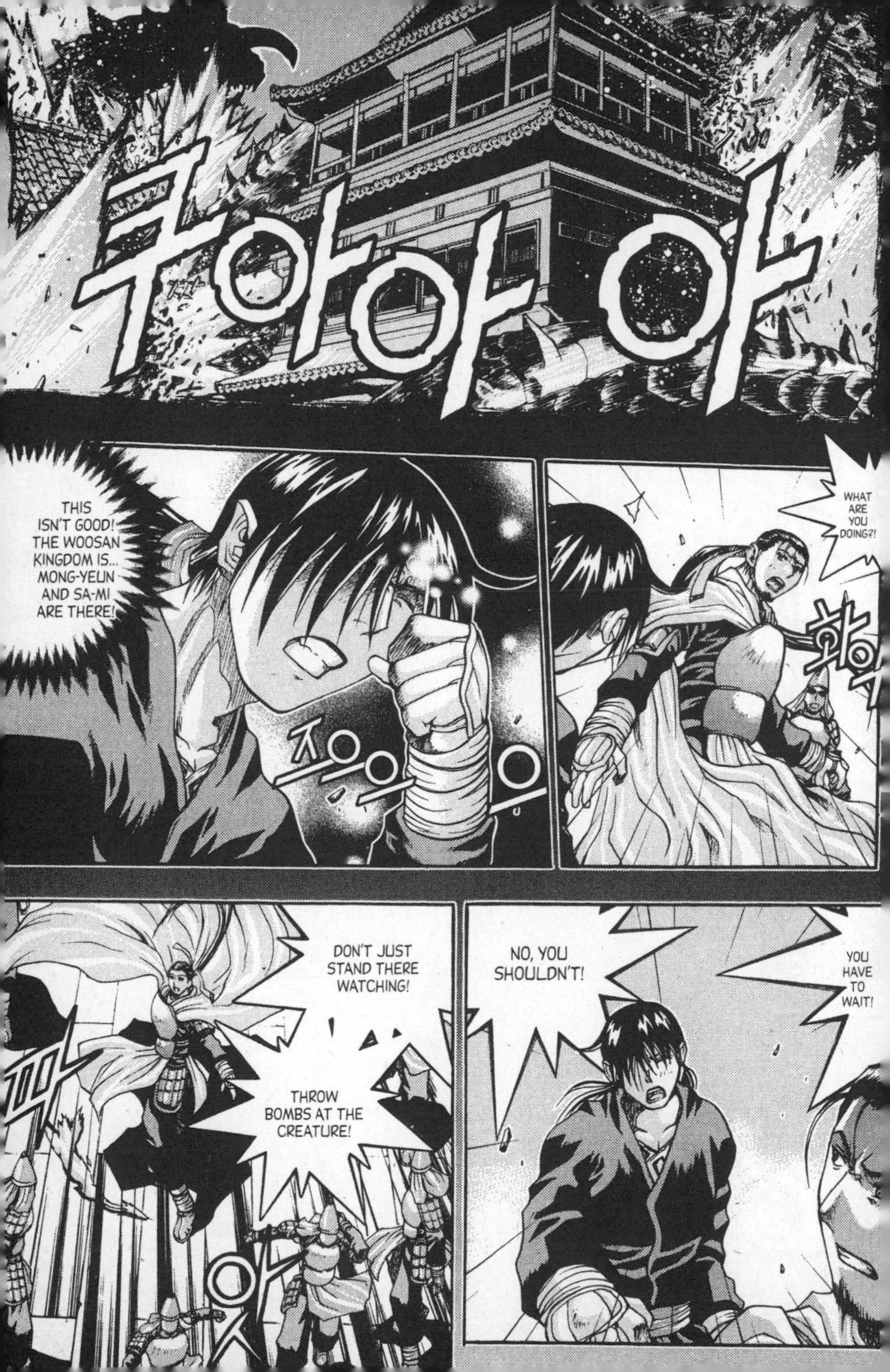
THIS ISN'T GOOD! THE WOOSAN KINGDOM IS... MONG-YEUN AND SA-MI ARE THERE!
WHAT ARE YOU DOING?!
DON'T JUST STAND THERE WATCHING!
THROW BOMBS AT THE CREATURE!
NO, YOU SHOULDN'T!
YOU HAVE TO WAIT!

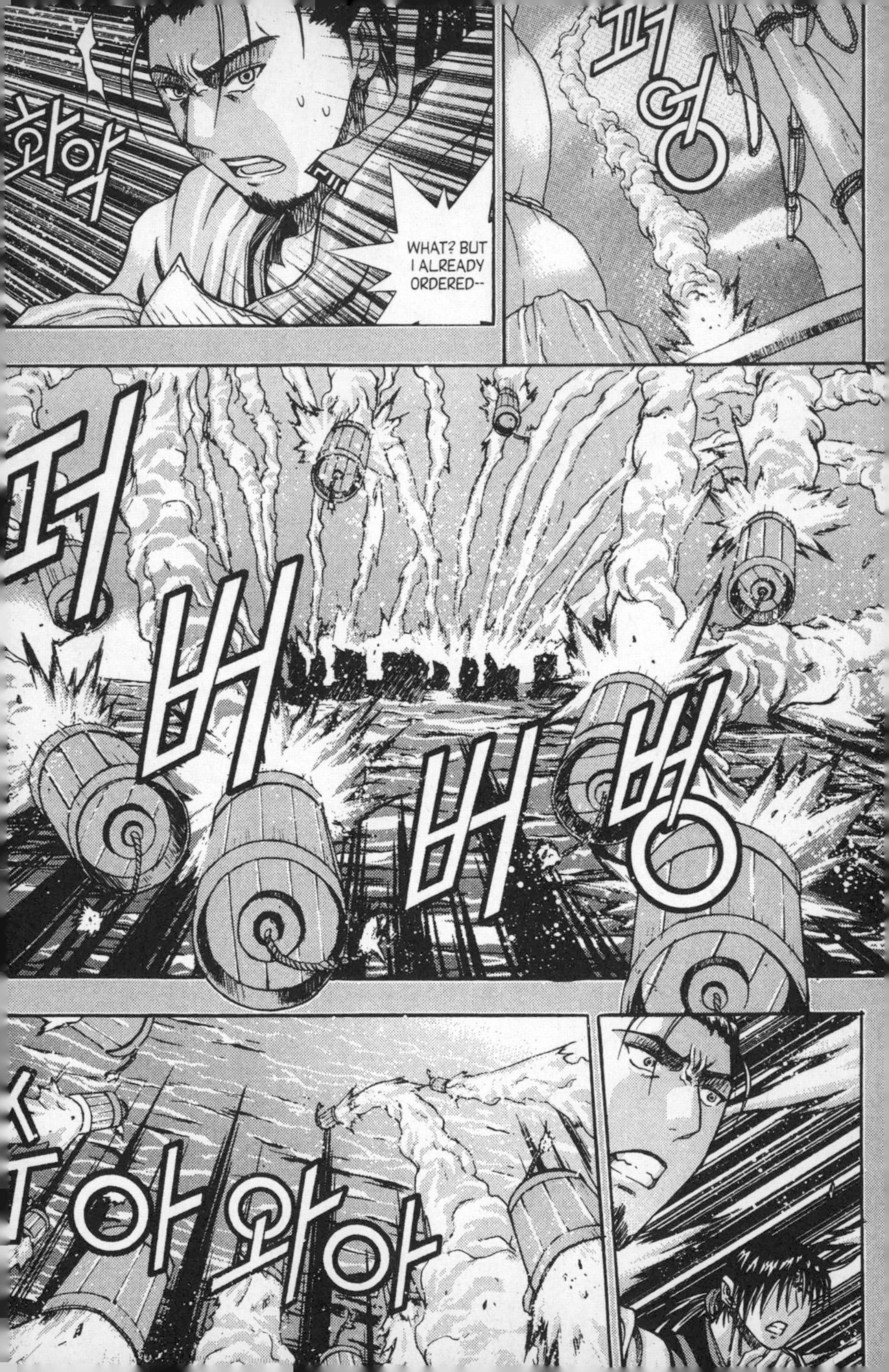
화악
WHAT? BUT I ALREADY ORDERED--
피잉
퍼버버벙

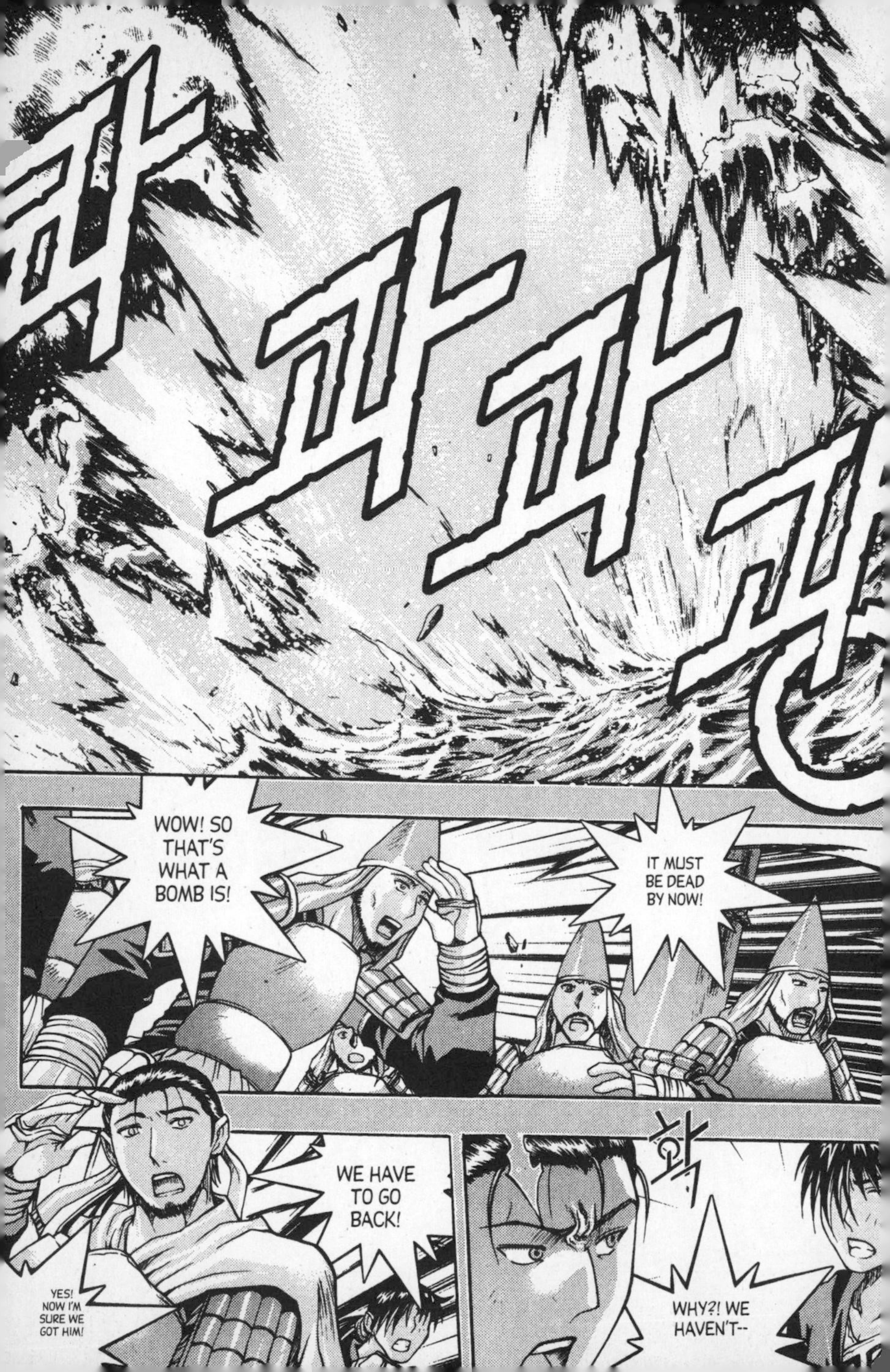
WOW! SO THAT'S WHAT A BOMB IS!
IT MUST BE DEAD BY NOW!
WE HAVE TO GO BACK!
YES! NOW I'M SURE WE GOT HIM!
WHY?! WE HAVEN'T--

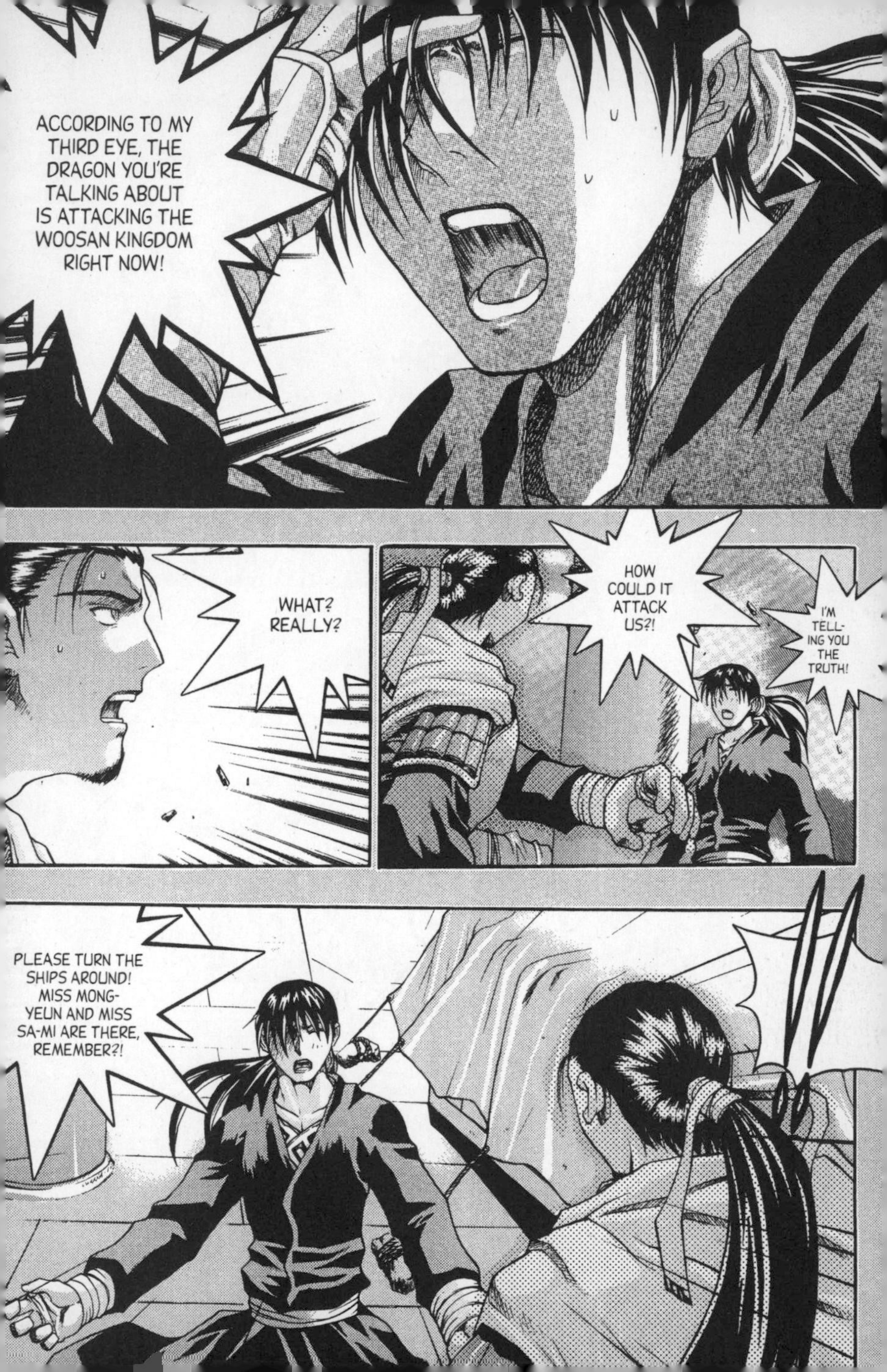
ACCORDING TO MY THIRD EYE, THE DRAGON YOU'RE TALKING ABOUT IS ATTACKING THE WOOSAN KINGDOM RIGHT NOW!
WHAT? REALLY?
HOW COULD IT ATTACK US?!
I'M TELL-ING YOU THE TRUTH!
PLEASE TURN THE SHIPS AROUND! MISS MONG-YEUN AND MISS SA-MI ARE THERE, REMEMBER?!

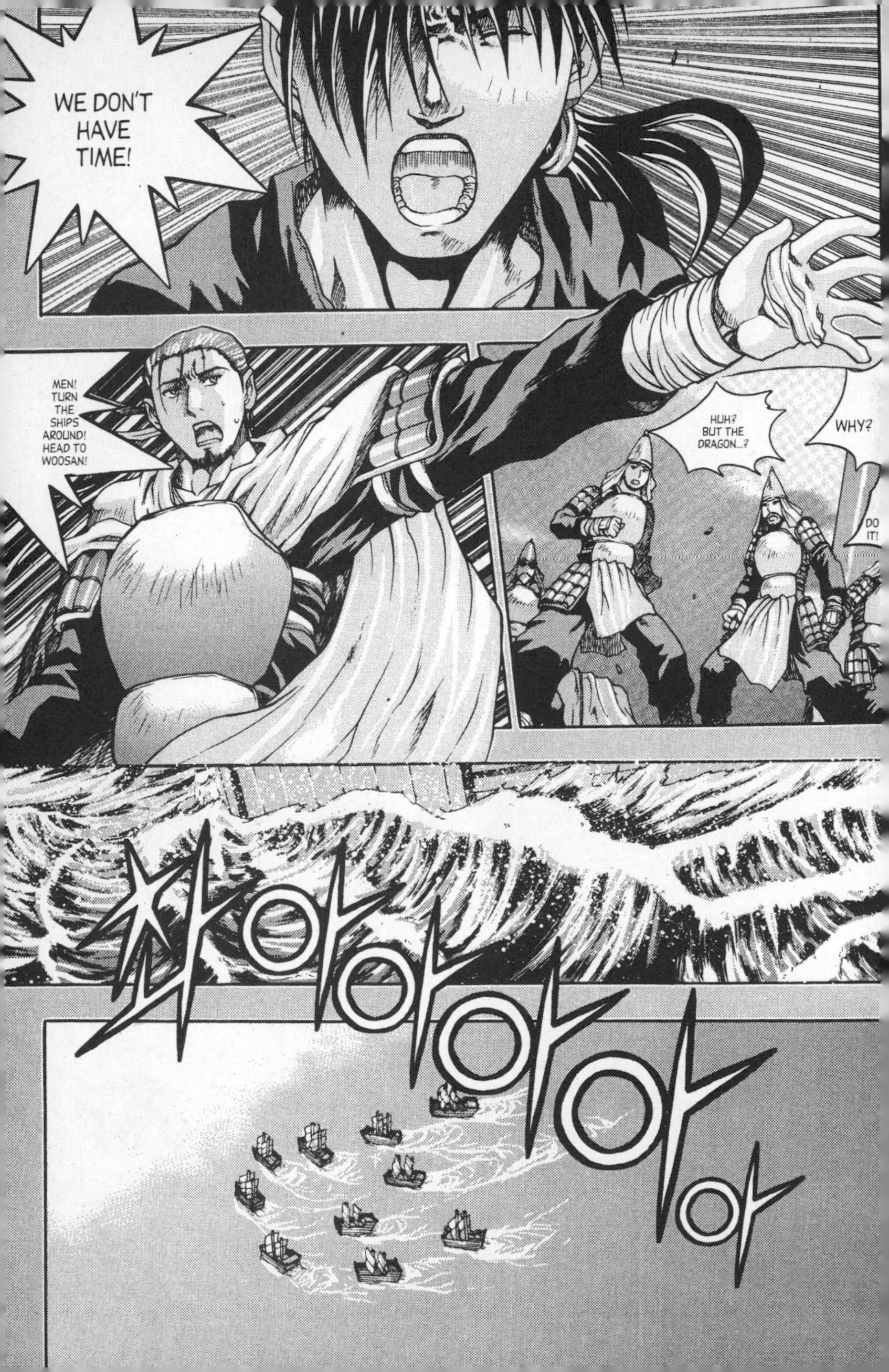
WE DON'T HAVE TIME!
MEN! TURN THE SHIPS AROUND! HEAD TO WOOSAN!
HUH? BUT THE DRAGON...?
WHY?
DO IT!

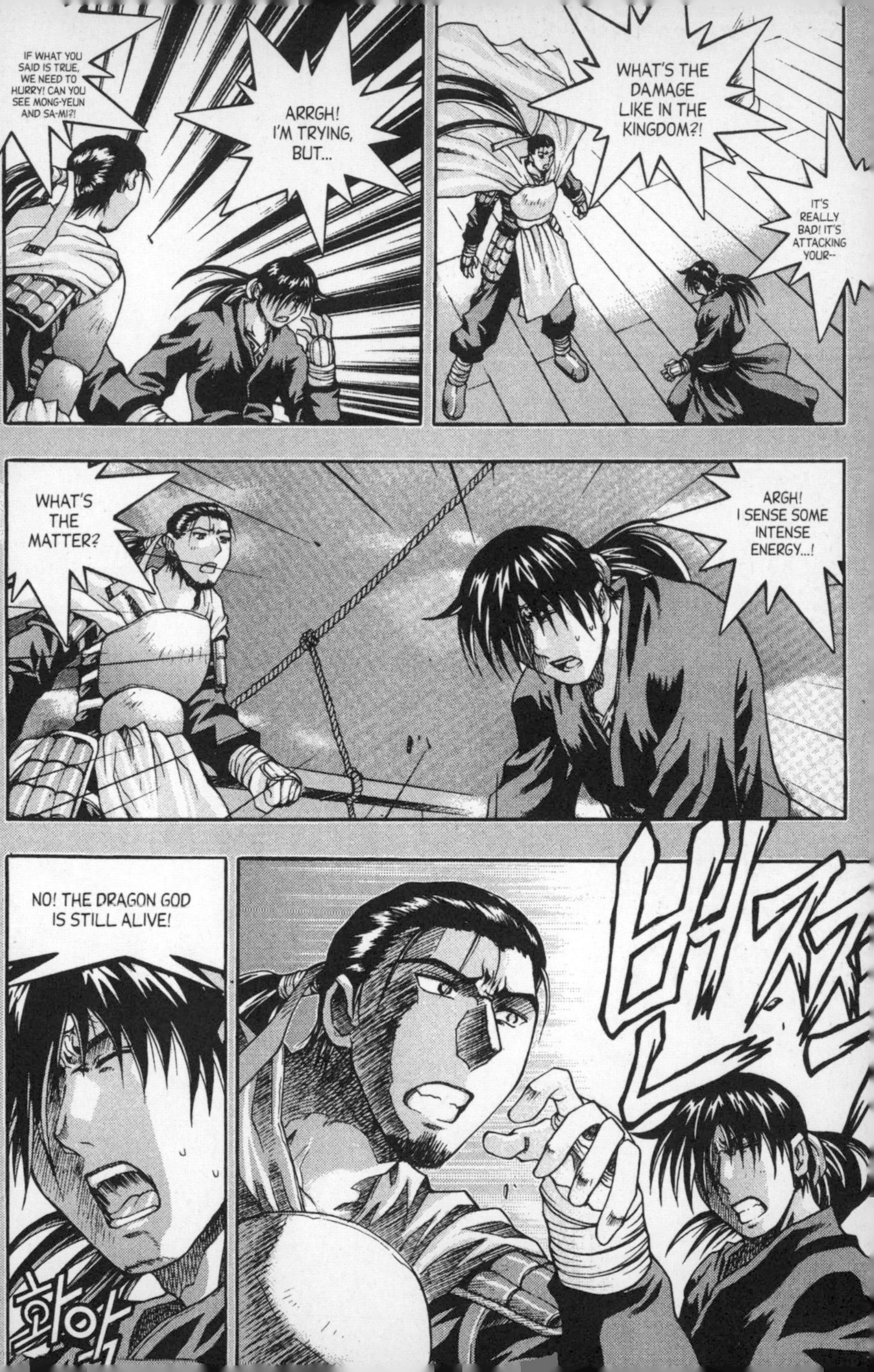

IF WHAT YOU SAID IS TRUE, WE NEED TO HURRY! CAN YOU SEE MONG-YEUN AND SA-MI?!
ARRGH! I'M TRYING, BUT...
WHAT'S THE DAMAGE LIKE IN THE KINGDOM?!
IT'S REALLY BAD! IT'S ATTACKING YOUR--
WHAT'S THE MATTER?
ARGH! I SENSE SOME INTENSE ENERGY...!
NO! THE DRAGON GOD IS STILL ALIVE!

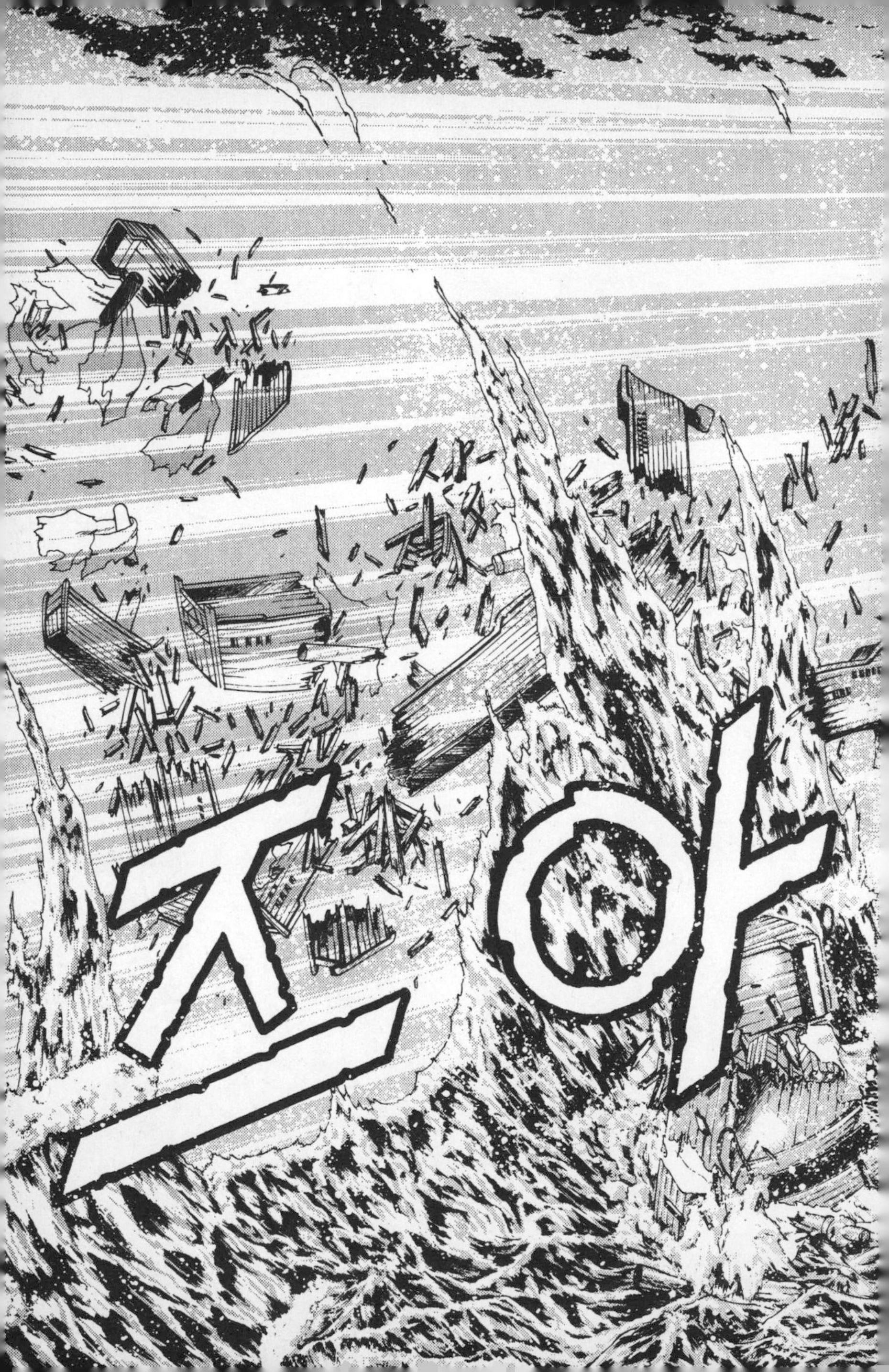
즈아

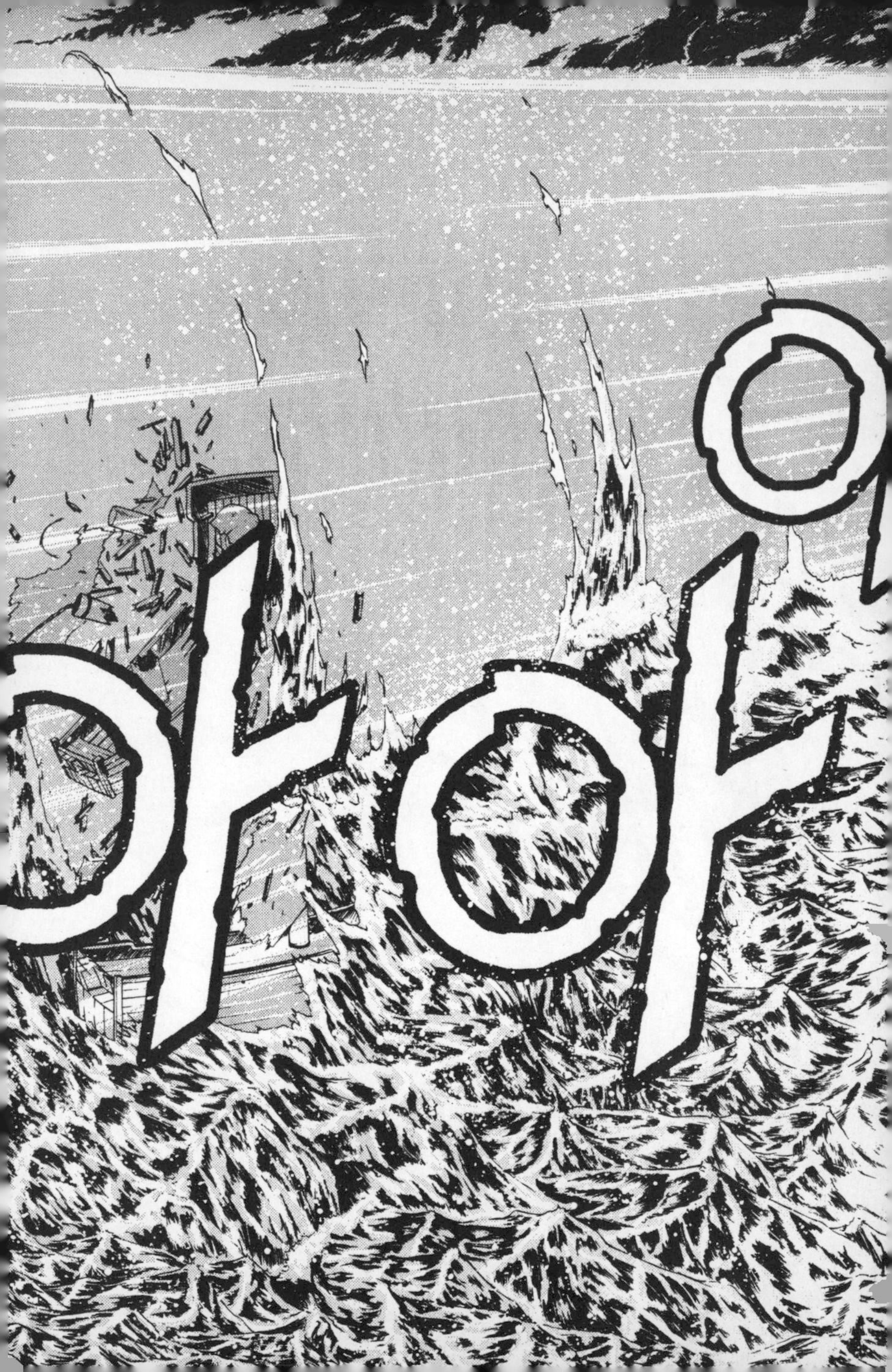

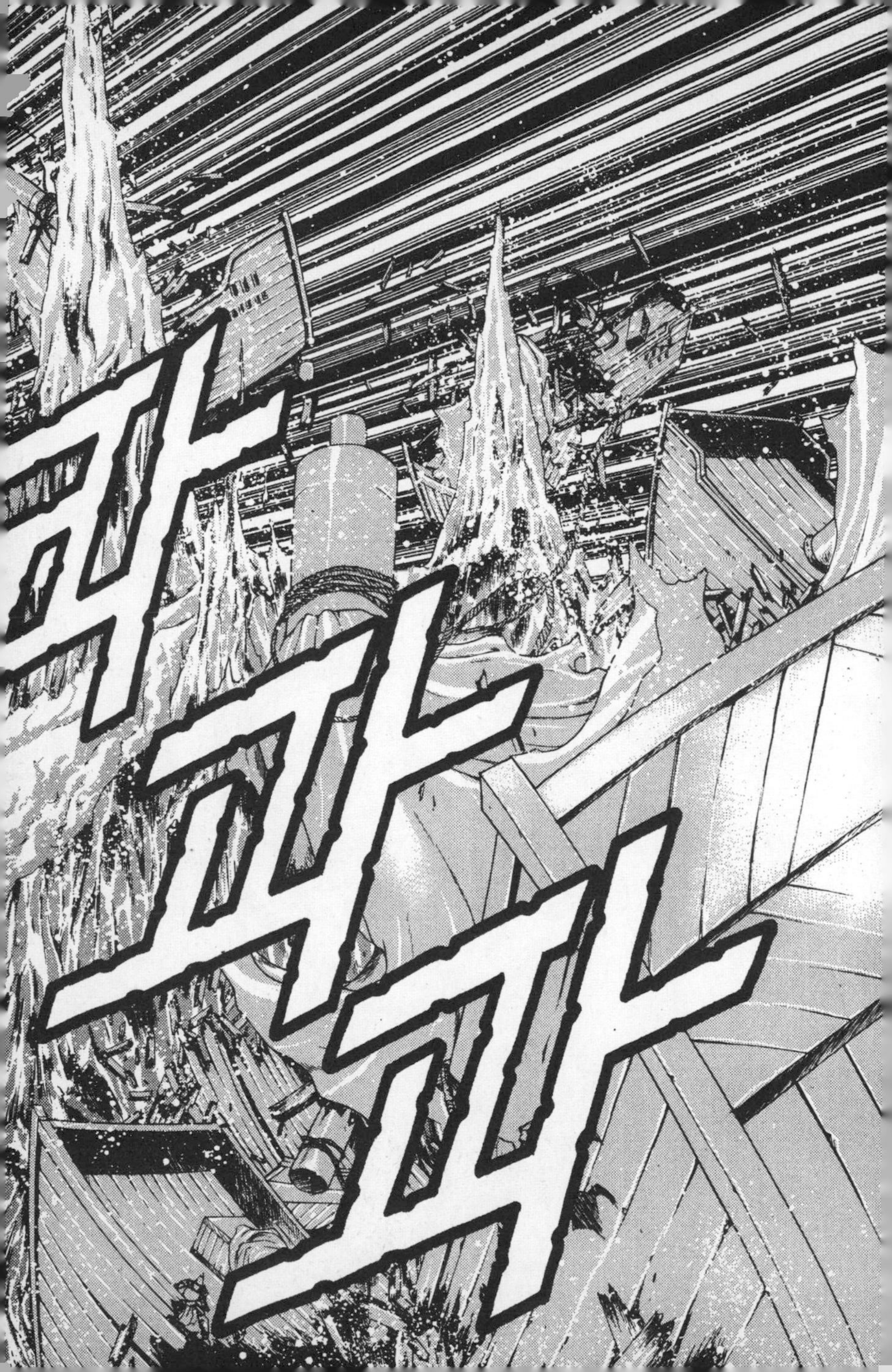

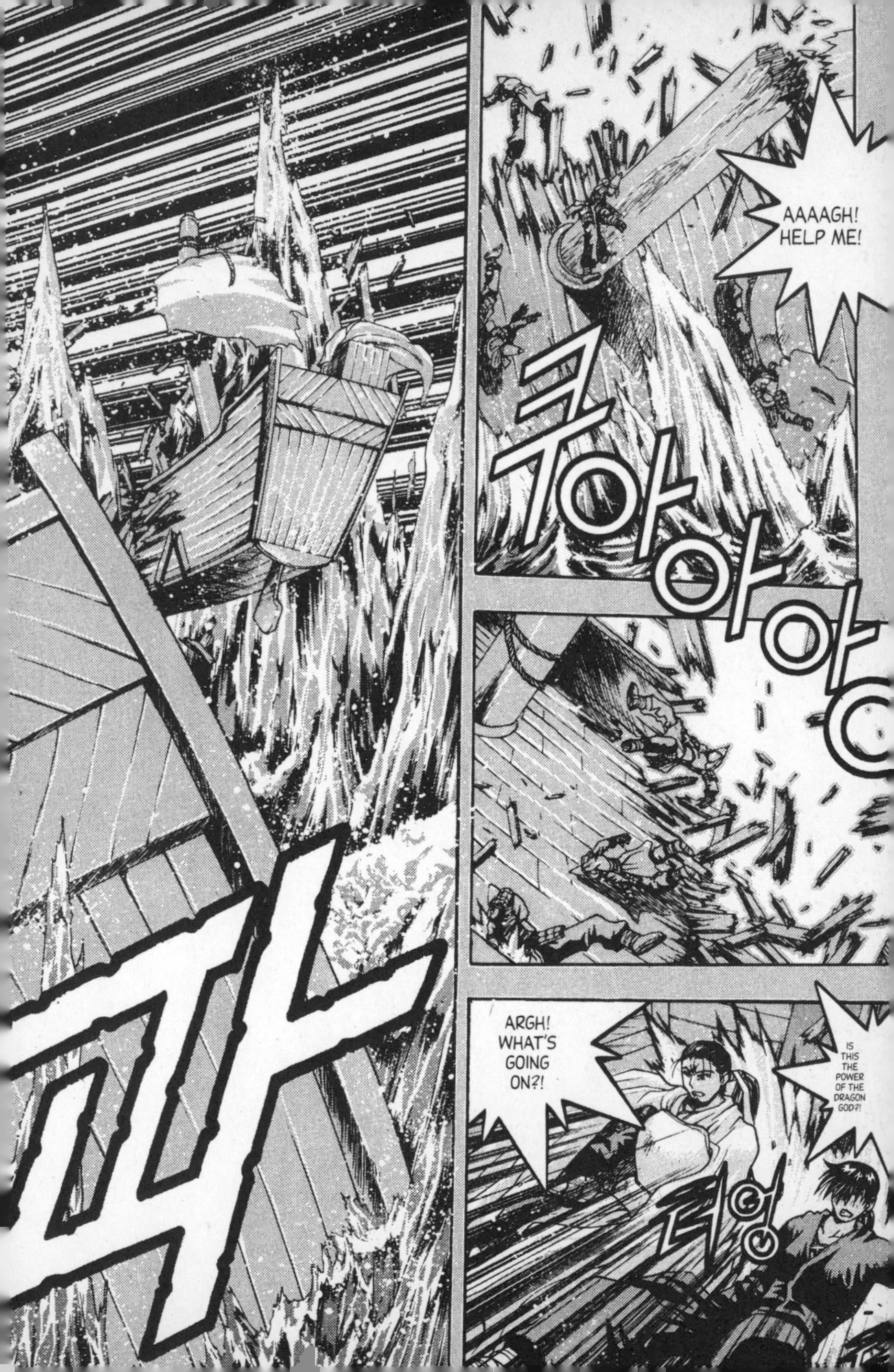
AAAAGH! HELP ME!
ARGH! WHAT'S GOING ON?!
IS THIS THE POWER OF THE DRAGON GOD?!

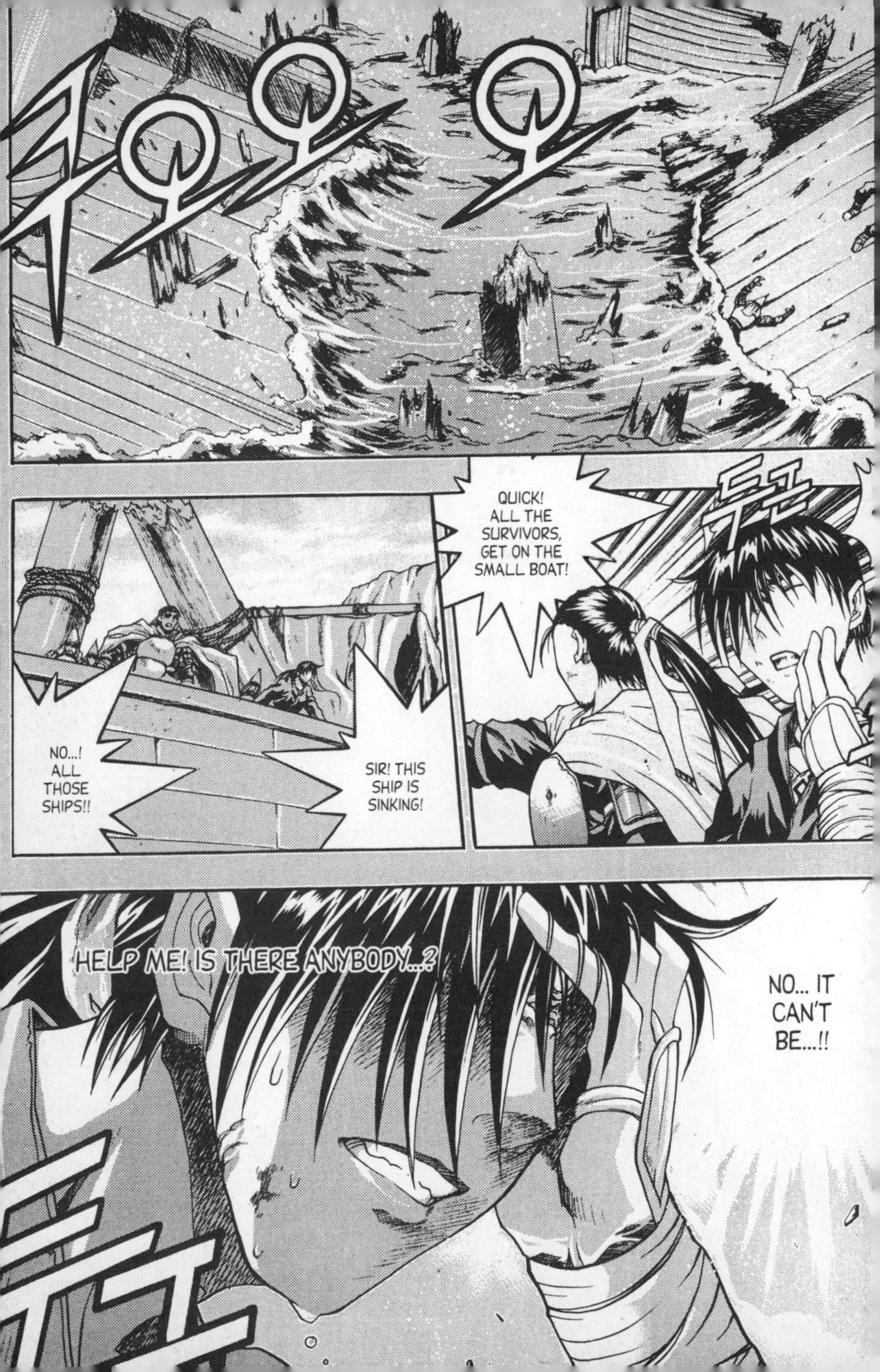
NO...! ALL THOSE SHIPS!!
SIR! THIS SHIP IS SINKING!
QUICK! ALL THE SURVIVORS, GET ON THE SMALL BOAT!
HELP ME! IS THERE ANYBODY...?
NO... IT CAN'T BE...!!

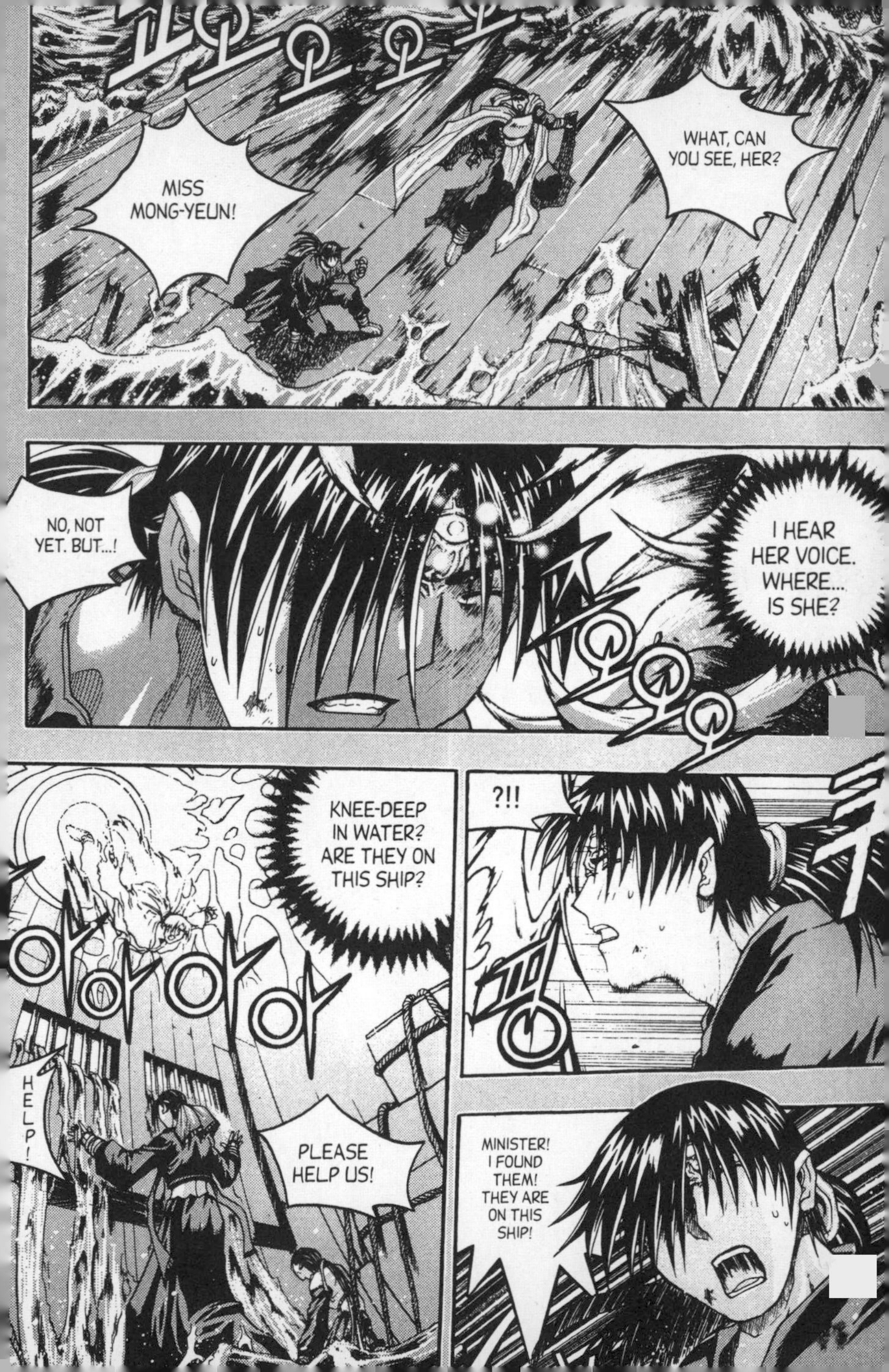
MISS MONG-YEUN!
WHAT, CAN YOU SEE, HER?
NO, NOT YET. BUT...!
I HEAR HER VOICE. WHERE... IS SHE?
KNEE-DEEP IN WATER? ARE THEY ON THIS SHIP?
HELP!
PLEASE HELP US!
?!!
MINISTER! I FOUND THEM! THEY ARE ON THIS SHIP!

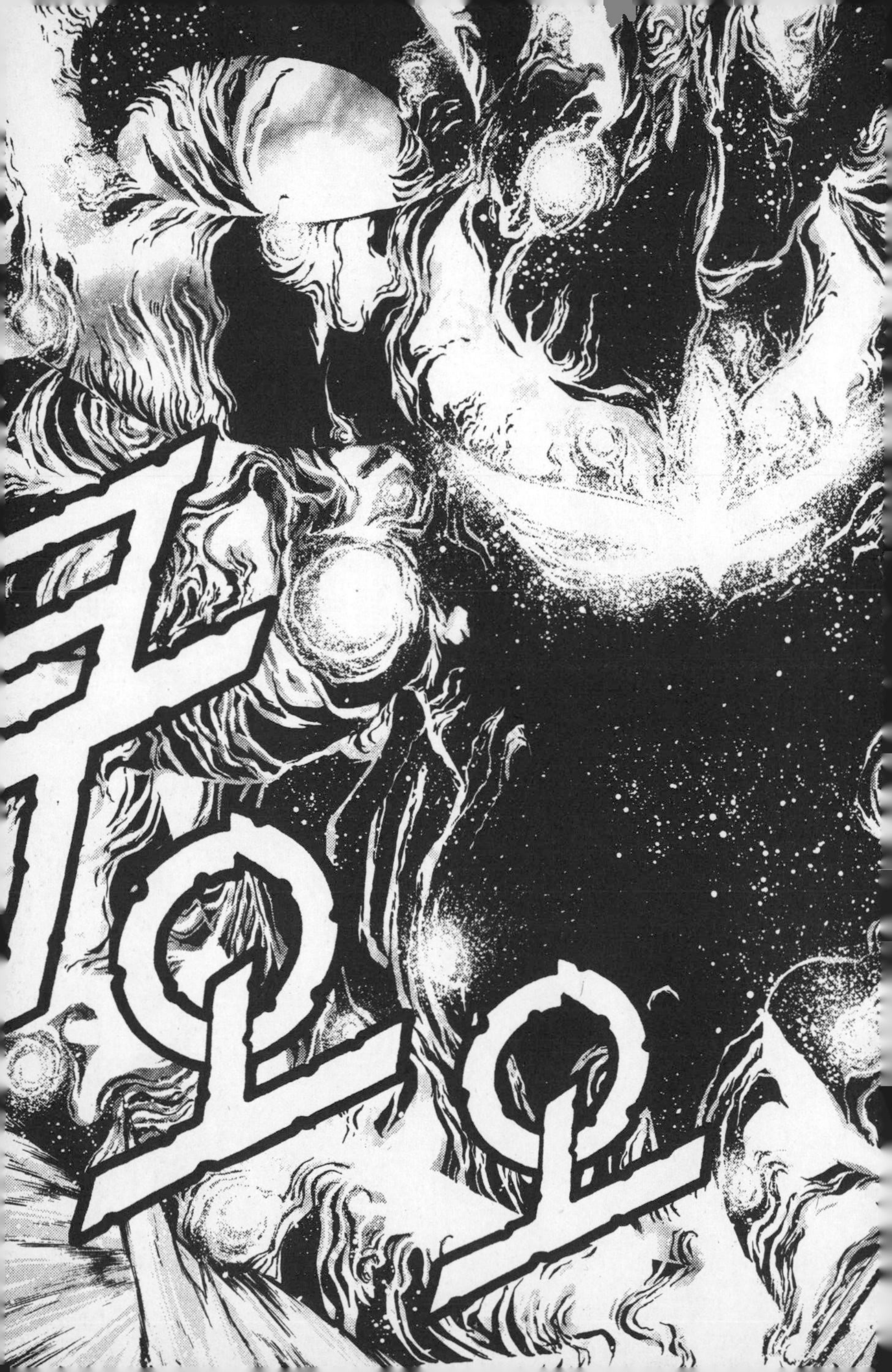

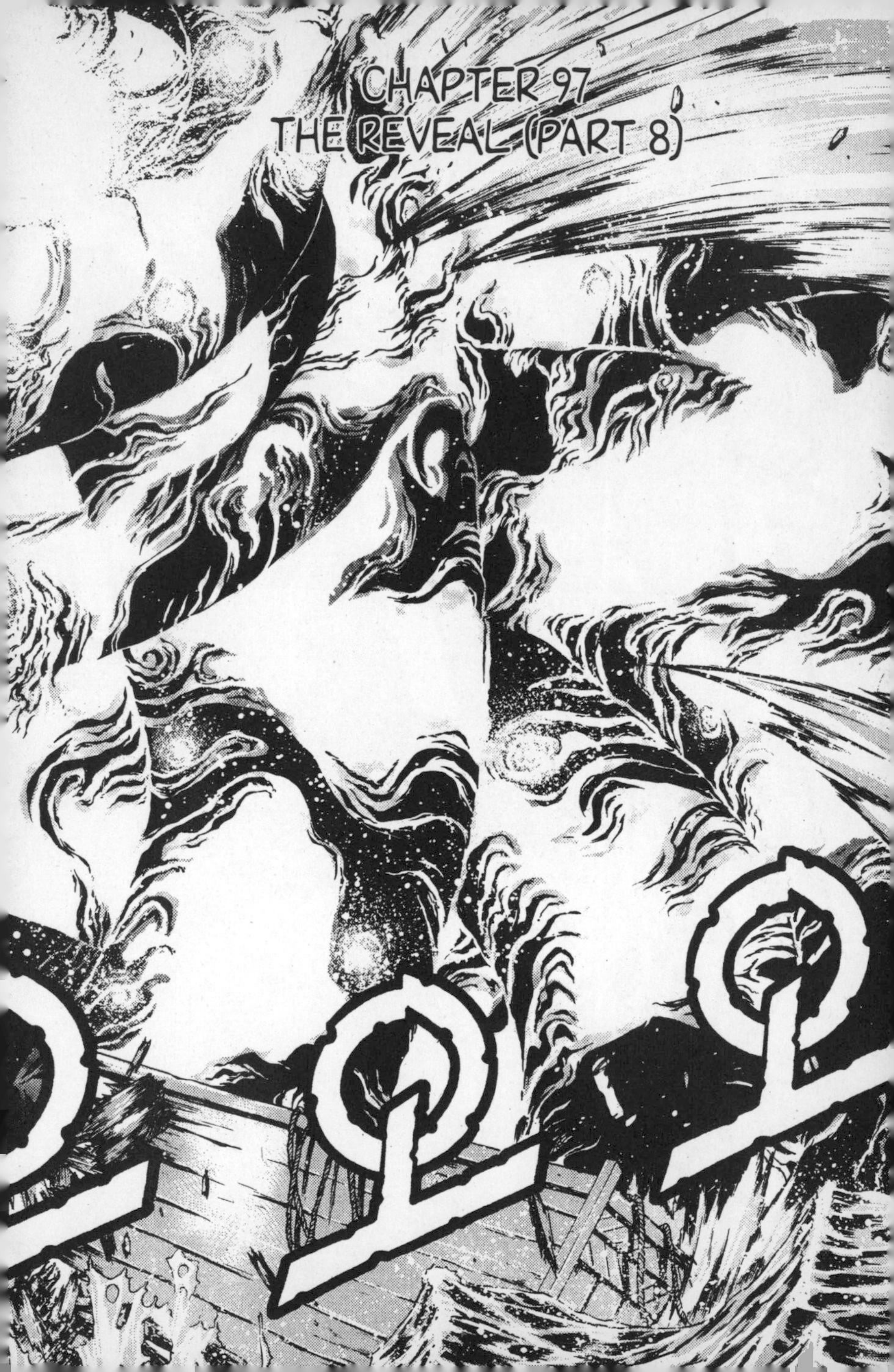
CHAPTER 97
THE REVEAL (PART 8)

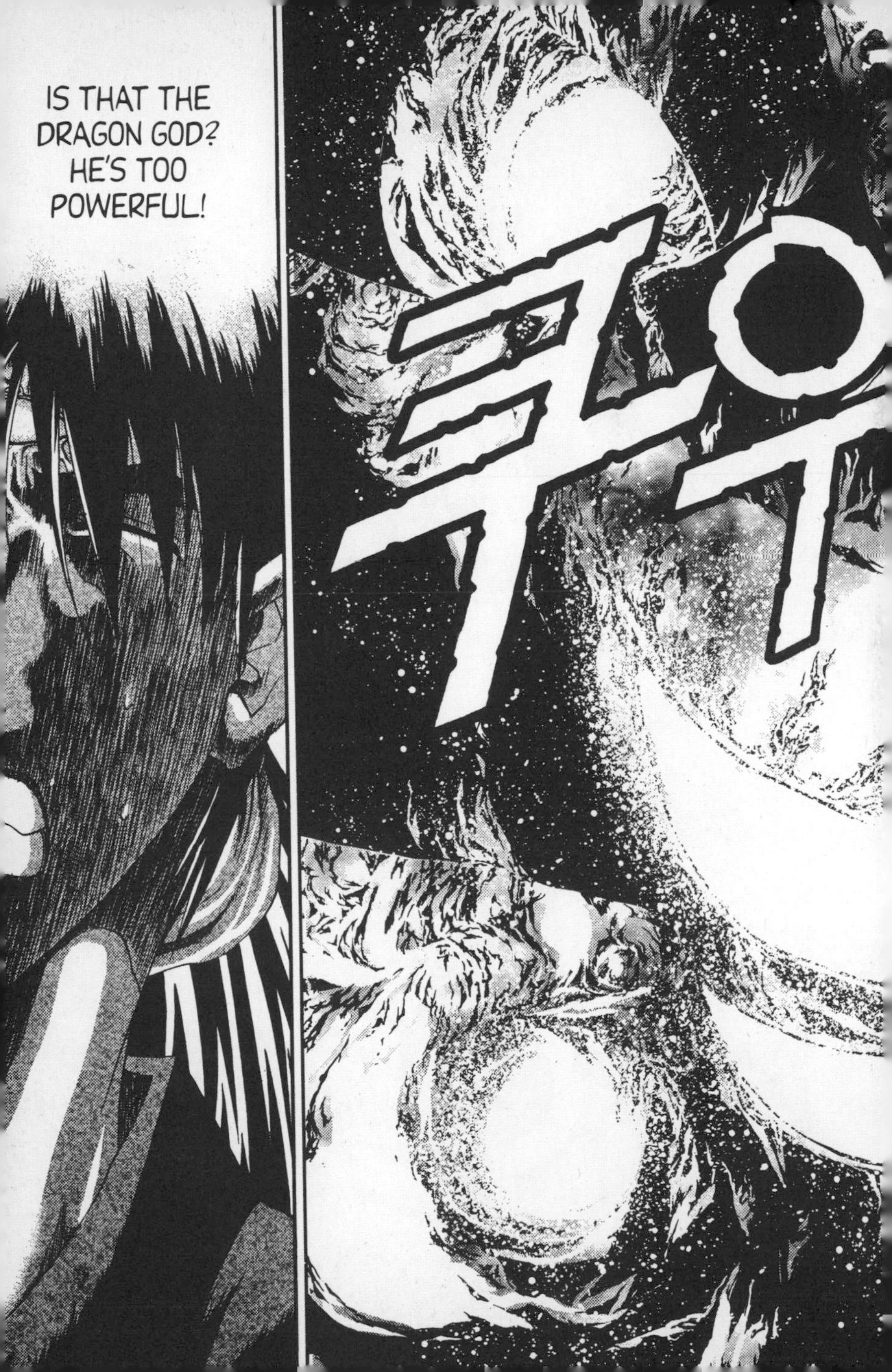
IS THAT THE DRAGON GOD? HE'S TOO POWERFUL!

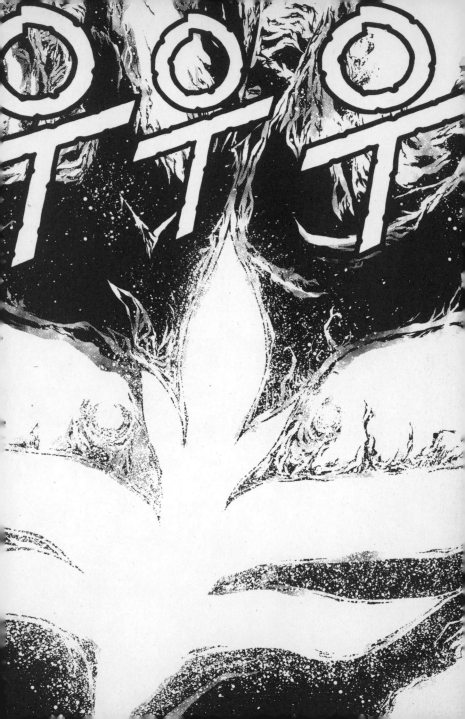

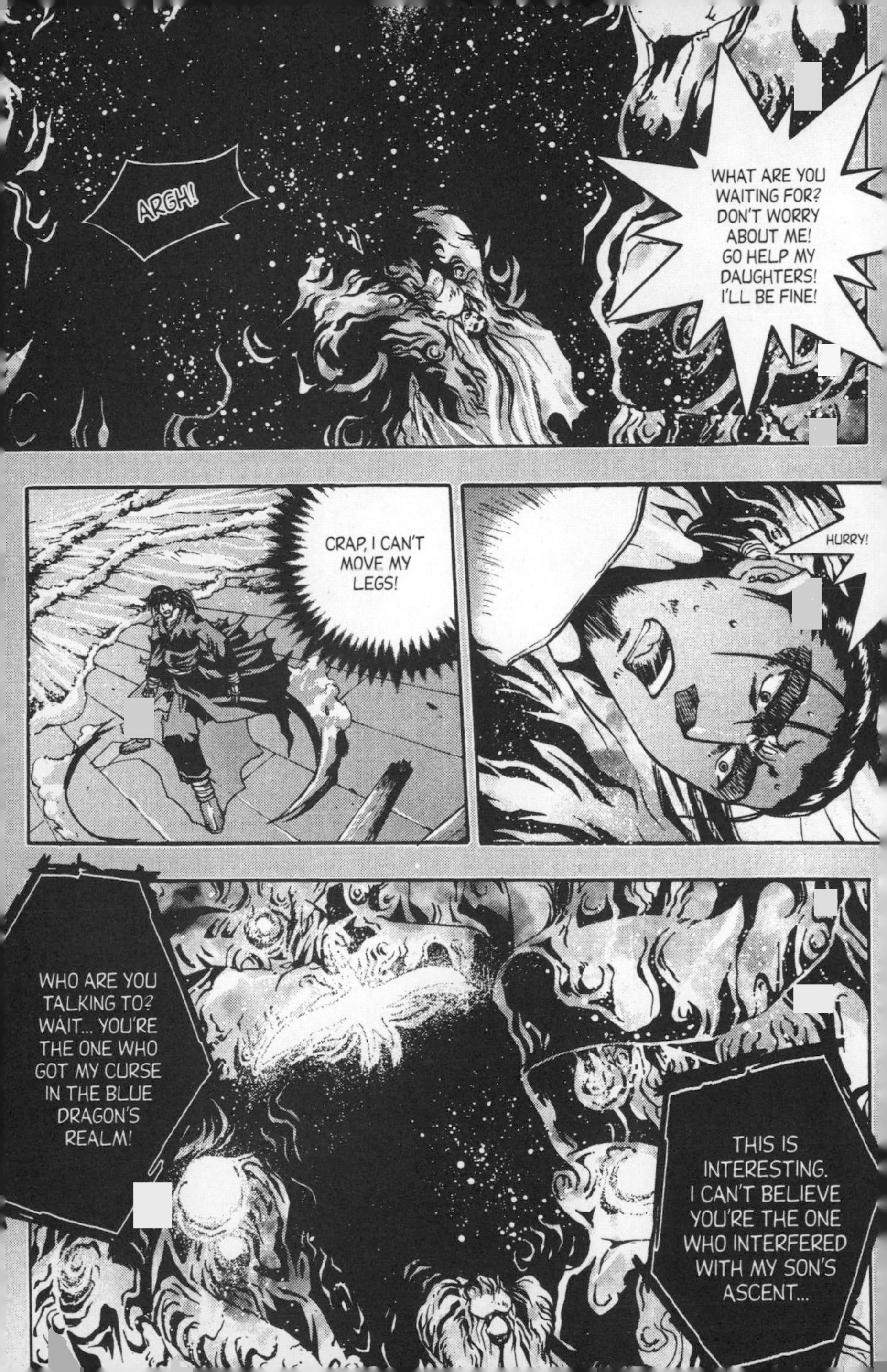
ARGH!
WHAT ARE YOU WAITING FOR? DON'T WORRY ABOUT ME! GO HELP MY DAUGHTERS! I'LL BE FINE!
CRAP, I CAN'T MOVE MY LEGS!
HURRY!
WHO ARE YOU TALKING TO? WAIT... YOU'RE THE ONE WHO GOT MY CURSE IN THE BLUE DRAGON'S REALM!
THIS IS INTERESTING. I CAN'T BELIEVE YOU'RE THE ONE WHO INTERFERED WITH MY SON'S ASCENT...

ARGH! HIS VOICE IS ECHOING IN MY HEAD!

BUT...CAN'T THE DRAGON GOD SEE ME?

HUH! I'M BACK TO SPIRIT FORM LIKE WHEN I FIRST CAME HERE.

ARE MONG-YEUN AND SA-MI'S MEMORIES BACK TO NORMAL, AS WELL?

THEN, IS THIS THE POINT WHERE THE DRAGON GOD SEALS THE DRAGON REVEAL SPELL IN THEIR MEMORY?

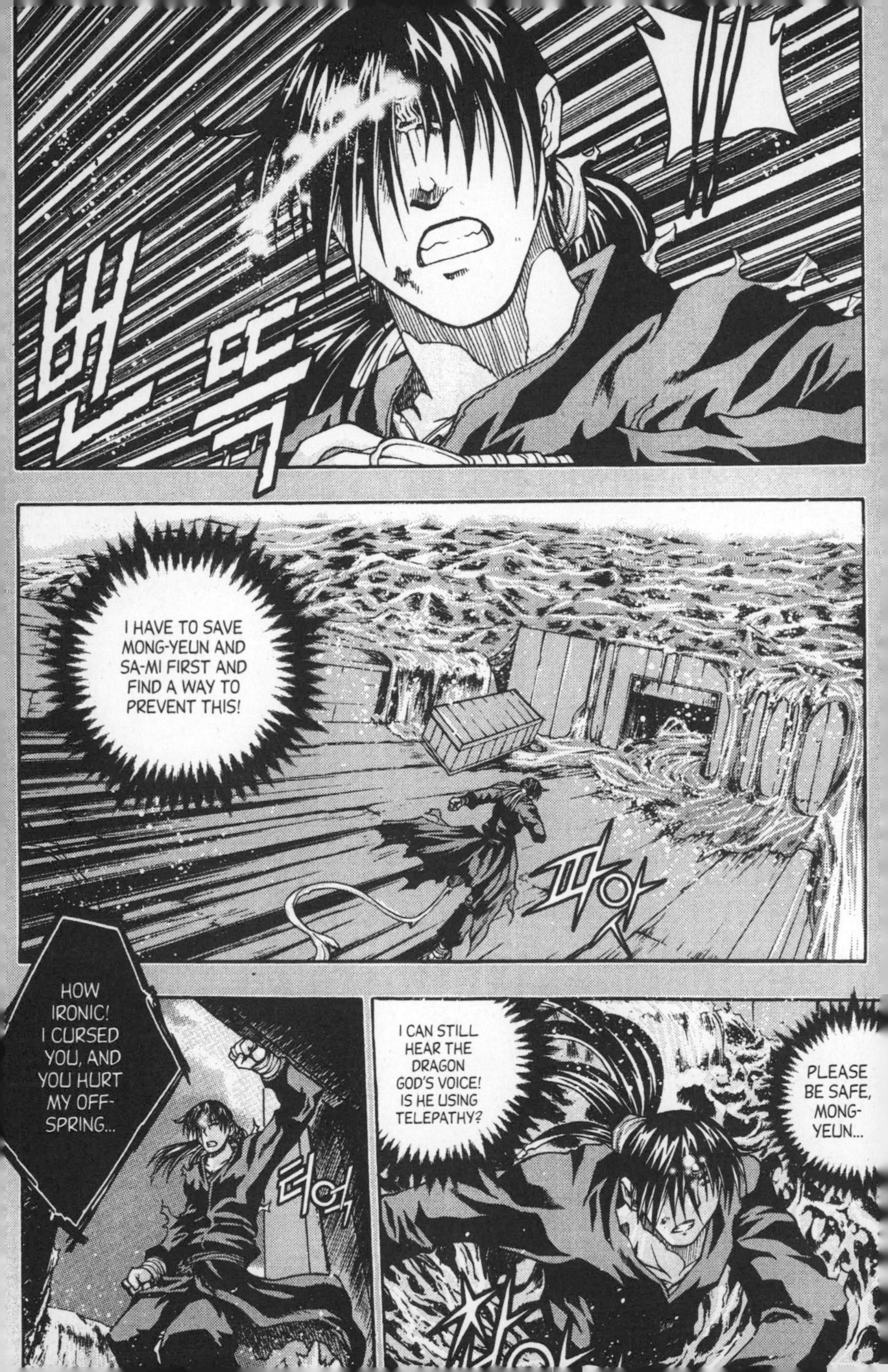
I HAVE TO SAVE MONG-YEUN AND SA-MI FIRST AND FIND A WAY TO PREVENT THIS!
HOW IRONIC! I CURSED YOU, AND YOU HURT MY OFF-SPRING...
I CAN STILL HEAR THE DRAGON GOD'S VOICE! IS HE USING TELEPATHY?
PLEASE BE SAFE, MONG-YEUN...

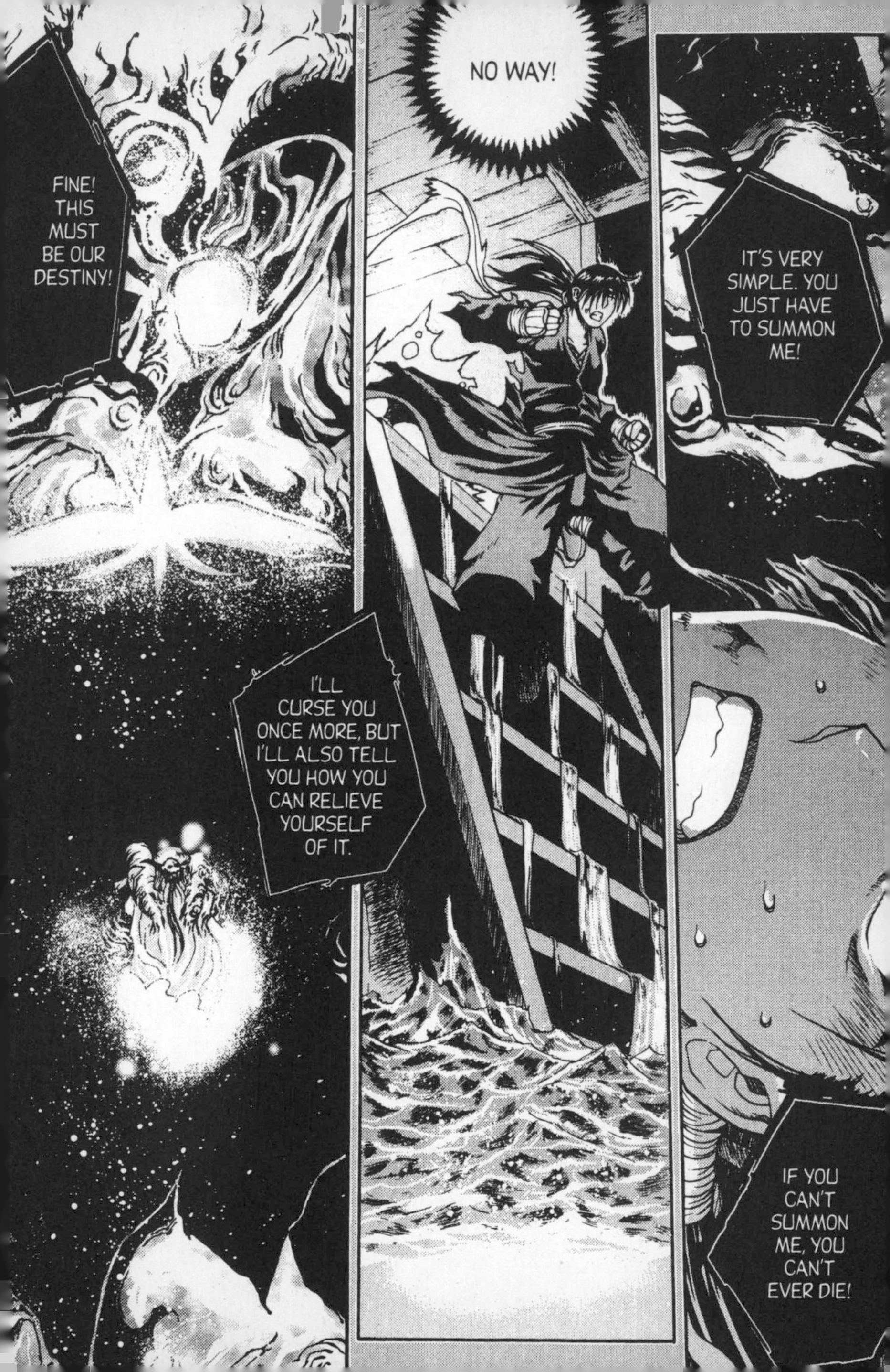
FINE! THIS MUST BE OUR DESTINY!
I'LL CURSE YOU ONCE MORE, BUT I'LL ALSO TELL YOU HOW YOU CAN RELIEVE YOURSELF OF IT.
NO WAY!
IT'S VERY SIMPLE. YOU JUST HAVE TO SUMMON ME!
IF YOU CAN'T SUMMON ME, YOU CAN'T EVER DIE!

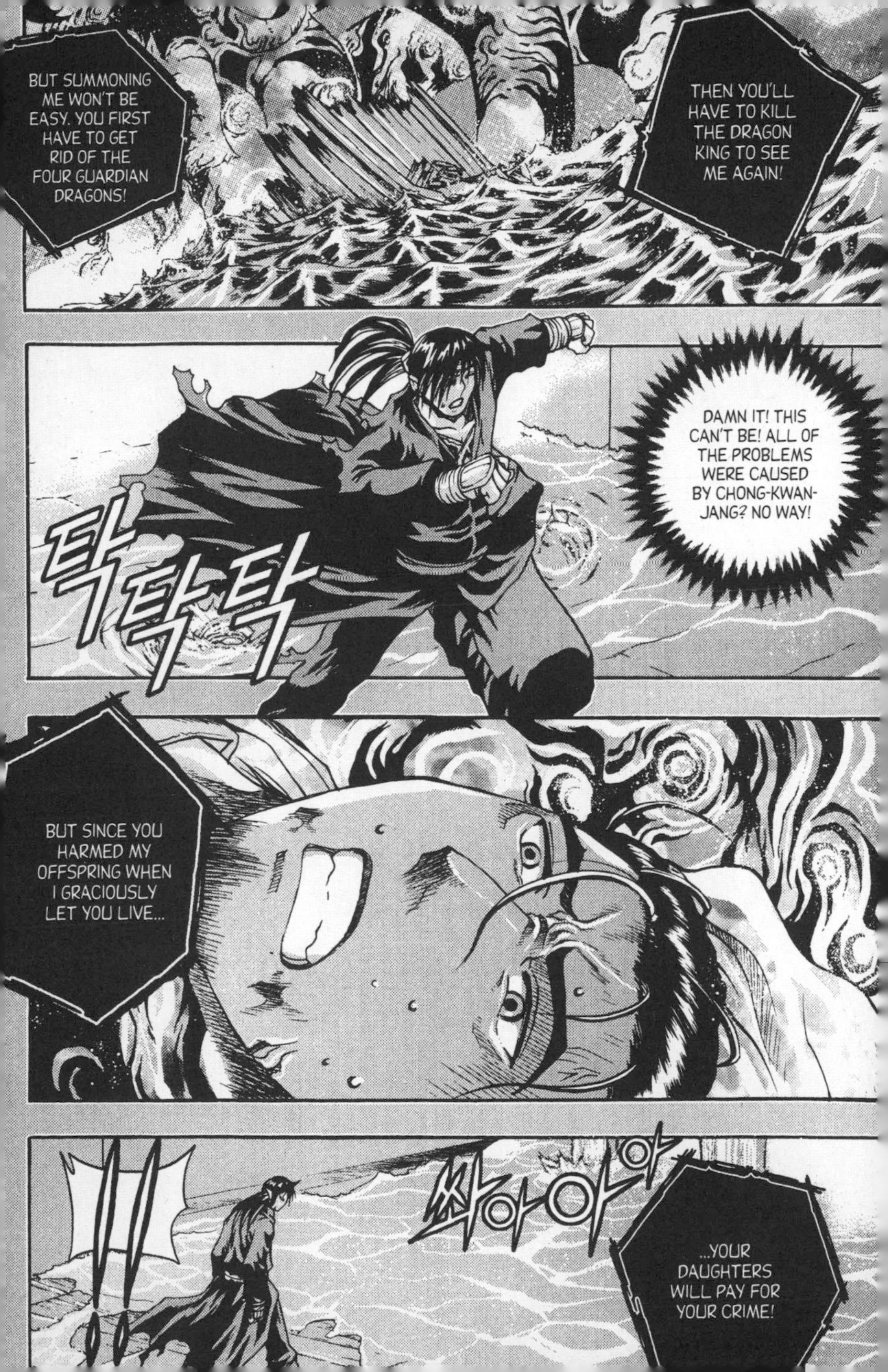
BUT SUMMONING ME WON'T BE EASY. YOU FIRST HAVE TO GET RID OF THE FOUR GUARDIAN DRAGONS!
THEN YOU'LL HAVE TO KILL THE DRAGON KING TO SEE ME AGAIN!
탁탁탁
DAMN IT! THIS CAN'T BE! ALL OF THE PROBLEMS WERE CAUSED BY CHONG-KWAN-JANG? NO WAY!
BUT SINCE YOU HARMED MY OFFSPRING WHEN I GRACIOUSLY LET YOU LIVE...
!!
쏴아아아
...YOUR DAUGHTERS WILL PAY FOR YOUR CRIME!

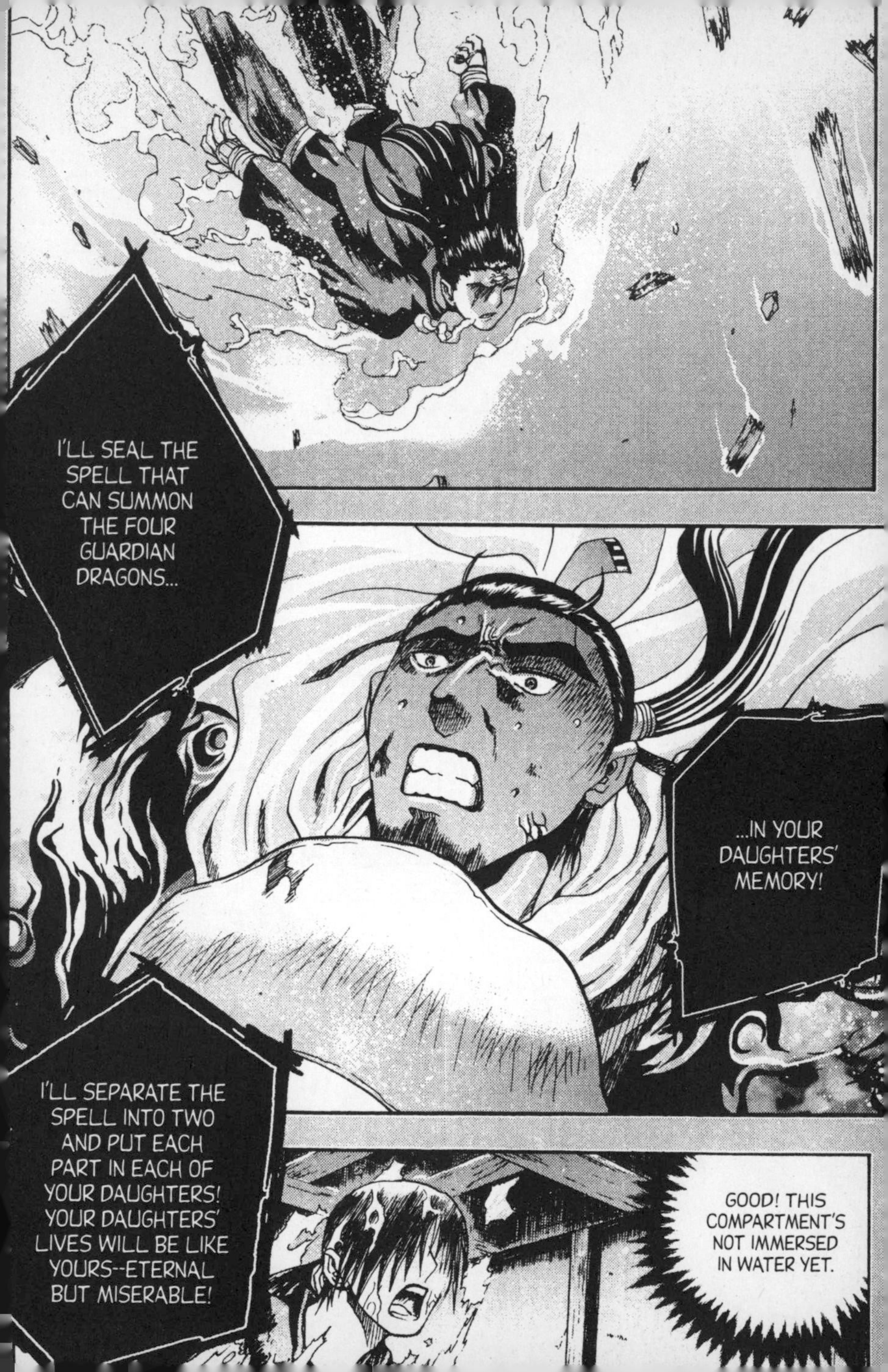
I'LL SEAL THE SPELL THAT CAN SUMMON THE FOUR GUARDIAN DRAGONS...
...IN YOUR DAUGHTERS' MEMORY!
I'LL SEPARATE THE SPELL INTO TWO AND PUT EACH PART IN EACH OF YOUR DAUGHTERS! YOUR DAUGHTERS' LIVES WILL BE LIKE YOURS--ETERNAL BUT MISERABLE!
GOOD! THIS COMPARTMENT'S NOT IMMERSED IN WATER YET.

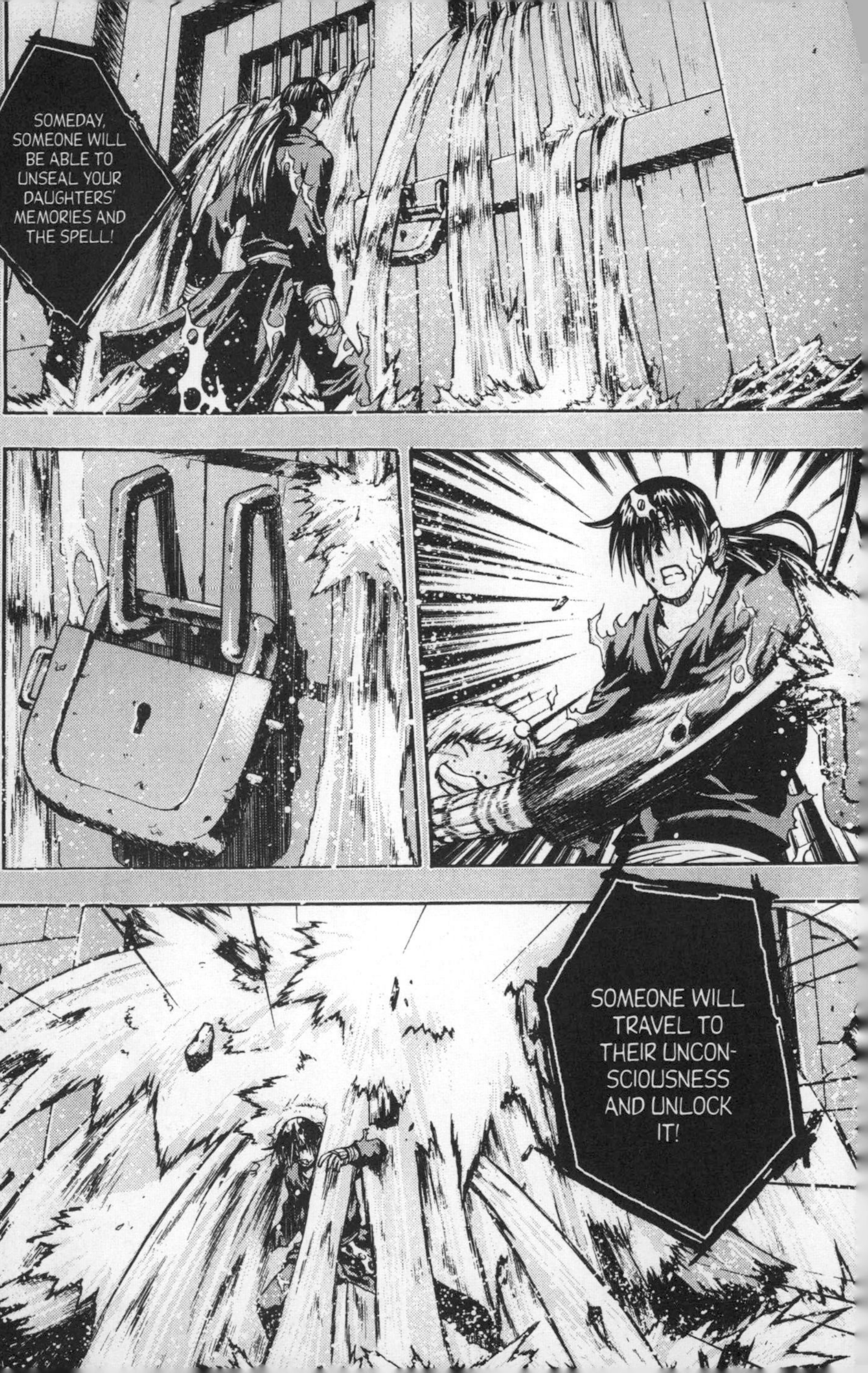
SOMEDAY, SOMEONE WILL BE ABLE TO UNSEAL YOUR DAUGHTERS' MEMORIES AND THE SPELL!
SOMEONE WILL TRAVEL TO THEIR UNCON-SCIOUSNESS AND UNLOCK IT!

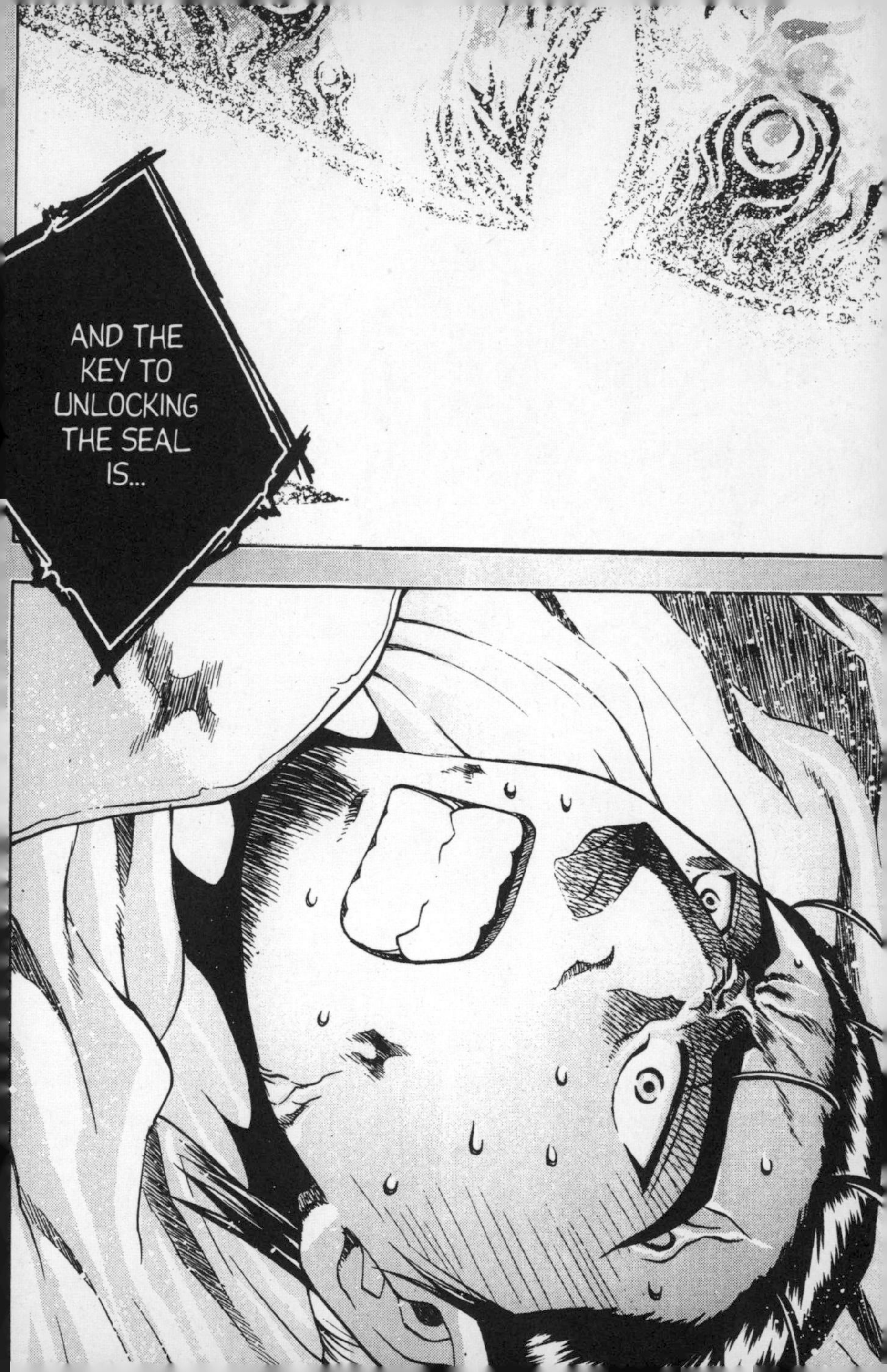
AND THE KEY TO UNLOCKING THE SEAL IS...

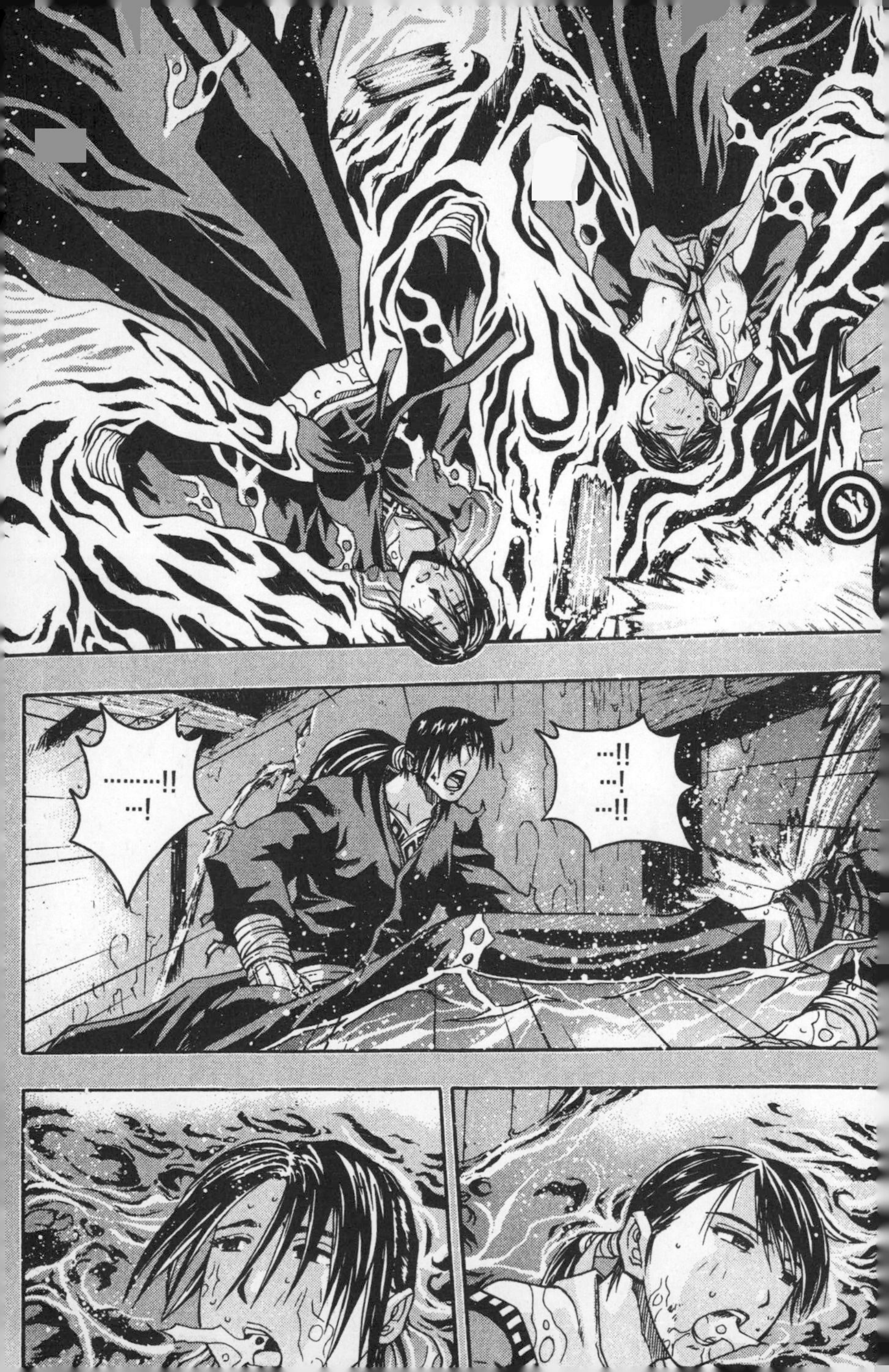
........!!
...!
...!!
...!
...!!

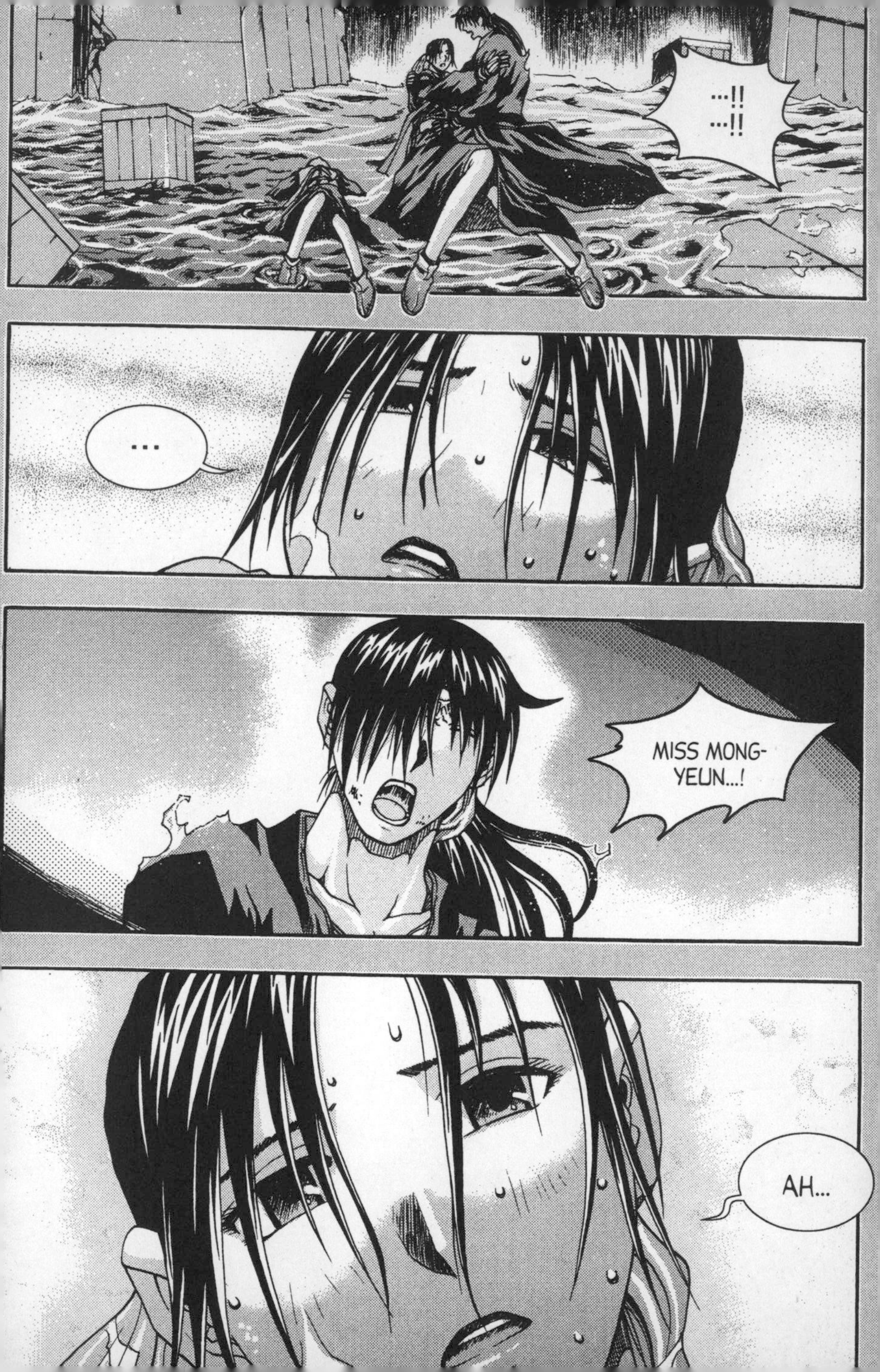
...!!
...!!
...
MISS MONG-YEUN...!
AH...

...IS THE VOICE OF YOUR DAUGHTER AS SHE UTTERS THE NAME OF THE ONE WHO AWAKES HER.

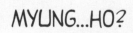

MYUNG...HO?

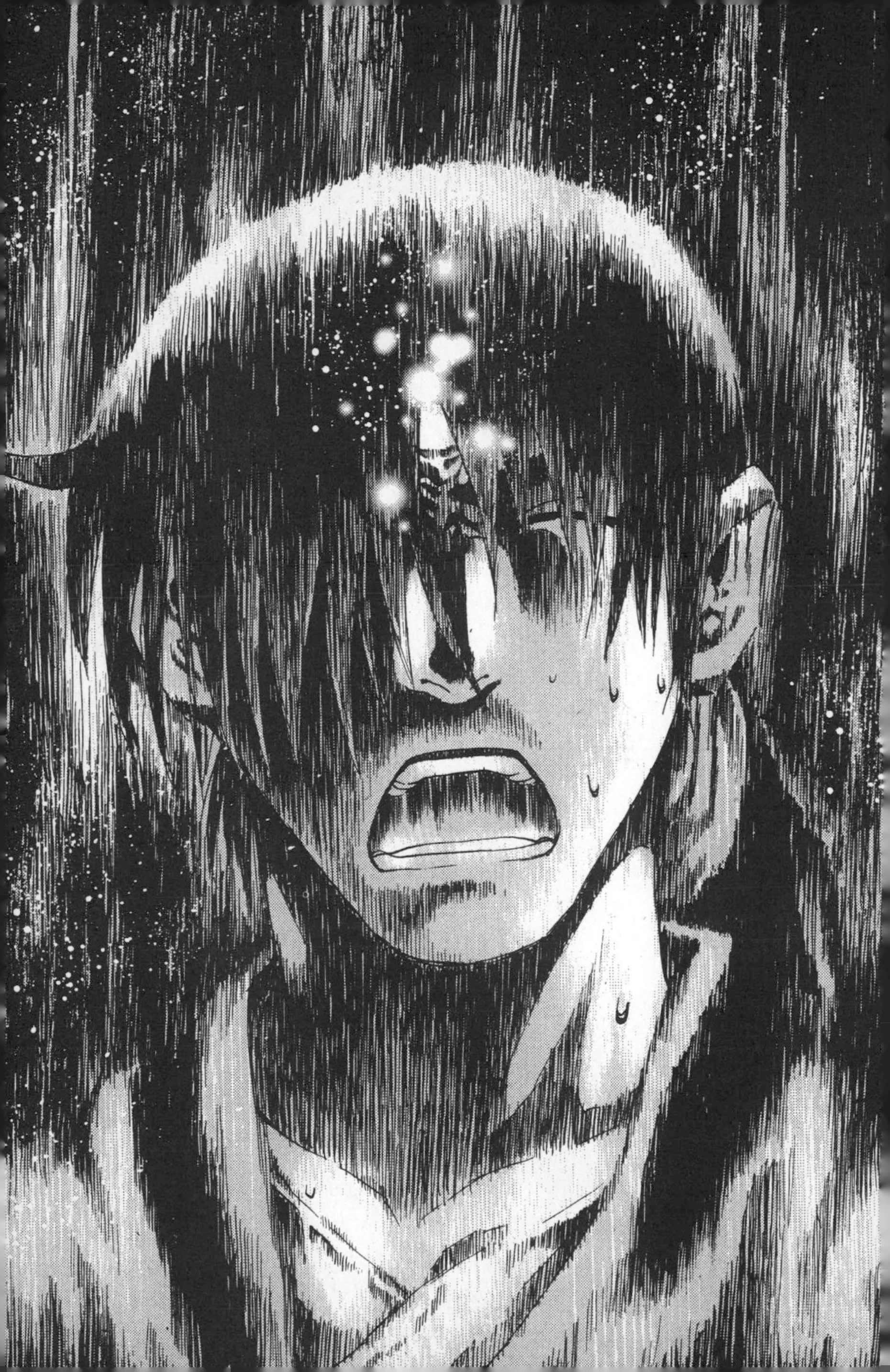

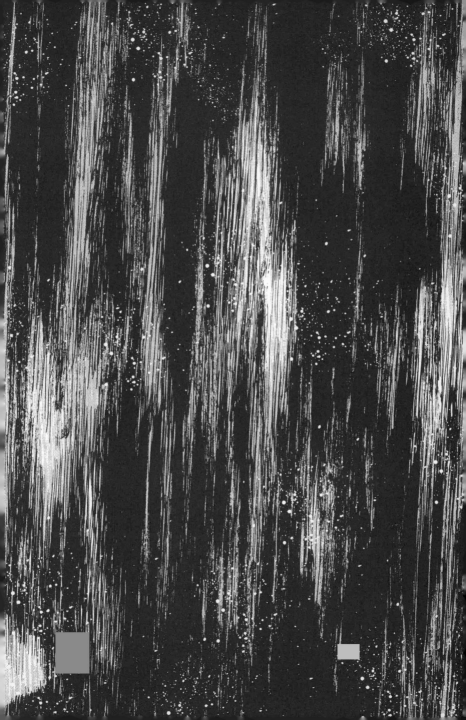

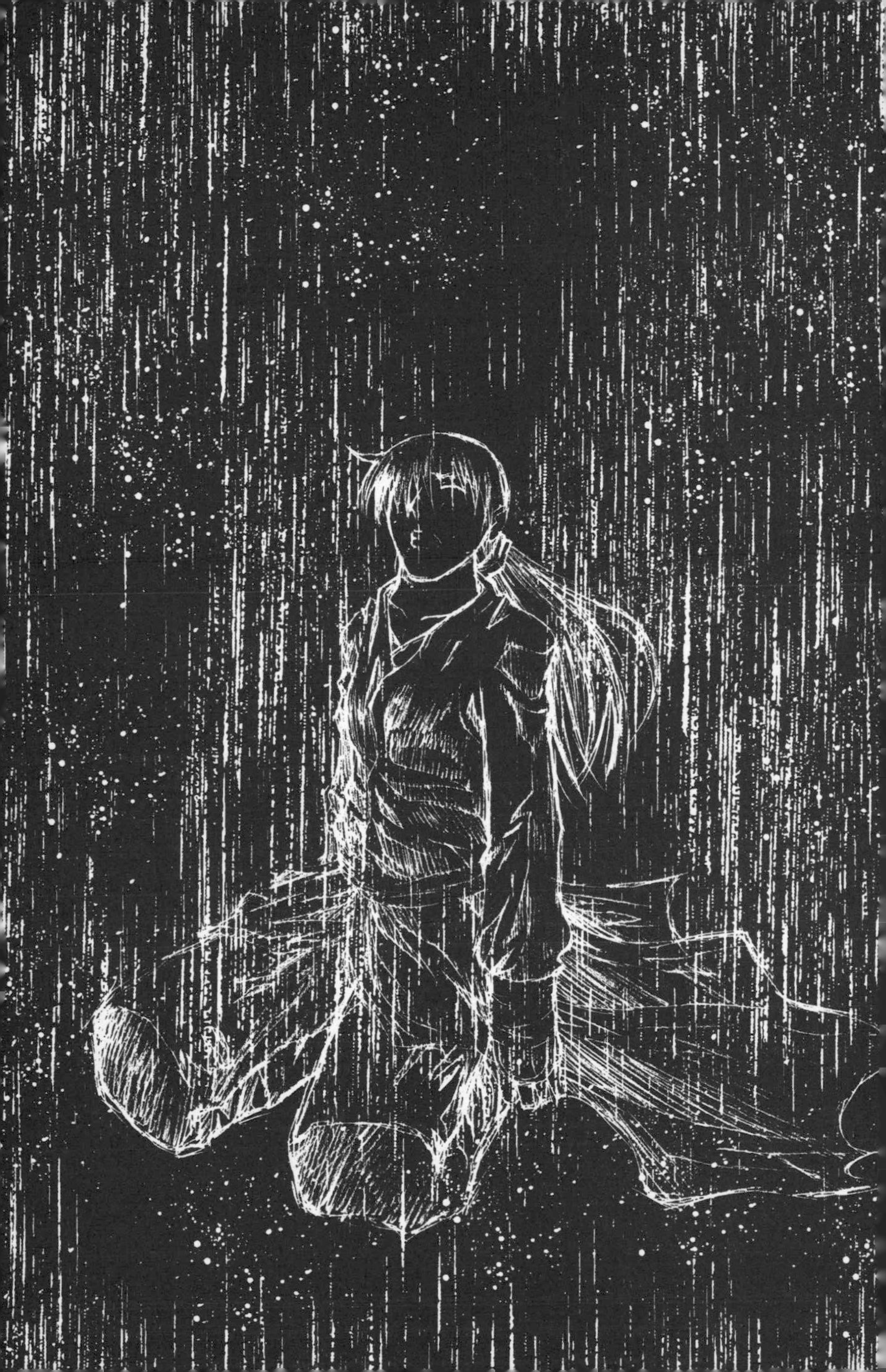

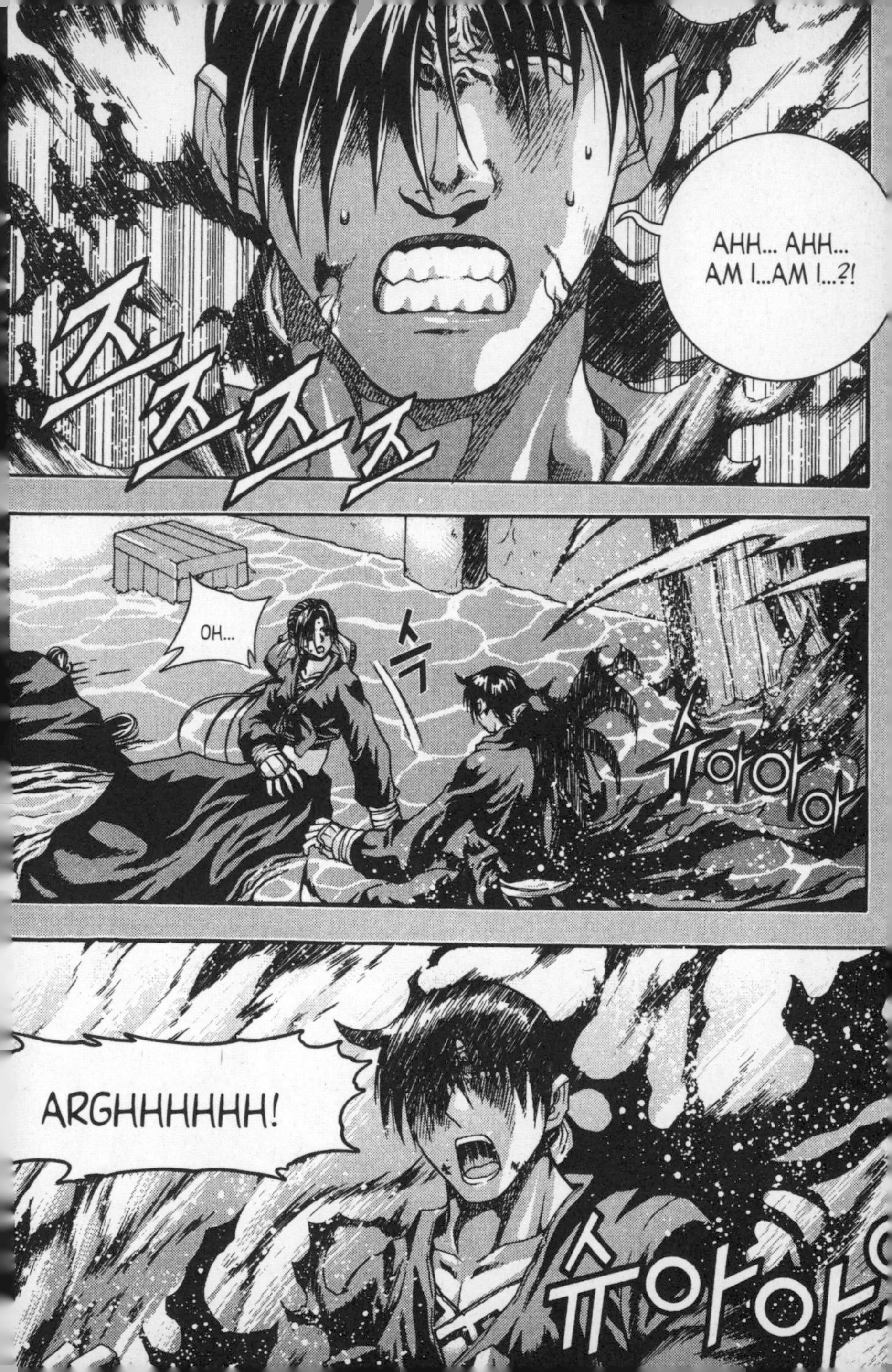
AHH... AHH...
AM I...AM I...?!
OH...
슈아아아아
ARGHHHHHH!

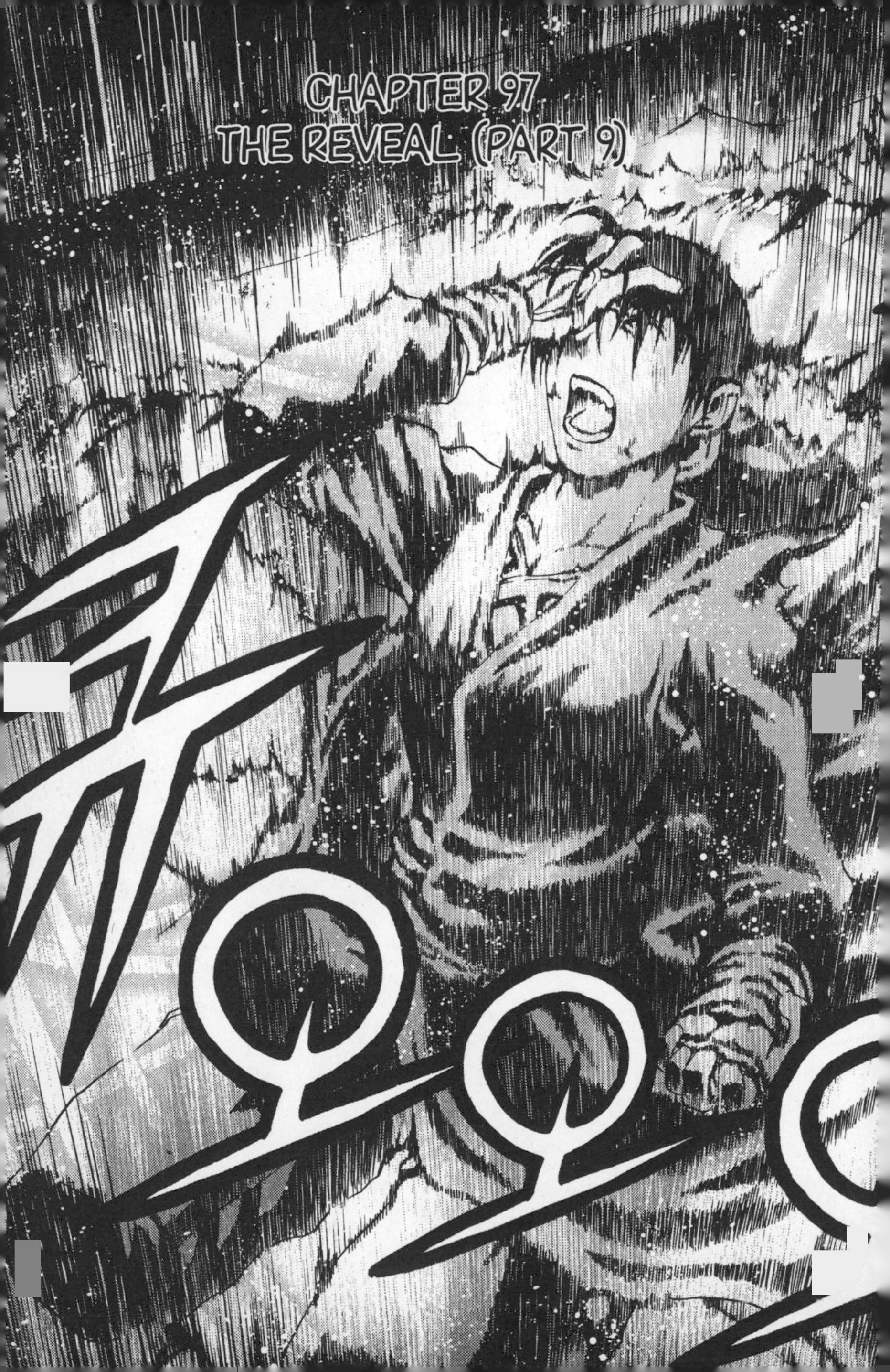
CHAPTER 97
THE REVEAL (PART 9)

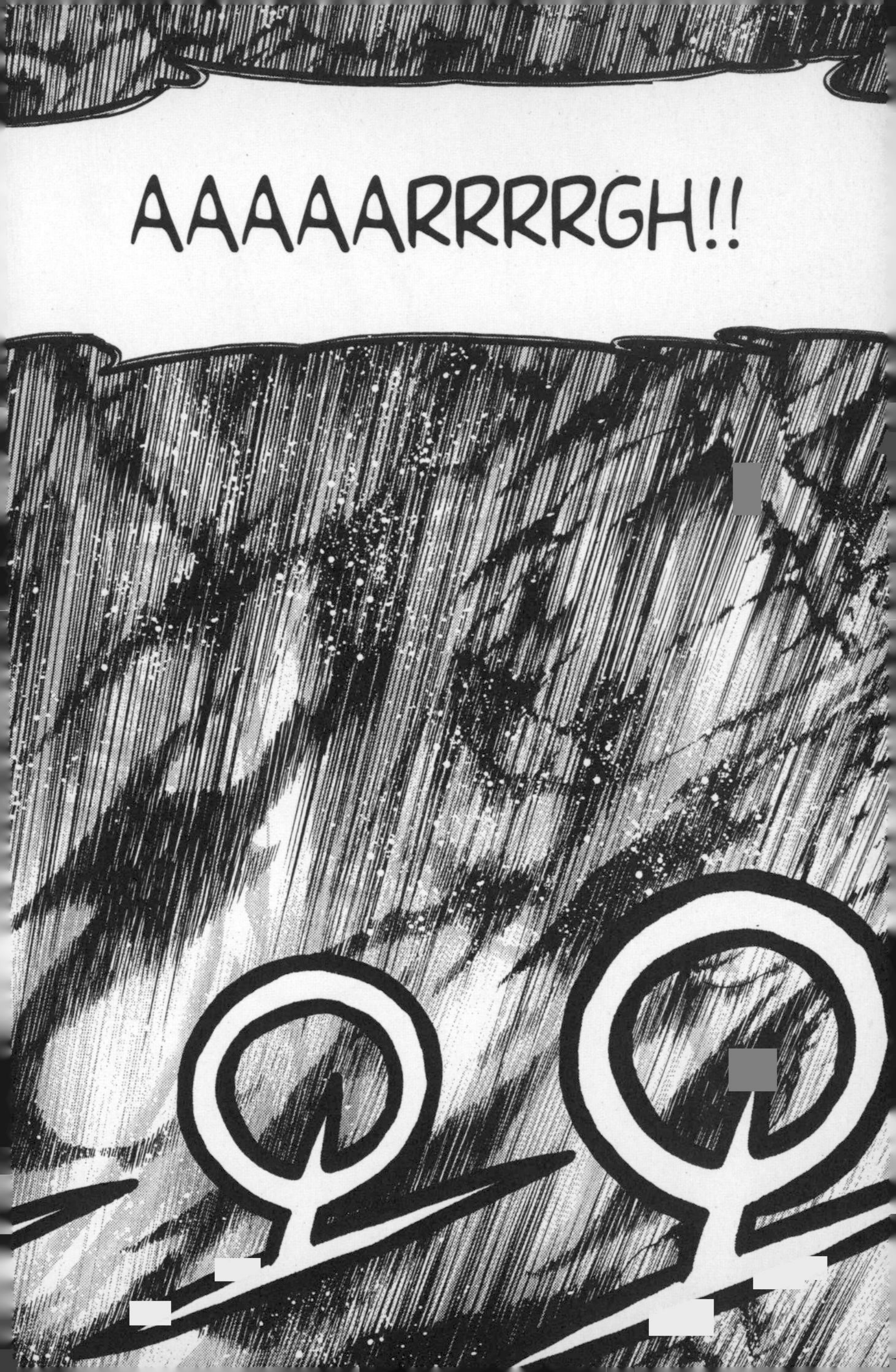
AAAAARRRRGH!!

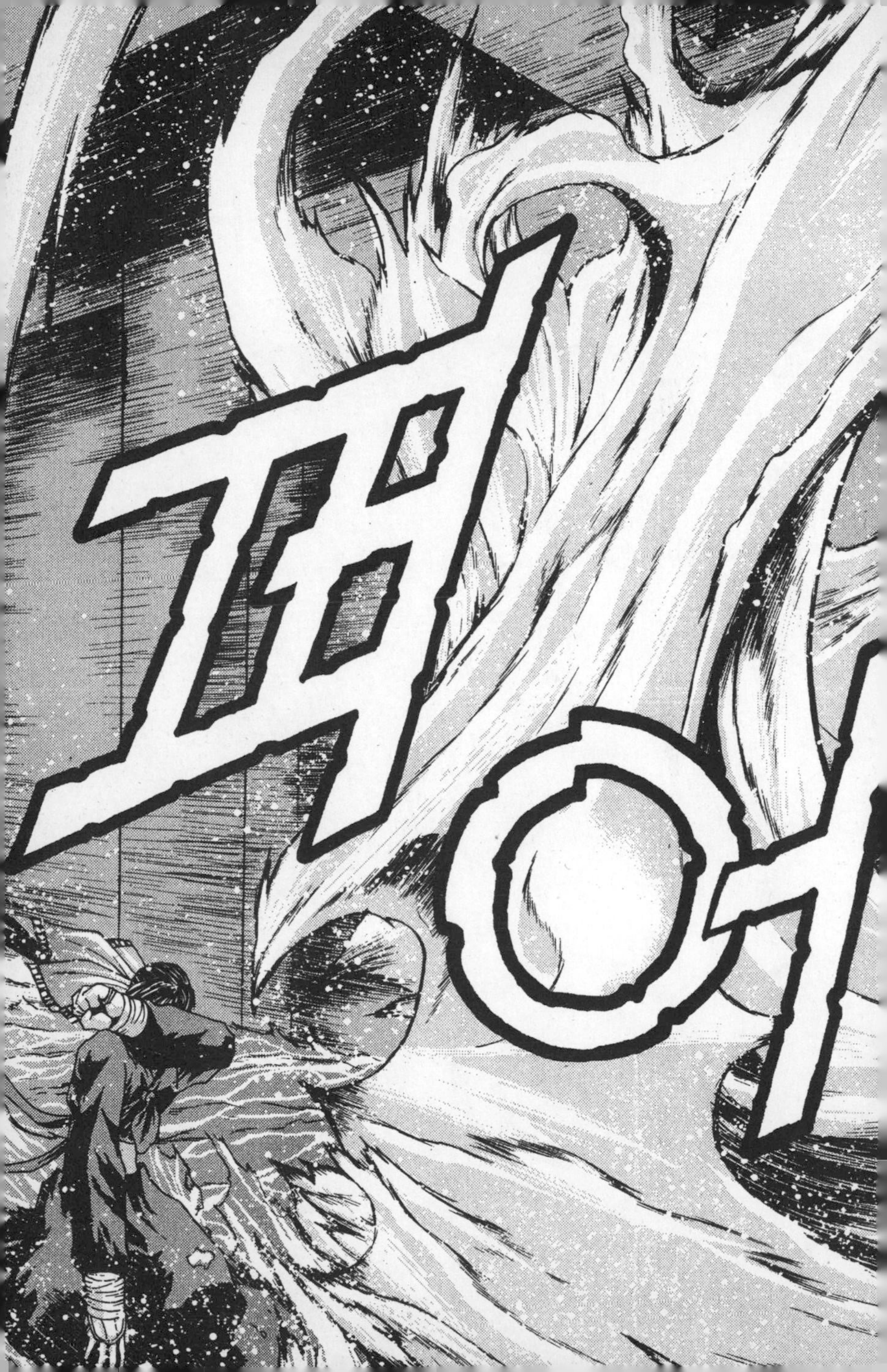
퍼어

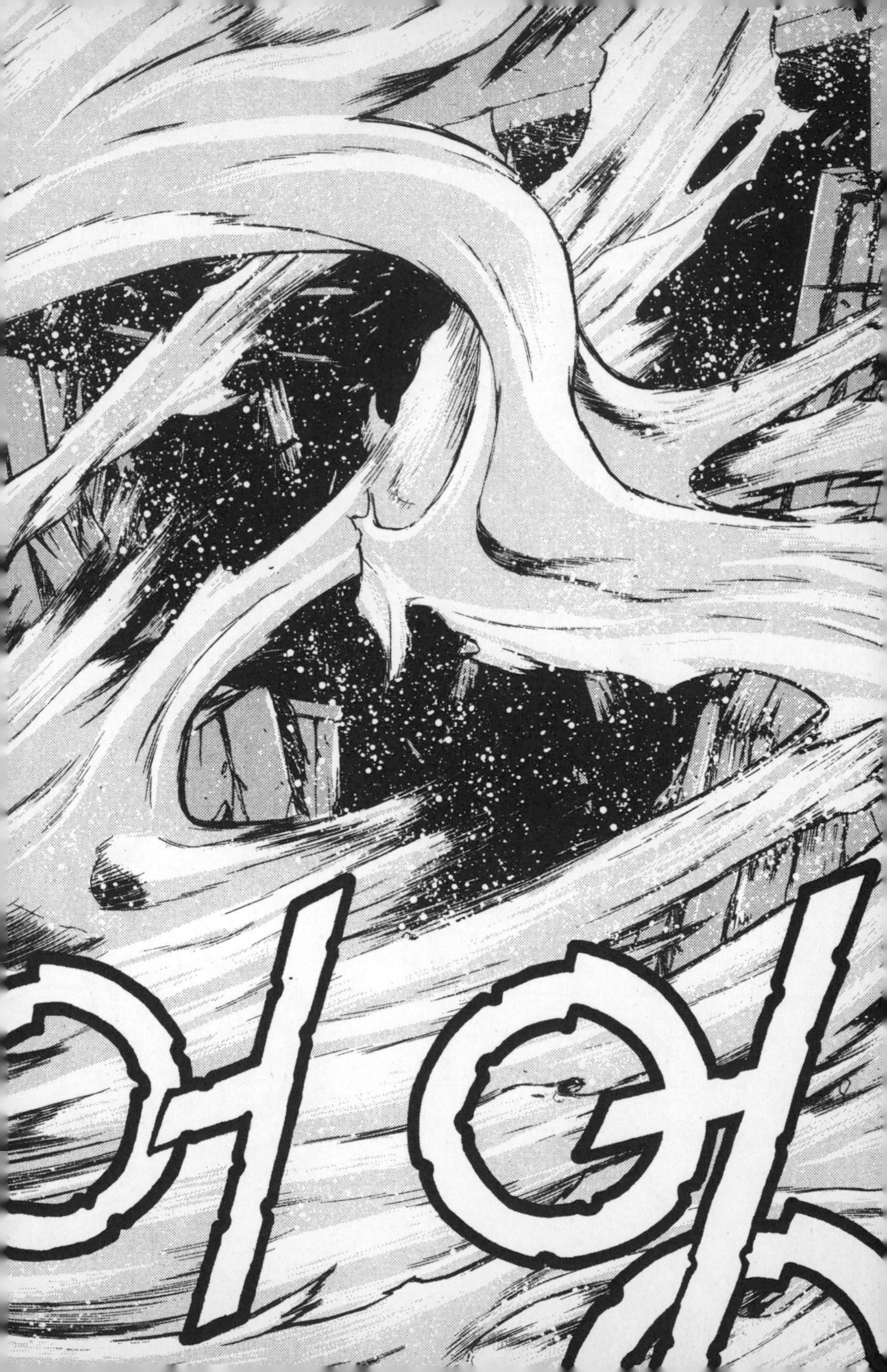

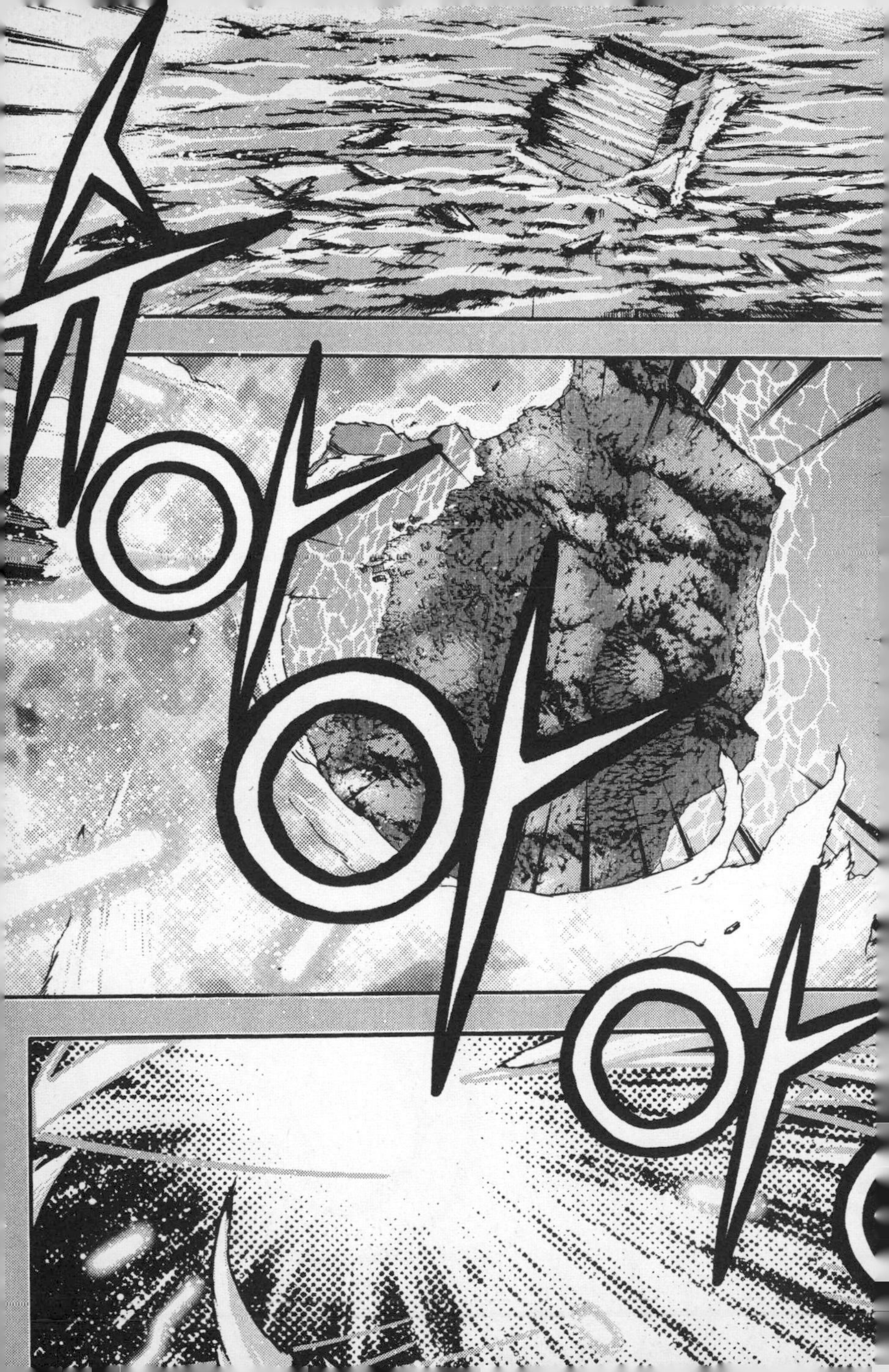
WOOOO

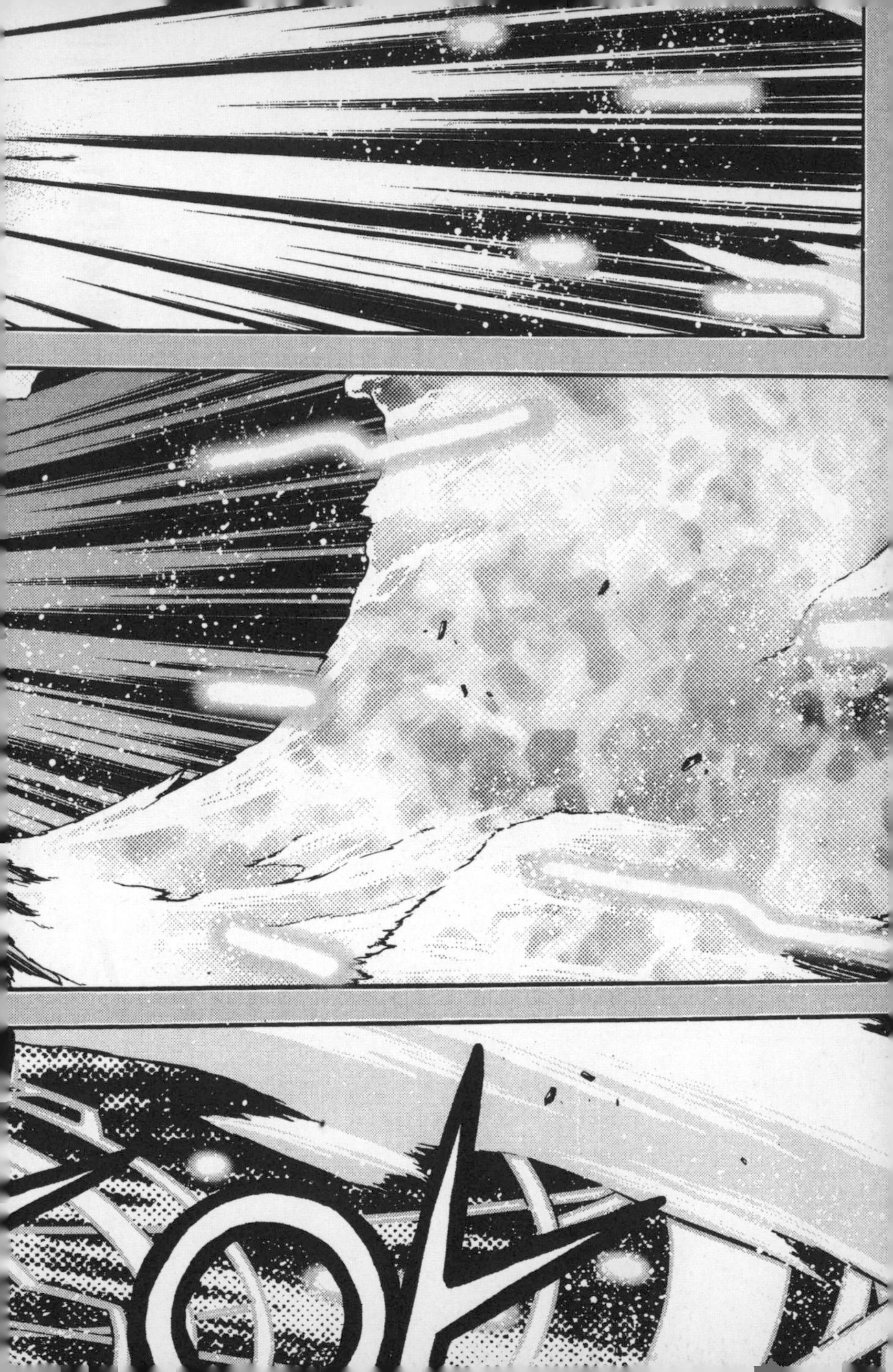

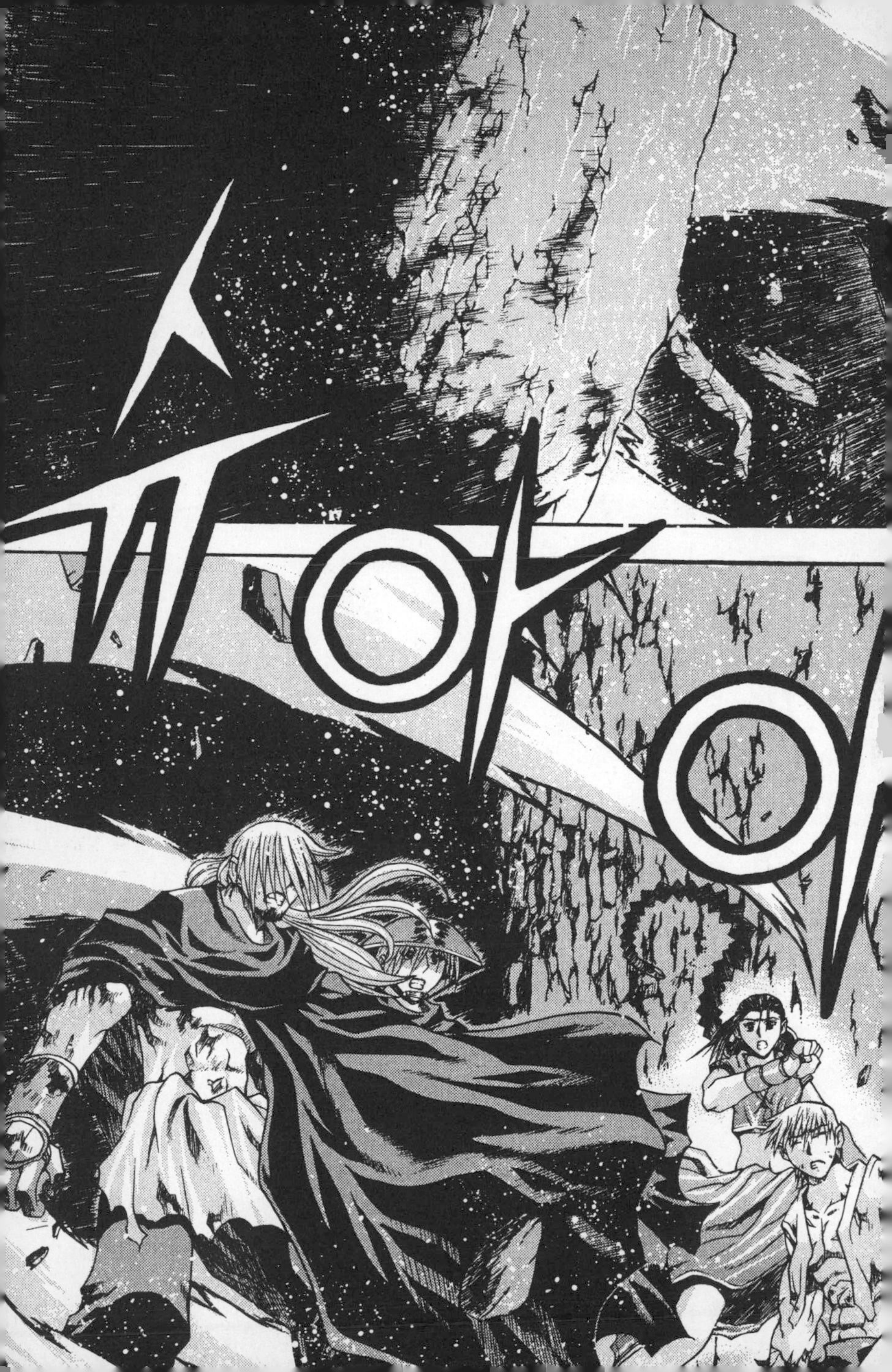

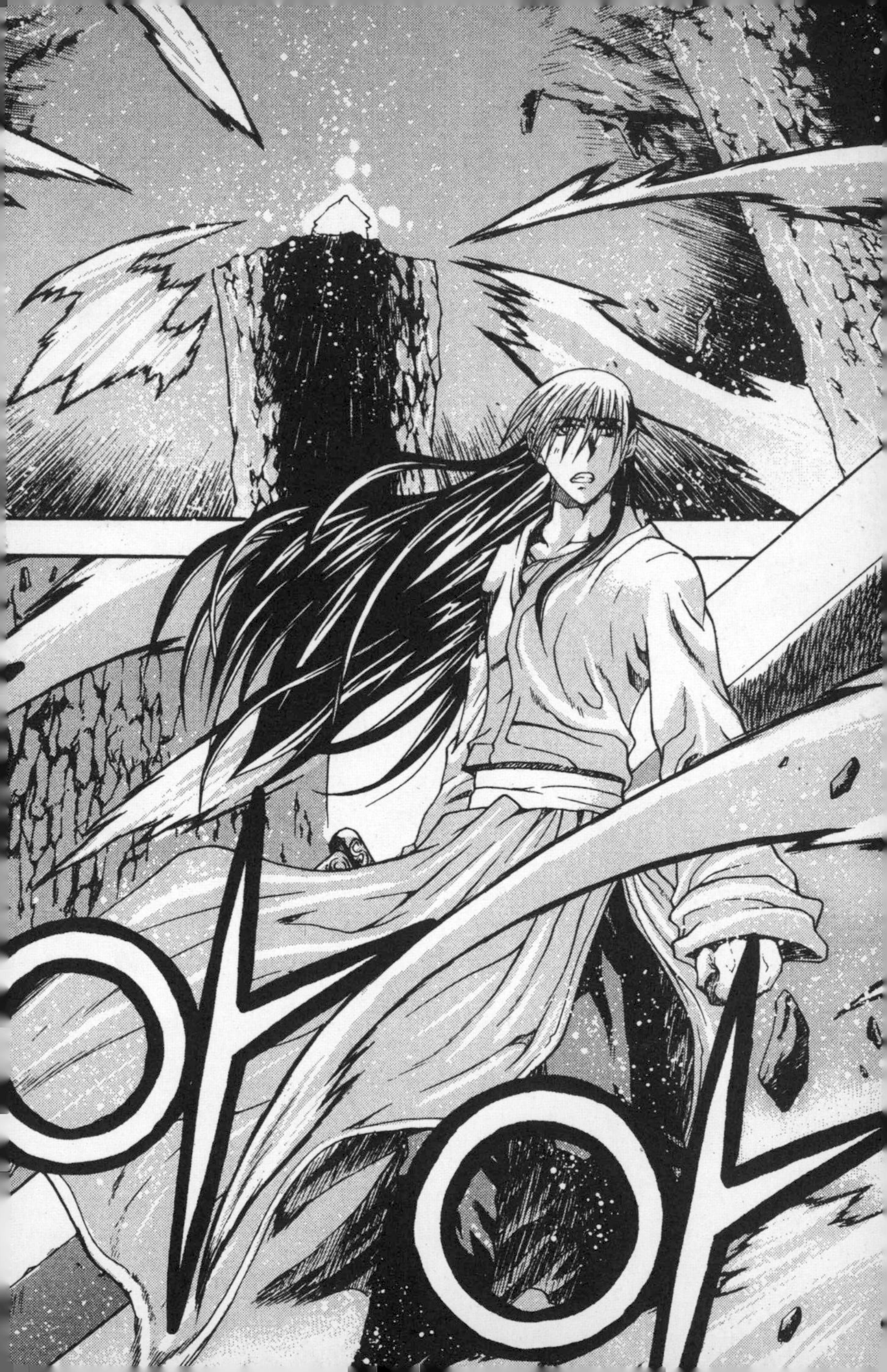

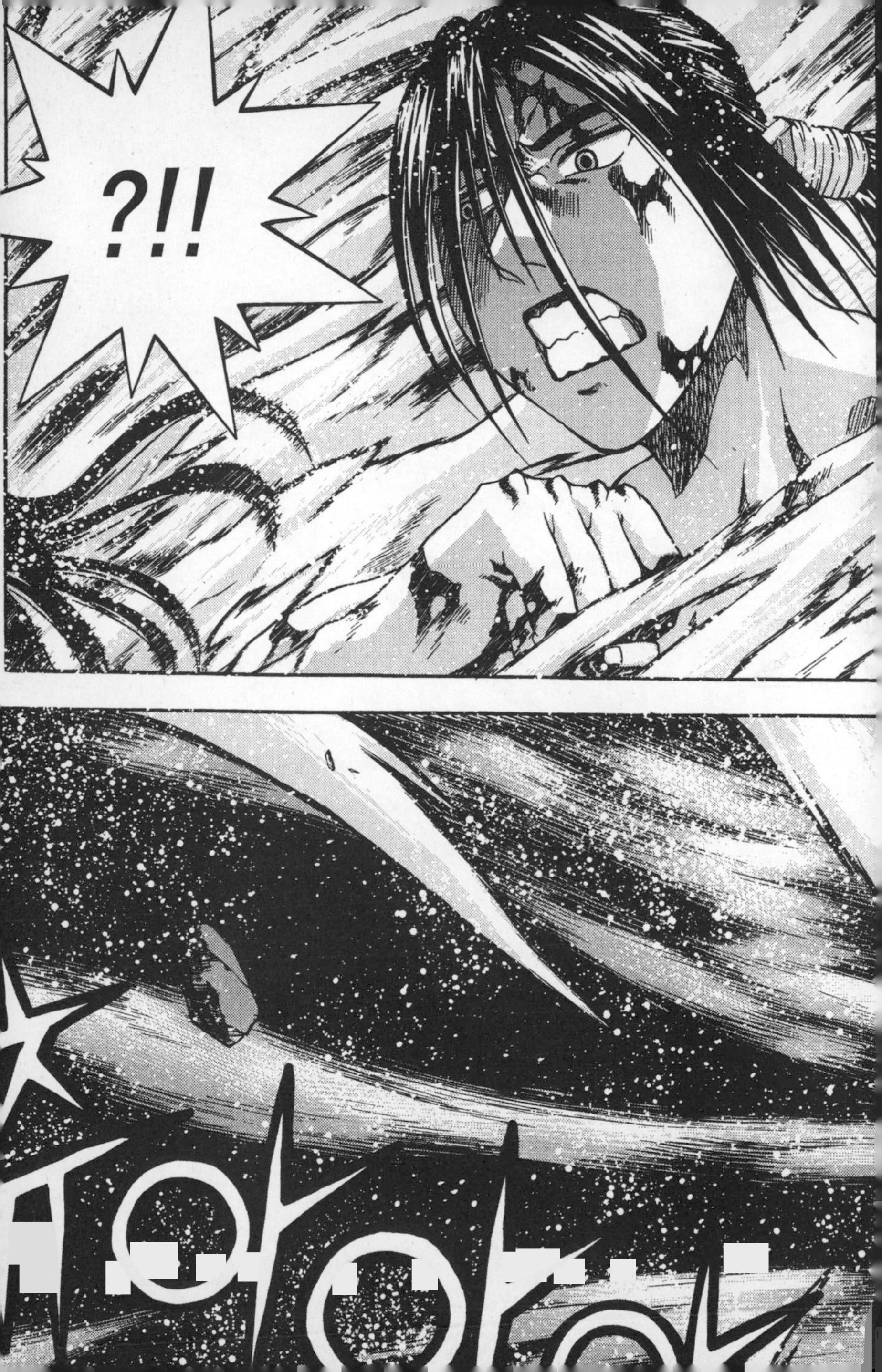
?!!

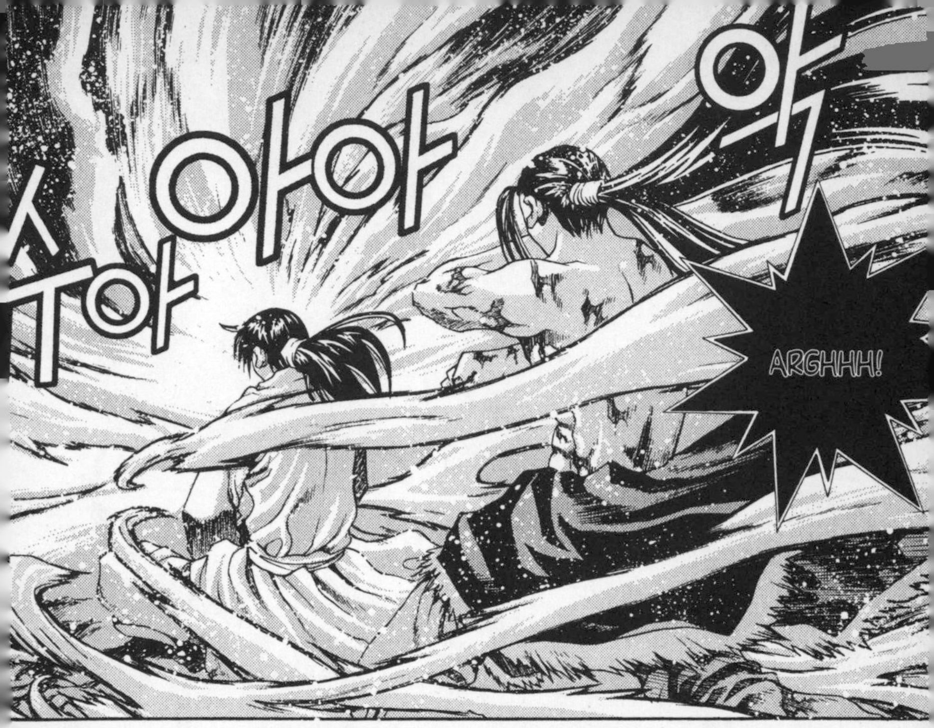
ARGHHH!
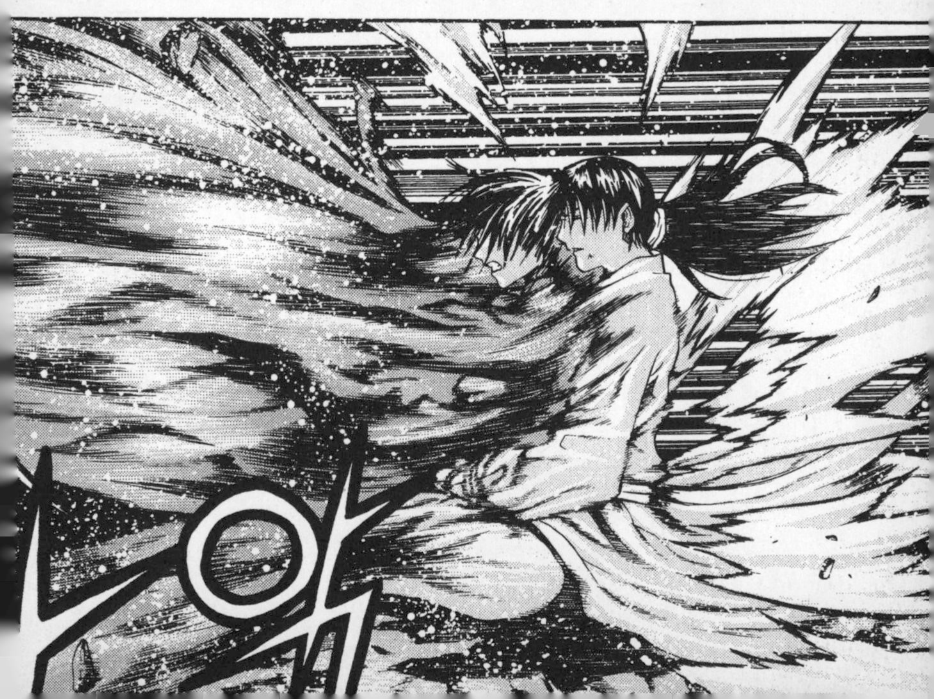

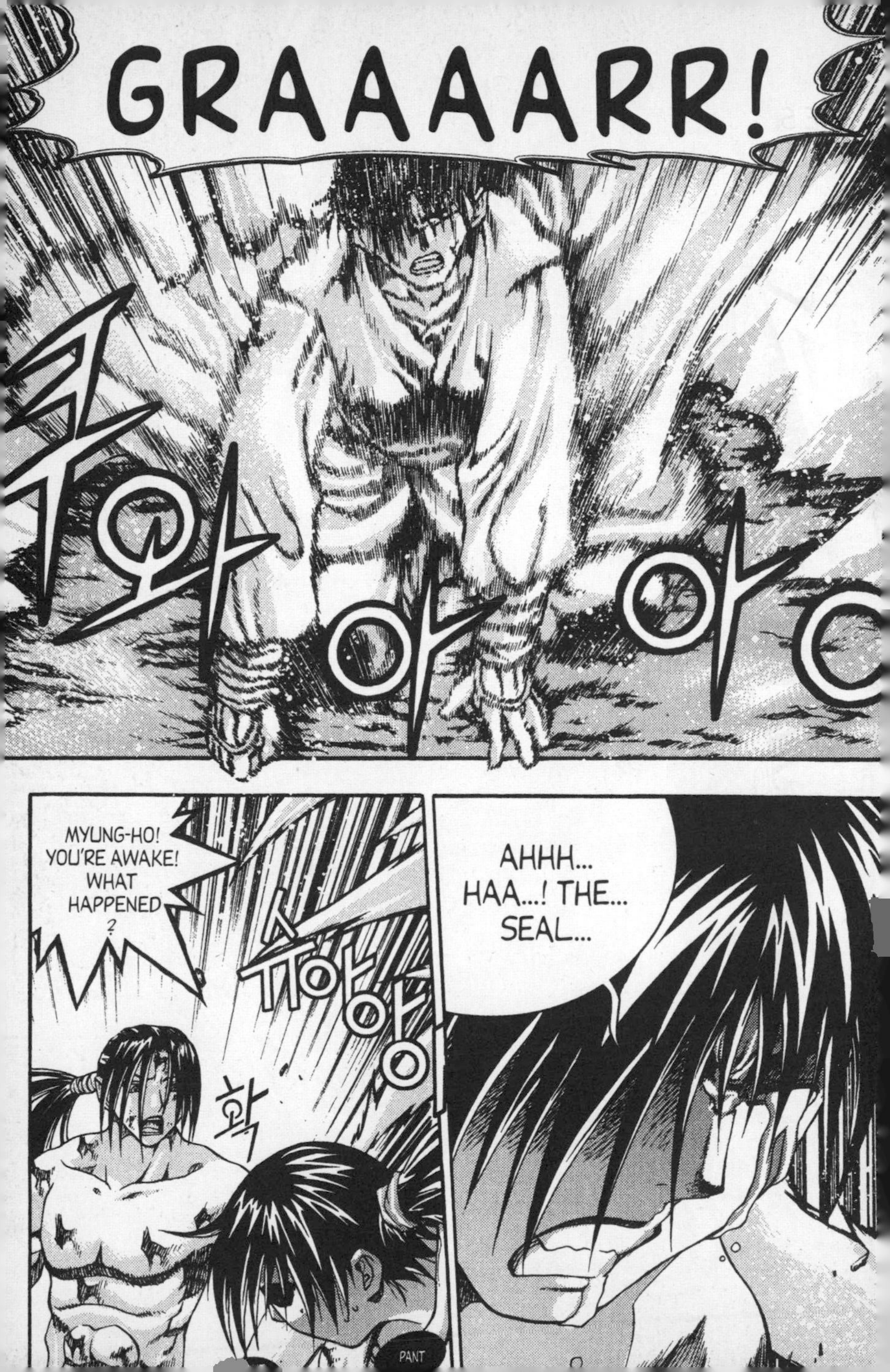
GRAAAARR!
MYUNG-HO! YOU'RE AWAKE! WHAT HAPPENED?
AHHH... HAA...! THE... SEAL...
PANT

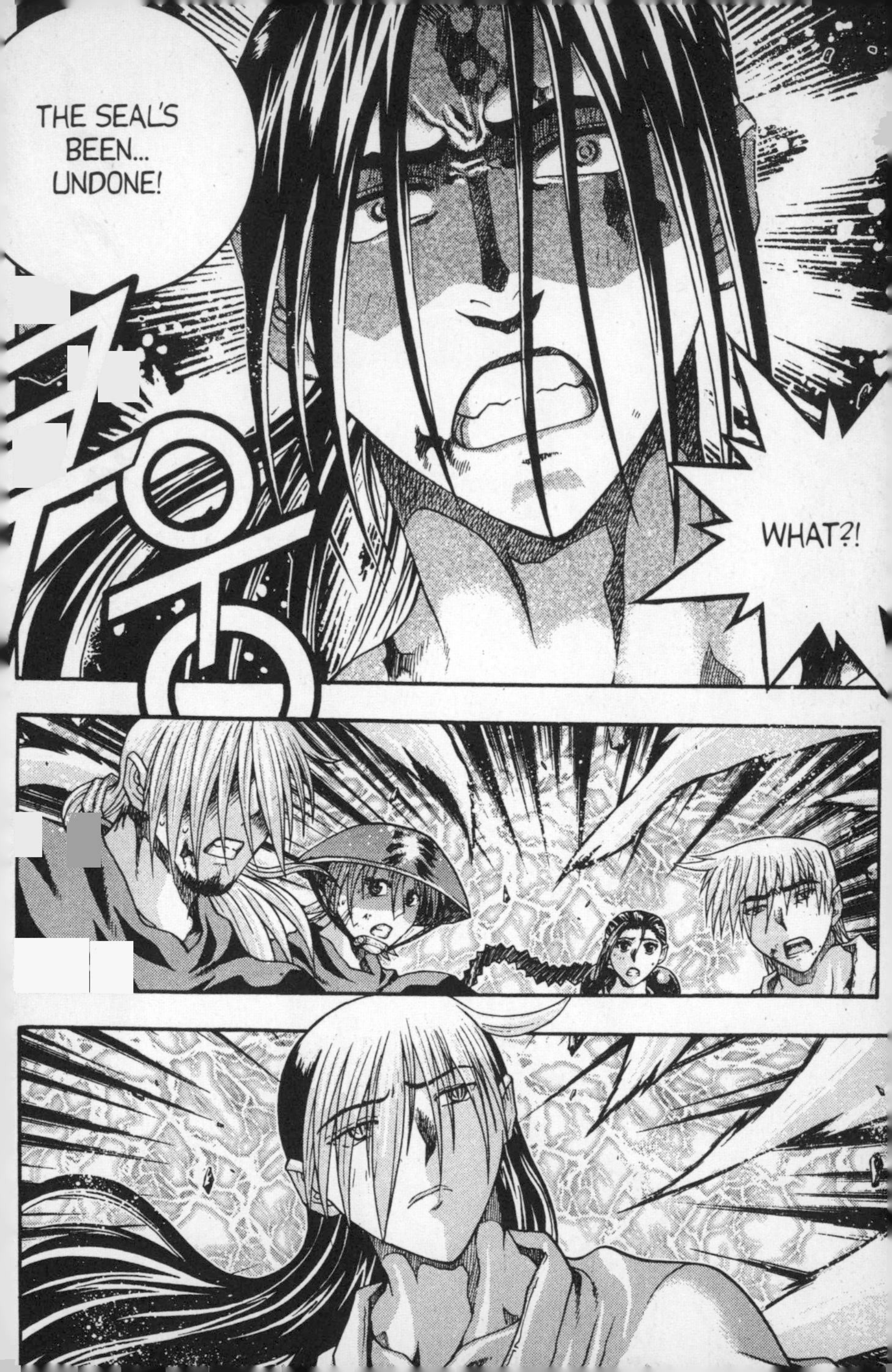
THE SEAL'S BEEN... UNDONE!
WHAT?!

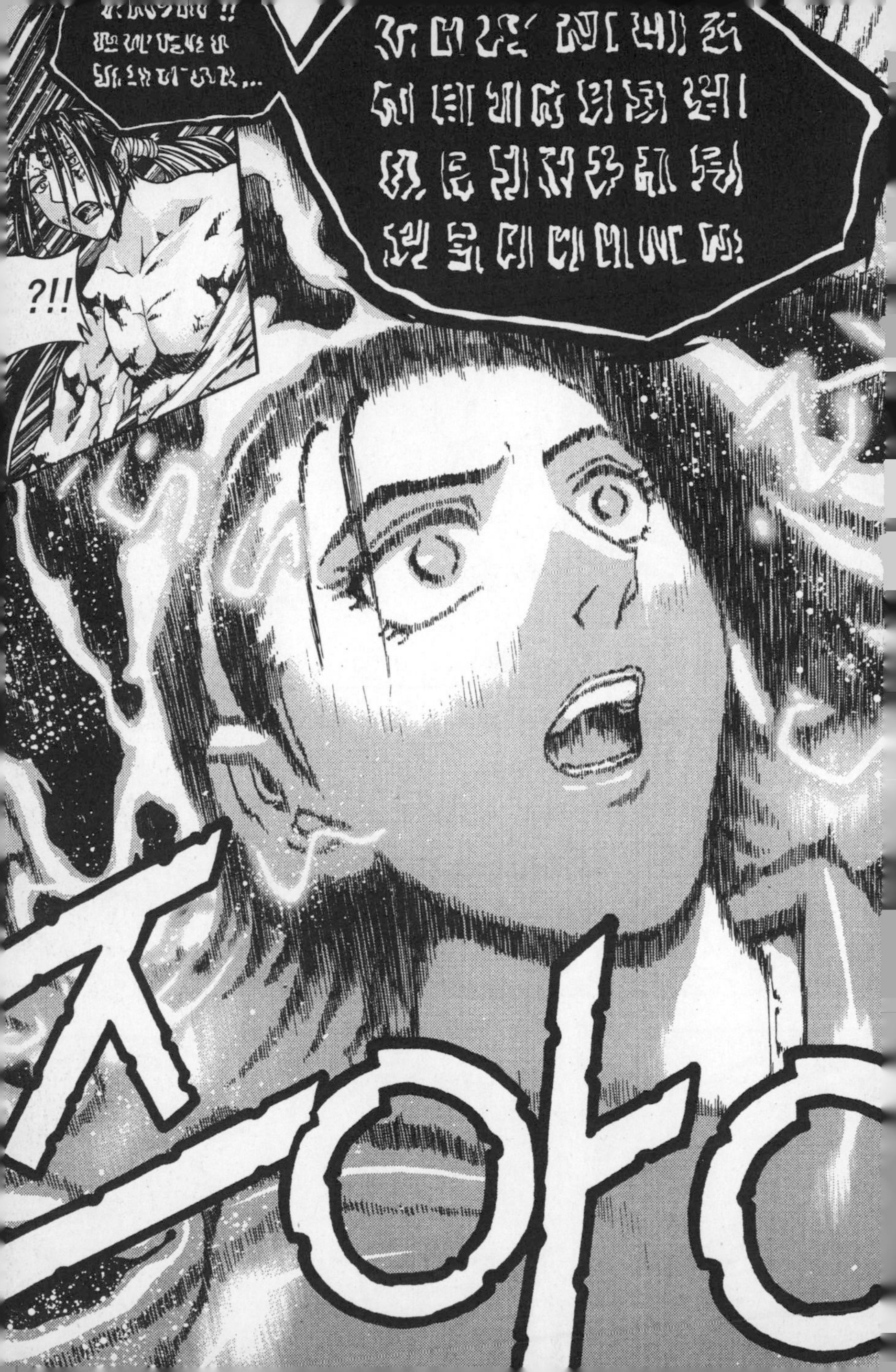

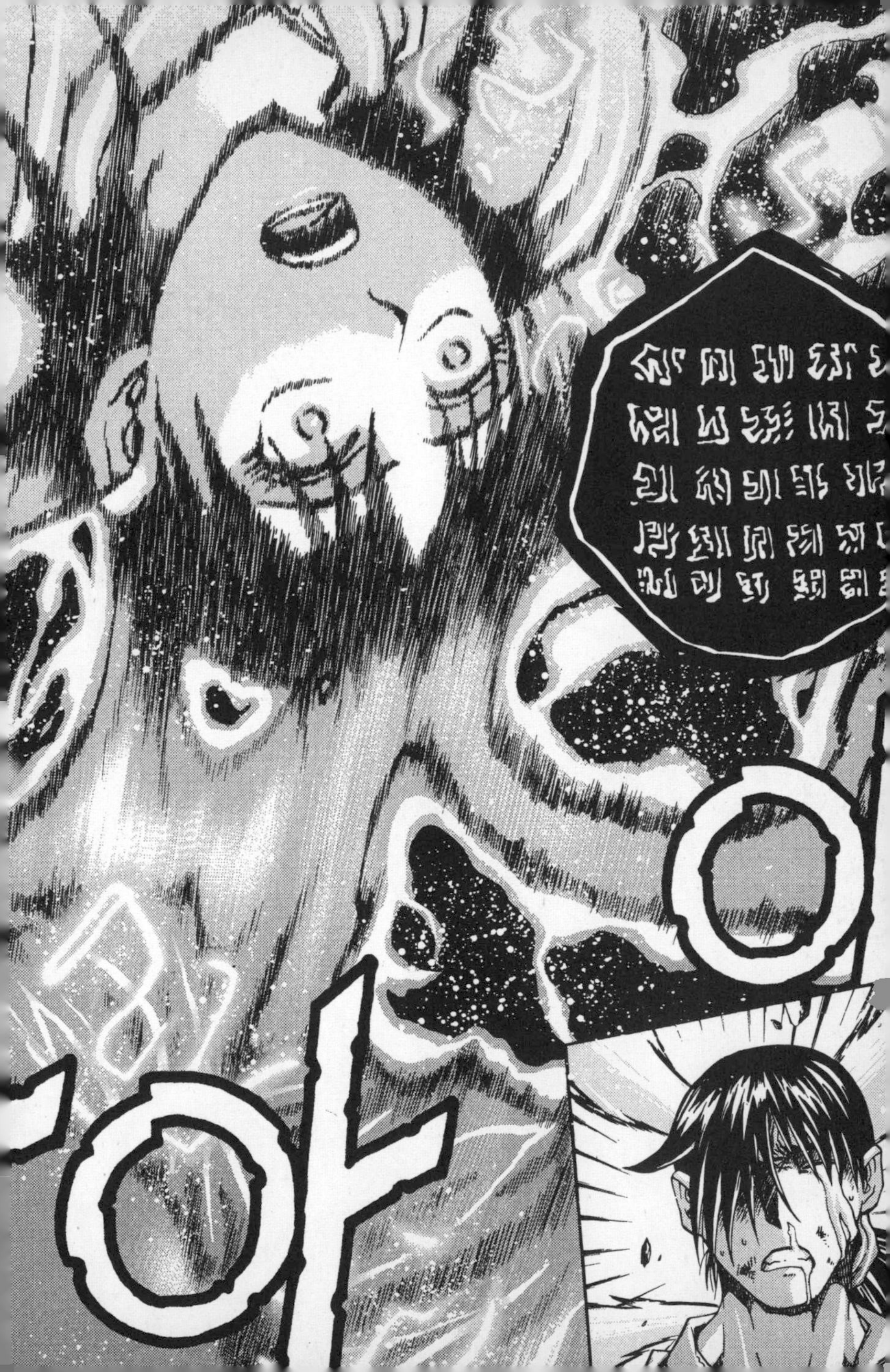

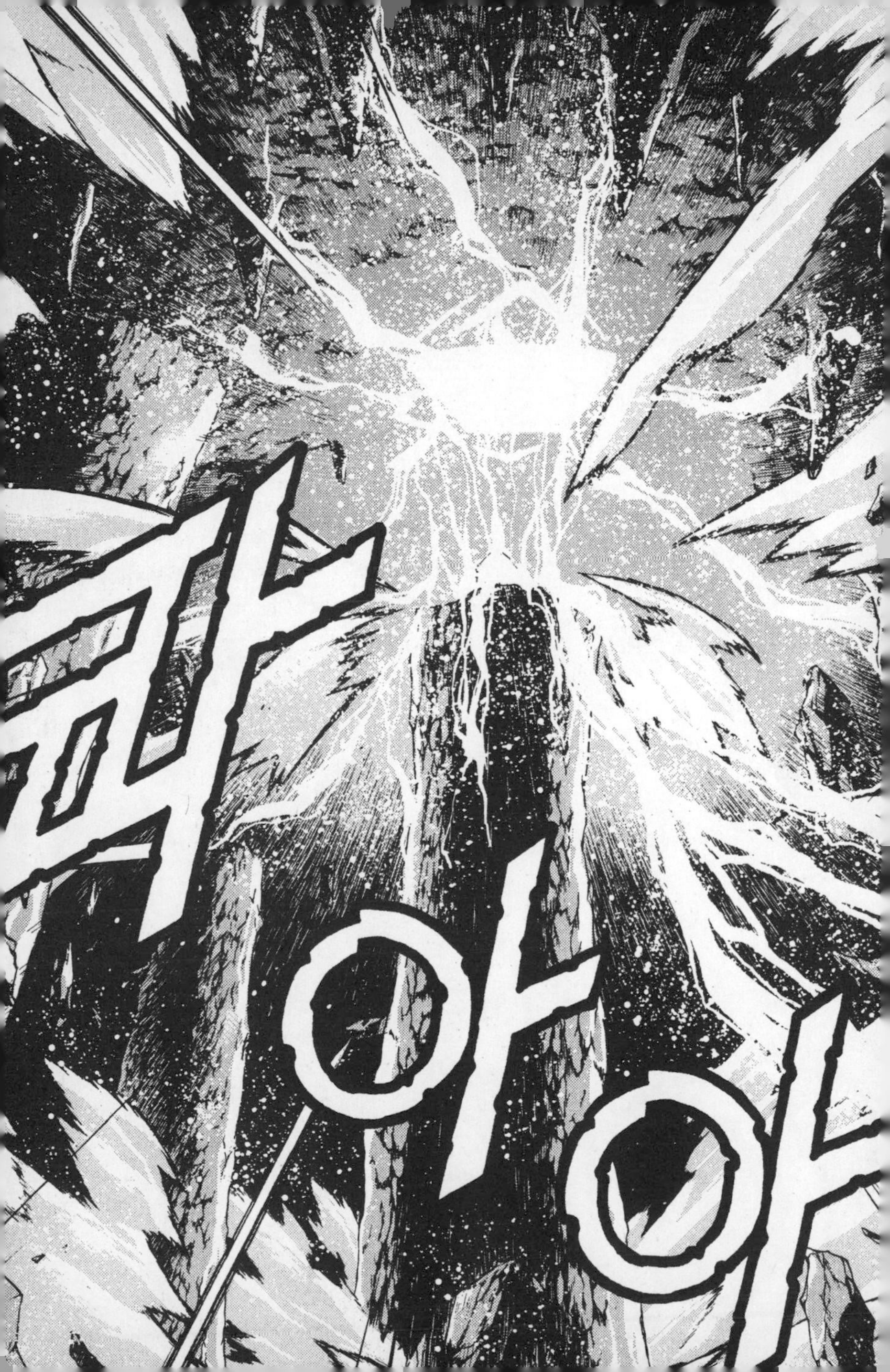
카아아

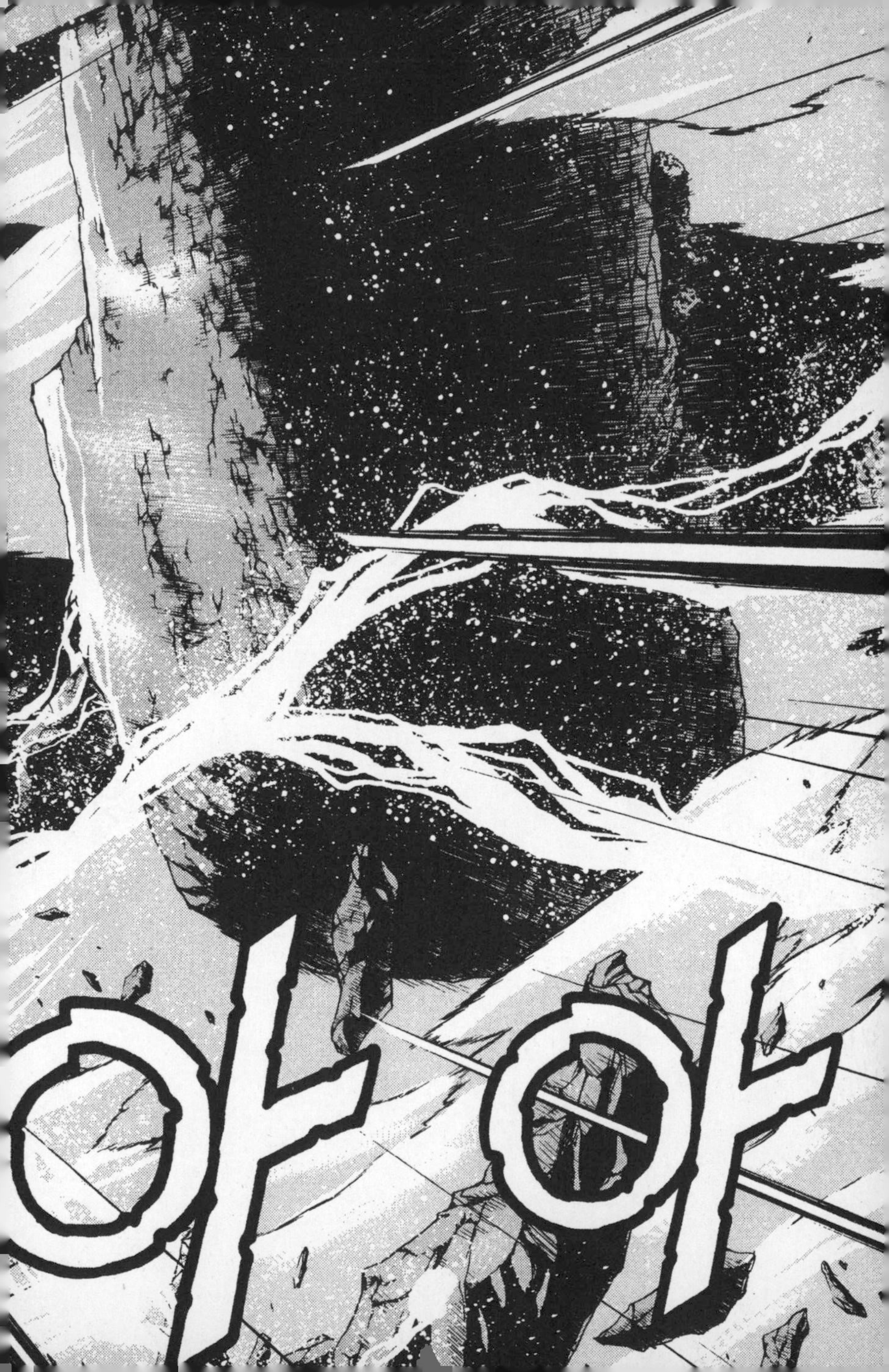
아아

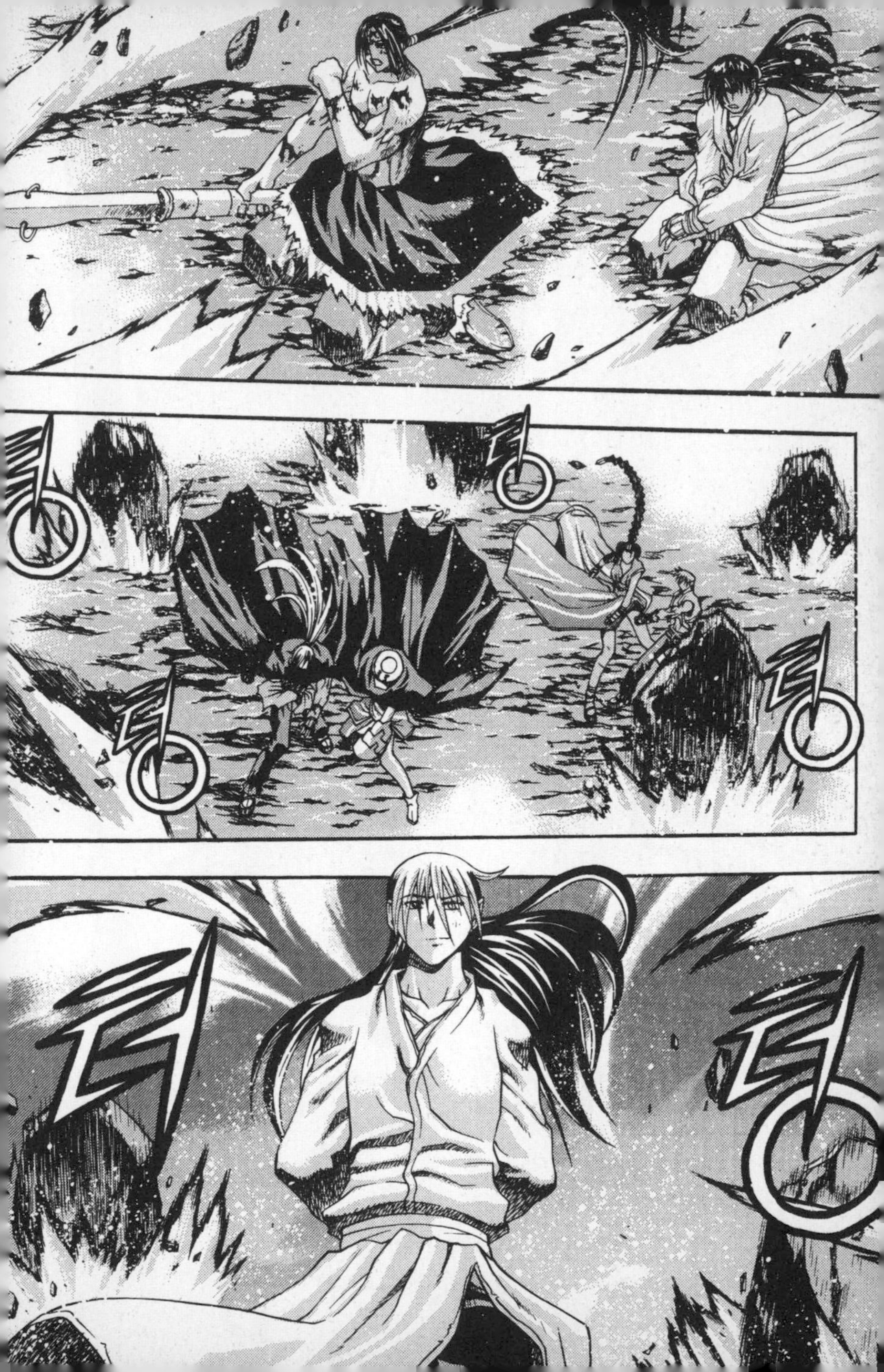

CHAPTER 97
THE REVEAL (PART 10)

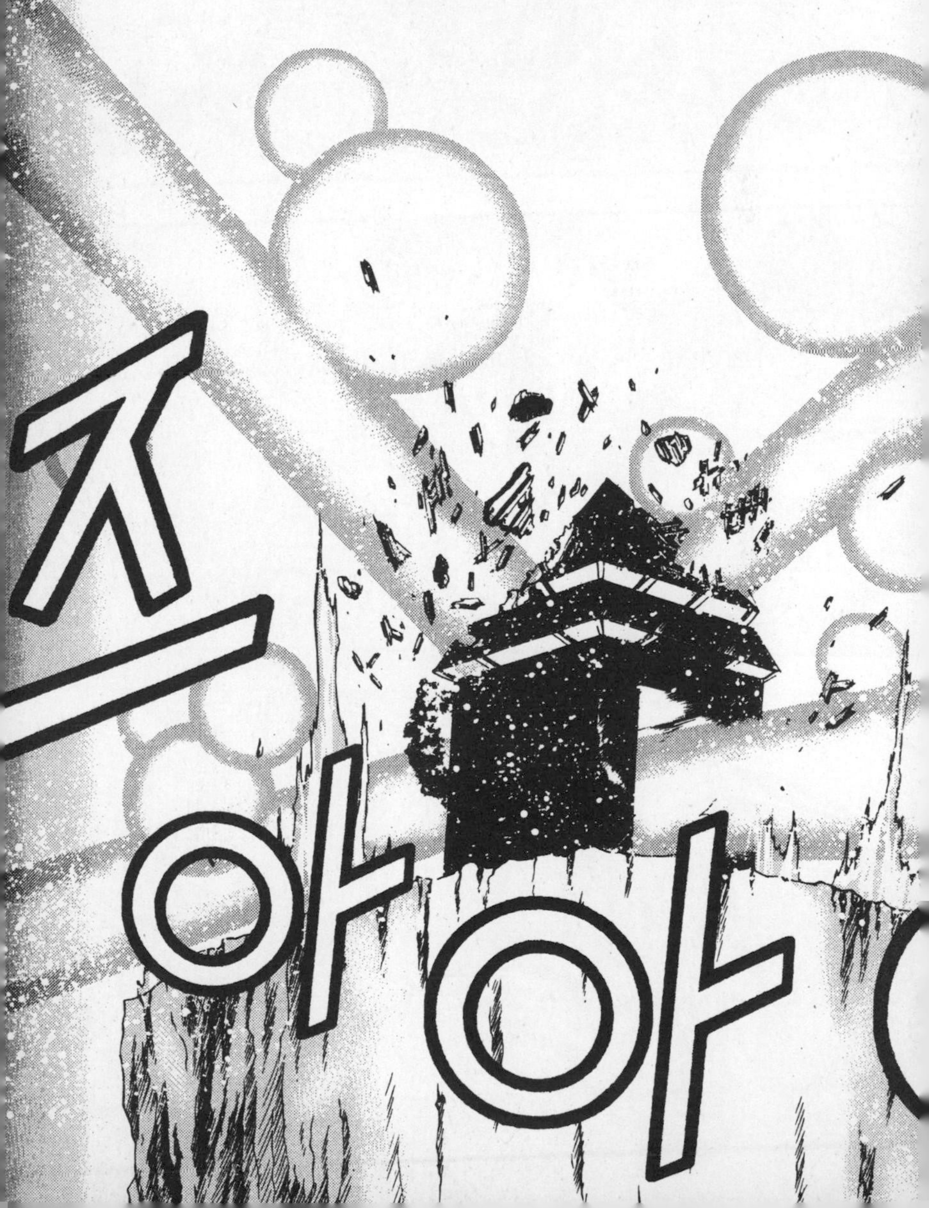
스아아

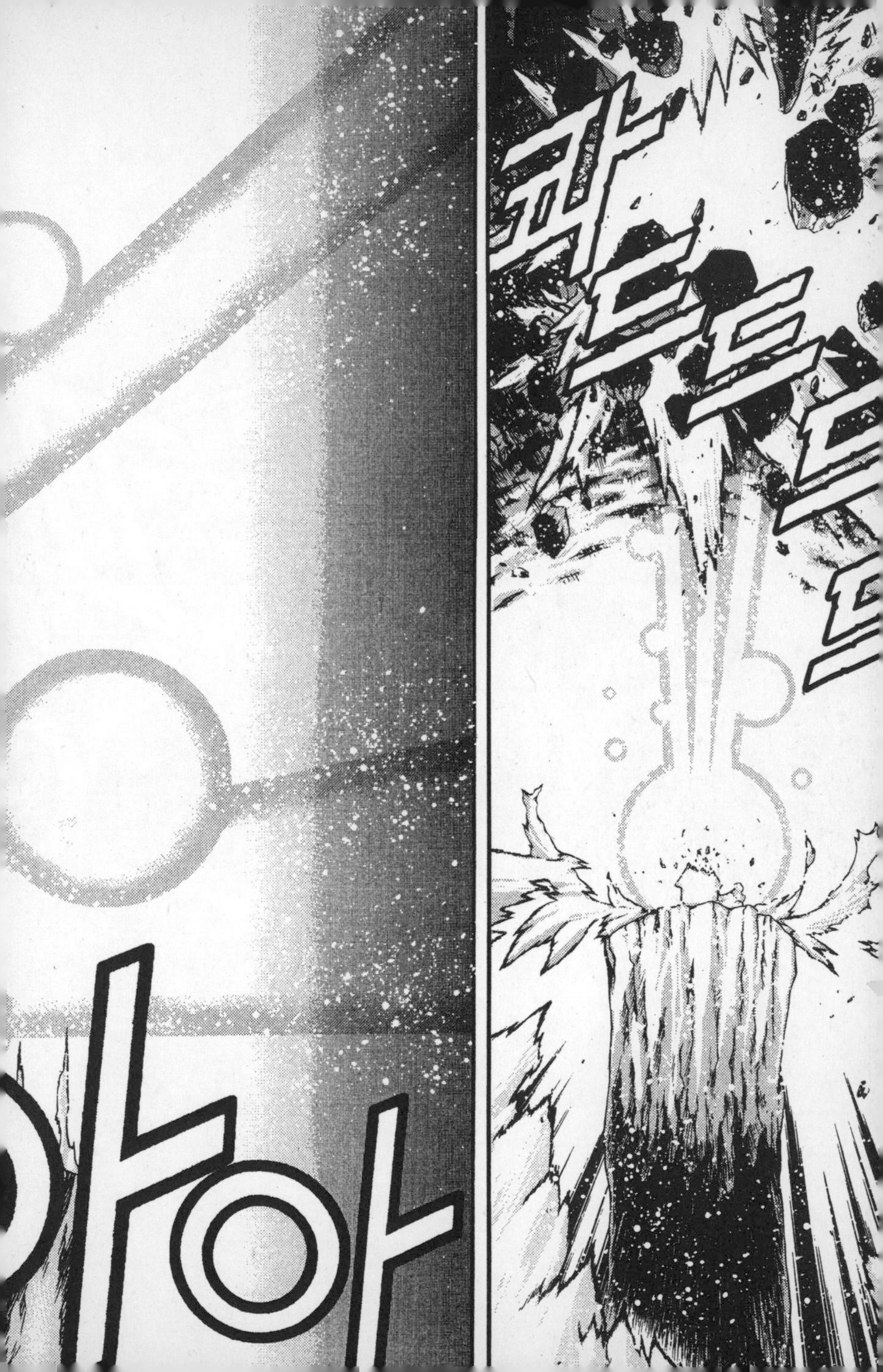
아아
콰드드드드

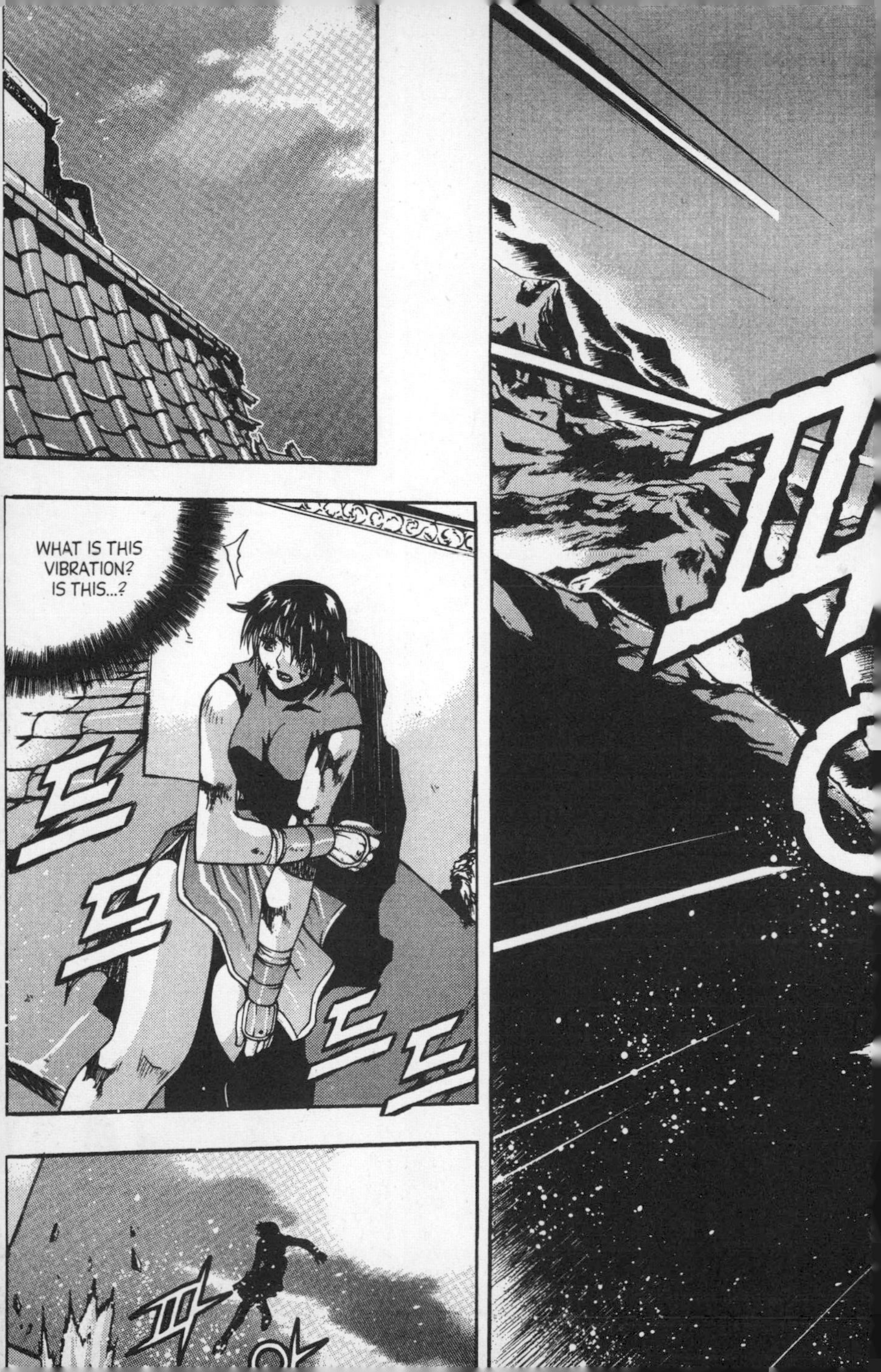
WHAT IS THIS VIBRATION? IS THIS...?

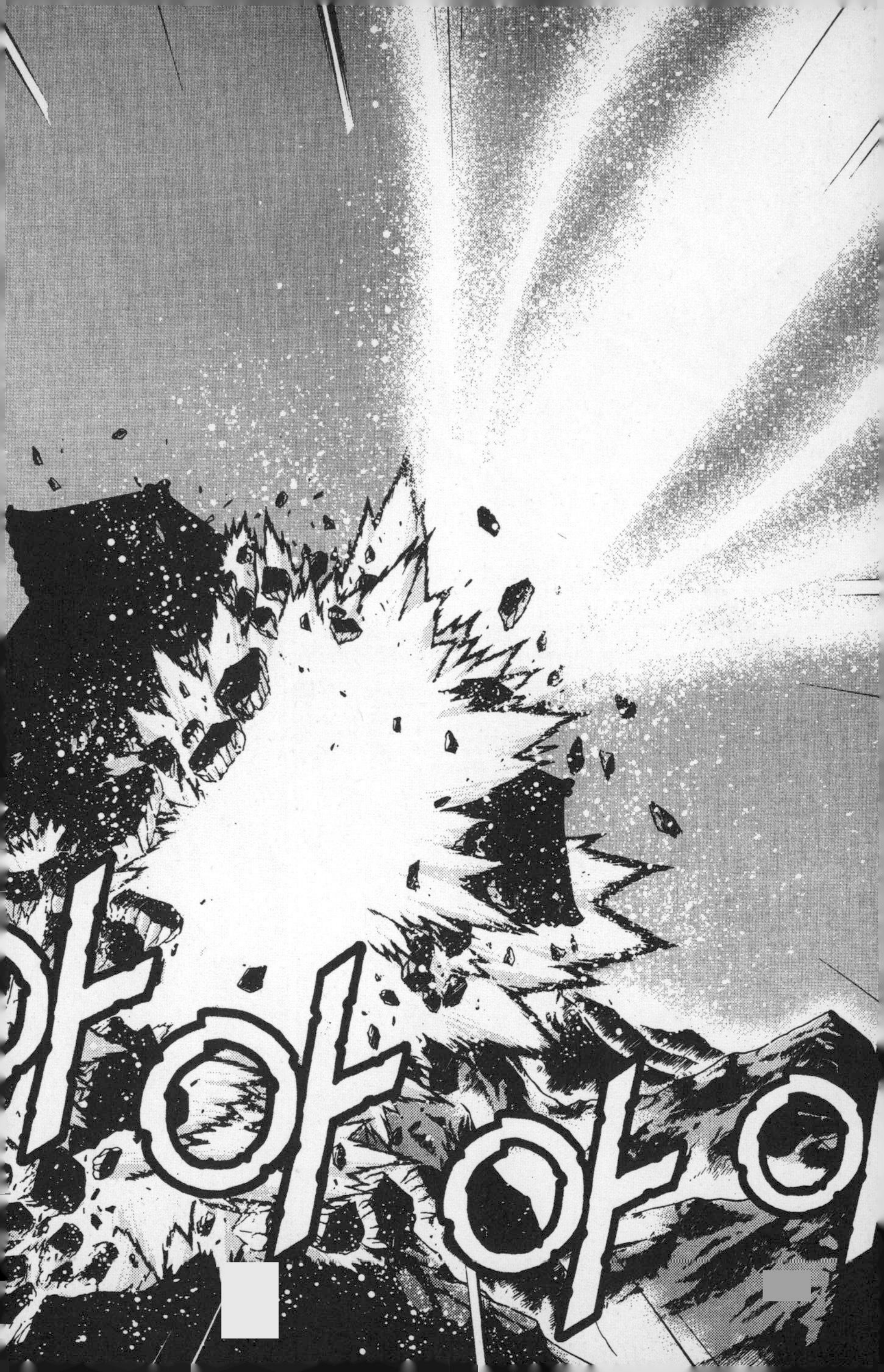

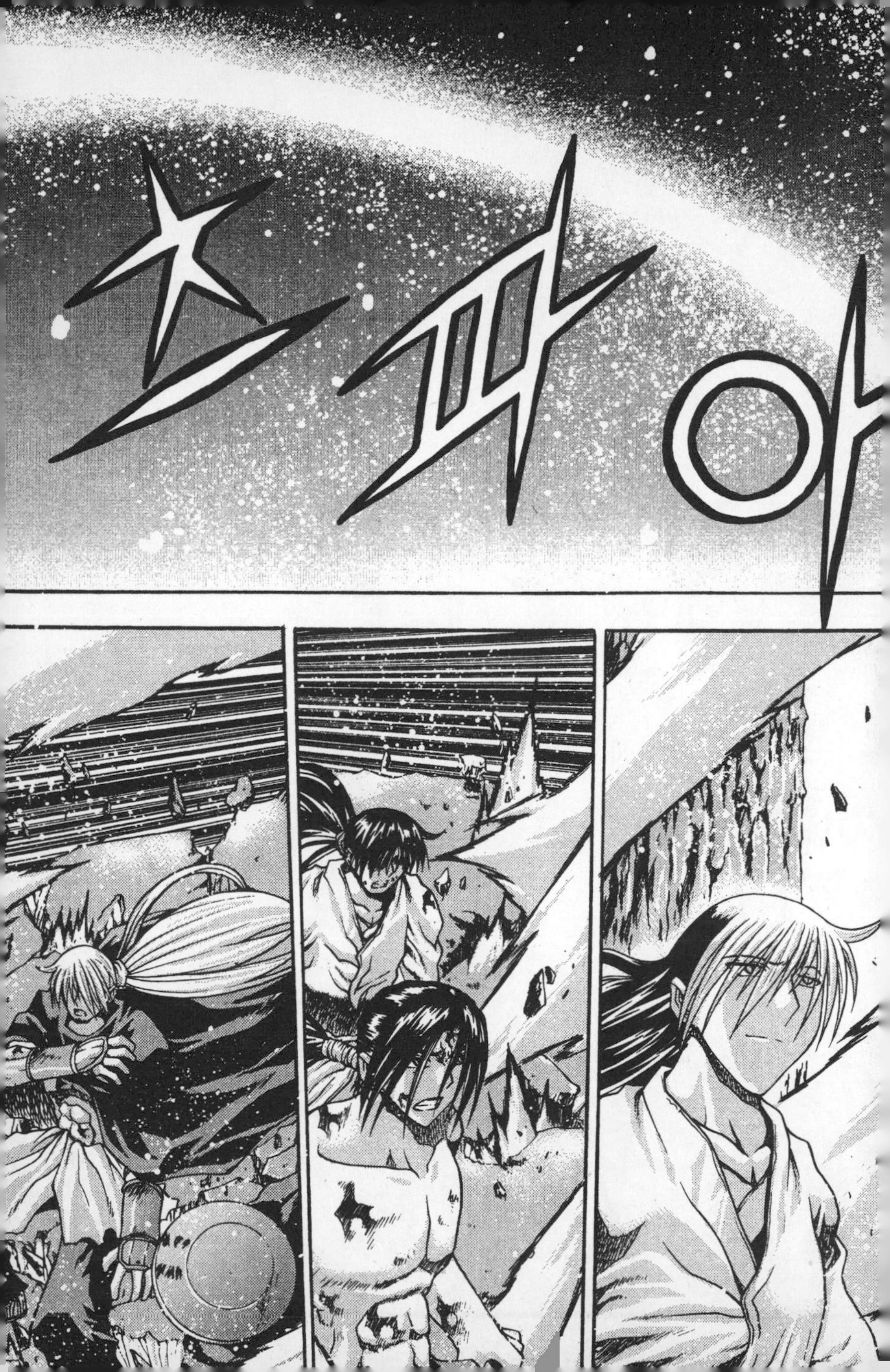
츠파아

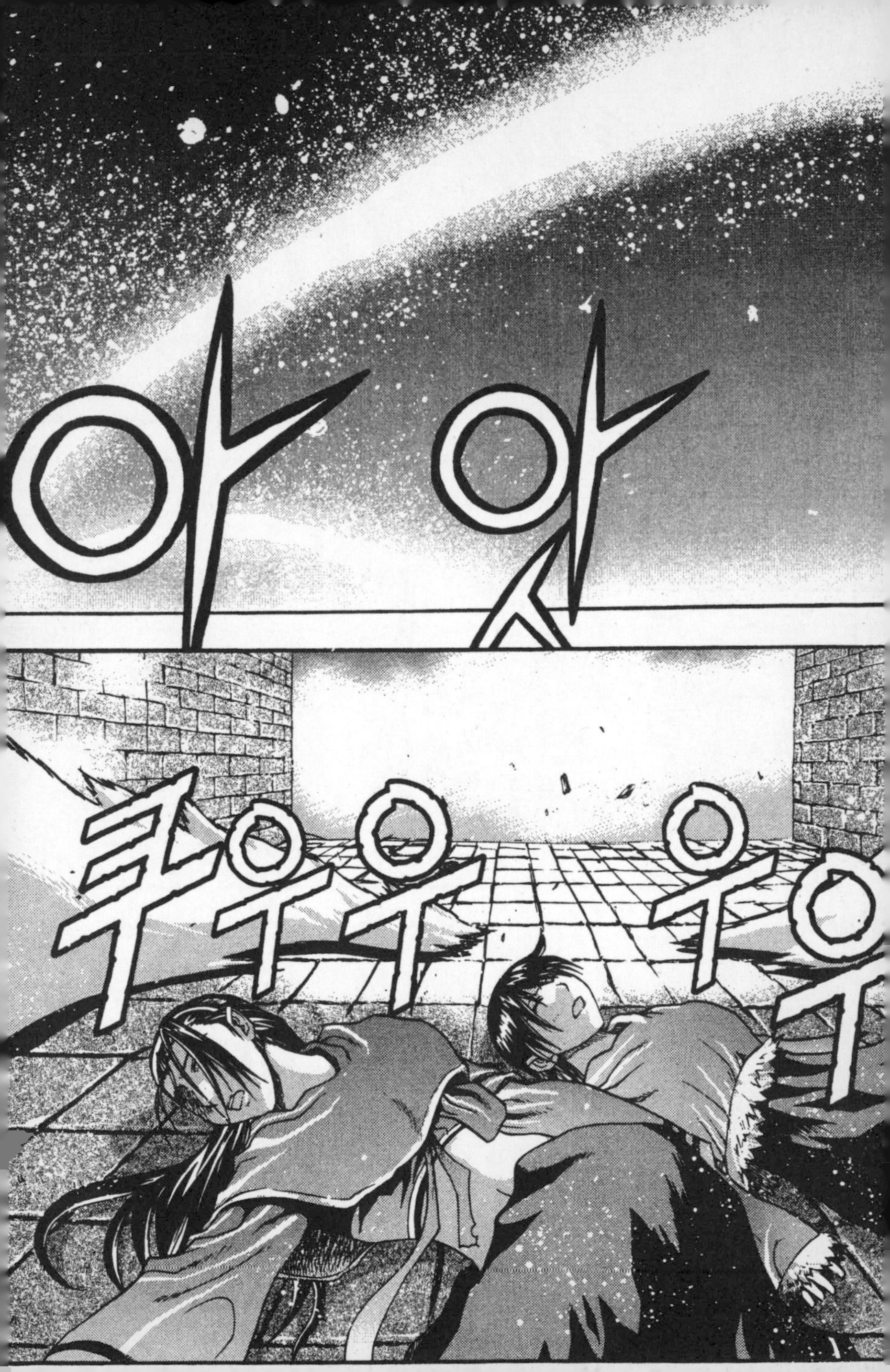
아앗
쿠우우우우

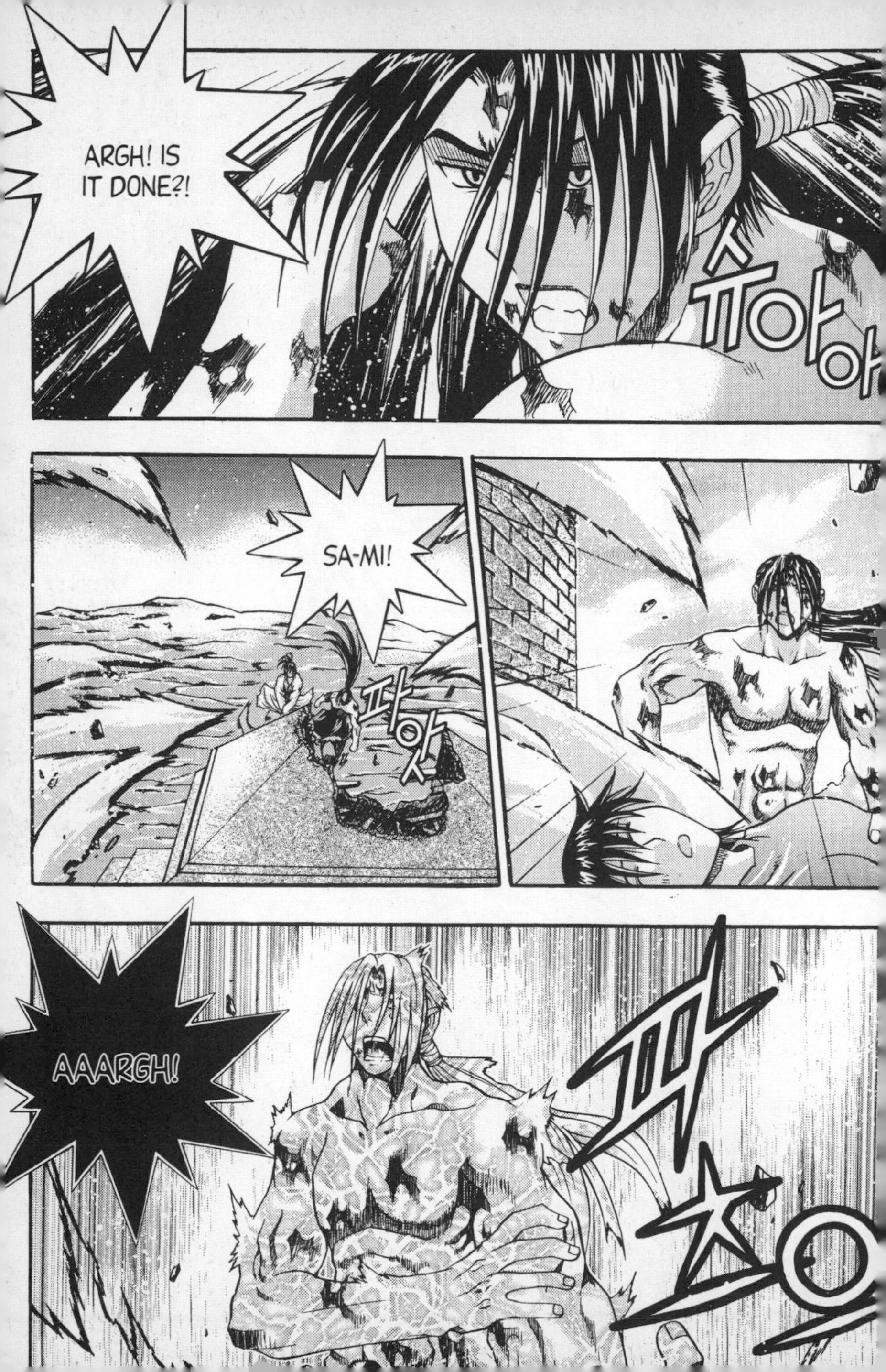
ARGH! IS IT DONE?!
SA-MI!
AAARGH!

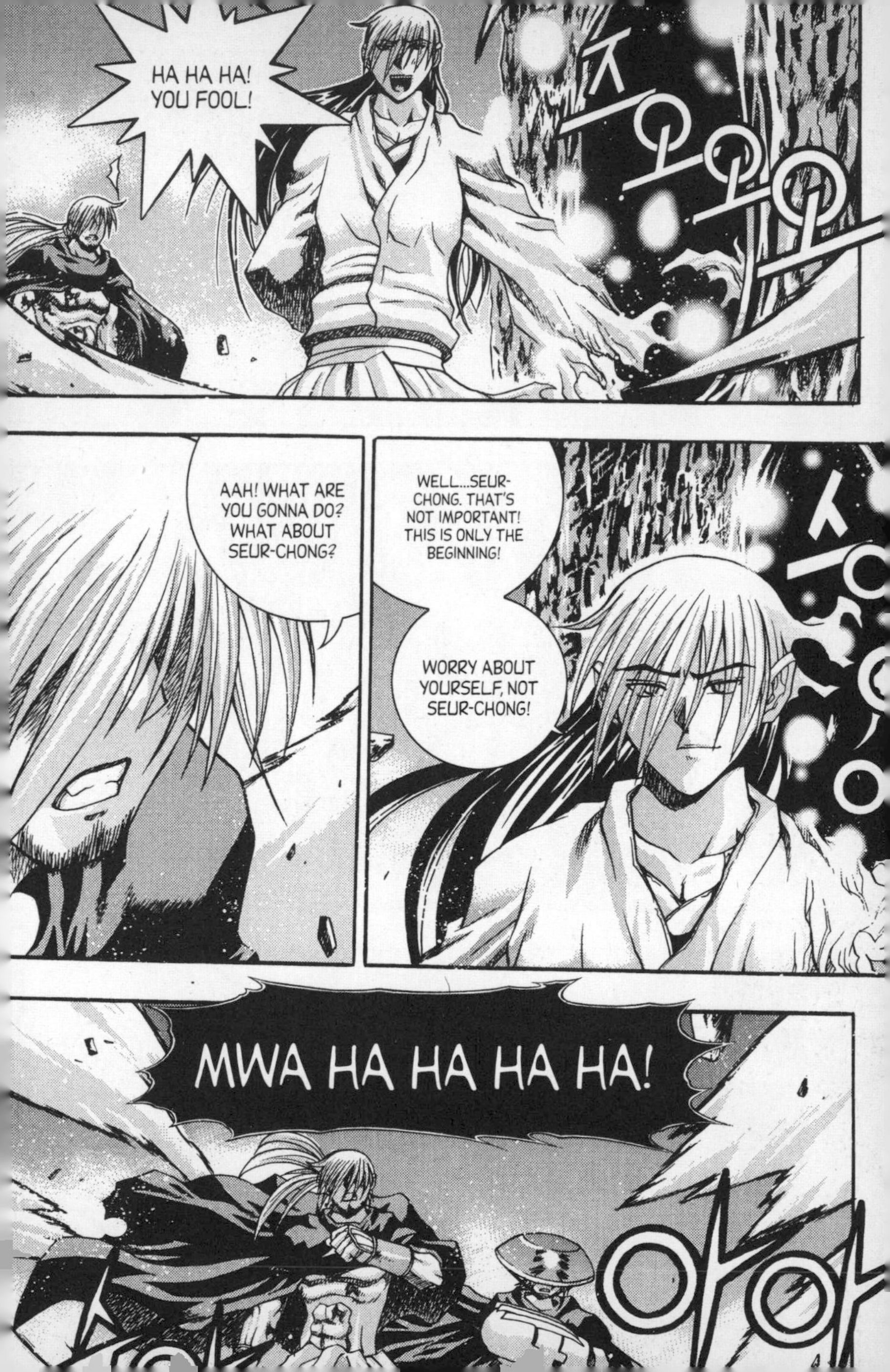
HA HA HA! YOU FOOL!
AAH! WHAT ARE YOU GONNA DO? WHAT ABOUT SEUR-CHONG?
WELL...SEUR-CHONG. THAT'S NOT IMPORTANT! THIS IS ONLY THE BEGINNING!
WORRY ABOUT YOURSELF, NOT SEUR-CHONG!
MWA HA HA HA HA!

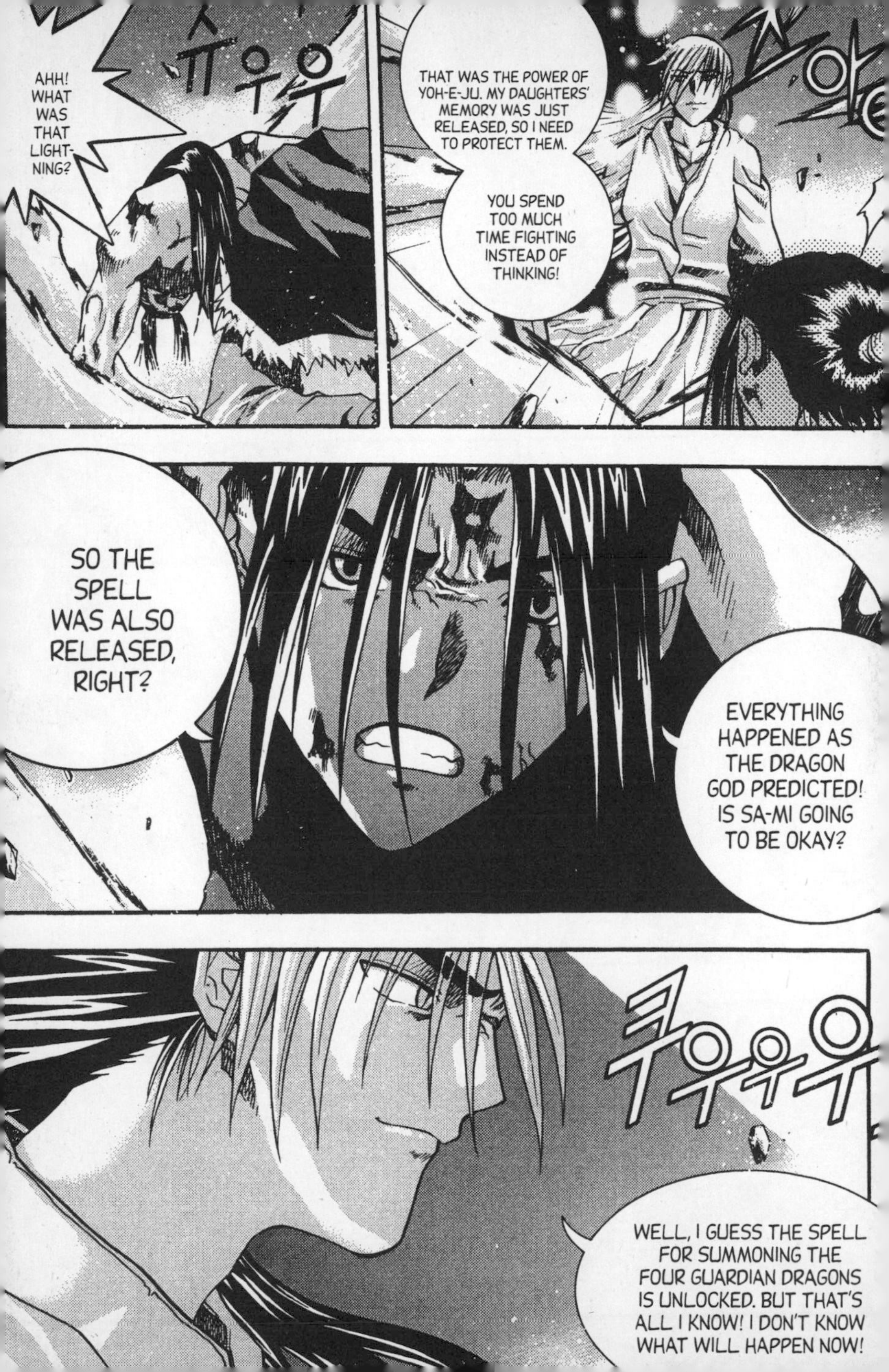
AHH! WHAT WAS THAT LIGHTNING?
슈우우
THAT WAS THE POWER OF YOH-E-JU. MY DAUGHTERS' MEMORY WAS JUST RELEASED, SO I NEED TO PROTECT THEM.
YOU SPEND TOO MUCH TIME FIGHTING INSTEAD OF THINKING!
SO THE SPELL WAS ALSO RELEASED, RIGHT?
EVERYTHING HAPPENED AS THE DRAGON GOD PREDICTED! IS SA-MI GOING TO BE OKAY?
쿠우우우
WELL, I GUESS THE SPELL FOR SUMMONING THE FOUR GUARDIAN DRAGONS IS UNLOCKED. BUT THAT'S ALL I KNOW! I DON'T KNOW WHAT WILL HAPPEN NOW!

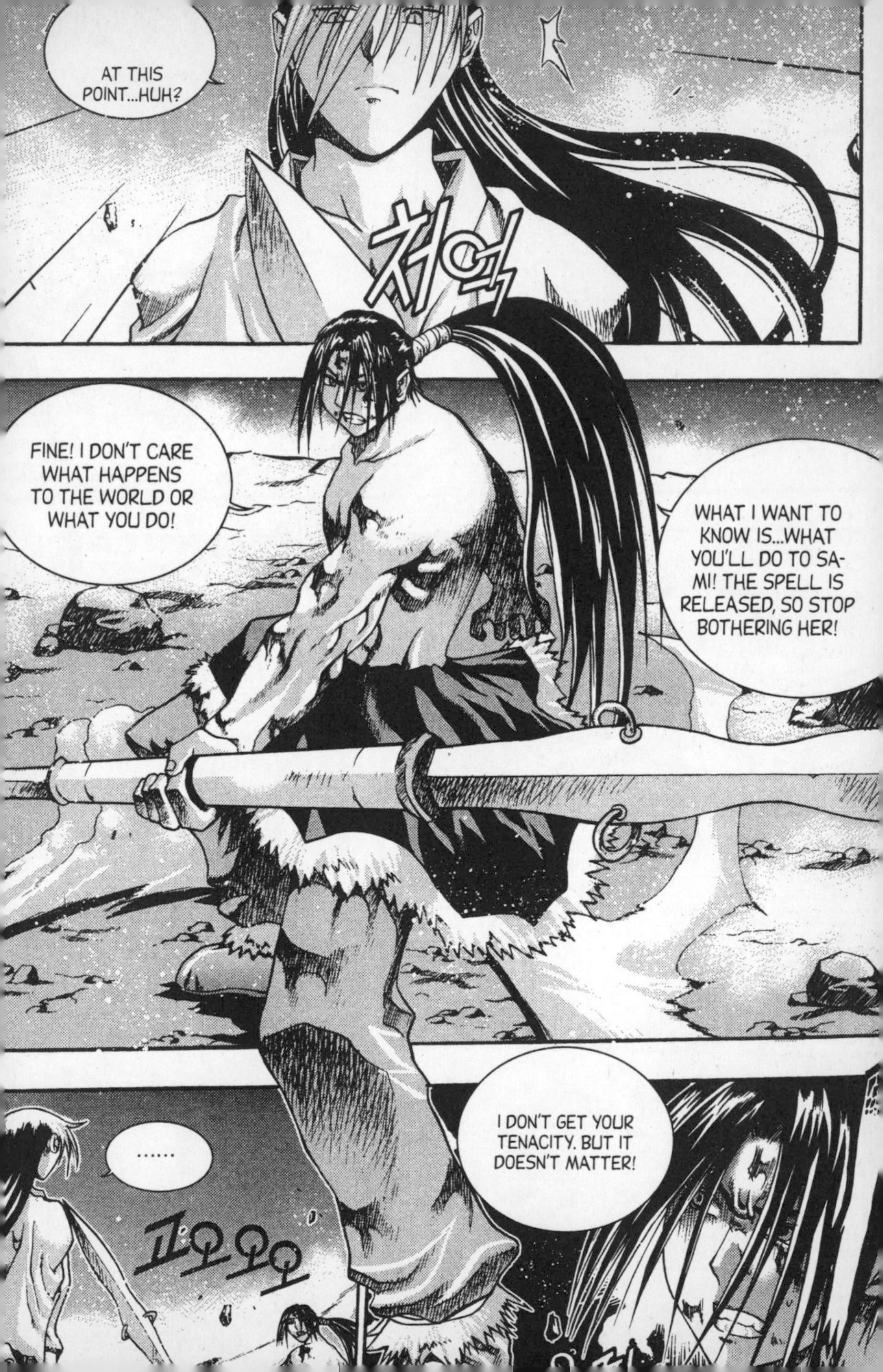
AT THIS POINT...HUH?
FINE! I DON'T CARE WHAT HAPPENS TO THE WORLD OR WHAT YOU DO!
WHAT I WANT TO KNOW IS...WHAT YOU'LL DO TO SA-MI! THE SPELL IS RELEASED, SO STOP BOTHERING HER!
......
I DON'T GET YOUR TENACITY. BUT IT DOESN'T MATTER!

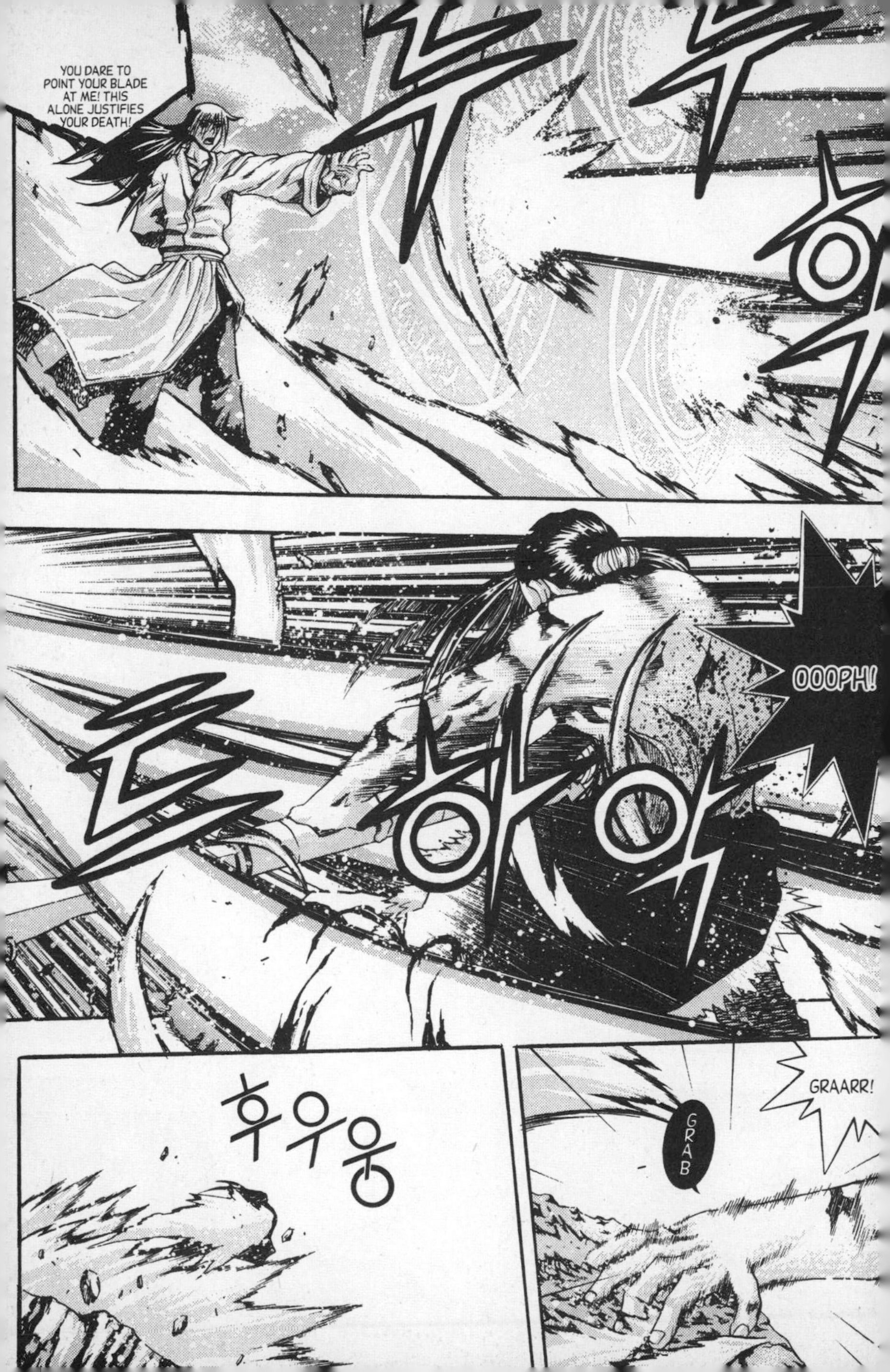
YOU DARE TO POINT YOUR BLADE AT ME! THIS ALONE JUSTIFIES YOUR DEATH!
OOOPH!
후우웅
GRAB
GRAARR!

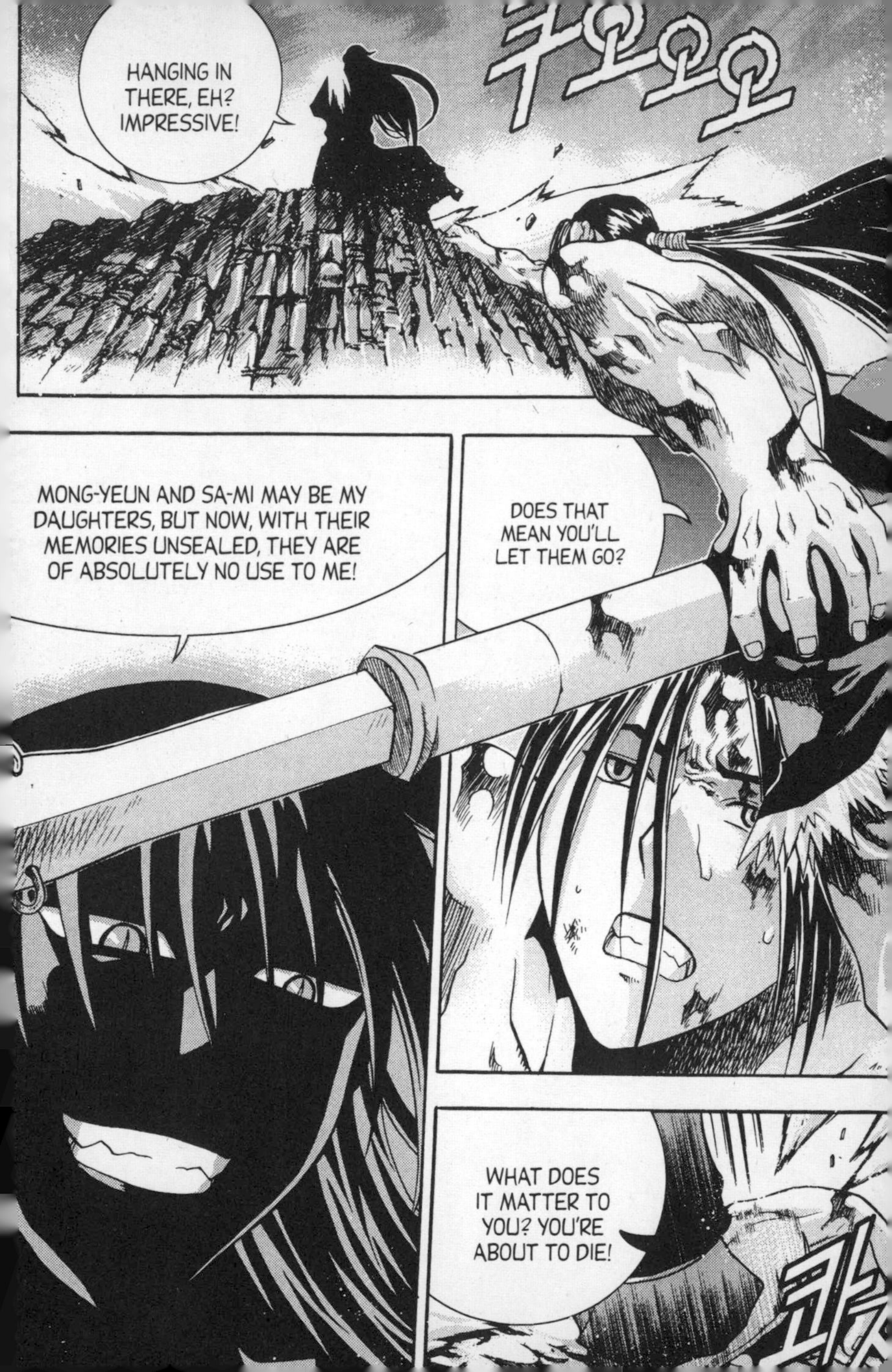
HANGING IN THERE, EH? IMPRESSIVE!
쿠오오오
MONG-YEUN AND SA-MI MAY BE MY DAUGHTERS, BUT NOW, WITH THEIR MEMORIES UNSEALED, THEY ARE OF ABSOLUTELY NO USE TO ME!
DOES THAT MEAN YOU'LL LET THEM GO?
WHAT DOES IT MATTER TO YOU? YOU'RE ABOUT TO DIE!

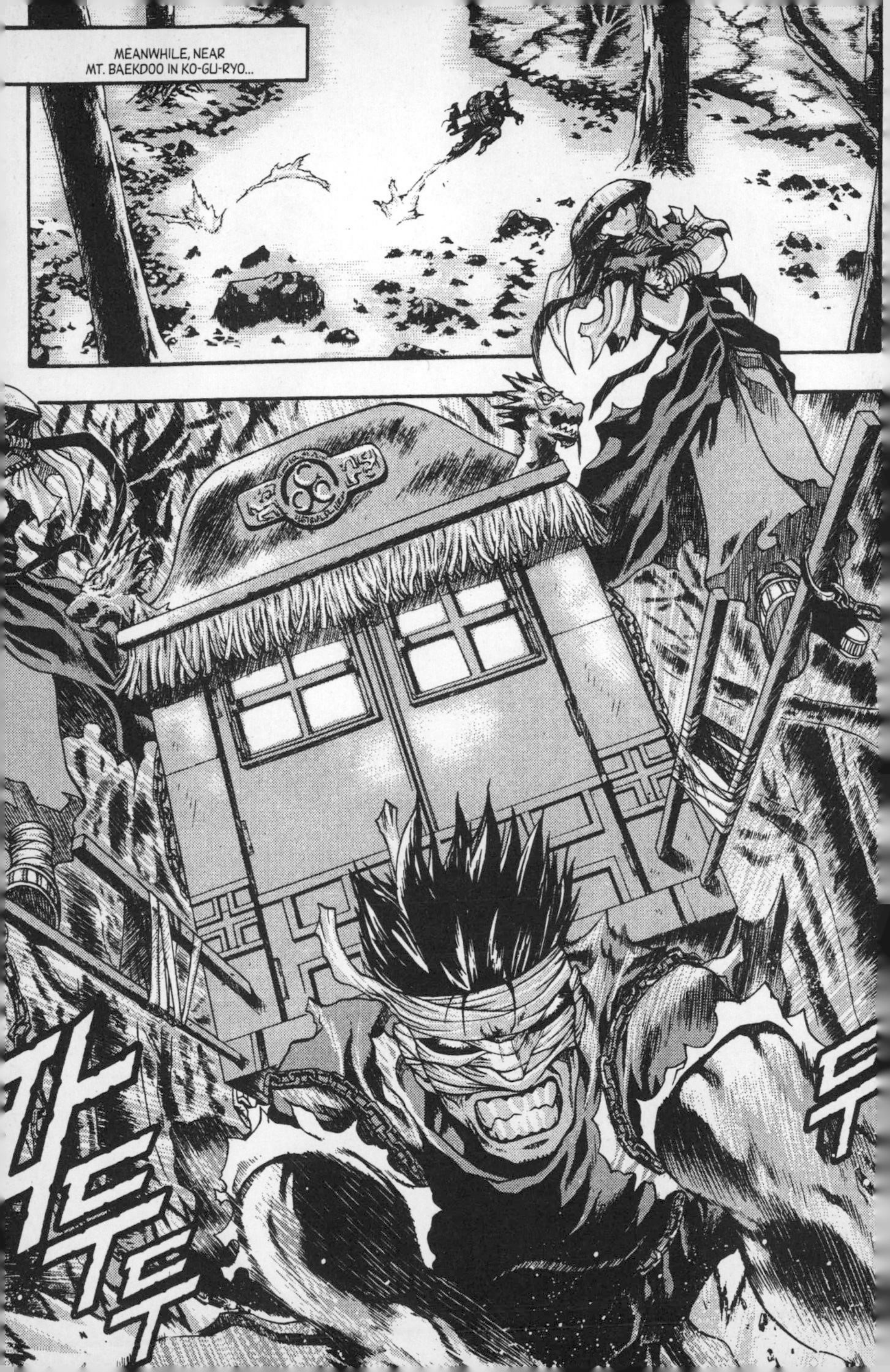
MEANWHILE, NEAR
MT. BAEKDOO IN KO-GU-RYO...

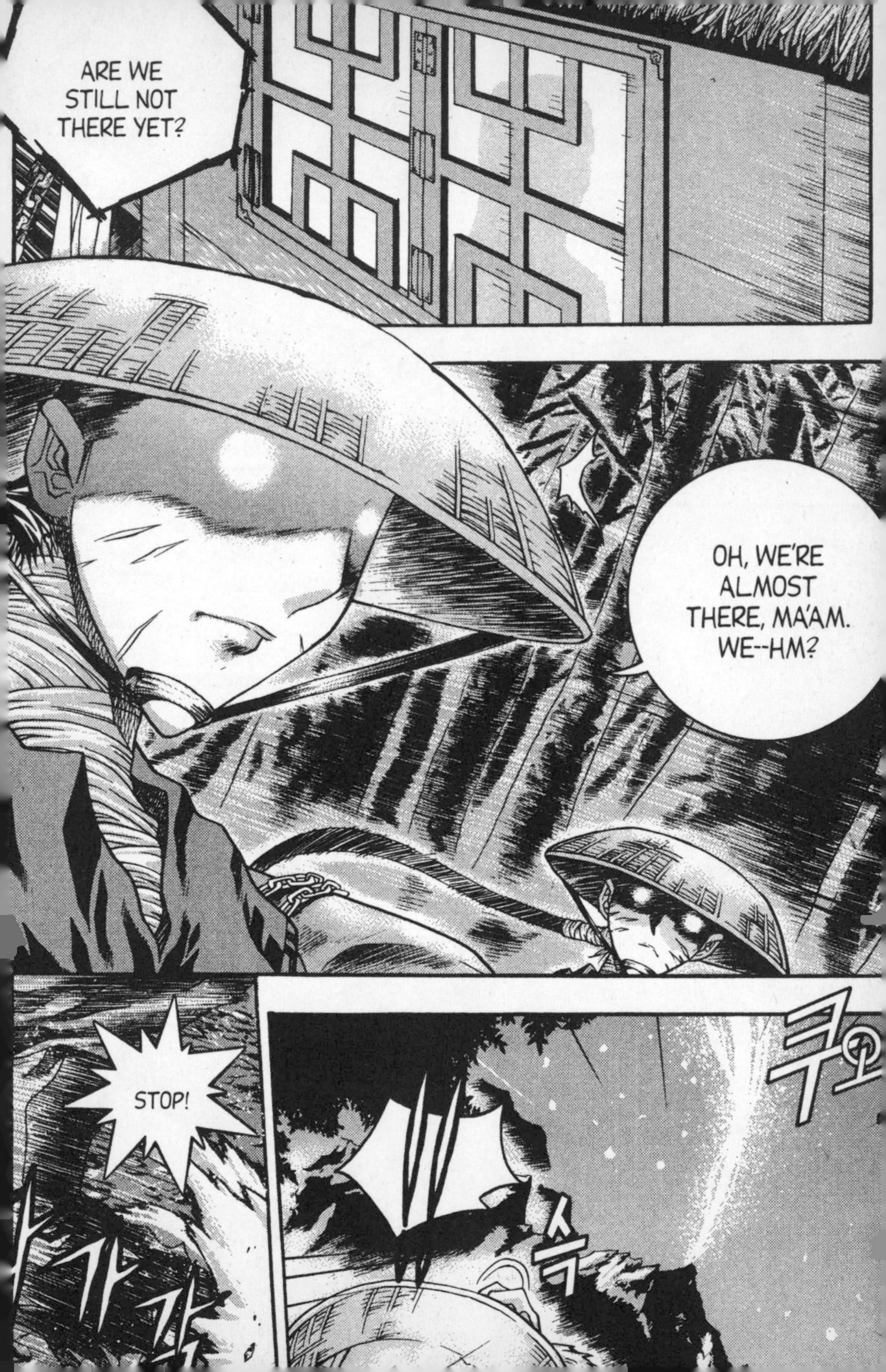
ARE WE STILL NOT THERE YET?
OH, WE'RE ALMOST THERE, MA'AM. WE--HM?
STOP!

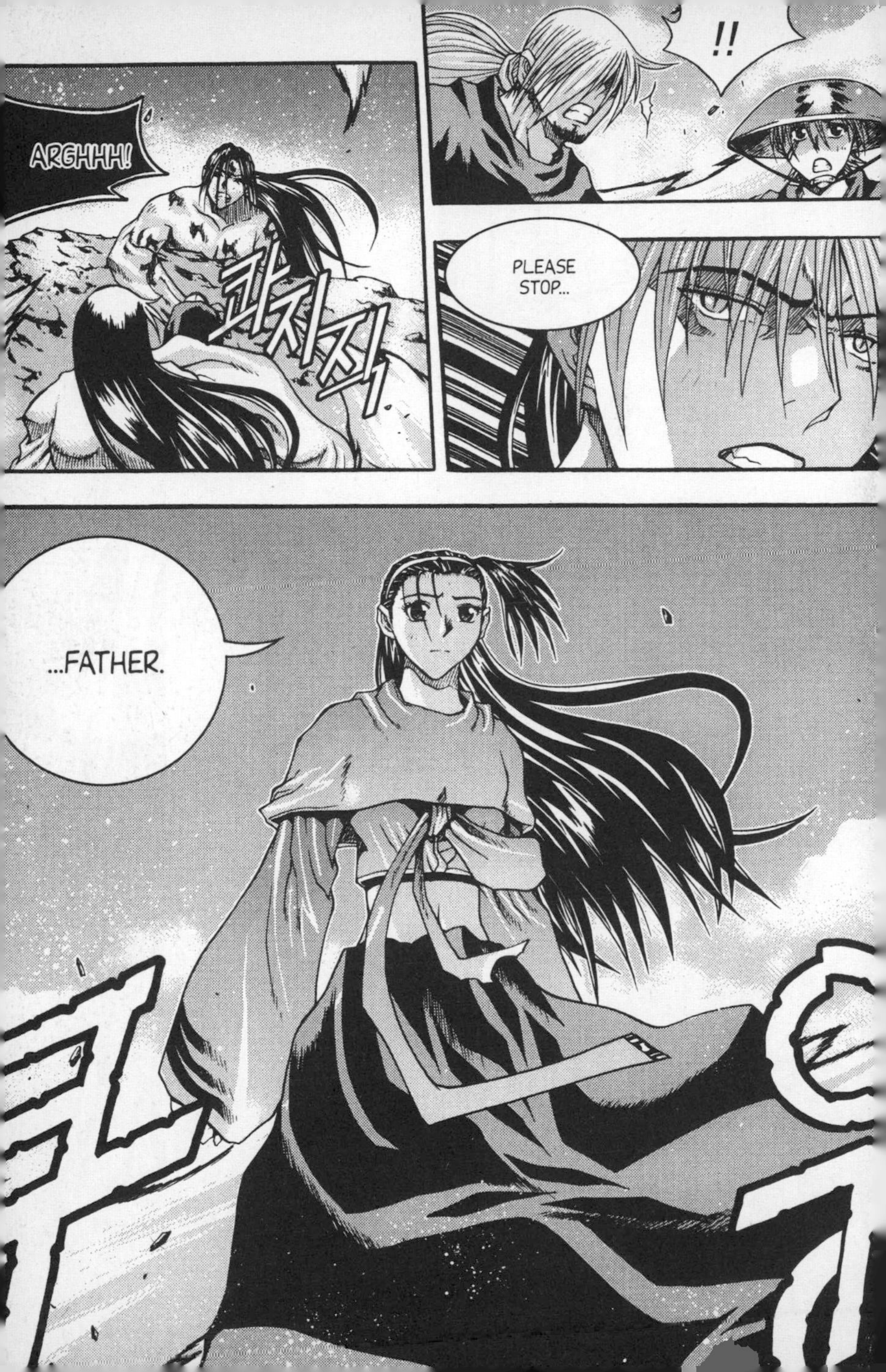
ARGHHH!
!!
PLEASE STOP...
...FATHER.

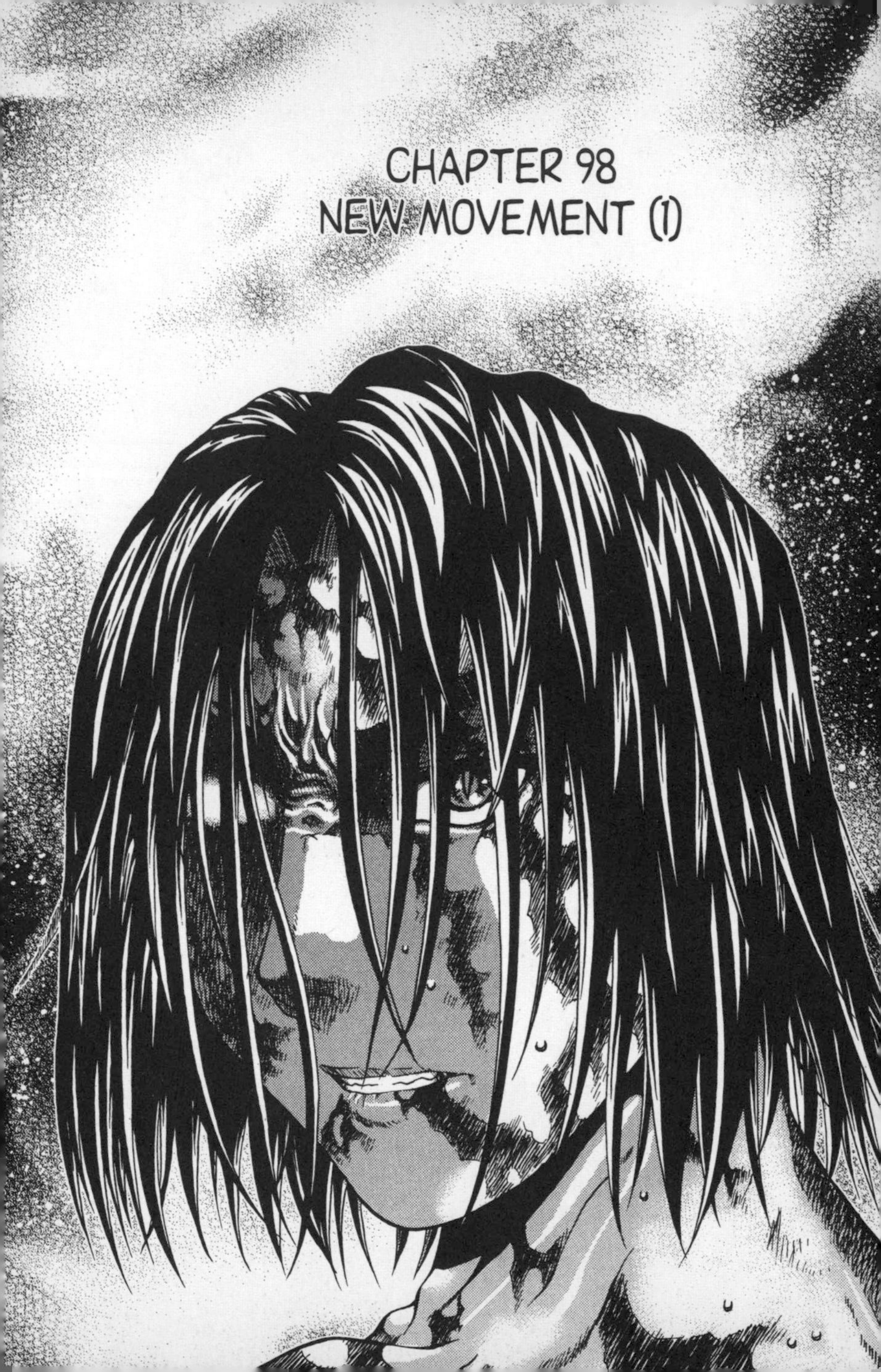
CHAPTER 98
NEW MOVEMENT (1)

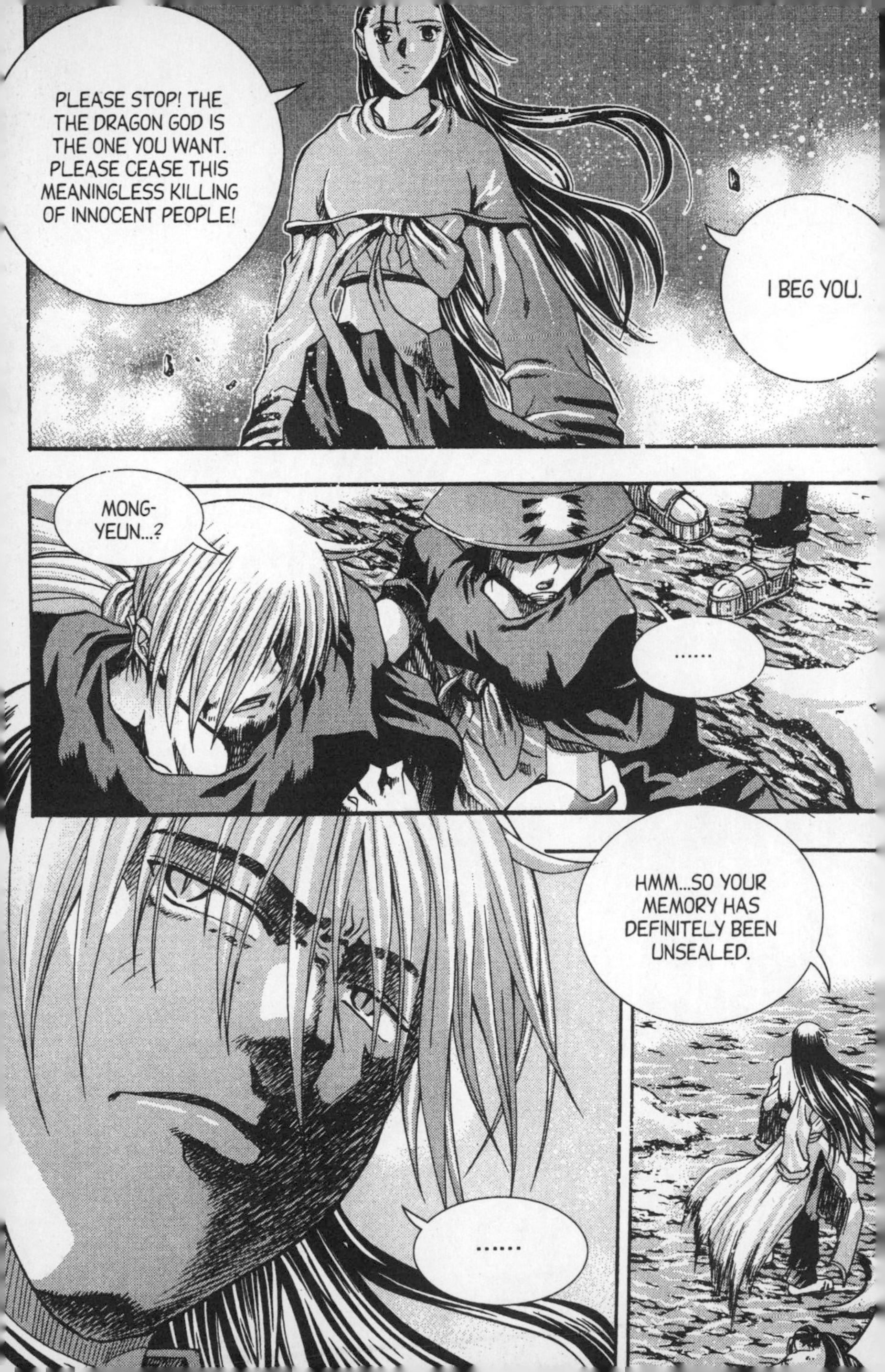
PLEASE STOP! THE THE DRAGON GOD IS THE ONE YOU WANT. PLEASE CEASE THIS MEANINGLESS KILLING OF INNOCENT PEOPLE!
I BEG YOU.
MONG-YEUN...?
......
HMM...SO YOUR MEMORY HAS DEFINITELY BEEN UNSEALED.
......

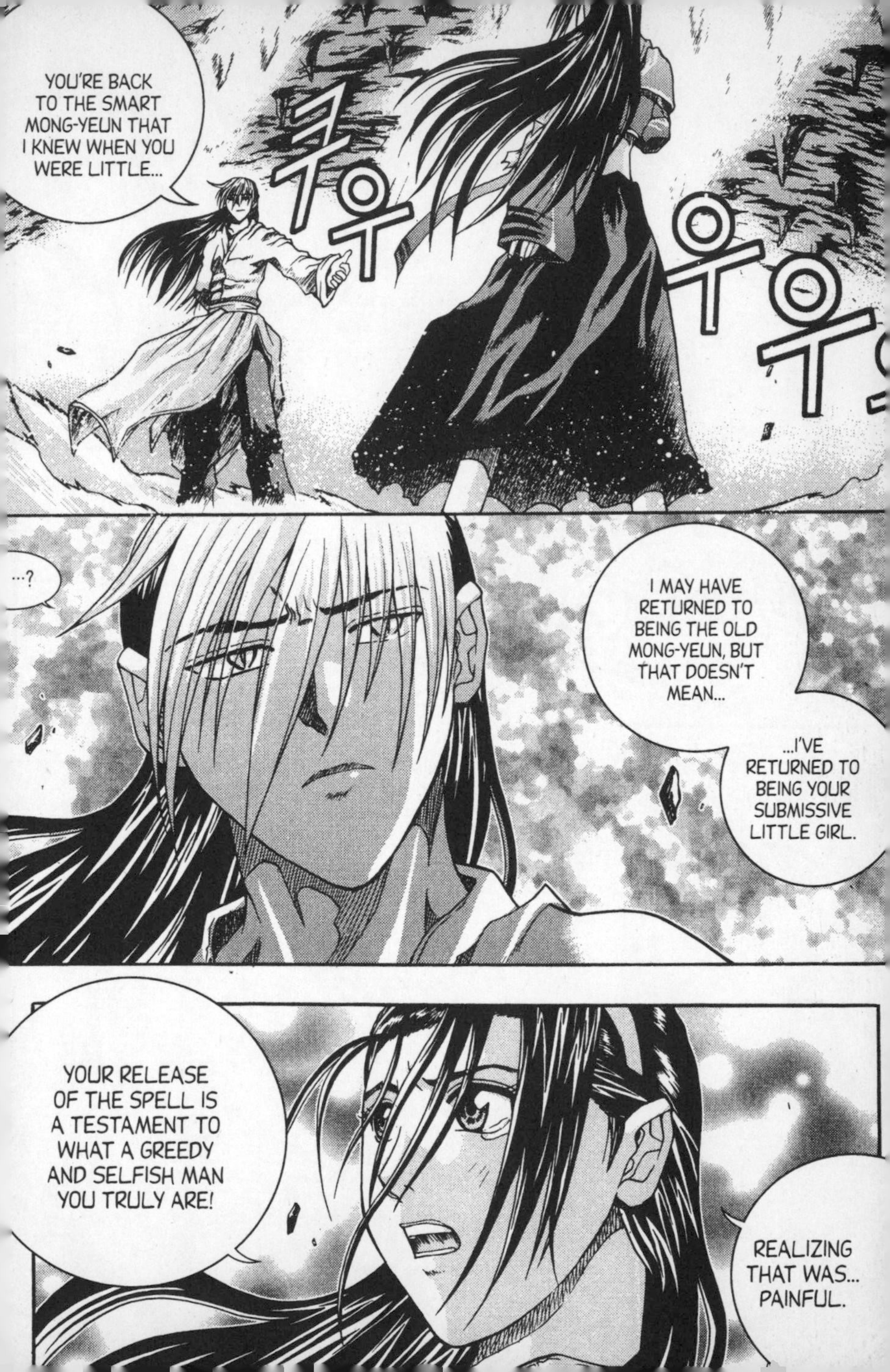
YOU'RE BACK TO THE SMART MONG-YEUN THAT I KNEW WHEN YOU WERE LITTLE...
쿠우우우
...?
I MAY HAVE RETURNED TO BEING THE OLD MONG-YEUN, BUT THAT DOESN'T MEAN...
...I'VE RETURNED TO BEING YOUR SUBMISSIVE LITTLE GIRL.
YOUR RELEASE OF THE SPELL IS A TESTAMENT TO WHAT A GREEDY AND SELFISH MAN YOU TRULY ARE!
REALIZING THAT WAS... PAINFUL.

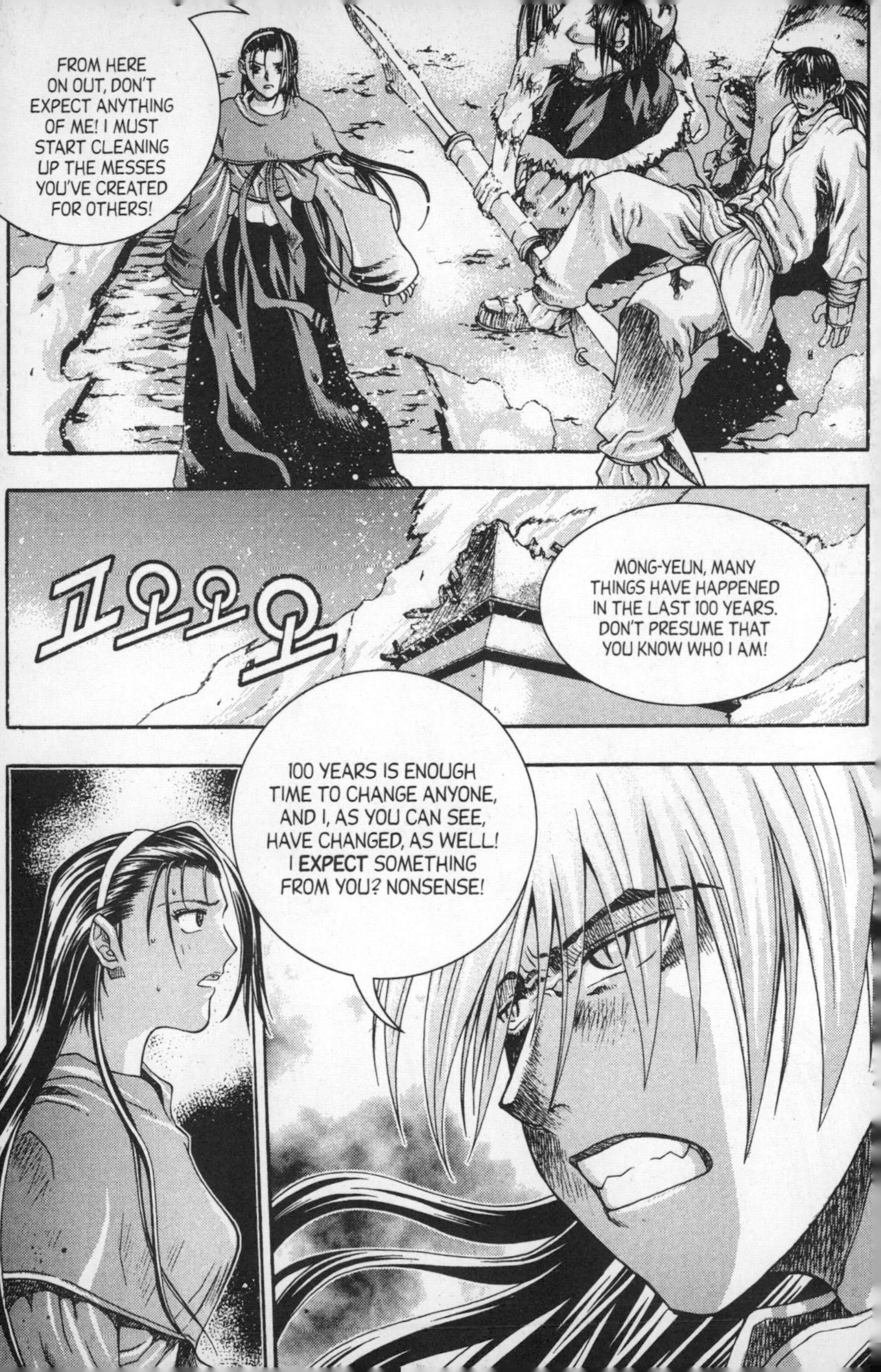
FROM HERE ON OUT, DON'T EXPECT ANYTHING OF ME! I MUST START CLEANING UP THE MESSES YOU'VE CREATED FOR OTHERS!
MONG-YEUN, MANY THINGS HAVE HAPPENED IN THE LAST 100 YEARS. DON'T PRESUME THAT YOU KNOW WHO I AM!
100 YEARS IS ENOUGH TIME TO CHANGE ANYONE, AND I, AS YOU CAN SEE, HAVE CHANGED, AS WELL! I **EXPECT** SOMETHING FROM YOU? NONSENSE!

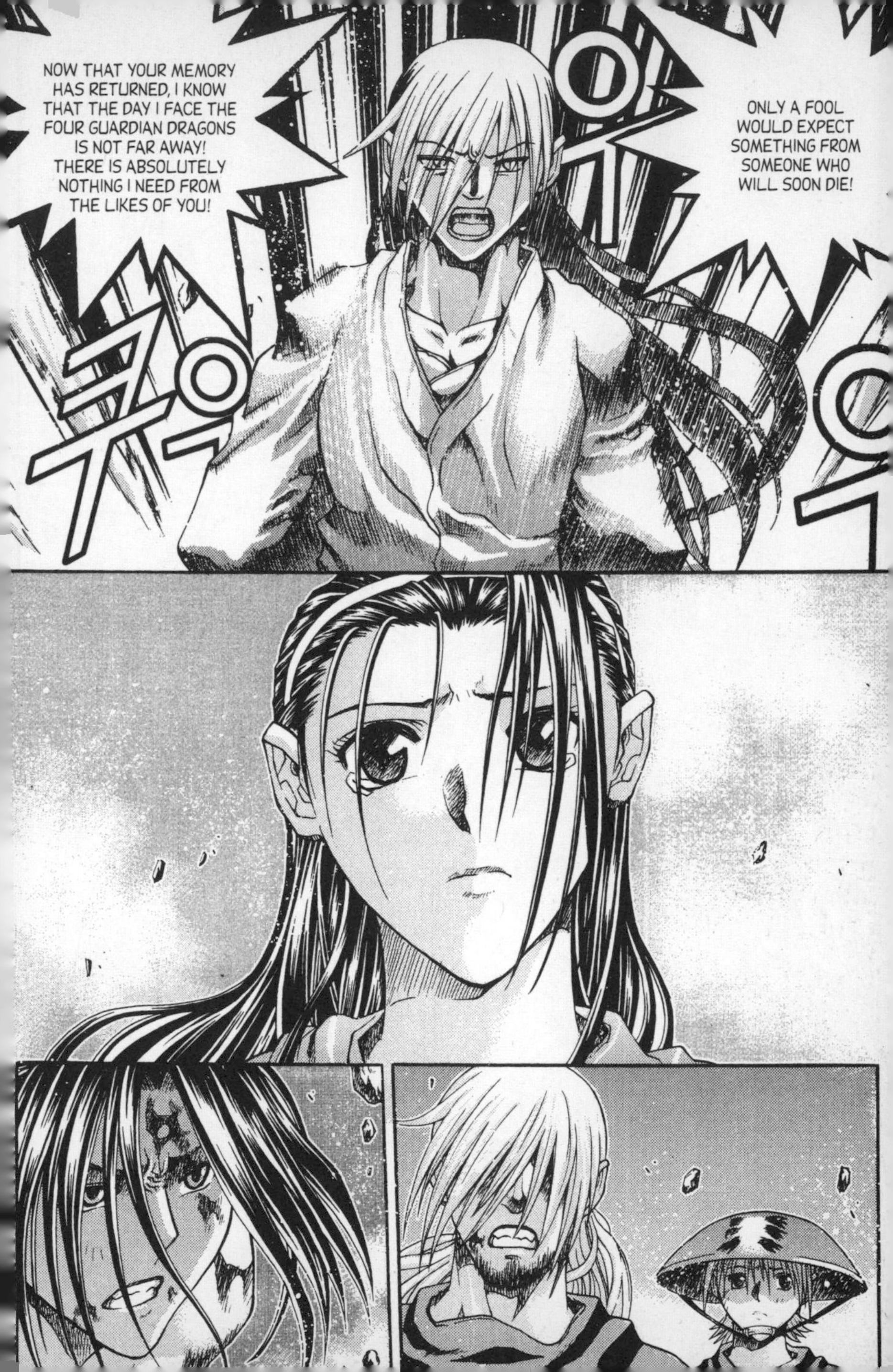
NOW THAT YOUR MEMORY HAS RETURNED, I KNOW THAT THE DAY I FACE THE FOUR GUARDIAN DRAGONS IS NOT FAR AWAY! THERE IS ABSOLUTELY NOTHING I NEED FROM THE LIKES OF YOU!
ONLY A FOOL WOULD EXPECT SOMETHING FROM SOMEONE WHO WILL SOON DIE!

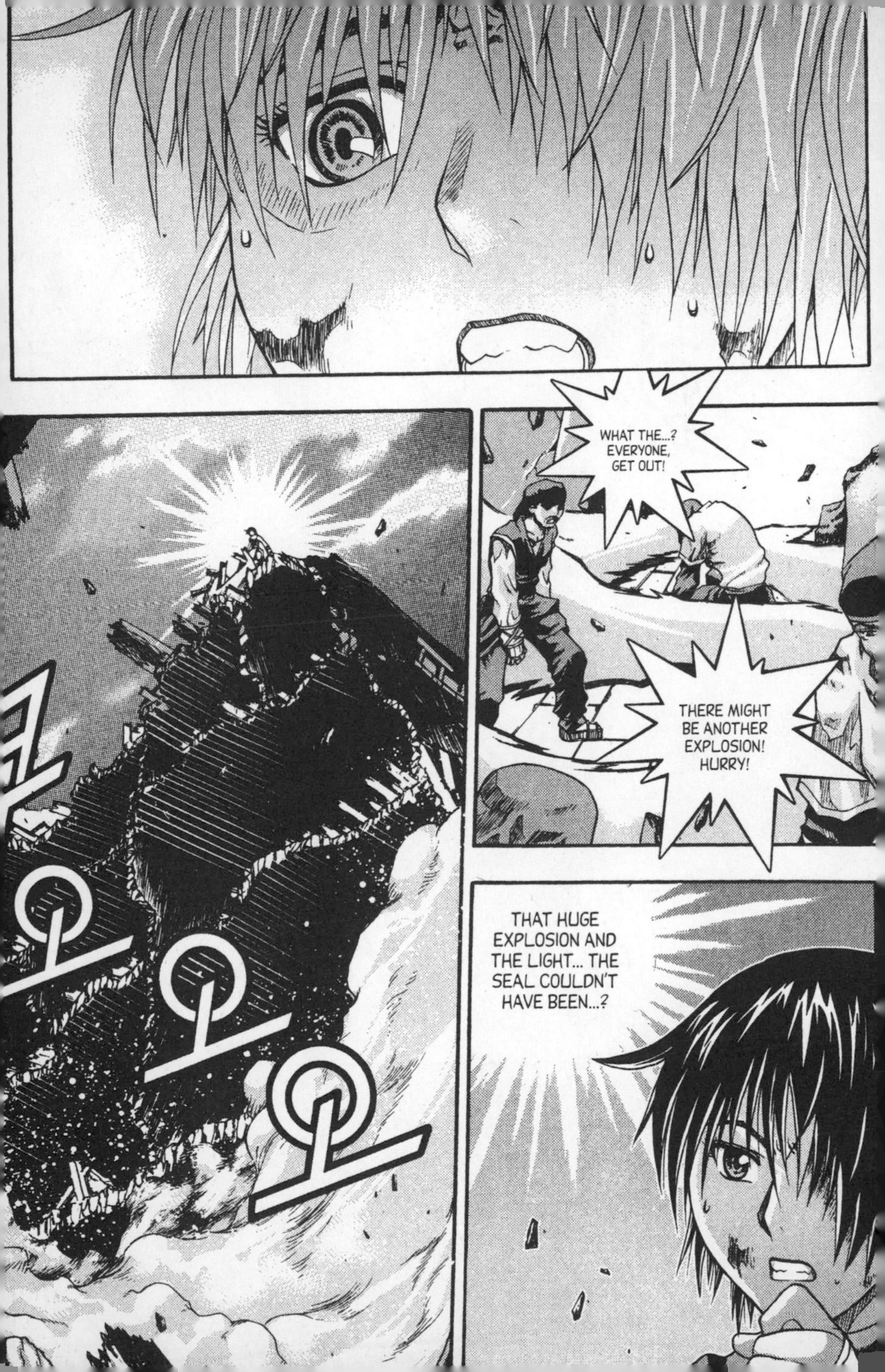
WHAT THE...? EVERYONE, GET OUT!
THERE MIGHT BE ANOTHER EXPLOSION! HURRY!
THAT HUGE EXPLOSION AND THE LIGHT... THE SEAL COULDN'T HAVE BEEN...?

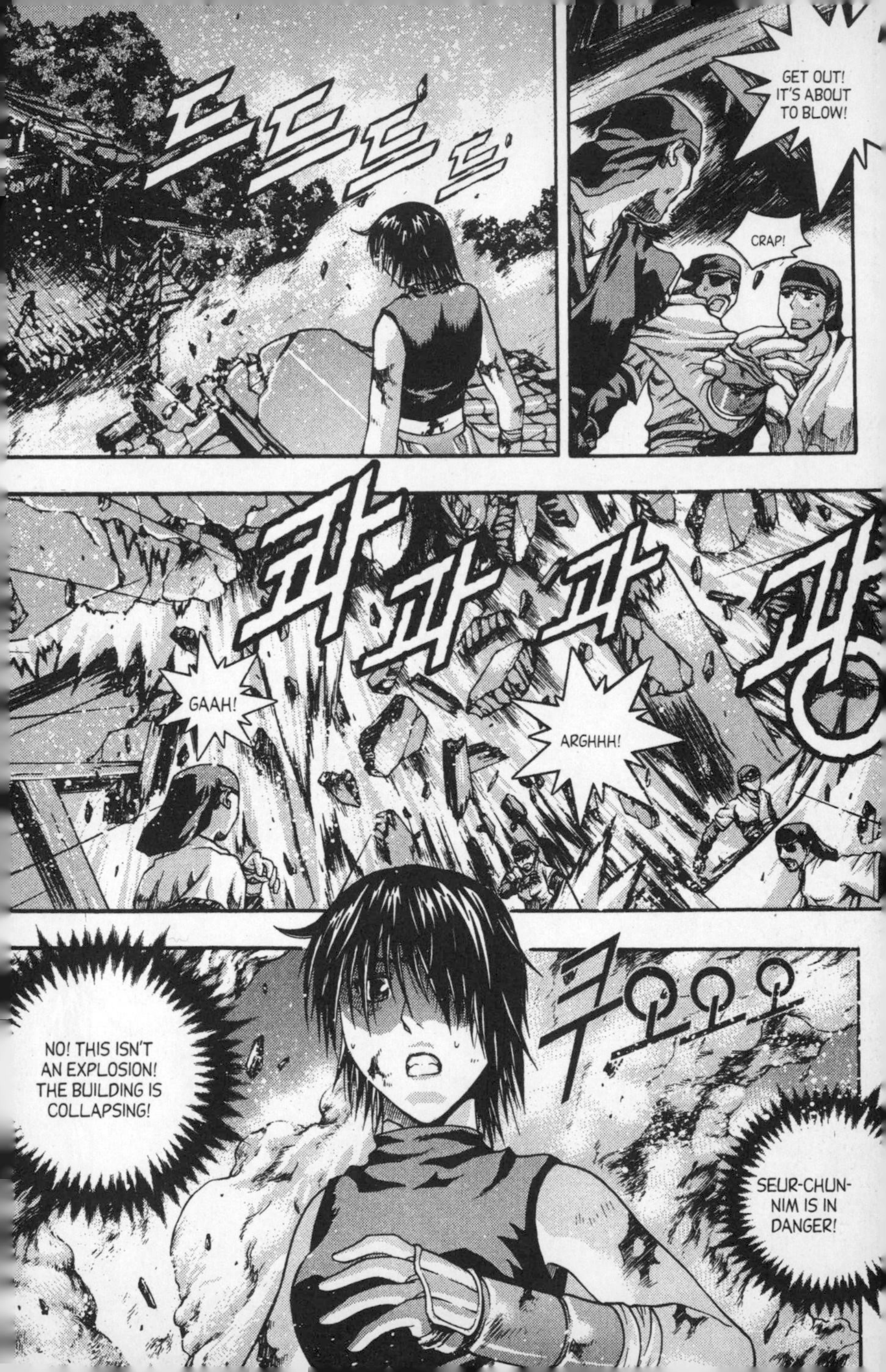
GET OUT! IT'S ABOUT TO BLOW!
CRAP!
GAAH!
ARGHHH!
NO! THIS ISN'T AN EXPLOSION! THE BUILDING IS COLLAPSING!
SEUR-CHUN-NIM IS IN DANGER!

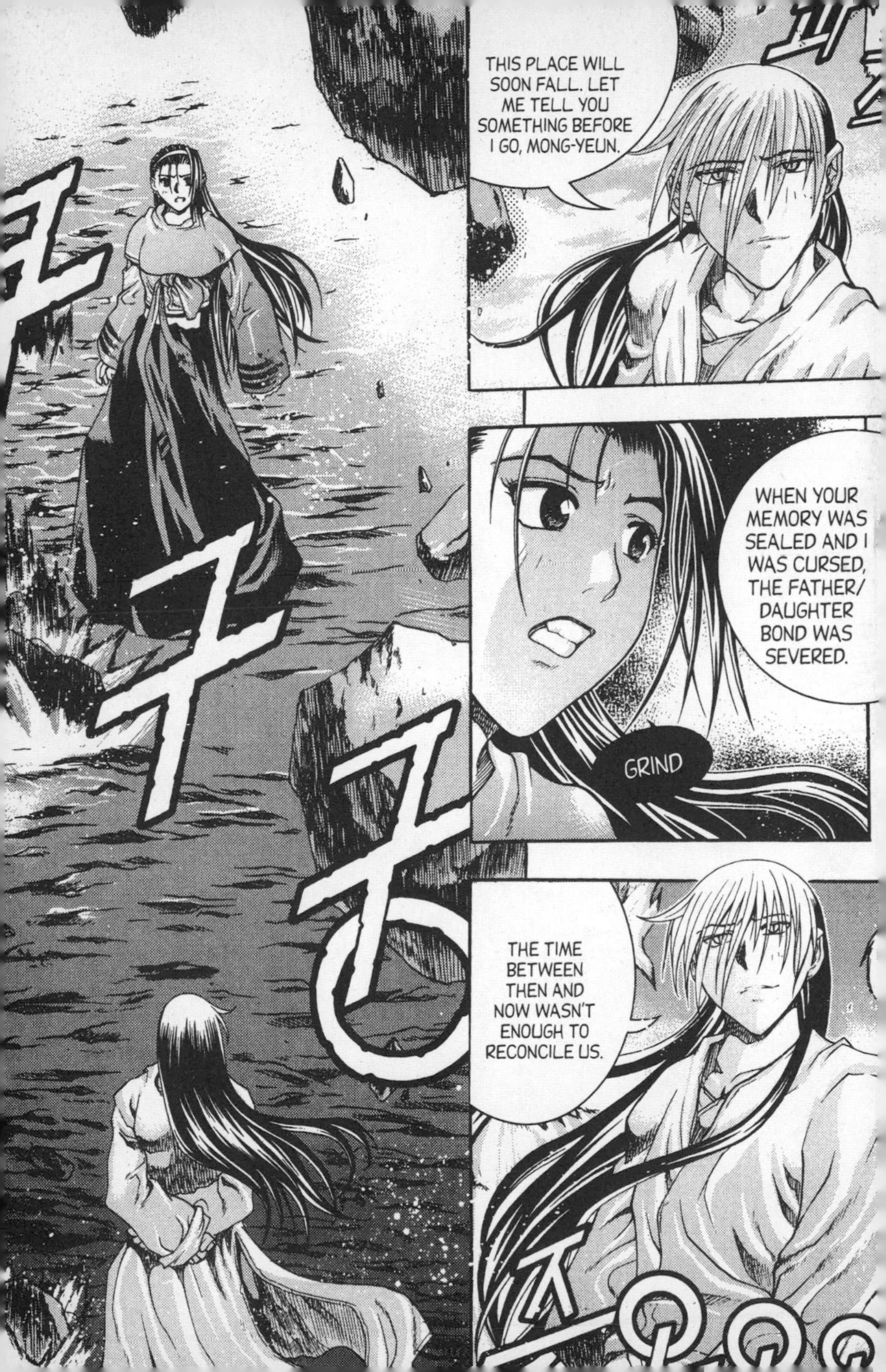
THIS PLACE WILL SOON FALL. LET ME TELL YOU SOMETHING BEFORE I GO, MONG-YEUN.
WHEN YOUR MEMORY WAS SEALED AND I WAS CURSED, THE FATHER/DAUGHTER BOND WAS SEVERED.
GRIND
THE TIME BETWEEN THEN AND NOW WASN'T ENOUGH TO RECONCILE US.

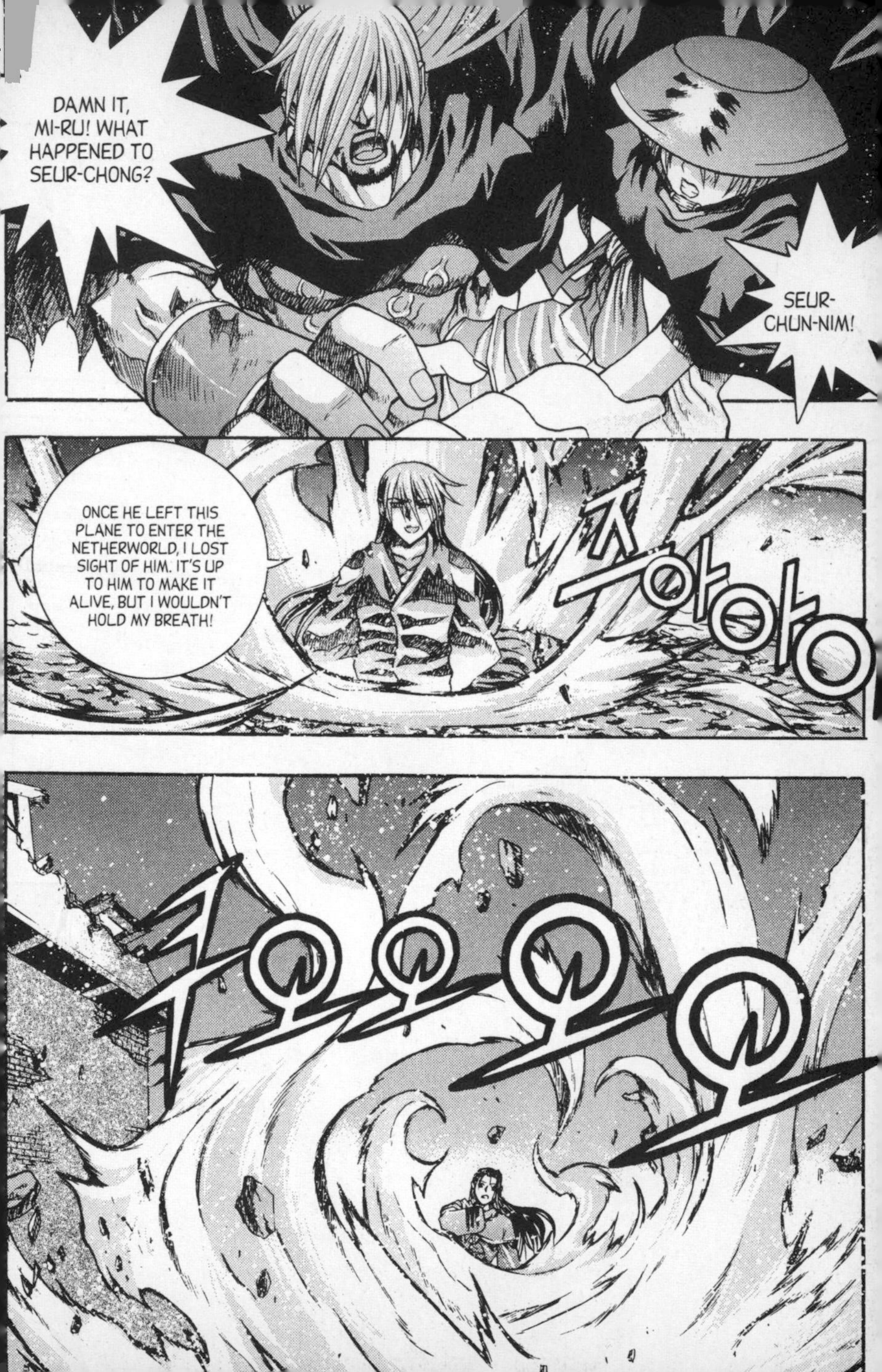
DAMN IT, MI-RU! WHAT HAPPENED TO SEUR-CHONG?
SEUR-CHUN-NIM!
ONCE HE LEFT THIS PLANE TO ENTER THE NETHERWORLD, I LOST SIGHT OF HIM. IT'S UP TO HIM TO MAKE IT ALIVE, BUT I WOULDN'T HOLD MY BREATH!

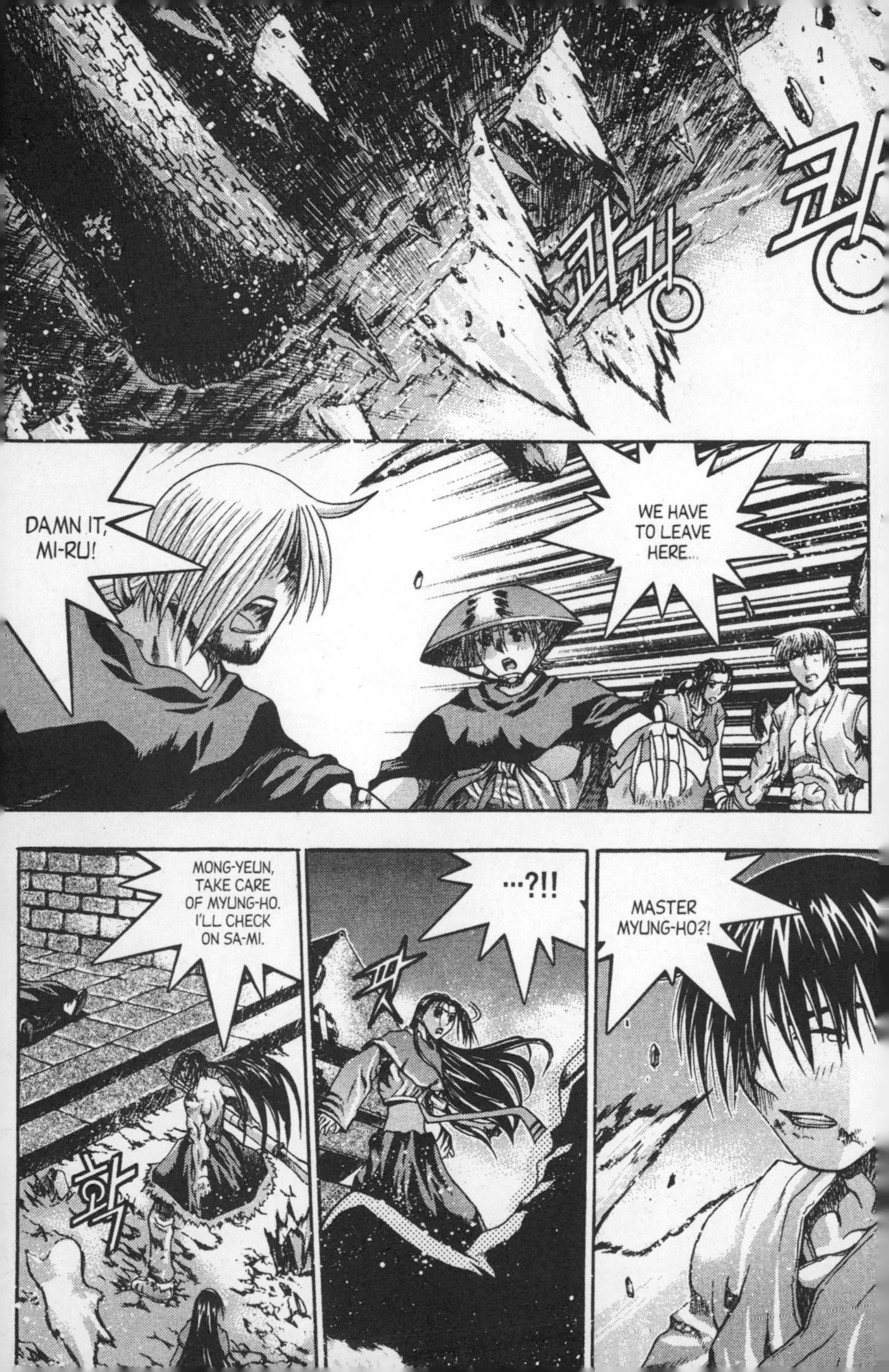
DAMN IT, MI-RU!
WE HAVE TO LEAVE HERE...
MONG-YEUN, TAKE CARE OF MYUNG-HO. I'LL CHECK ON SA-MI.
...?!!
MASTER MYUNG-HO?!

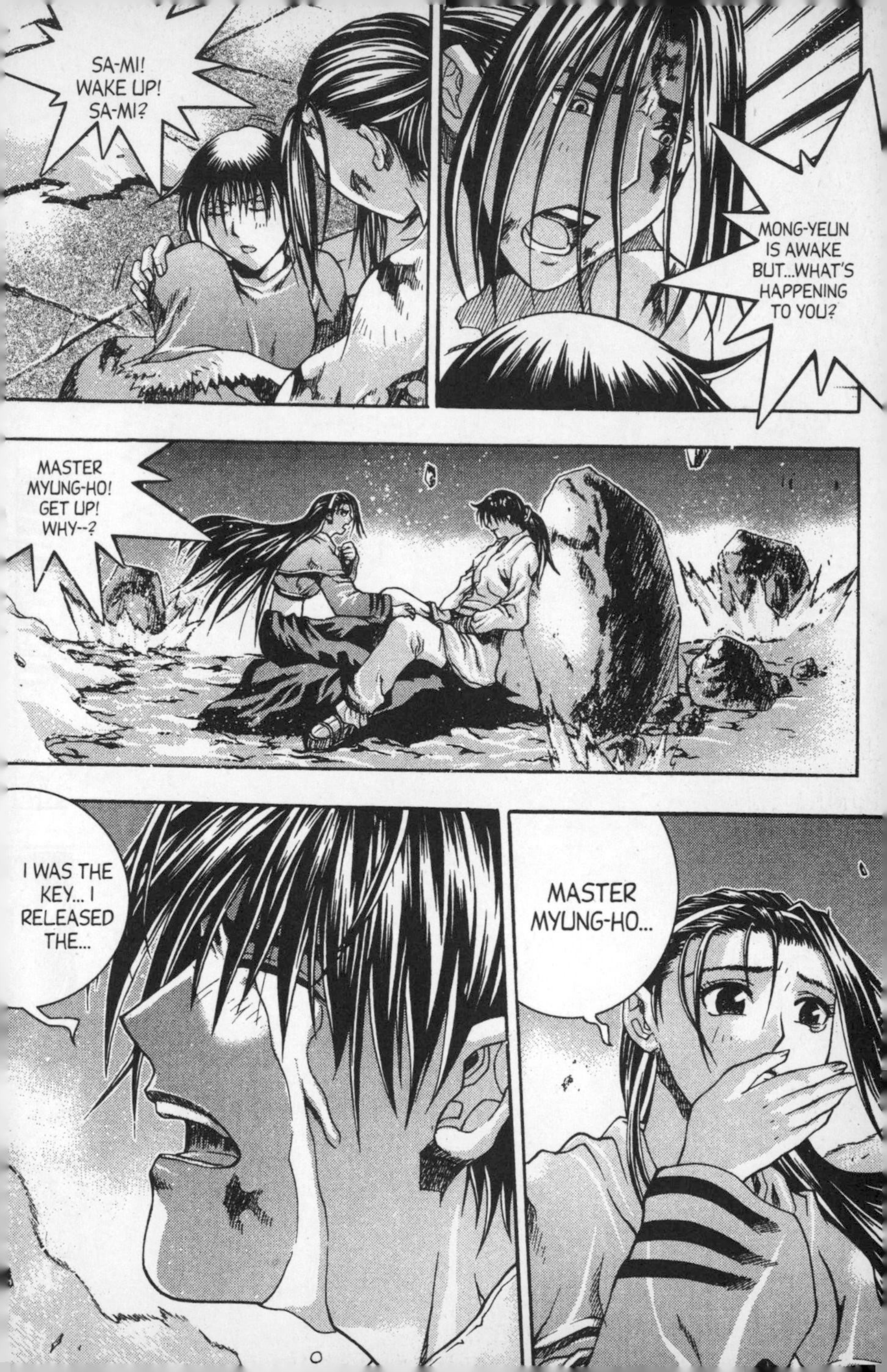
SA-MI! WAKE UP! SA-MI?
MONG-YEUN IS AWAKE BUT...WHAT'S HAPPENING TO YOU?
MASTER MYUNG-HO! GET UP! WHY--?
I WAS THE KEY... I RELEASED THE...
MASTER MYUNG-HO...

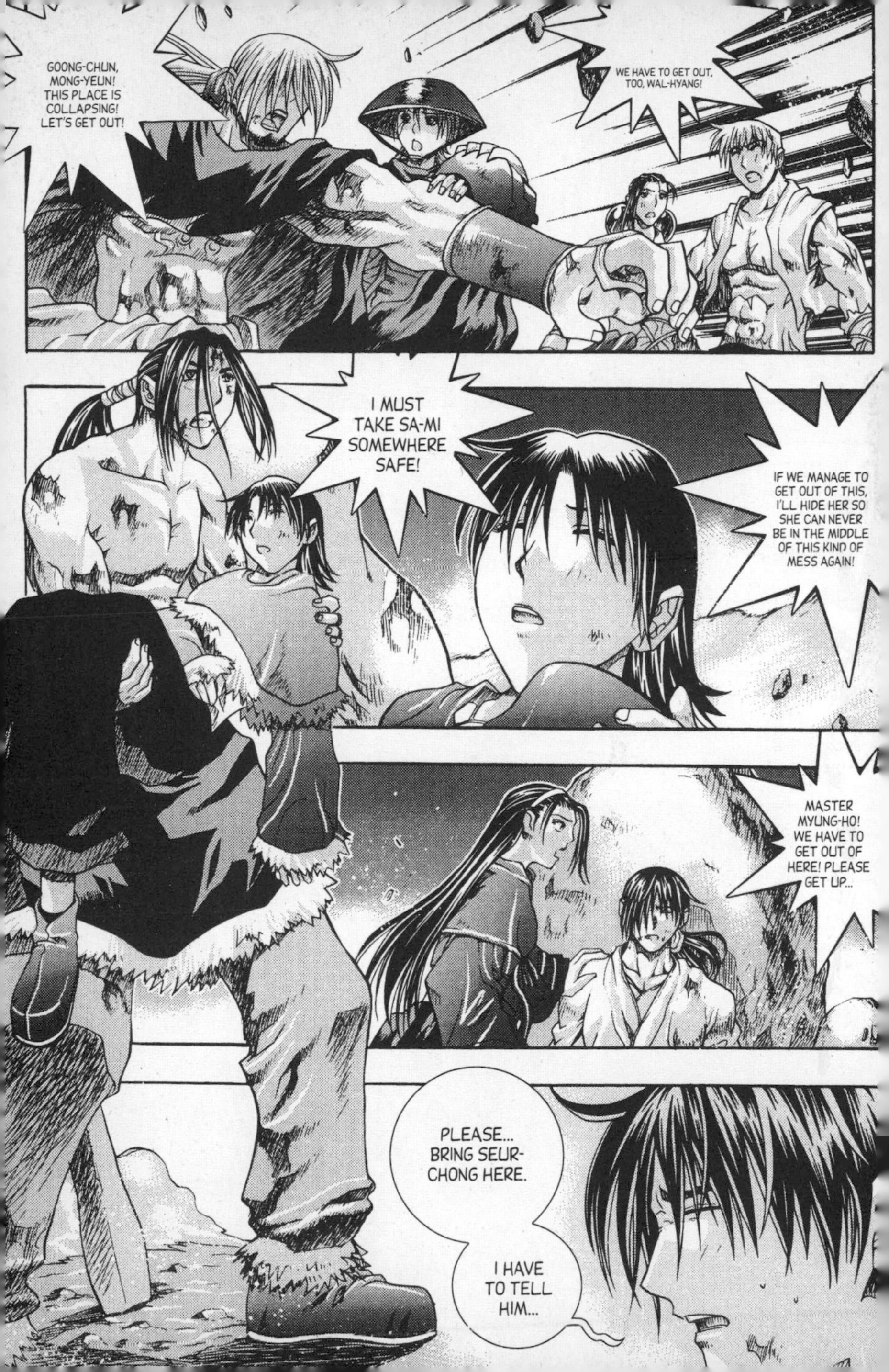
GOONG-CHUN, MONG-YEUN! THIS PLACE IS COLLAPSING! LET'S GET OUT!
WE HAVE TO GET OUT, TOO, WAL-HYANG!
I MUST TAKE SA-MI SOMEWHERE SAFE!
IF WE MANAGE TO GET OUT OF THIS, I'LL HIDE HER SO SHE CAN NEVER BE IN THE MIDDLE OF THIS KIND OF MESS AGAIN!
MASTER MYUNG-HO! WE HAVE TO GET OUT OF HERE! PLEASE GET UP...
PLEASE... BRING SEUR-CHONG HERE.
I HAVE TO TELL HIM...

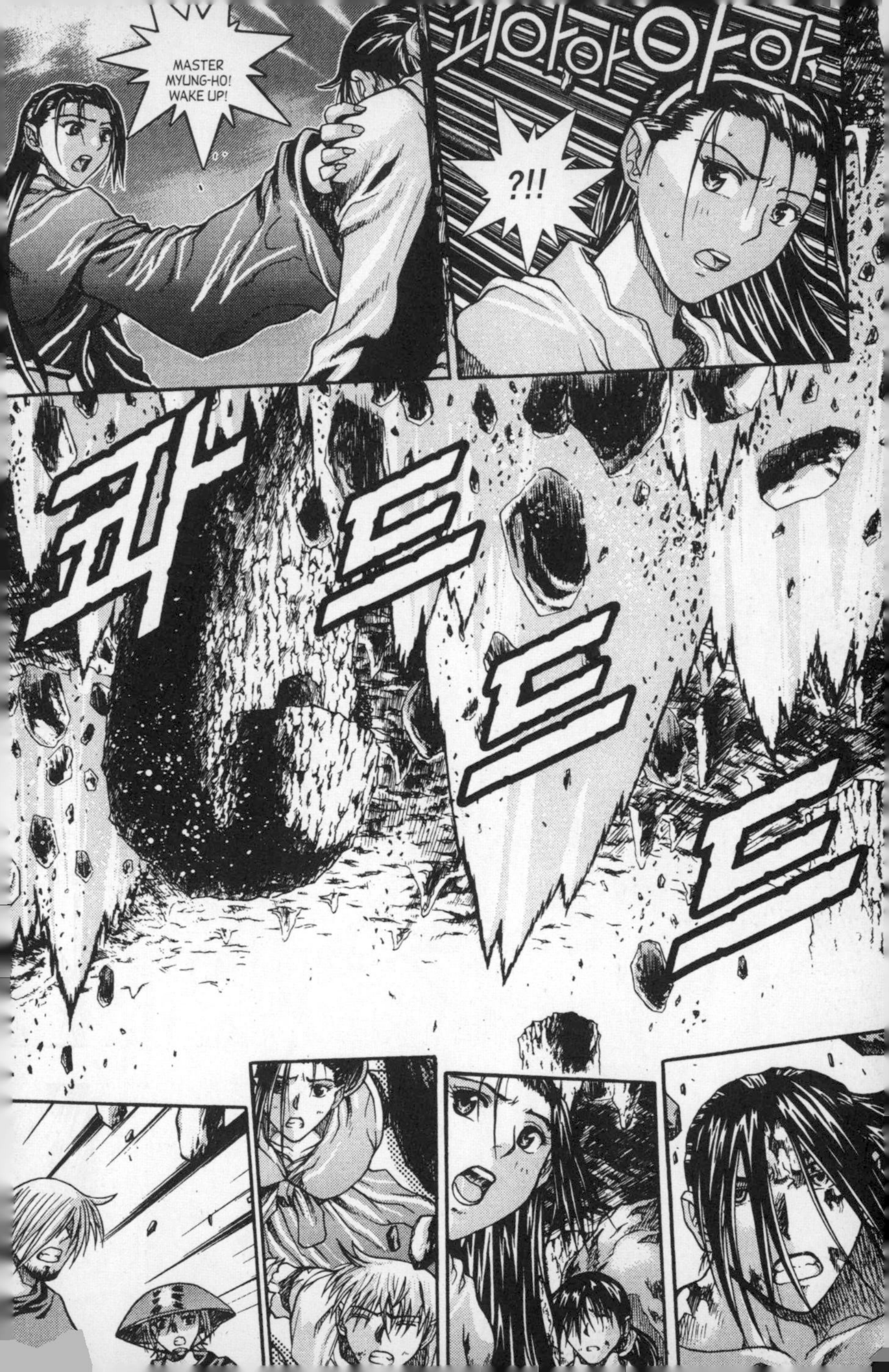
MASTER MYUNG-HO! WAKE UP!
?!!

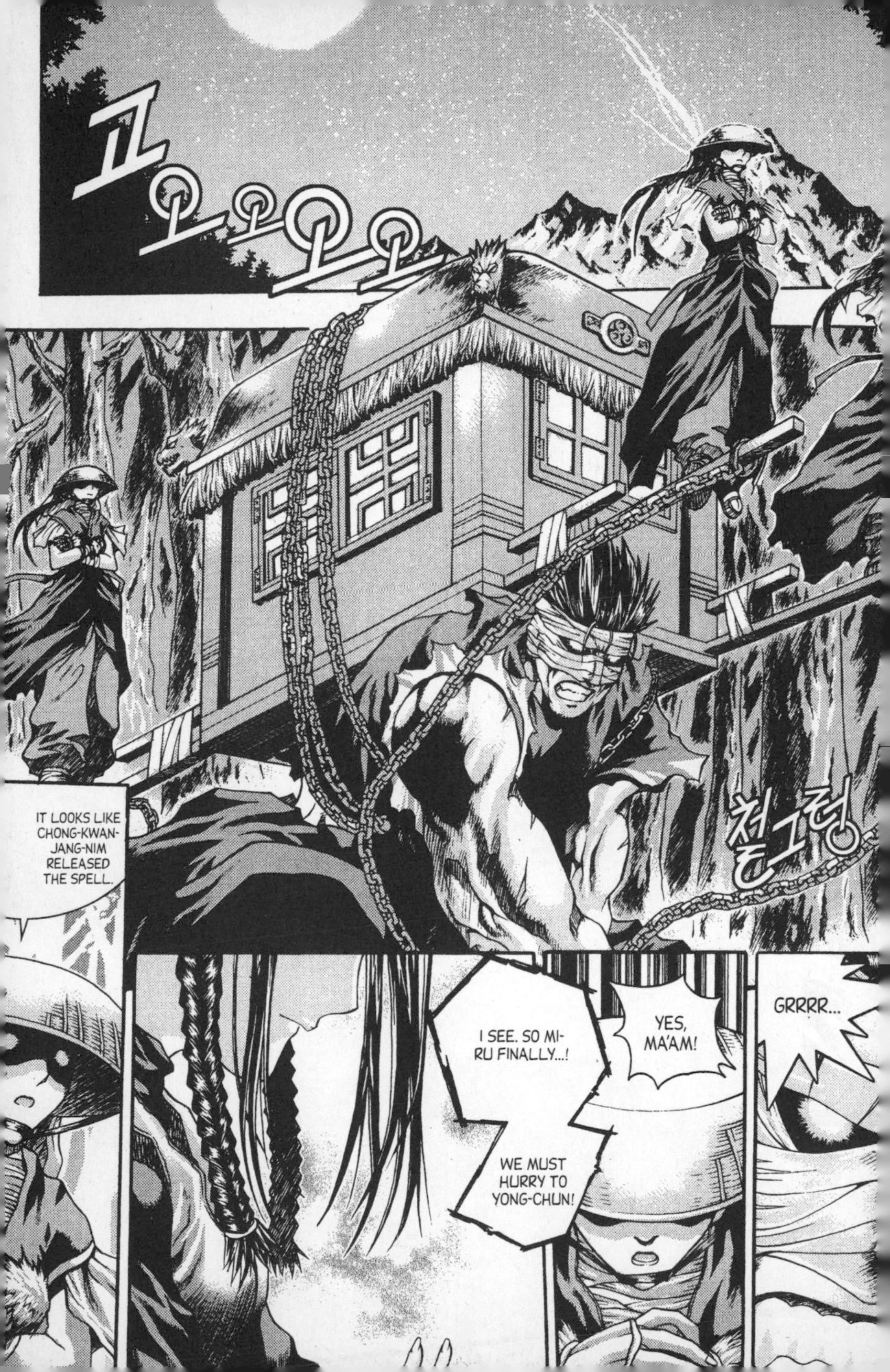

IT LOOKS LIKE CHONG-KWAN-JANG-NIM RELEASED THE SPELL.
철그렁
I SEE. SO MI-RU FINALLY...!
YES, MA'AM!
WE MUST HURRY TO YONG-CHUN!
GRRRR...

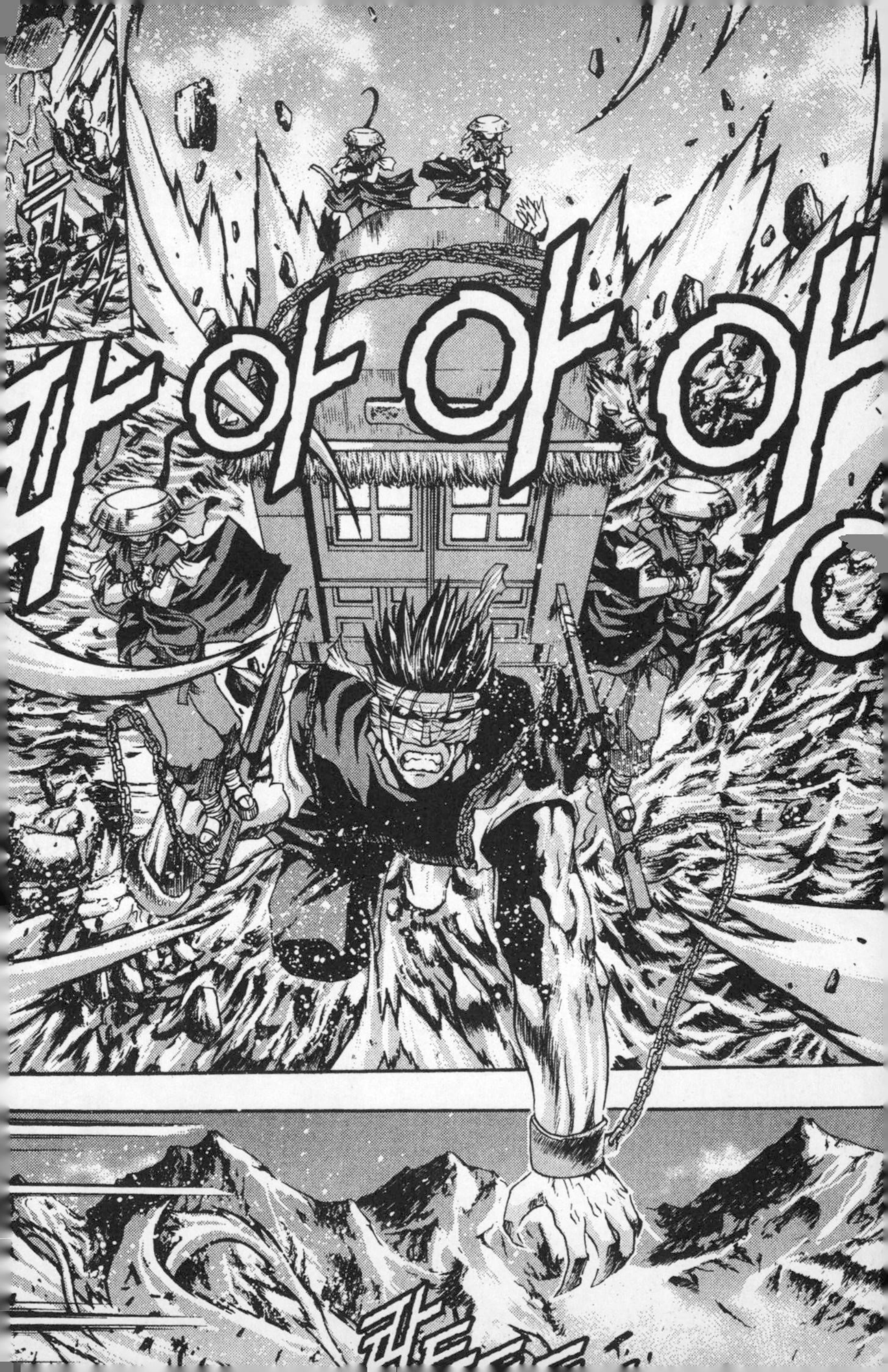
갸아아아

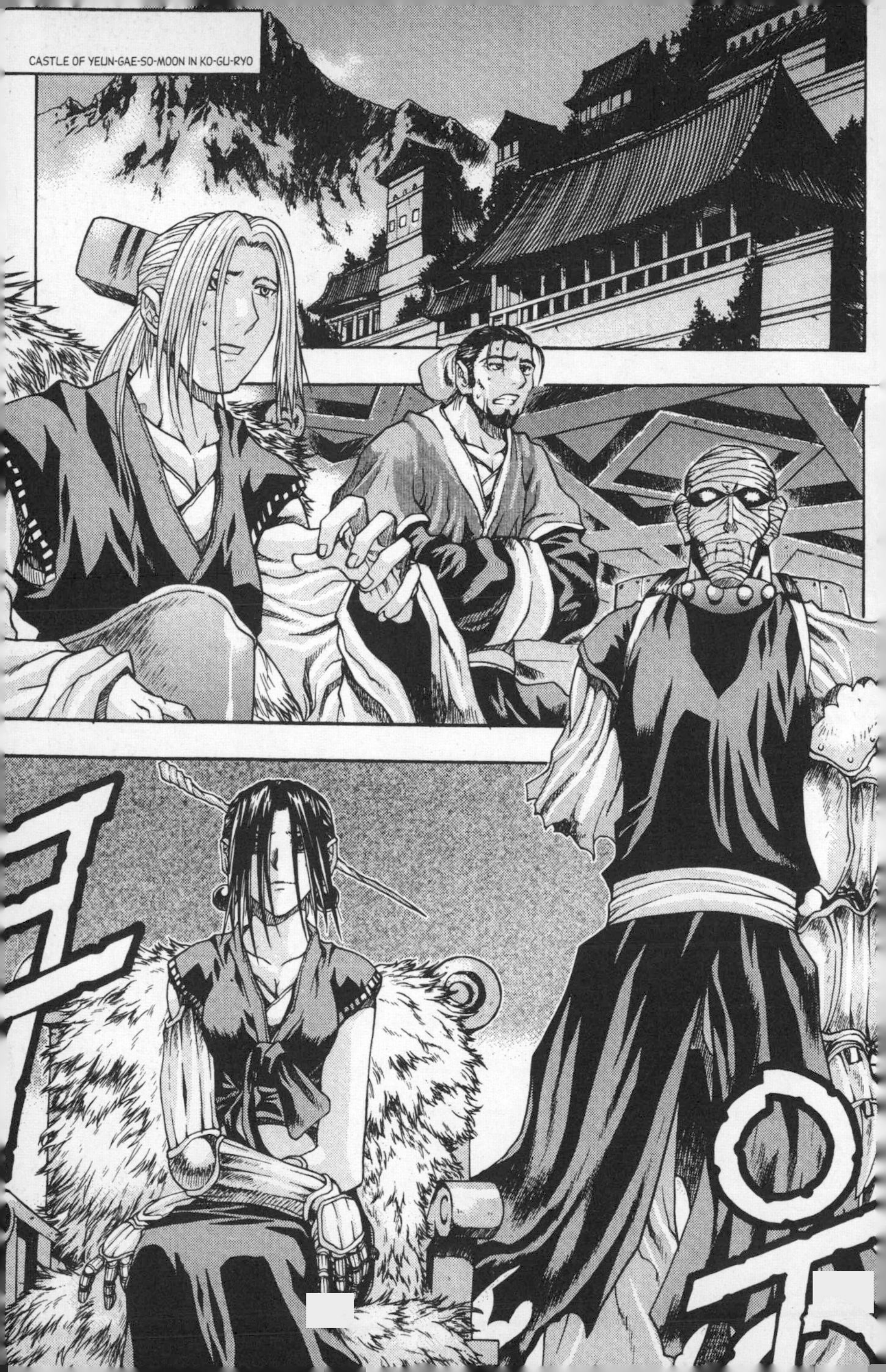
CASTLE OF YEUN-GAE-SO-MOON IN KO-GU-RYO

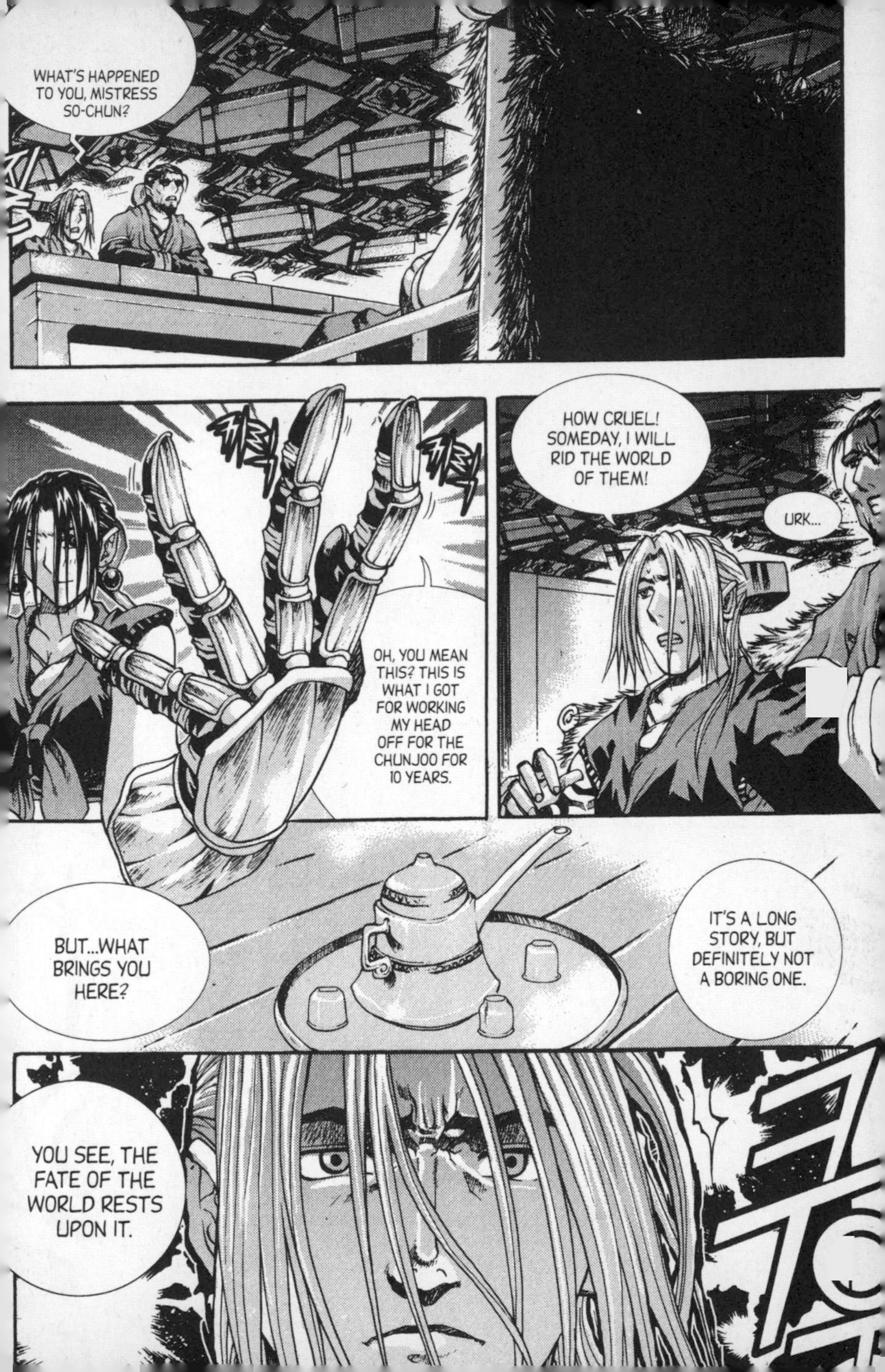
WHAT'S HAPPENED TO YOU, MISTRESS SO-CHUN?
OH, YOU MEAN THIS? THIS IS WHAT I GOT FOR WORKING MY HEAD OFF FOR THE CHUNJOO FOR 10 YEARS.
HOW CRUEL! SOMEDAY, I WILL RID THE WORLD OF THEM!
URK...
BUT...WHAT BRINGS YOU HERE?
IT'S A LONG STORY, BUT DEFINITELY NOT A BORING ONE.
YOU SEE, THE FATE OF THE WORLD RESTS UPON IT.

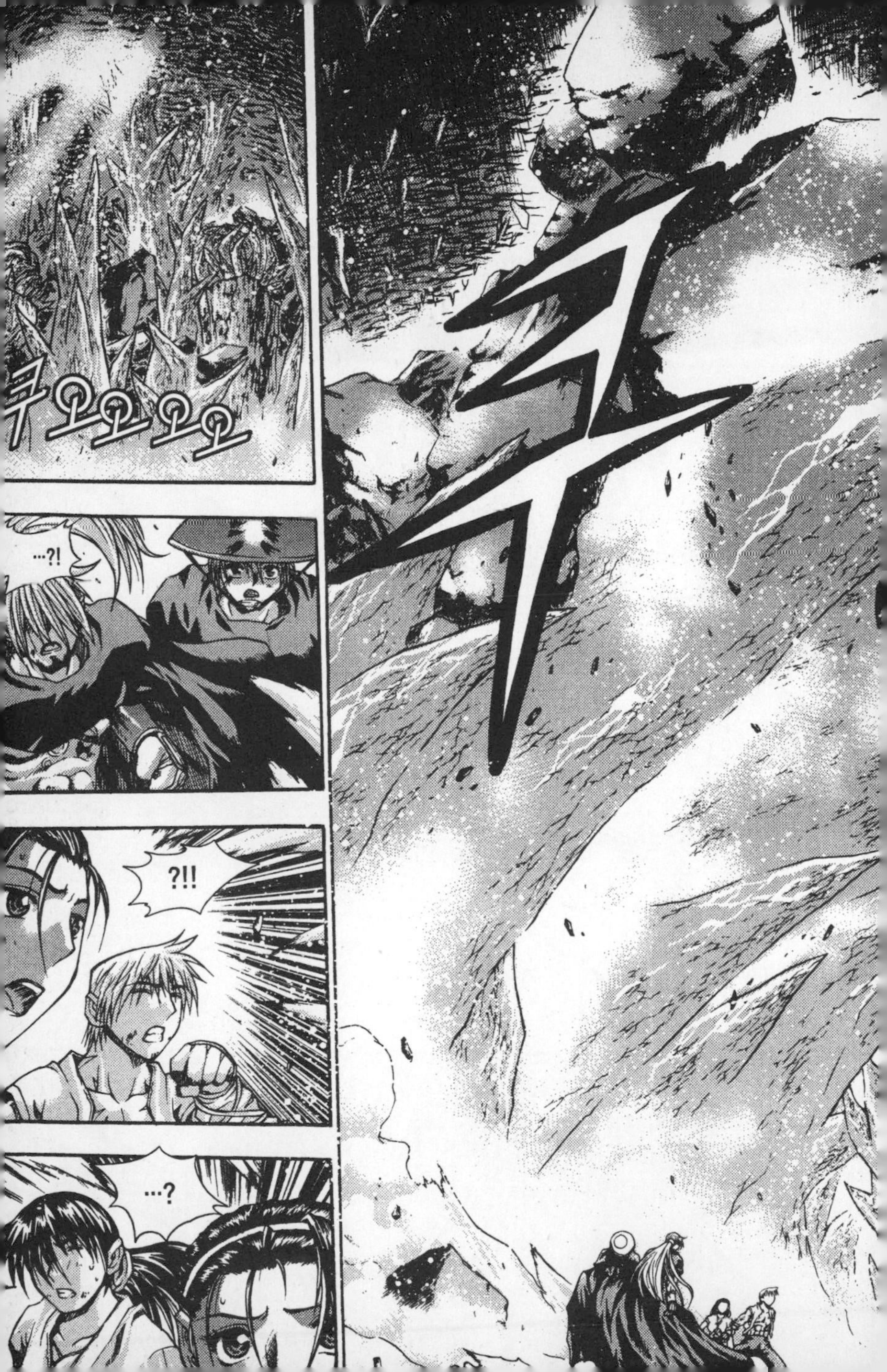
쿠오오오오
…?!
?!!
…?

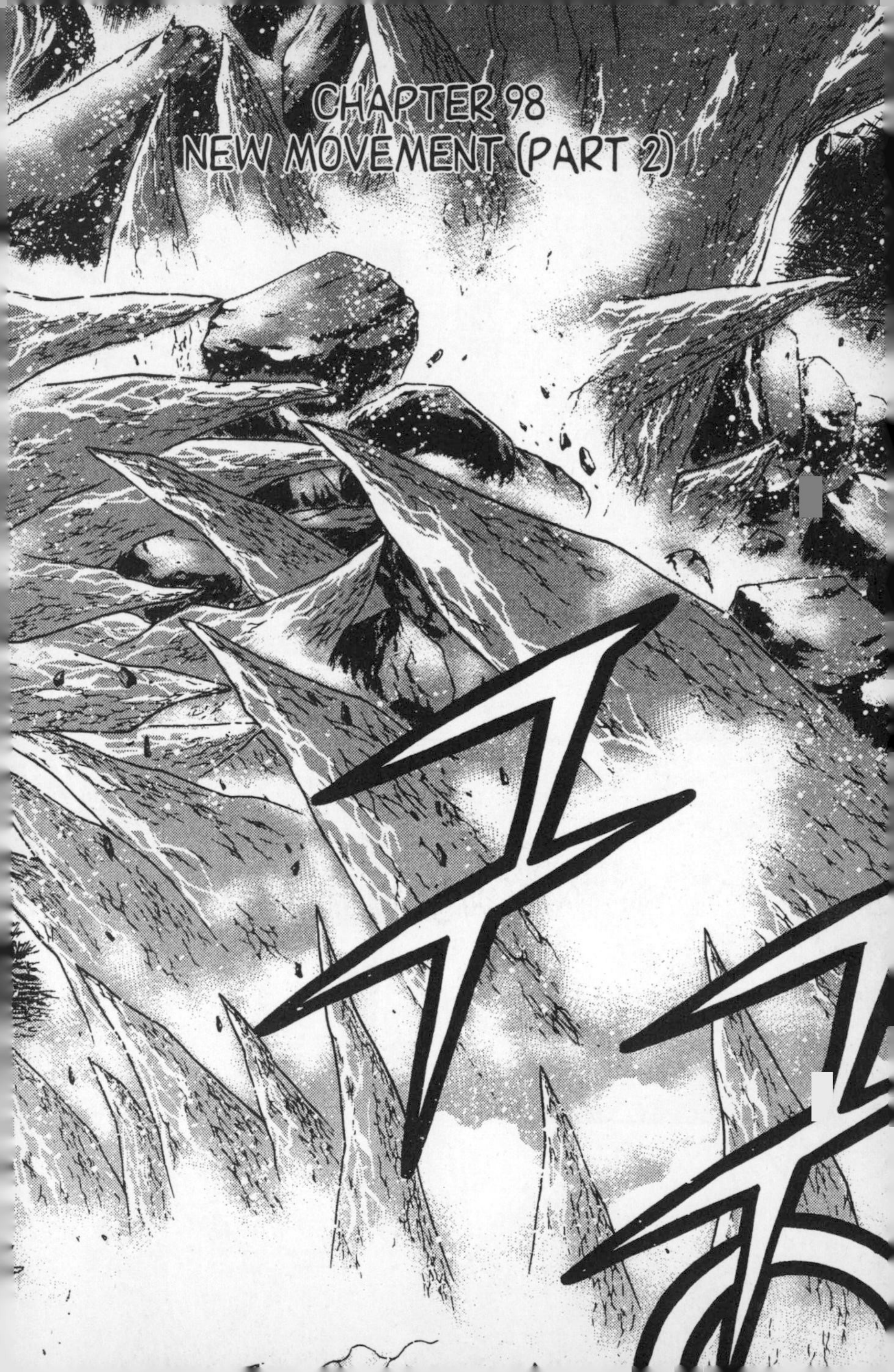
CHAPTER 98
NEW MOVEMENT (PART 2)

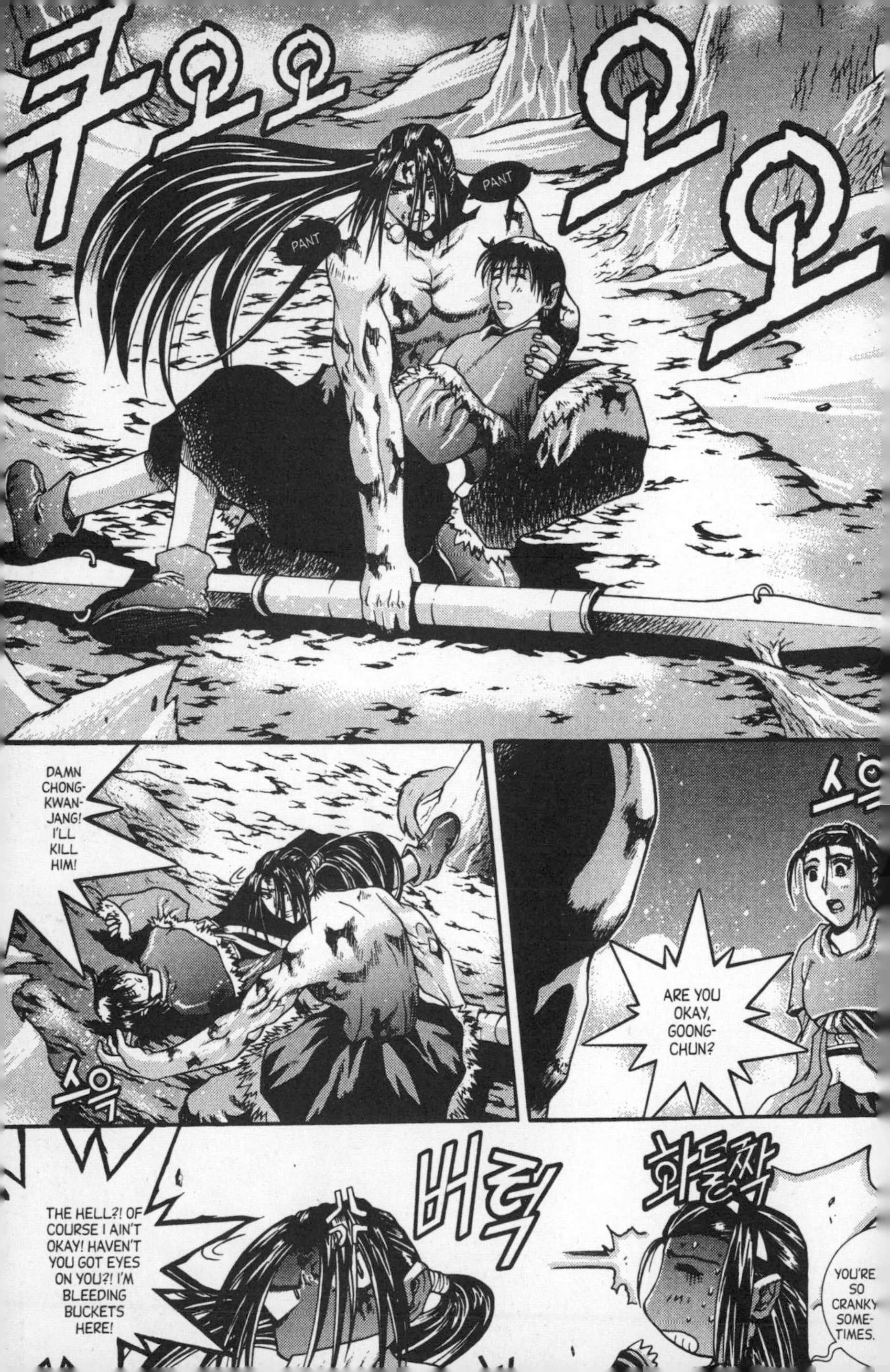
쿠오오
PANT
PANT
오오
DAMN CHONG-KWAN-JANG! I'LL KILL HIM!
스윽
스윽
ARE YOU OKAY, GOONG-CHUN?
THE HELL?! OF COURSE I AIN'T OKAY! HAVEN'T YOU GOT EYES ON YOU?! I'M BLEEDING BUCKETS HERE!
버럭
화들짝
YOU'RE SO CRANKY SOME-TIMES.

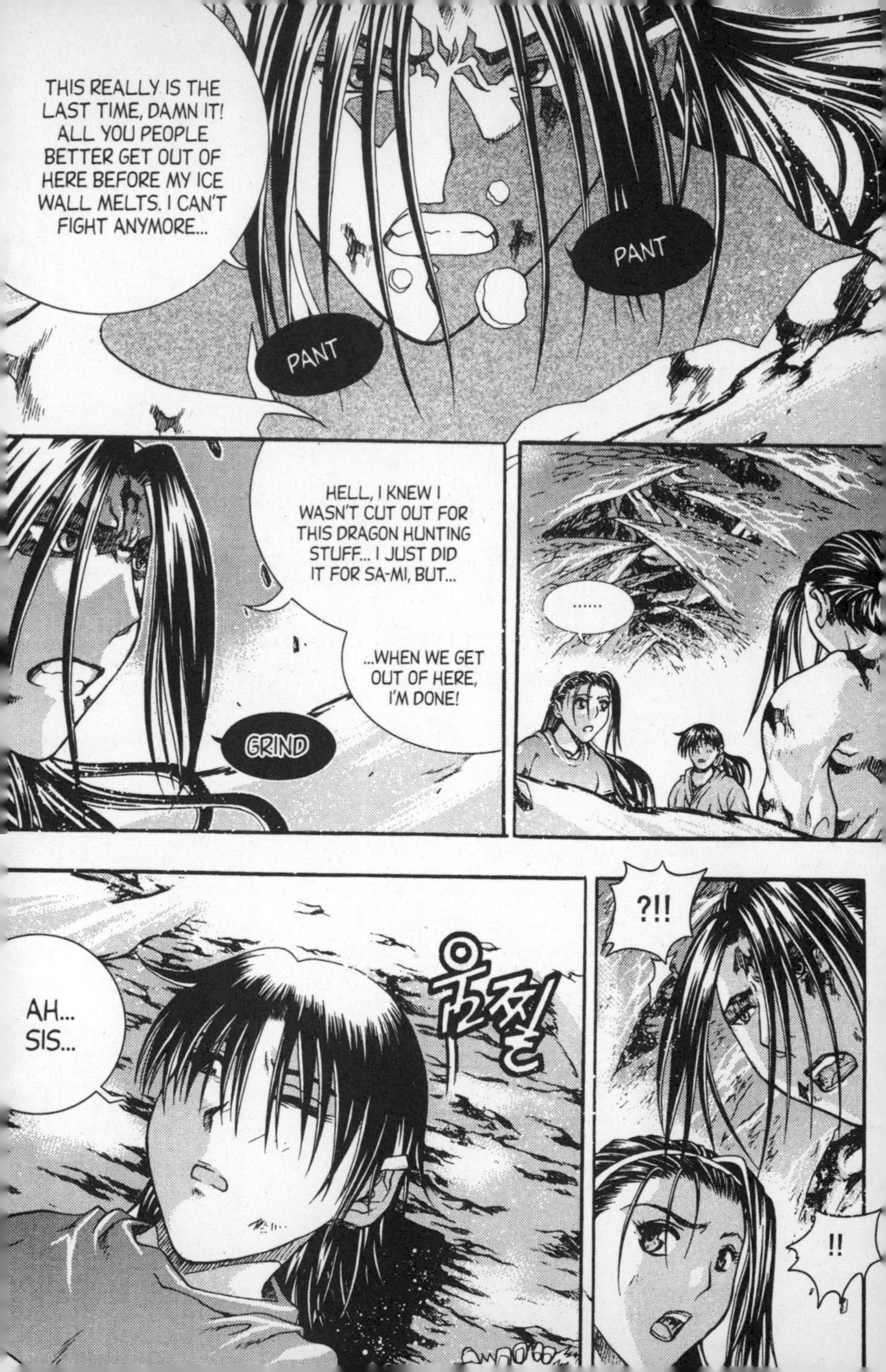
THIS REALLY IS THE LAST TIME, DAMN IT! ALL YOU PEOPLE BETTER GET OUT OF HERE BEFORE MY ICE WALL MELTS. I CAN'T FIGHT ANYMORE...
PANT
PANT
HELL, I KNEW I WASN'T CUT OUT FOR THIS DRAGON HUNTING STUFF... I JUST DID IT FOR SA-MI, BUT...
...WHEN WE GET OUT OF HERE, I'M DONE!
GRIND
......
AH... SIS...
움찔
?!!
!!

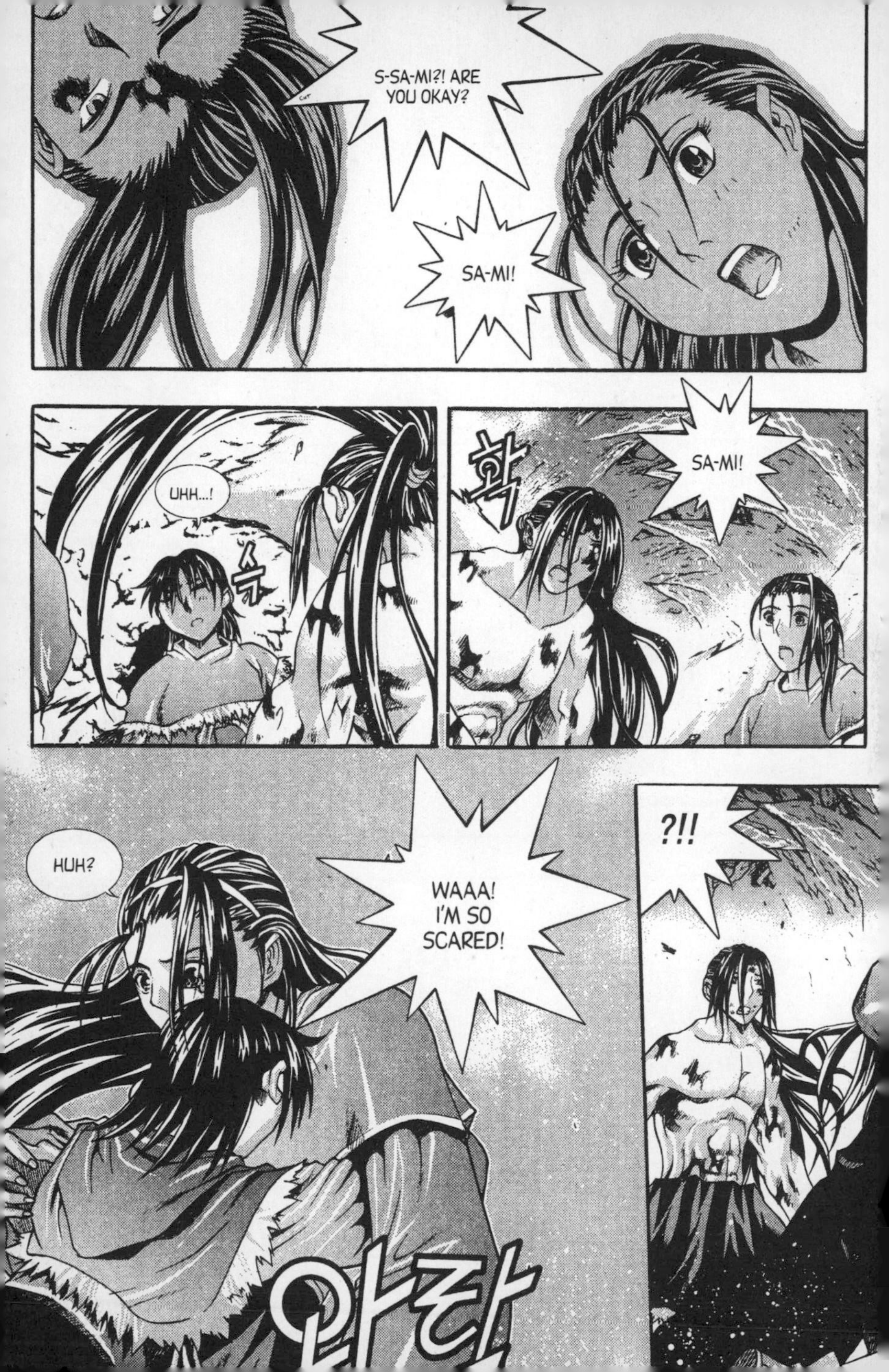
S-SA-MI?! ARE YOU OKAY?
SA-MI!
UHH...!
헉
SA-MI!
HUH?
WAAA! I'M SO SCARED!
?!!
와락

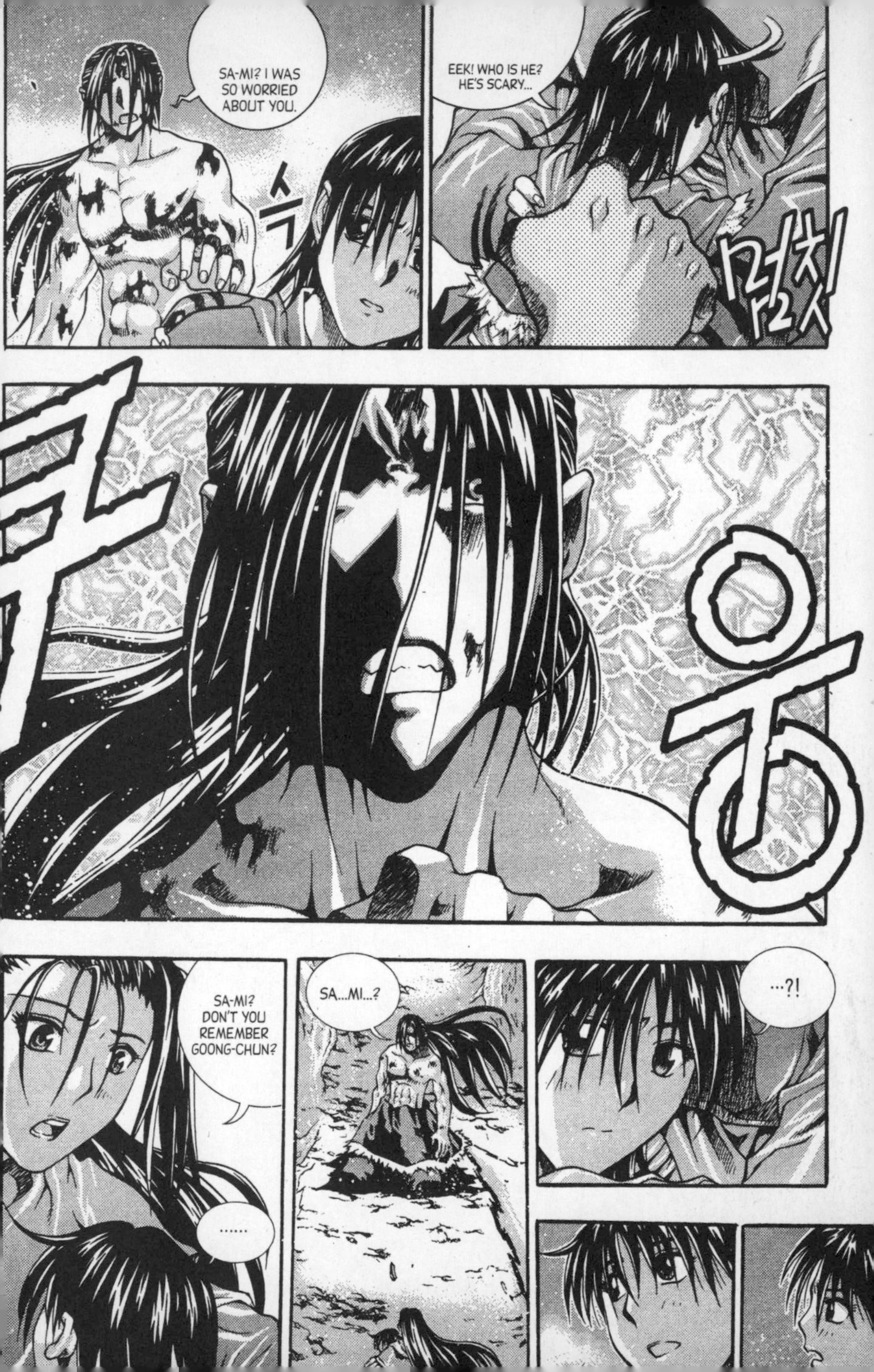
SA-MI? I WAS SO WORRIED ABOUT YOU.
EEK! WHO IS HE? HE'S SCARY...
SA-MI? DON'T YOU REMEMBER GOONG-CHUN?
......
SA...MI...?
...?!

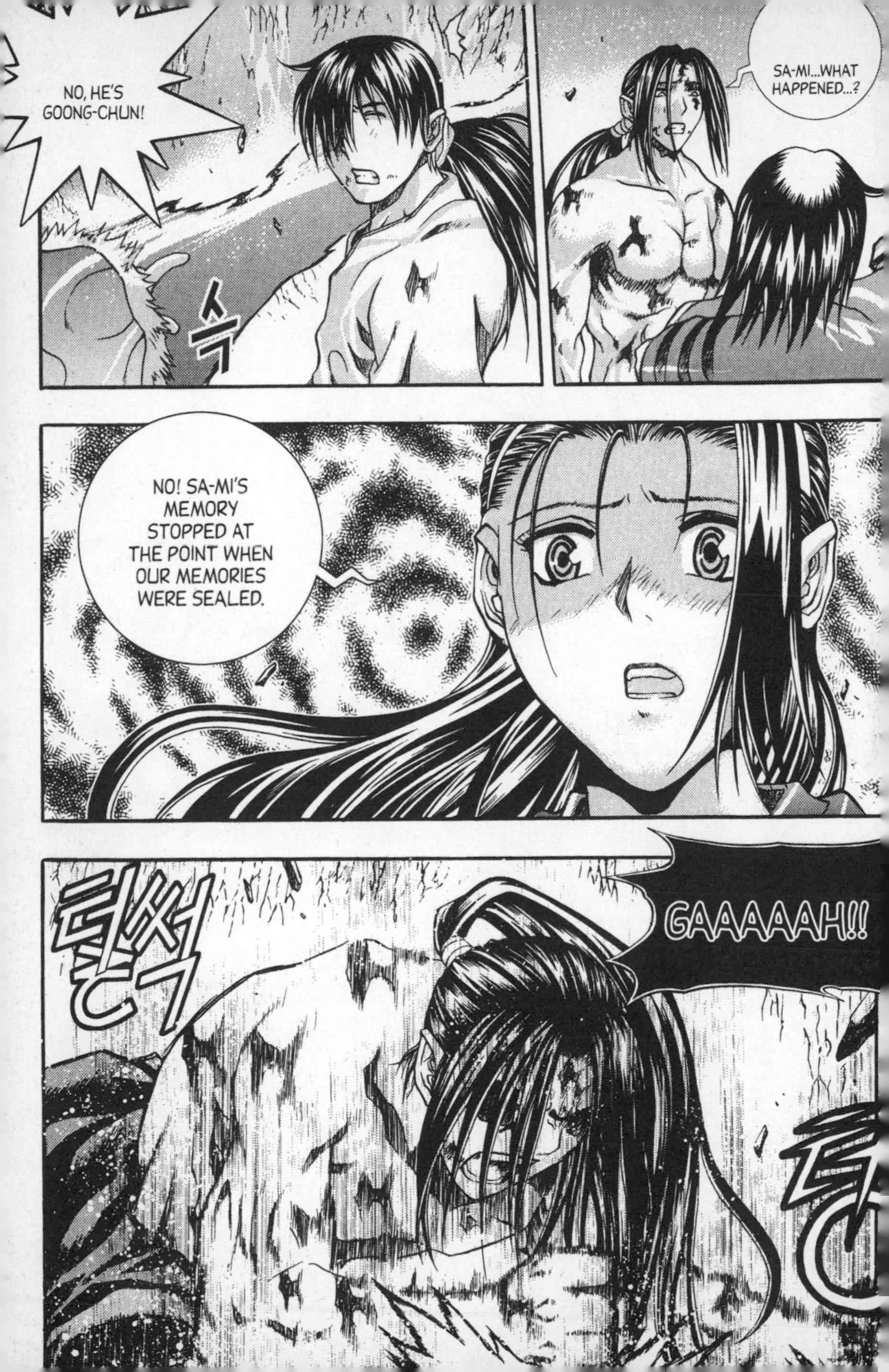
NO, HE'S GOONG-CHUN!
SA-MI...WHAT HAPPENED...?
NO! SA-MI'S MEMORY STOPPED AT THE POINT WHEN OUR MEMORIES WERE SEALED.
GAAAAAH!!

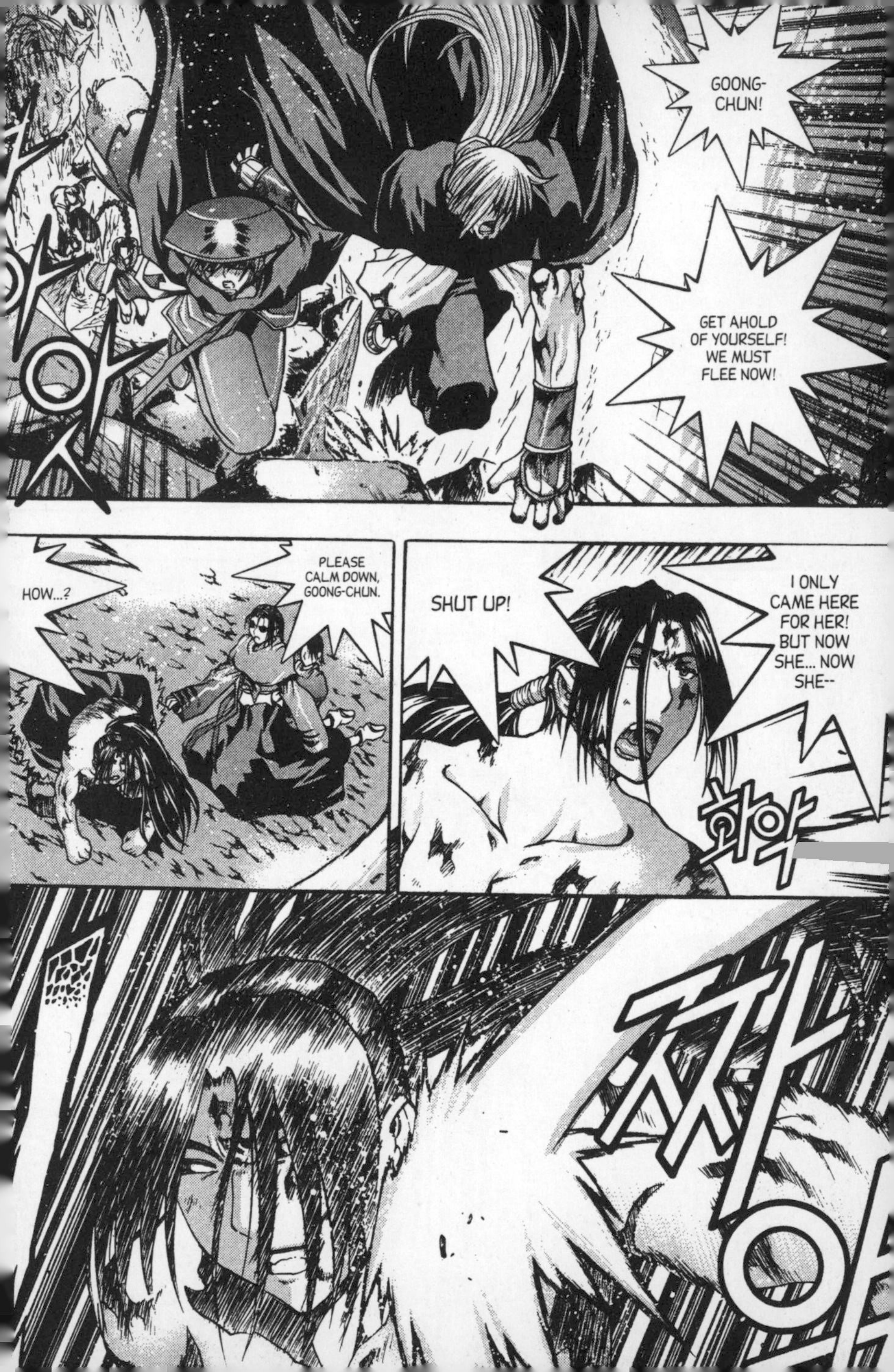
GOONG-CHUN!
GET AHOLD OF YOURSELF! WE MUST FLEE NOW!
HOW...?
PLEASE CALM DOWN, GOONG-CHUN.
SHUT UP!
I ONLY CAME HERE FOR HER! BUT NOW SHE... NOW SHE--
화악

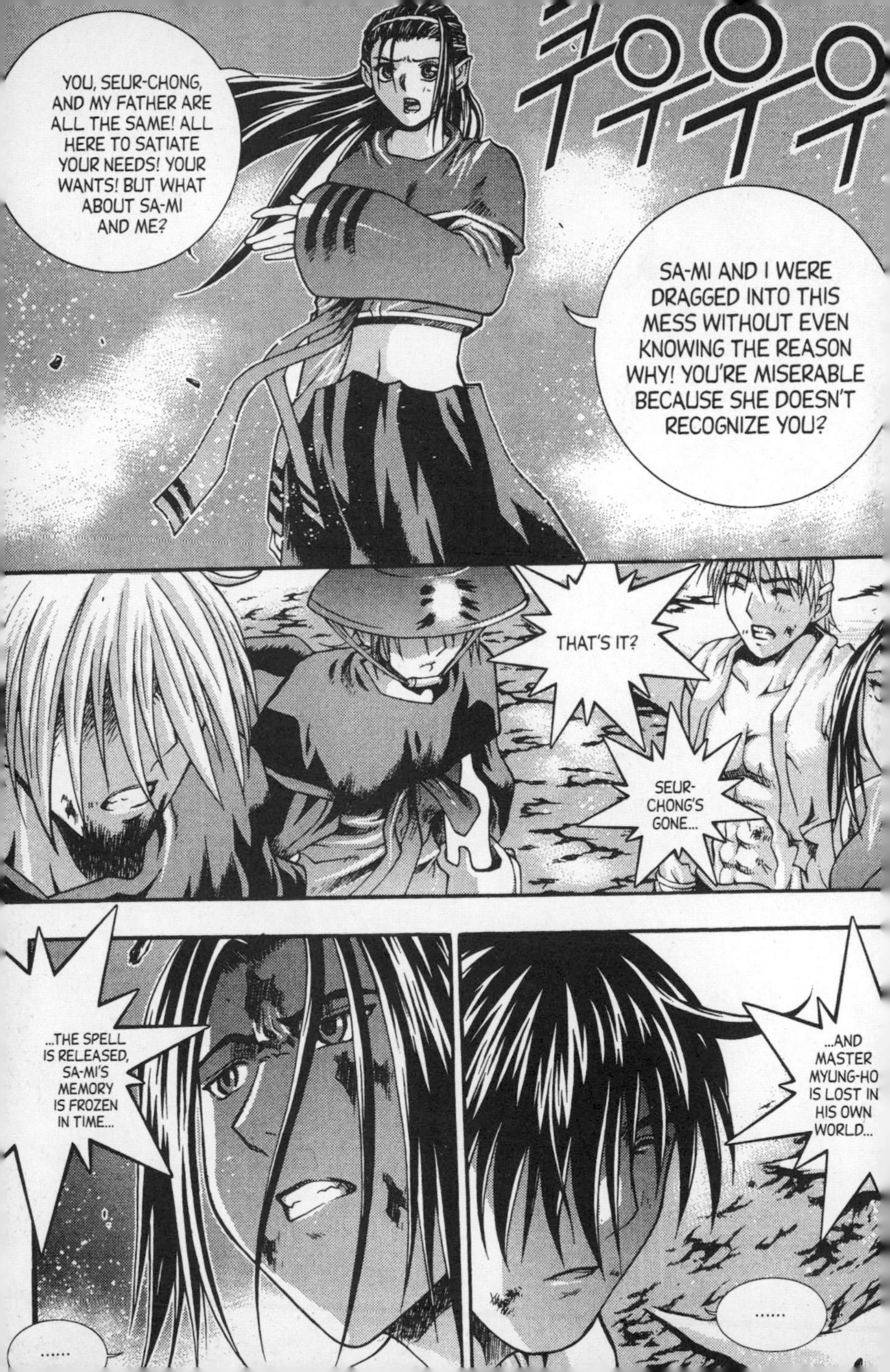
YOU, SEUR-CHONG, AND MY FATHER ARE ALL THE SAME! ALL HERE TO SATIATE YOUR NEEDS! YOUR WANTS! BUT WHAT ABOUT SA-MI AND ME?
SA-MI AND I WERE DRAGGED INTO THIS MESS WITHOUT EVEN KNOWING THE REASON WHY! YOU'RE MISERABLE BECAUSE SHE DOESN'T RECOGNIZE YOU?
THAT'S IT?
SEUR-CHONG'S GONE...
...THE SPELL IS RELEASED, SA-MI'S MEMORY IS FROZEN IN TIME...
...AND MASTER MYUNG-HO IS LOST IN HIS OWN WORLD...
......
......

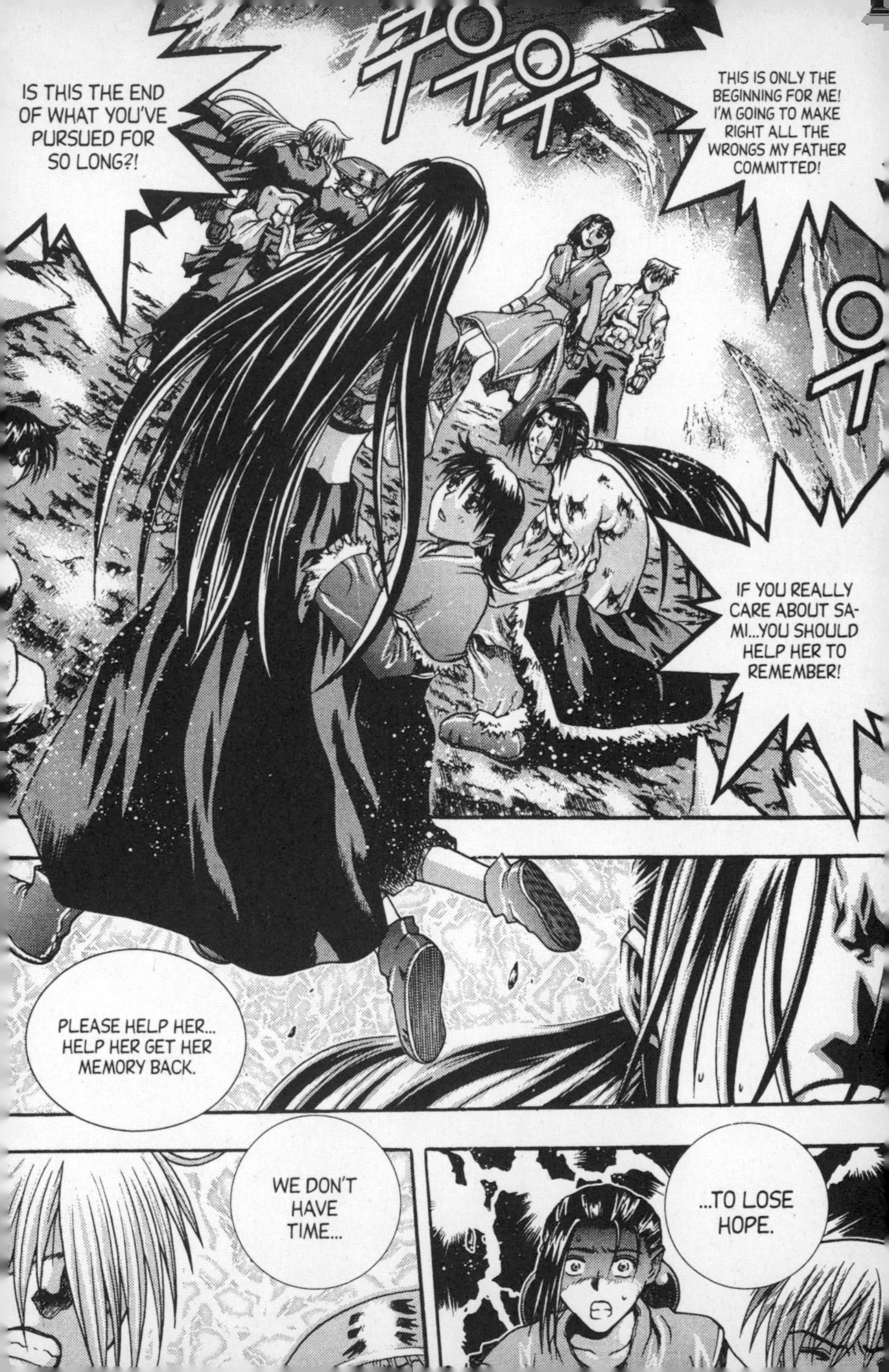
IS THIS THE END OF WHAT YOU'VE PURSUED FOR SO LONG?!
THIS IS ONLY THE BEGINNING FOR ME! I'M GOING TO MAKE RIGHT ALL THE WRONGS MY FATHER COMMITTED!
IF YOU REALLY CARE ABOUT SA-MI...YOU SHOULD HELP HER TO REMEMBER!
PLEASE HELP HER... HELP HER GET HER MEMORY BACK.
WE DON'T HAVE TIME...
...TO LOSE HOPE.

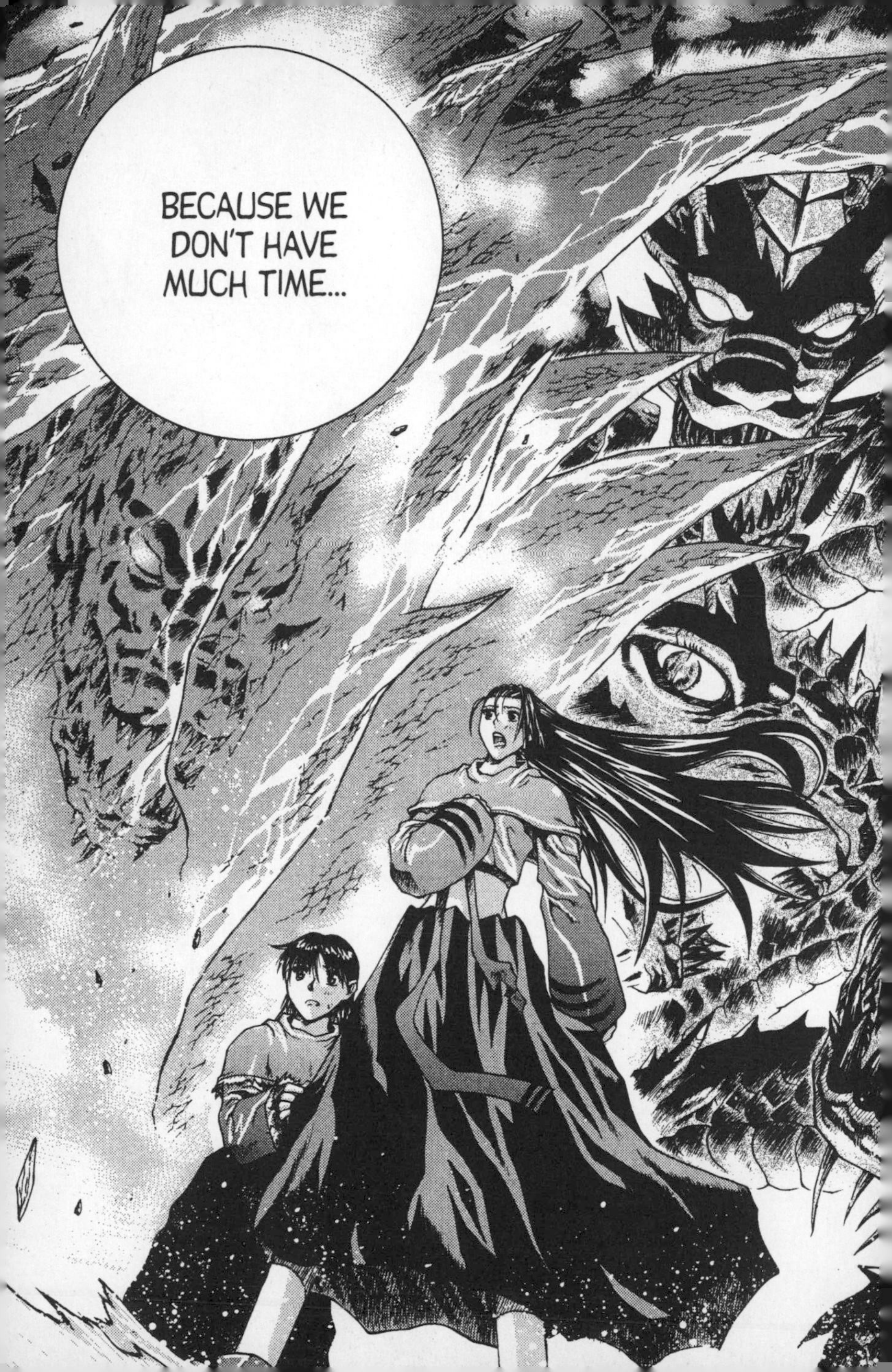
BECAUSE WE DON'T HAVE MUCH TIME...

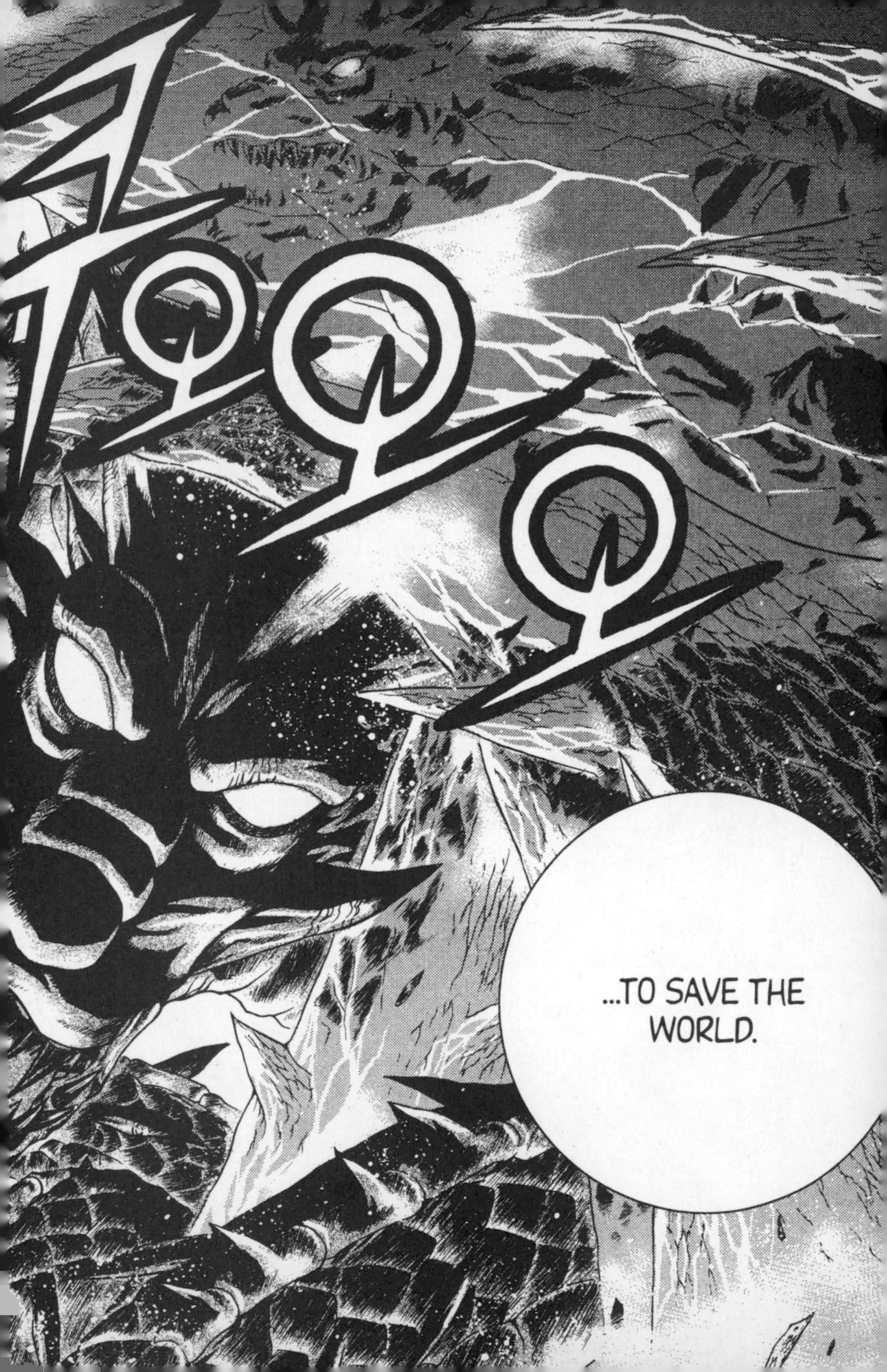
...TO SAVE THE WORLD.

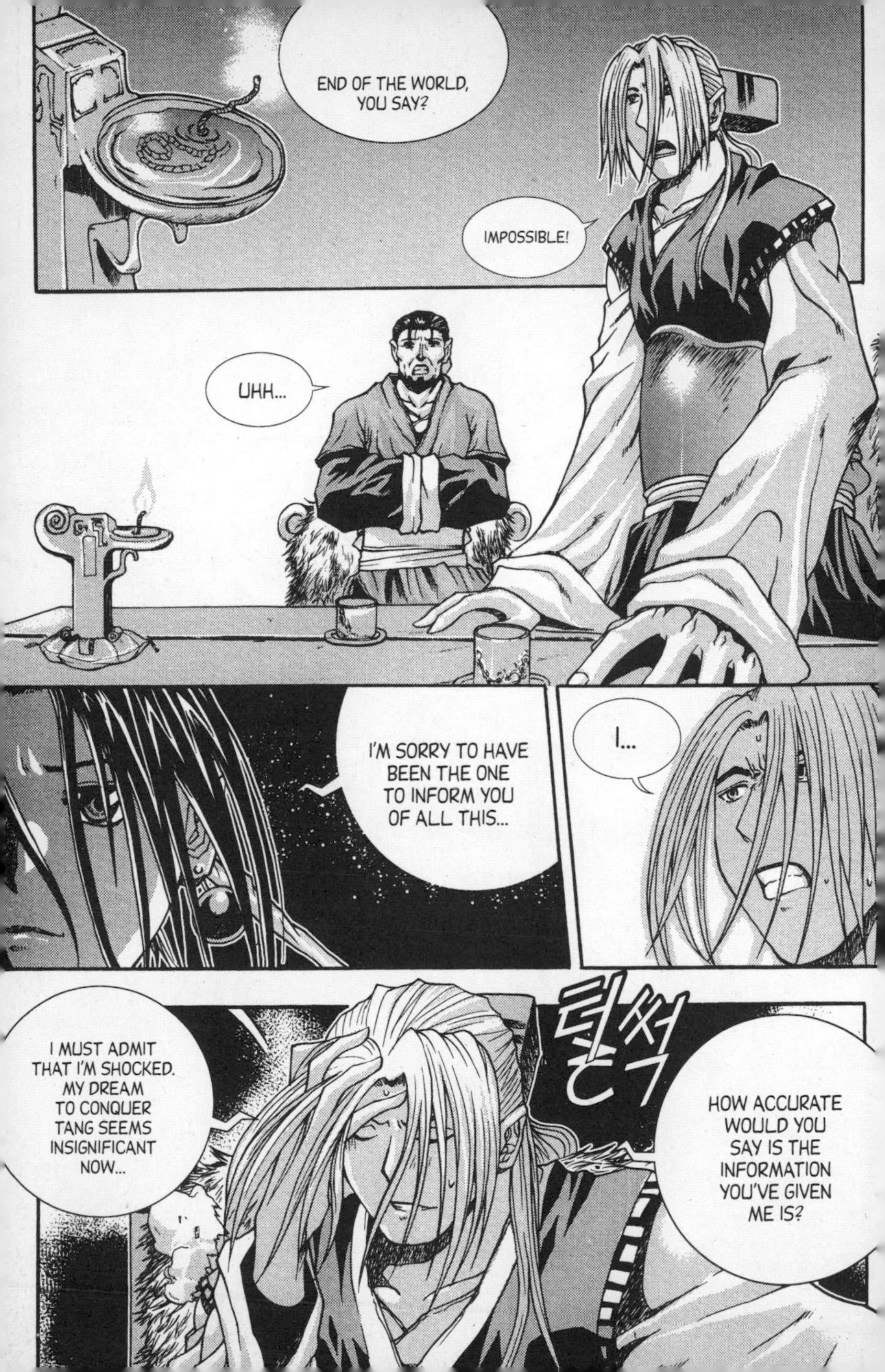
END OF THE WORLD, YOU SAY?
IMPOSSIBLE!
UHH...
I'M SORRY TO HAVE BEEN THE ONE TO INFORM YOU OF ALL THIS...
I...
I MUST ADMIT THAT I'M SHOCKED. MY DREAM TO CONQUER TANG SEEMS INSIGNIFICANT NOW...
털썩
HOW ACCURATE WOULD YOU SAY IS THE INFORMATION YOU'VE GIVEN ME IS?

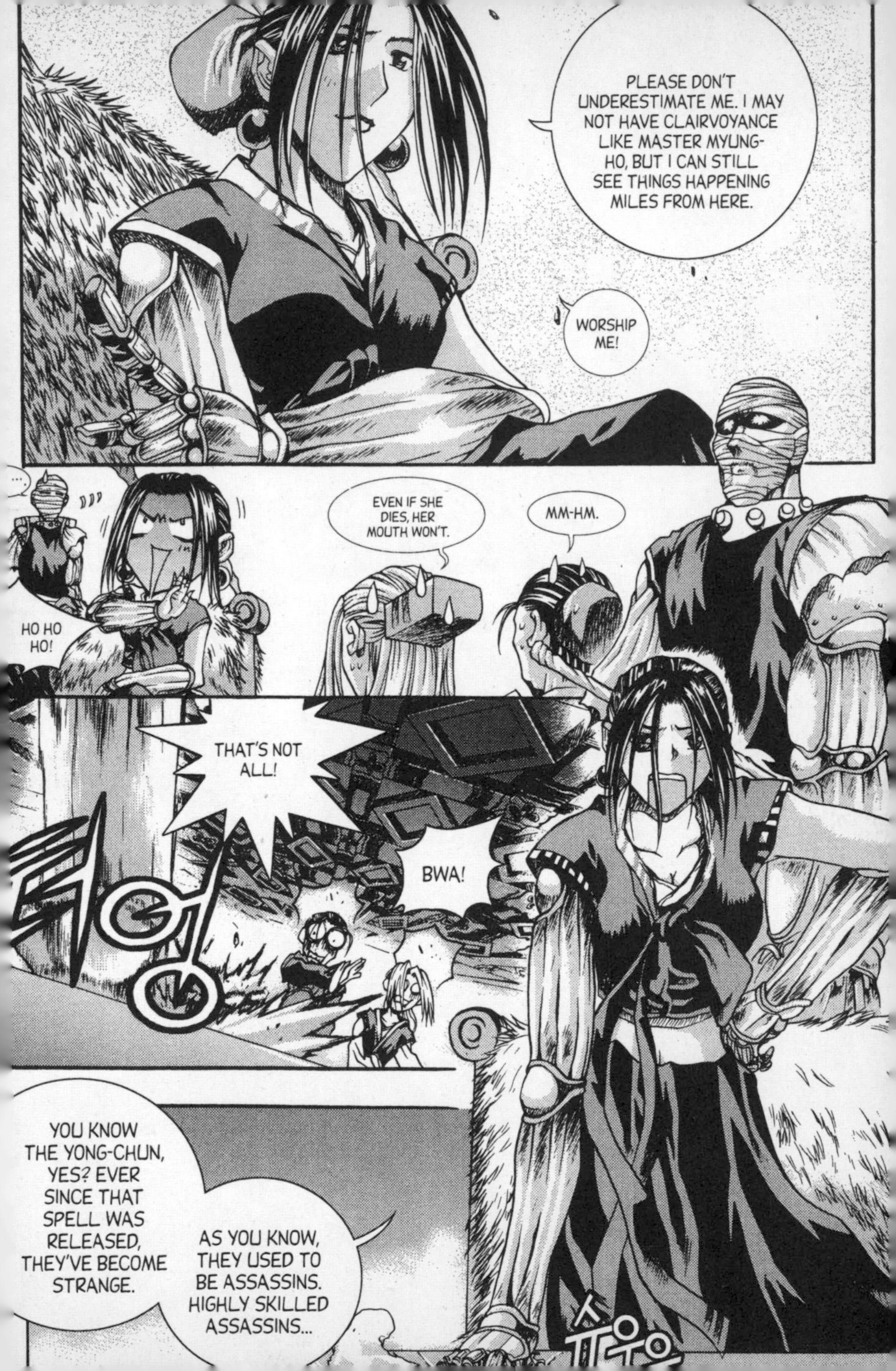

PLEASE DON'T UNDERESTIMATE ME. I MAY NOT HAVE CLAIRVOYANCE LIKE MASTER MYUNG-HO, BUT I CAN STILL SEE THINGS HAPPENING MILES FROM HERE.
WORSHIP ME!
...
HO HO HO!
EVEN IF SHE DIES, HER MOUTH WON'T.
MM-HM.
THAT'S NOT ALL!
BWA!
YOU KNOW THE YONG-CHUN, YES? EVER SINCE THAT SPELL WAS RELEASED, THEY'VE BECOME STRANGE.
AS YOU KNOW, THEY USED TO BE ASSASSINS. HIGHLY SKILLED ASSASSINS...

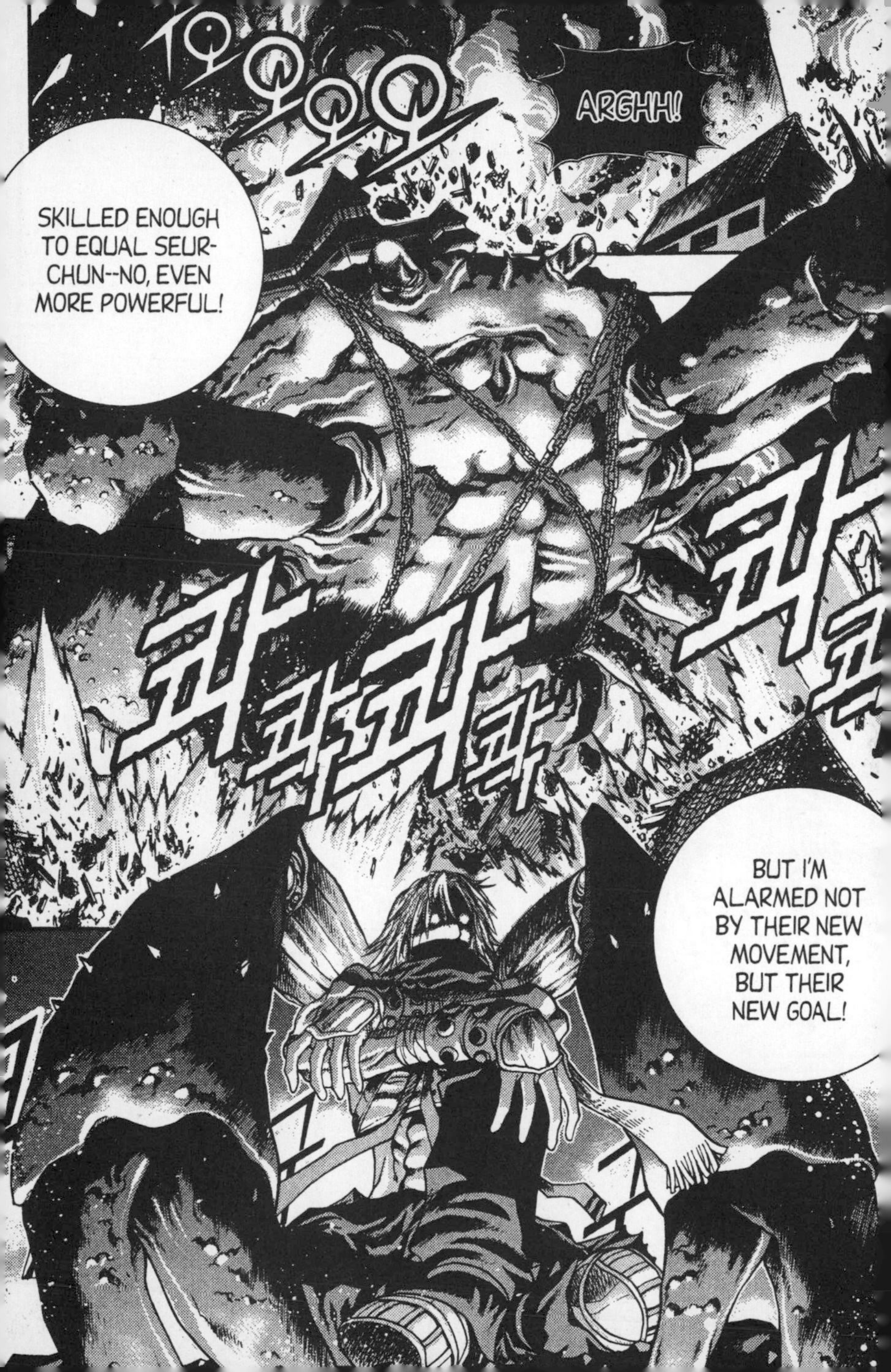
ARGHH!
SKILLED ENOUGH TO EQUAL SEUR-CHUN--NO, EVEN MORE POWERFUL!
BUT I'M ALARMED NOT BY THEIR NEW MOVEMENT, BUT THEIR NEW GOAL!

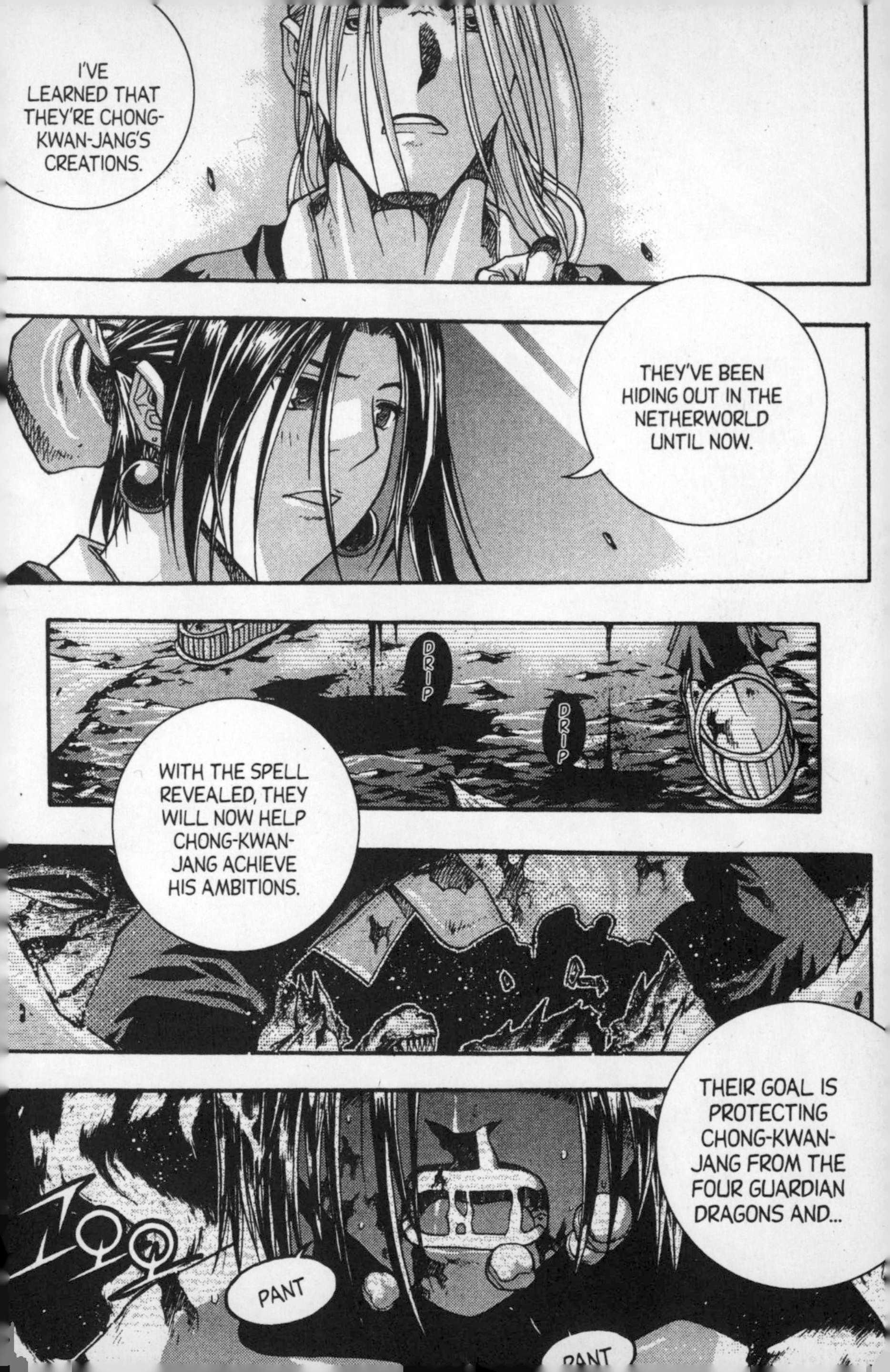
I'VE LEARNED THAT THEY'RE CHONG-KWAN-JANG'S CREATIONS.
THEY'VE BEEN HIDING OUT IN THE NETHERWORLD UNTIL NOW.
DRIP
DRIP
WITH THE SPELL REVEALED, THEY WILL NOW HELP CHONG-KWAN-JANG ACHIEVE HIS AMBITIONS.
THEIR GOAL IS PROTECTING CHONG-KWAN-JANG FROM THE FOUR GUARDIAN DRAGONS AND...
PANT
PANT

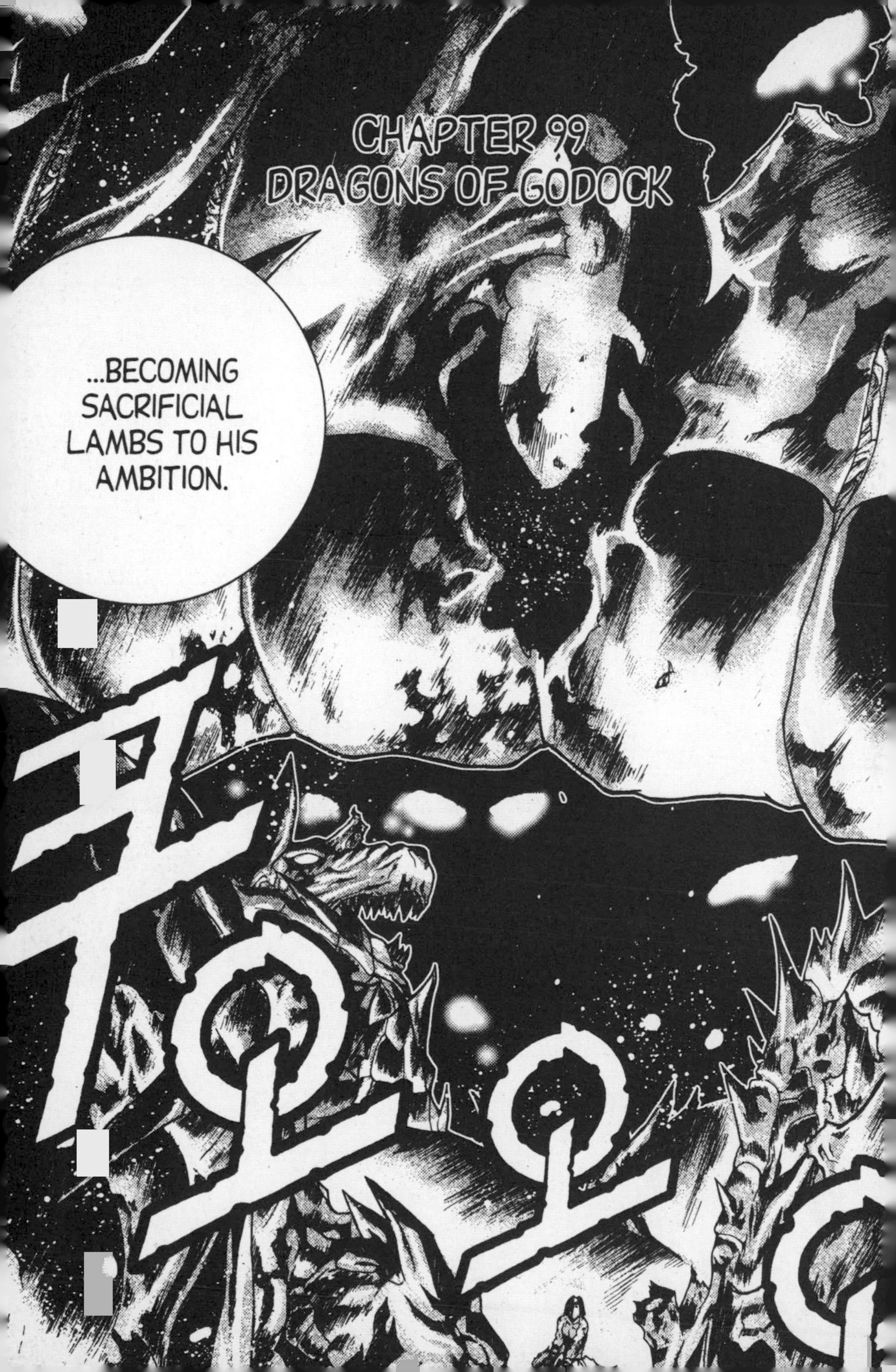
CHAPTER 99
DRAGONS OF GODOCK
...BECOMING SACRIFICIAL LAMBS TO HIS AMBITION.

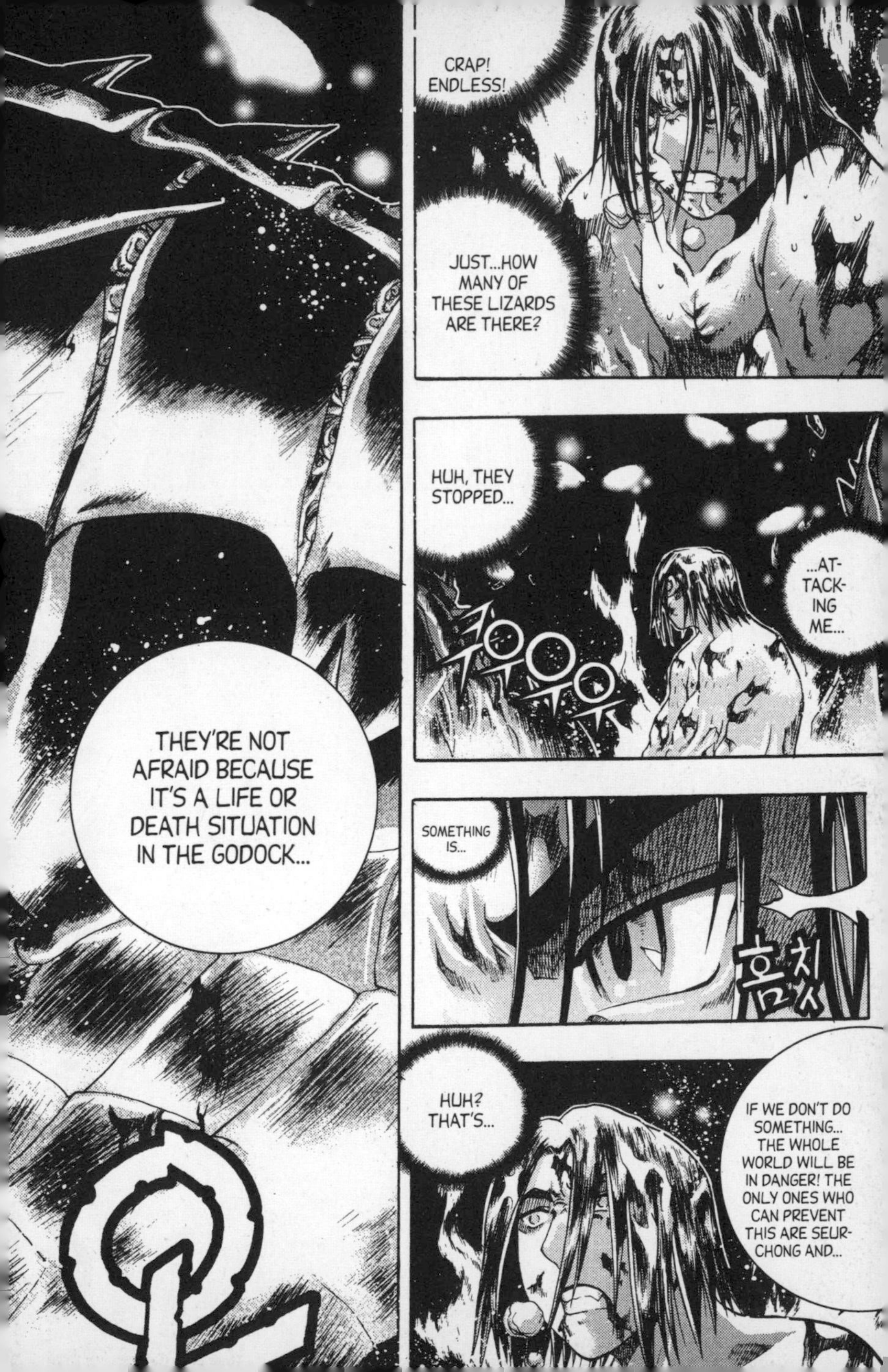
THEY'RE NOT AFRAID BECAUSE IT'S A LIFE OR DEATH SITUATION IN THE GODOCK...
CRAP! ENDLESS!
JUST...HOW MANY OF THESE LIZARDS ARE THERE?
HUH, THEY STOPPED...
...AT-TACK-ING ME...
SOMETHING IS...
흠칫
HUH? THAT'S...
IF WE DON'T DO SOMETHING... THE WHOLE WORLD WILL BE IN DANGER! THE ONLY ONES WHO CAN PREVENT THIS ARE SEUR-CHONG AND...

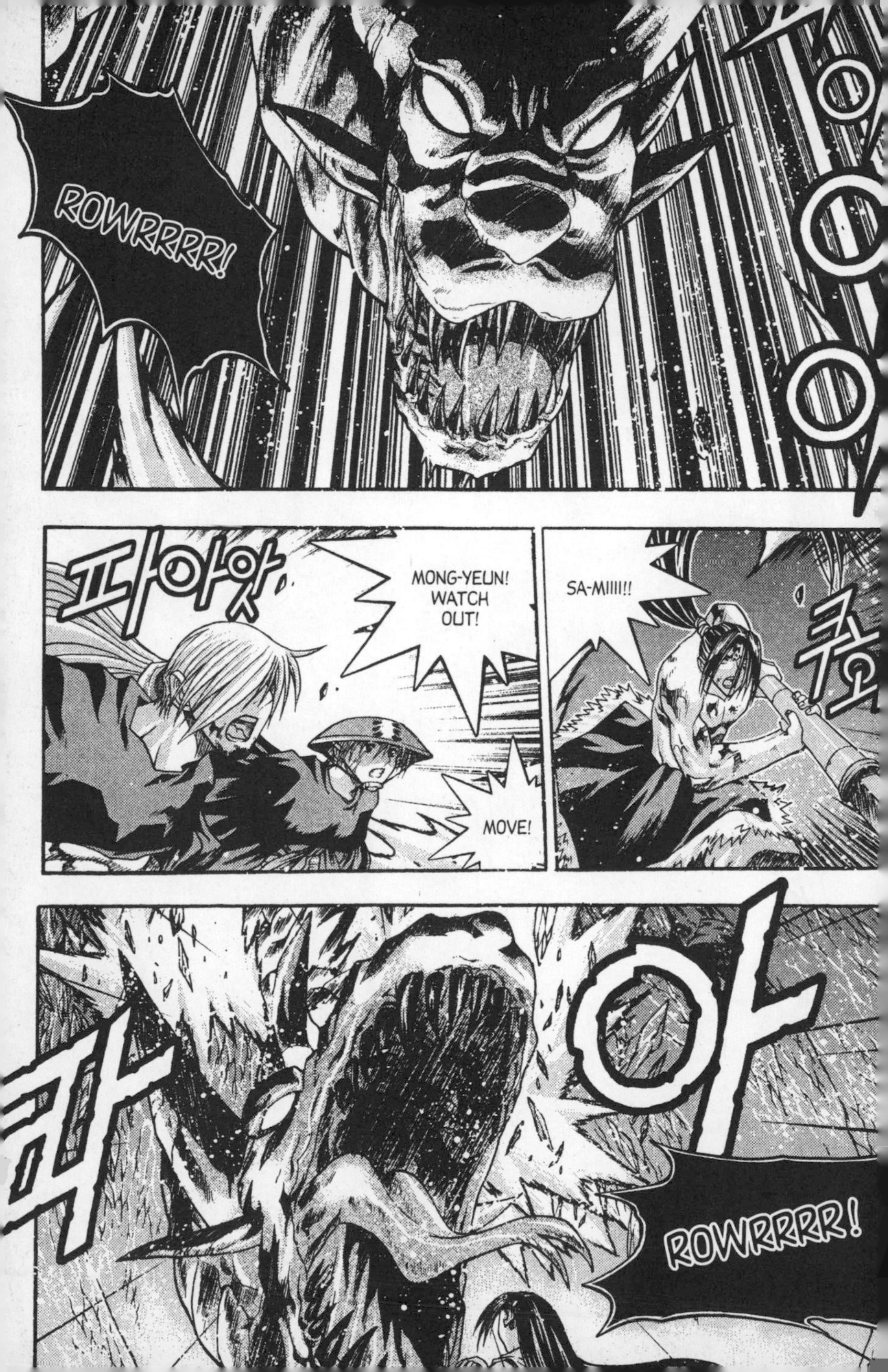
ROWRRRRR!
파아앗
MONG-YEUN! WATCH OUT!
MOVE!
SA-MIIII!!
ROWRRRR!

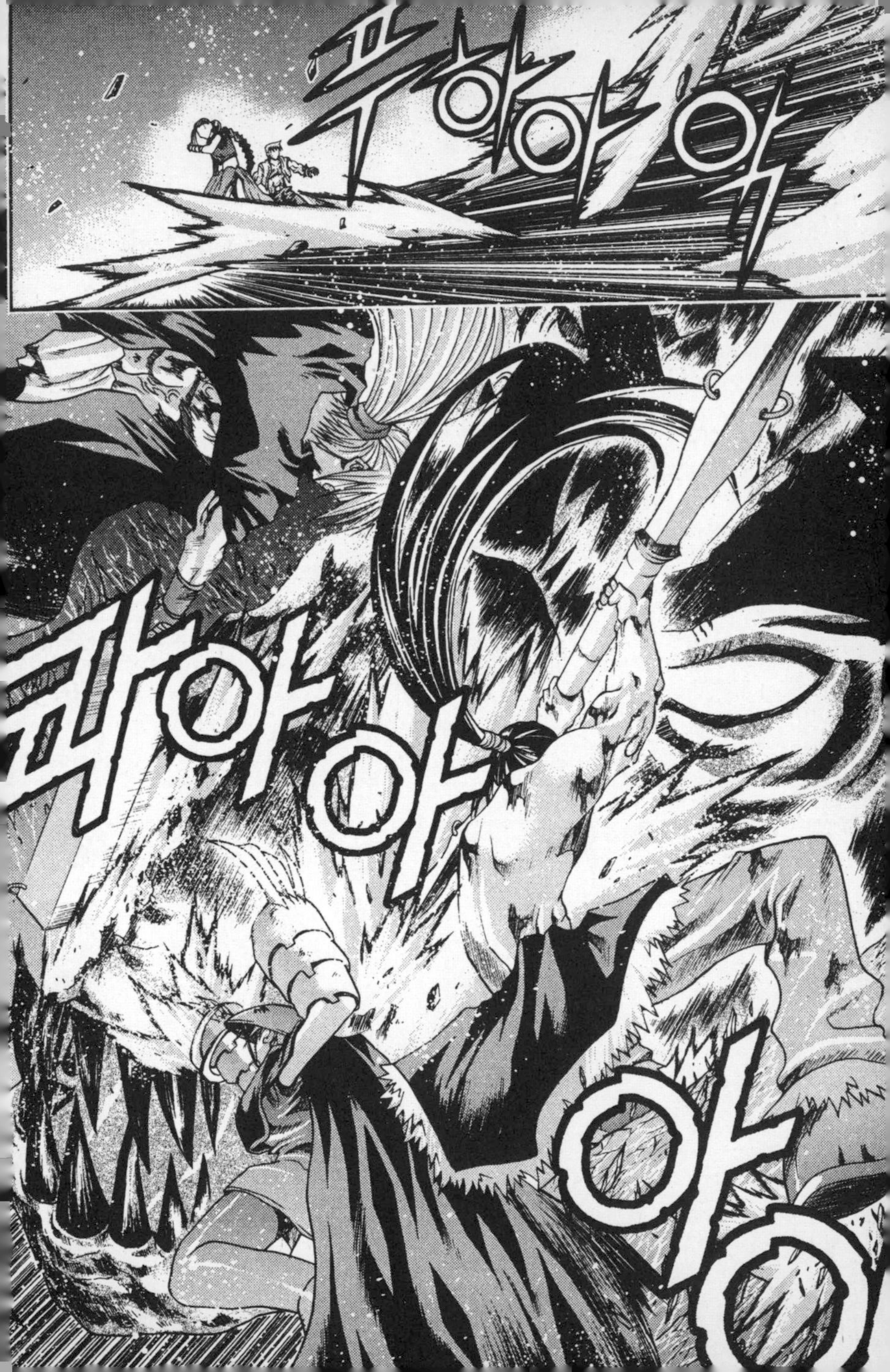

꾸아아악

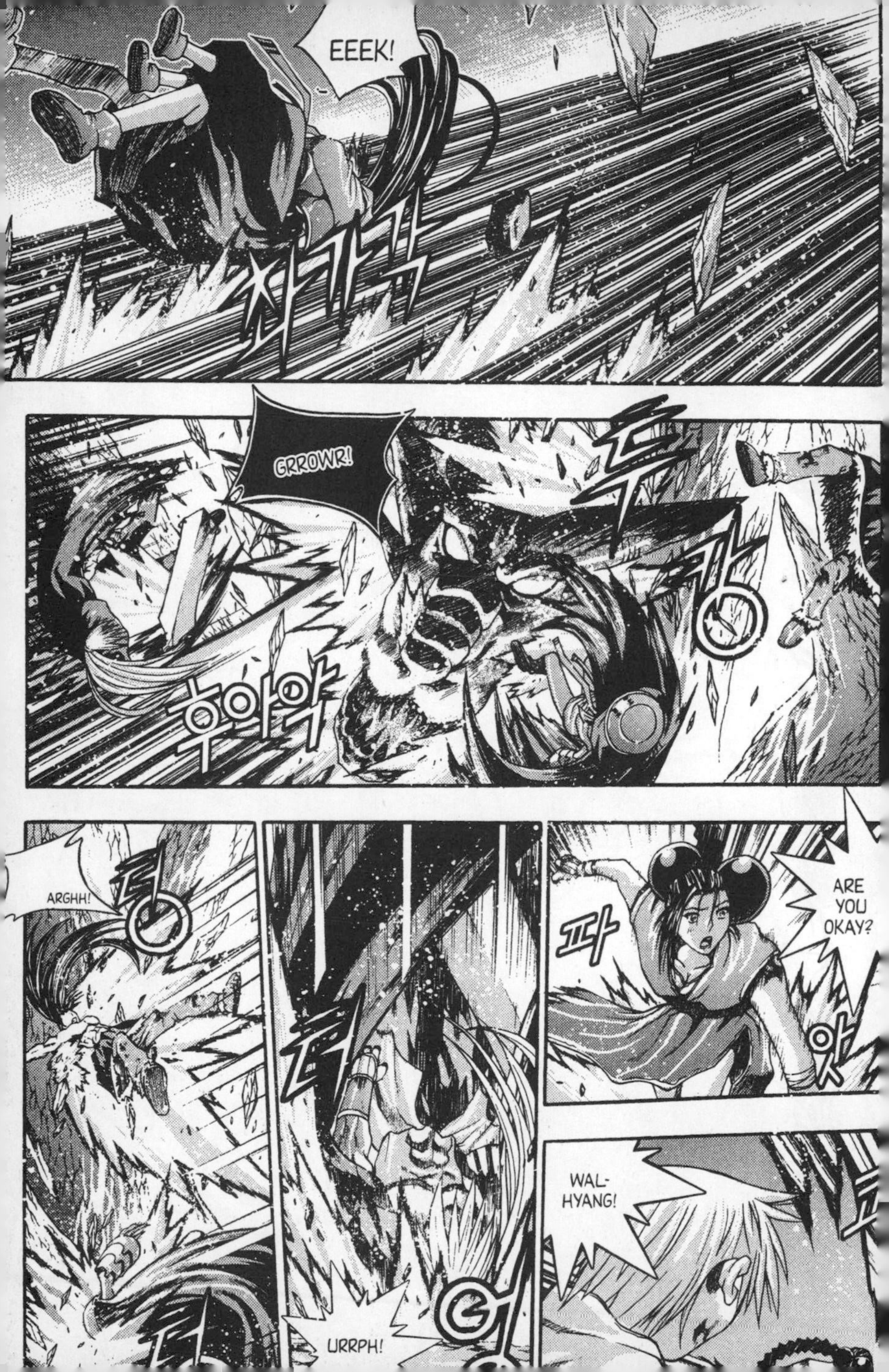
EEEK!
GRROWR!
후아악
ARGHH!
URRPH!
ARE YOU OKAY?
WAL-HYANG!

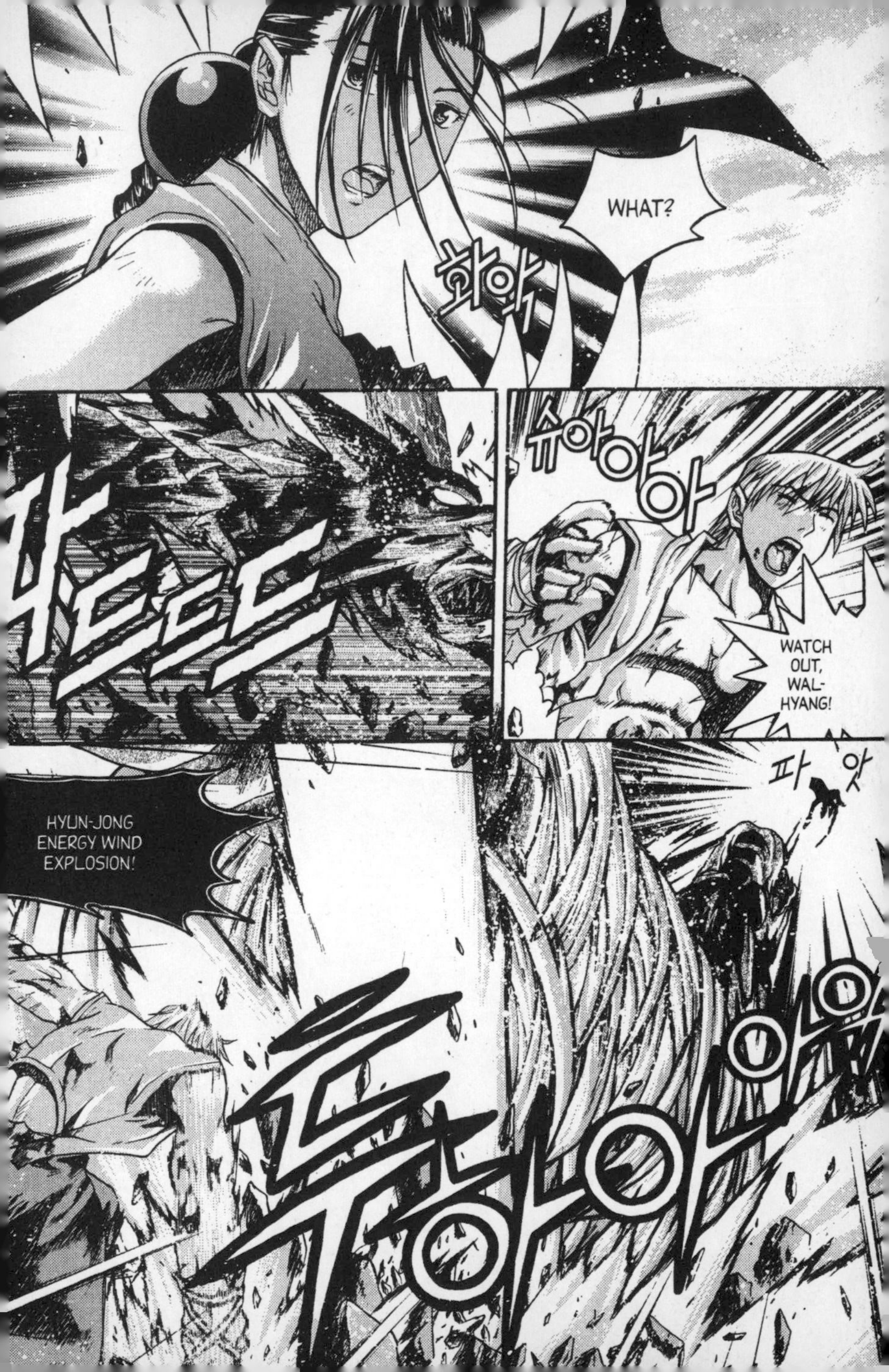
WHAT?
화악
콰드드드
슈아아아
WATCH OUT, WAL-HYANG!
HYUN-JONG ENERGY WIND EXPLOSION!
파앗

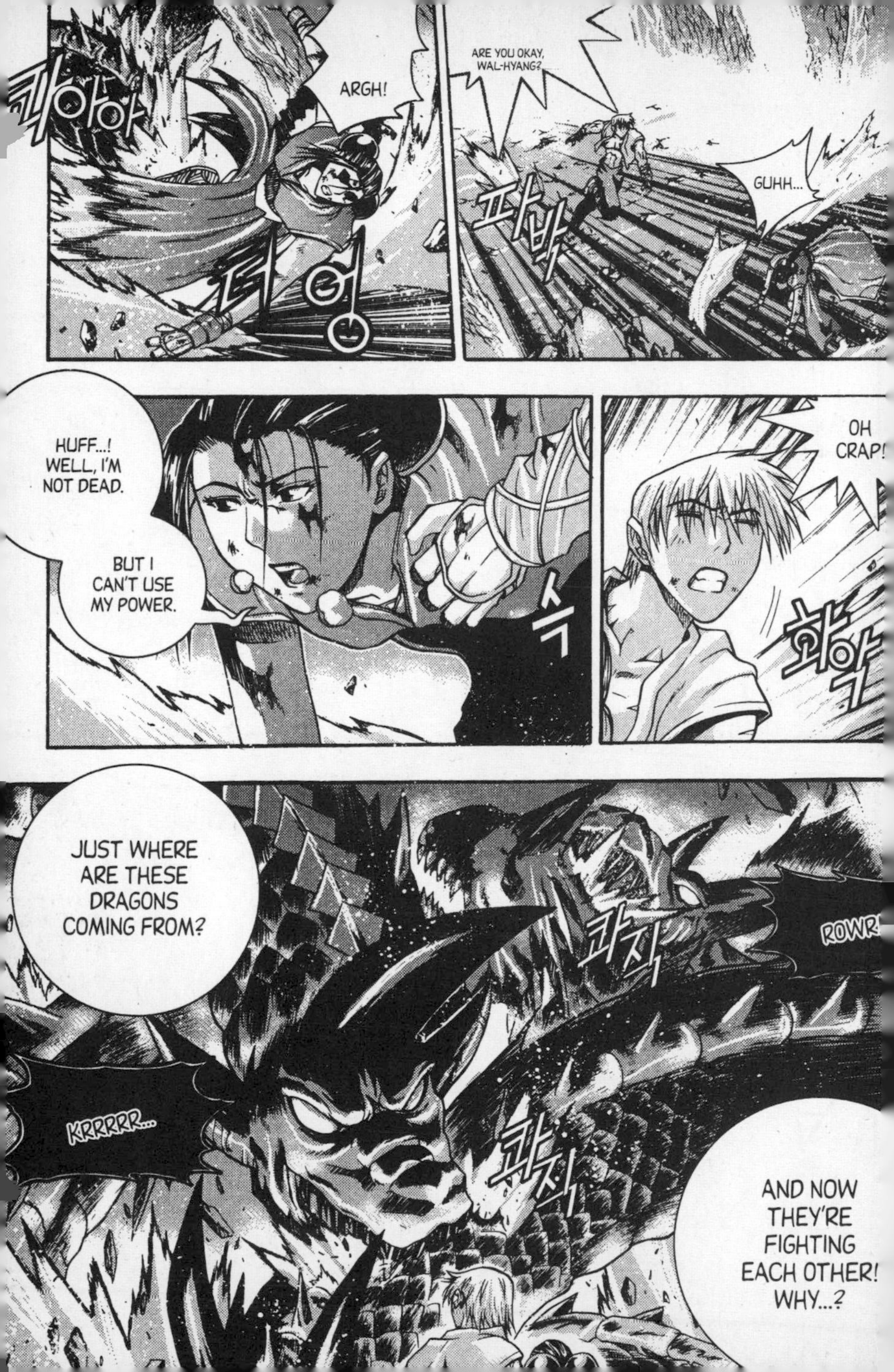
ARGH!
ARE YOU OKAY, WAL-HYANG?
GUHH...
HUFF...! WELL, I'M NOT DEAD.
BUT I CAN'T USE MY POWER.
OH CRAP!
JUST WHERE ARE THESE DRAGONS COMING FROM?
ROWR
KRRRRR...
AND NOW THEY'RE FIGHTING EACH OTHER! WHY...?

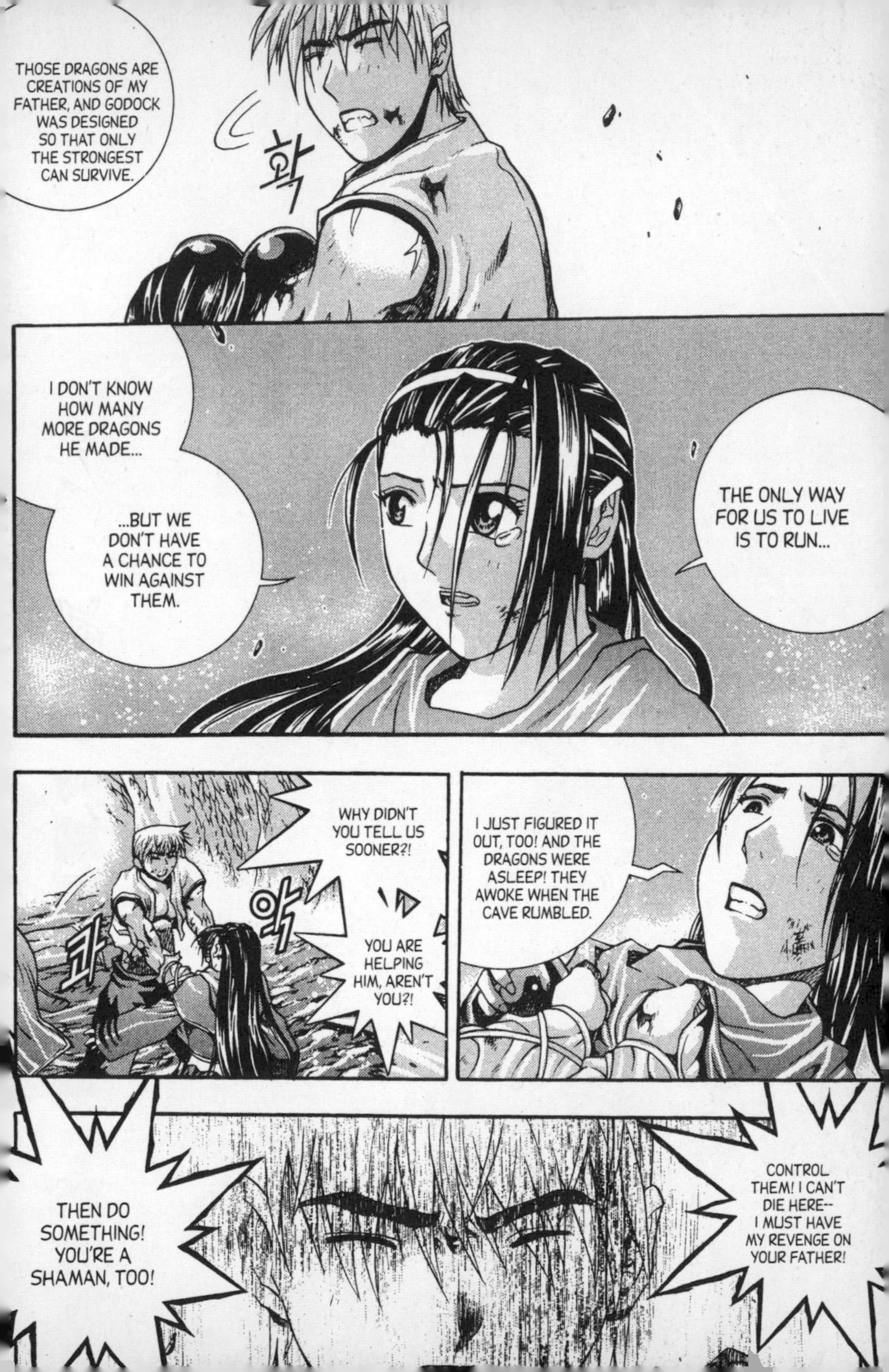
THOSE DRAGONS ARE CREATIONS OF MY FATHER, AND GODOCK WAS DESIGNED SO THAT ONLY THE STRONGEST CAN SURVIVE.
확
I DON'T KNOW HOW MANY MORE DRAGONS HE MADE...
...BUT WE DON'T HAVE A CHANCE TO WIN AGAINST THEM.
THE ONLY WAY FOR US TO LIVE IS TO RUN...
WHY DIDN'T YOU TELL US SOONER?!
YOU ARE HELPING HIM, AREN'T YOU?!
I JUST FIGURED IT OUT, TOO! AND THE DRAGONS WERE ASLEEP! THEY AWOKE WHEN THE CAVE RUMBLED.
THEN DO SOMETHING! YOU'RE A SHAMAN, TOO!
CONTROL THEM! I CAN'T DIE HERE-- I MUST HAVE MY REVENGE ON YOUR FATHER!

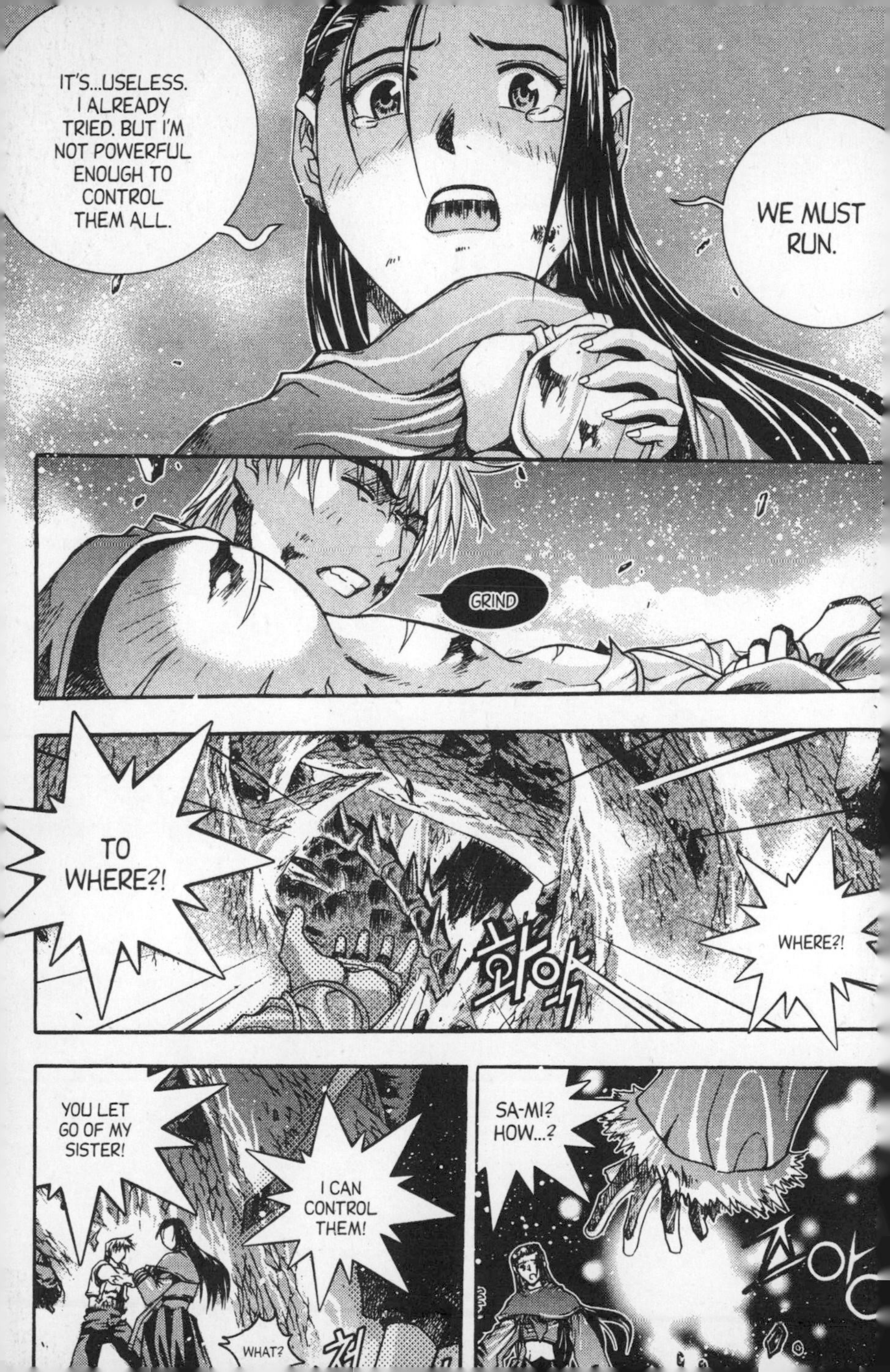
IT'S...USELESS. I ALREADY TRIED. BUT I'M NOT POWERFUL ENOUGH TO CONTROL THEM ALL.
WE MUST RUN.
GRIND
TO WHERE?!
화악
WHERE?!
YOU LET GO OF MY SISTER!
I CAN CONTROL THEM!
WHAT?
SA-MI? HOW...?

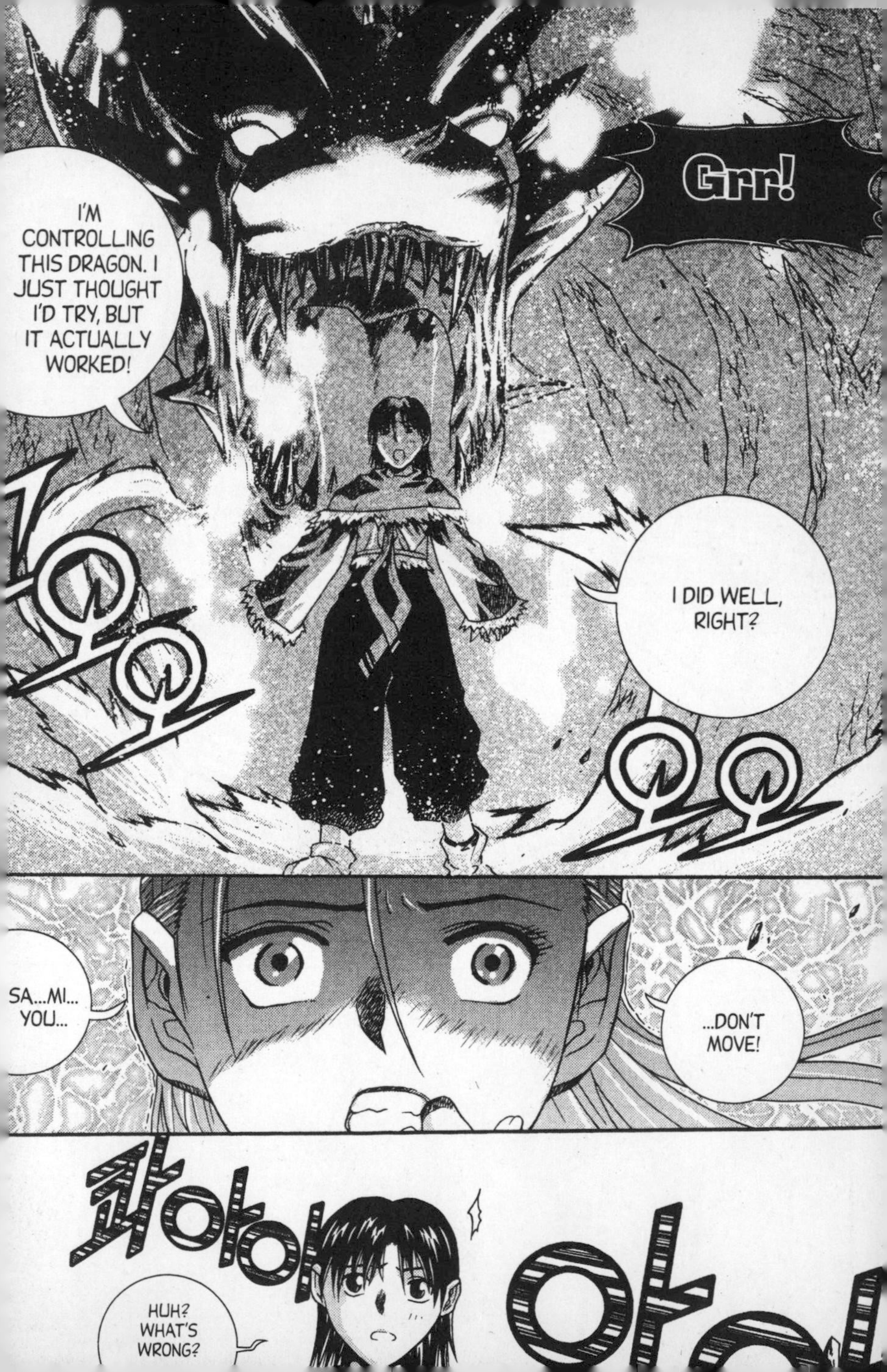
I'M CONTROLLING THIS DRAGON. I JUST THOUGHT I'D TRY, BUT IT ACTUALLY WORKED!
Grr!
I DID WELL, RIGHT?
SA...MI... YOU...
...DON'T MOVE!
HUH? WHAT'S WRONG?

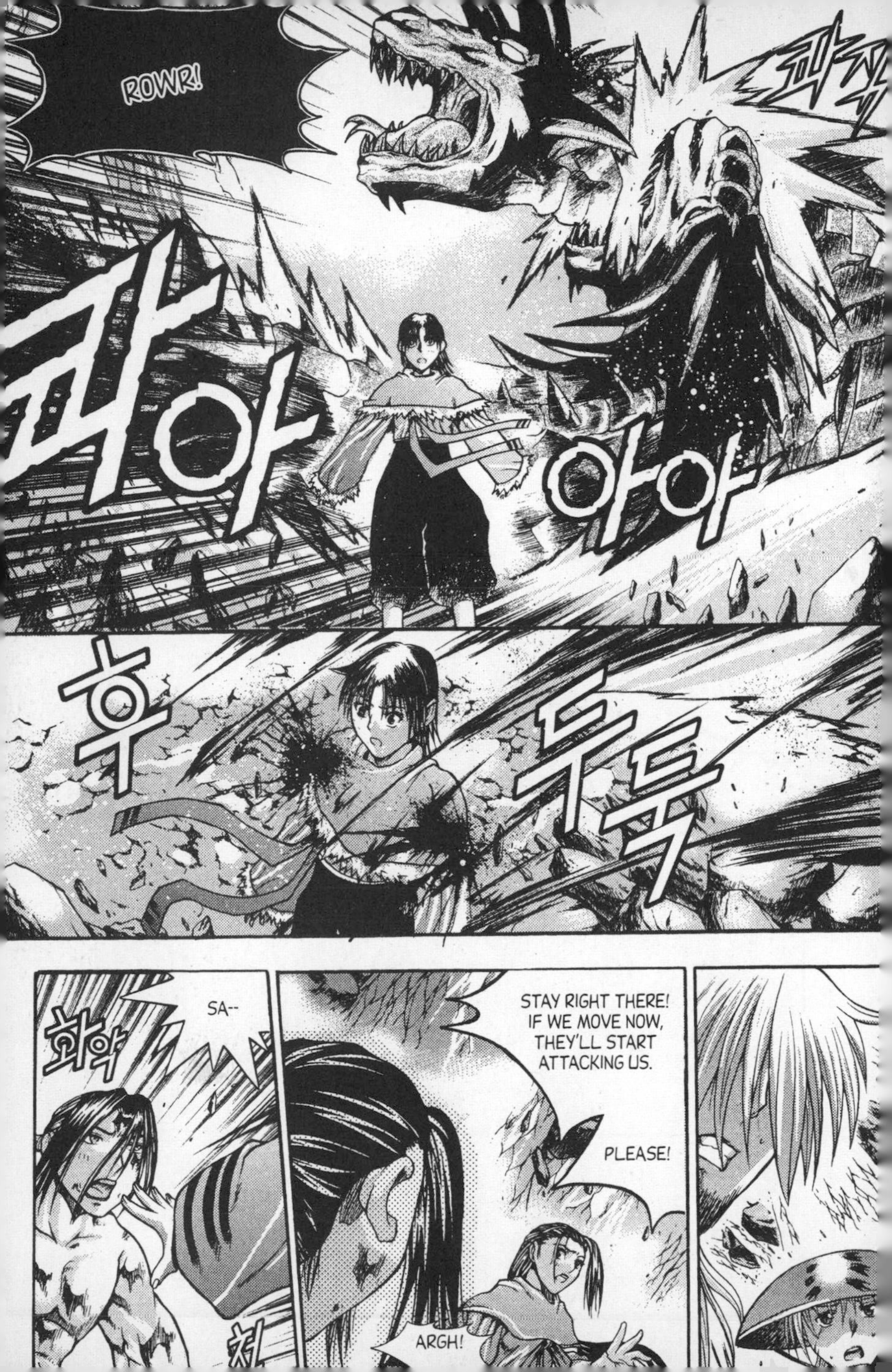
ROWR!
SA--
STAY RIGHT THERE! IF WE MOVE NOW, THEY'LL START ATTACKING US.
PLEASE!
ARGH!

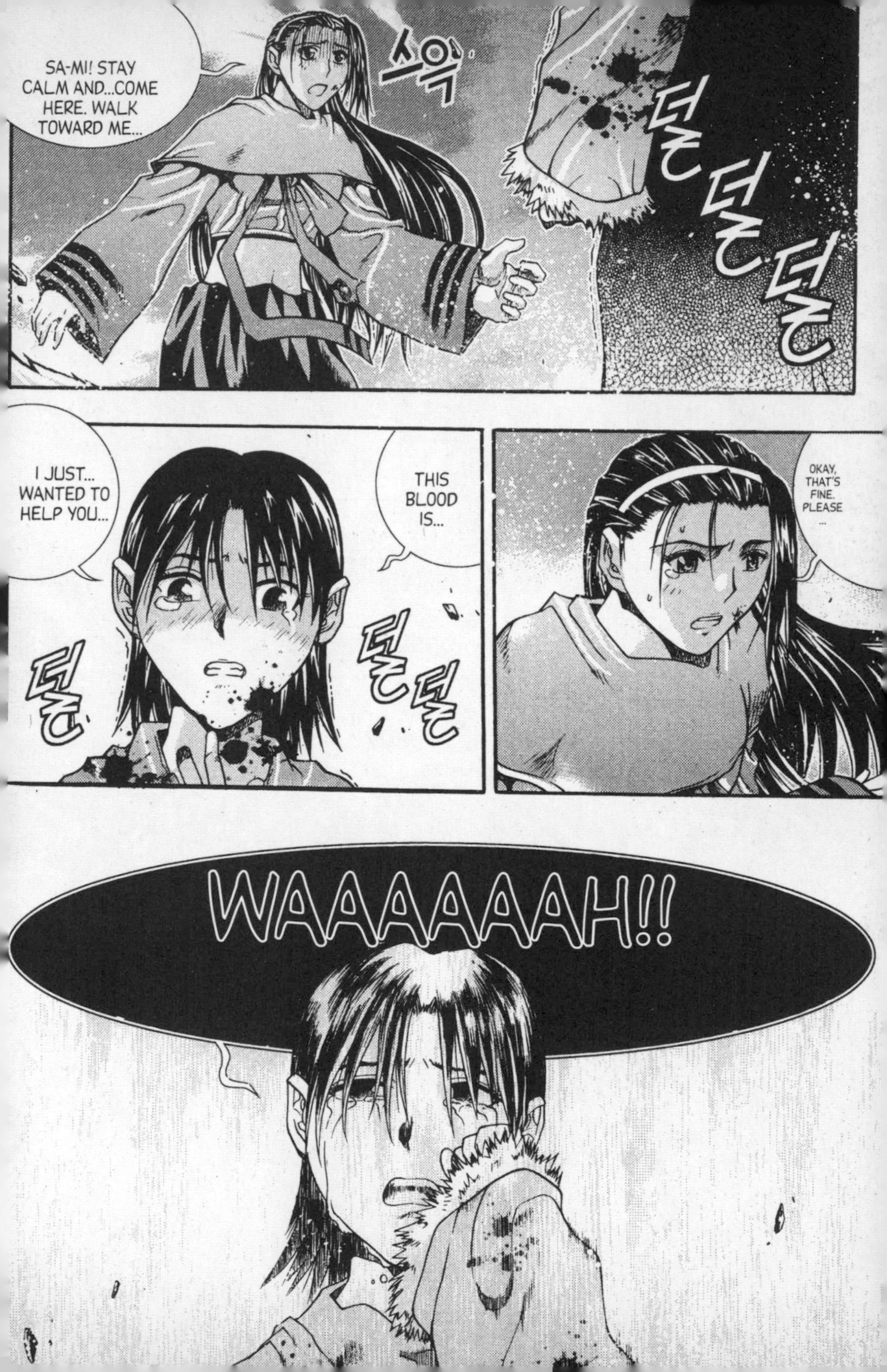
SA-MI! STAY CALM AND...COME HERE. WALK TOWARD ME...
스윽
덜덜덜덜
I JUST... WANTED TO HELP YOU...
THIS BLOOD IS...
덜
덜덜
OKAY, THAT'S FINE. PLEASE ...
WAAAAAAH!!

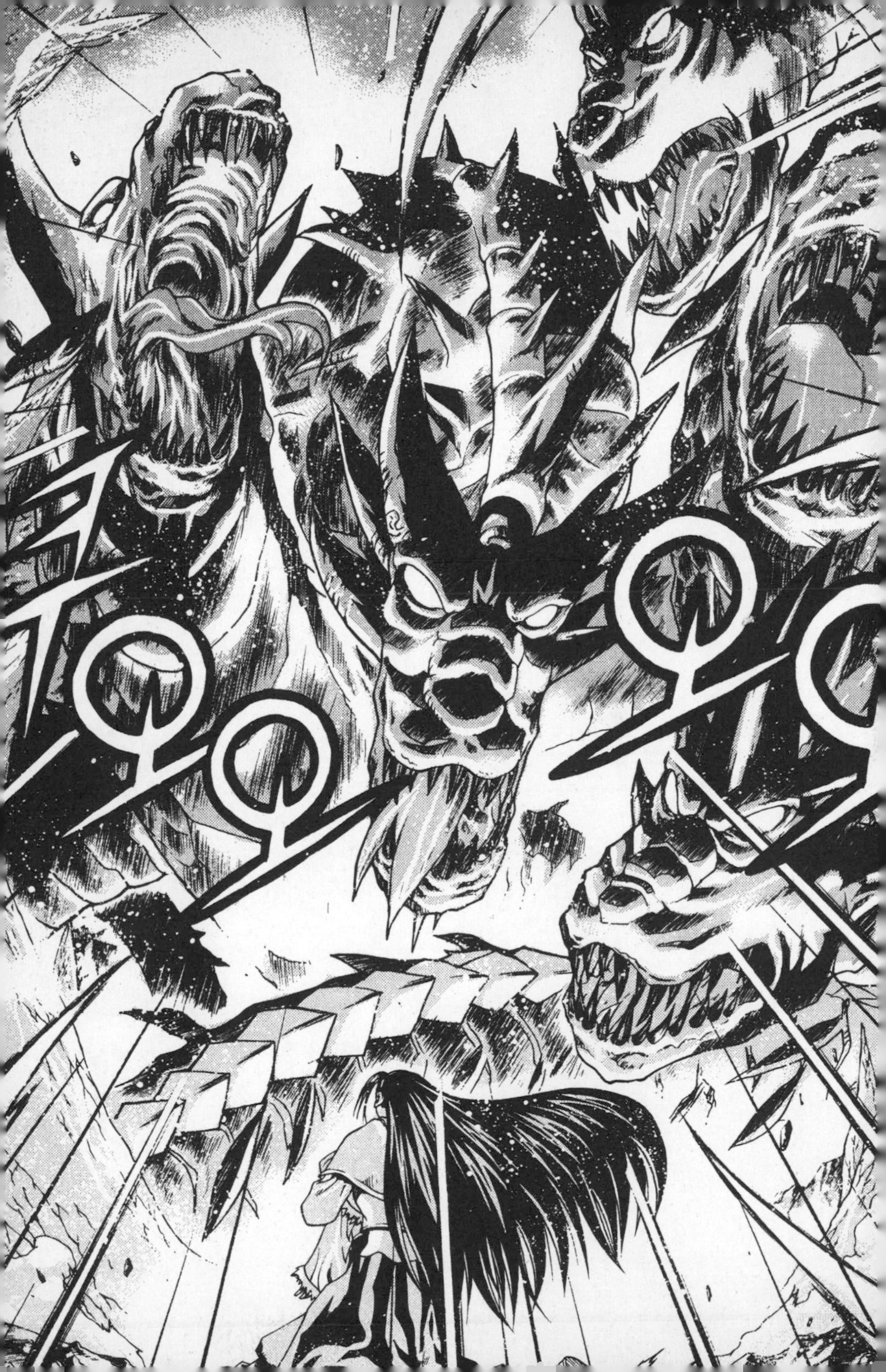

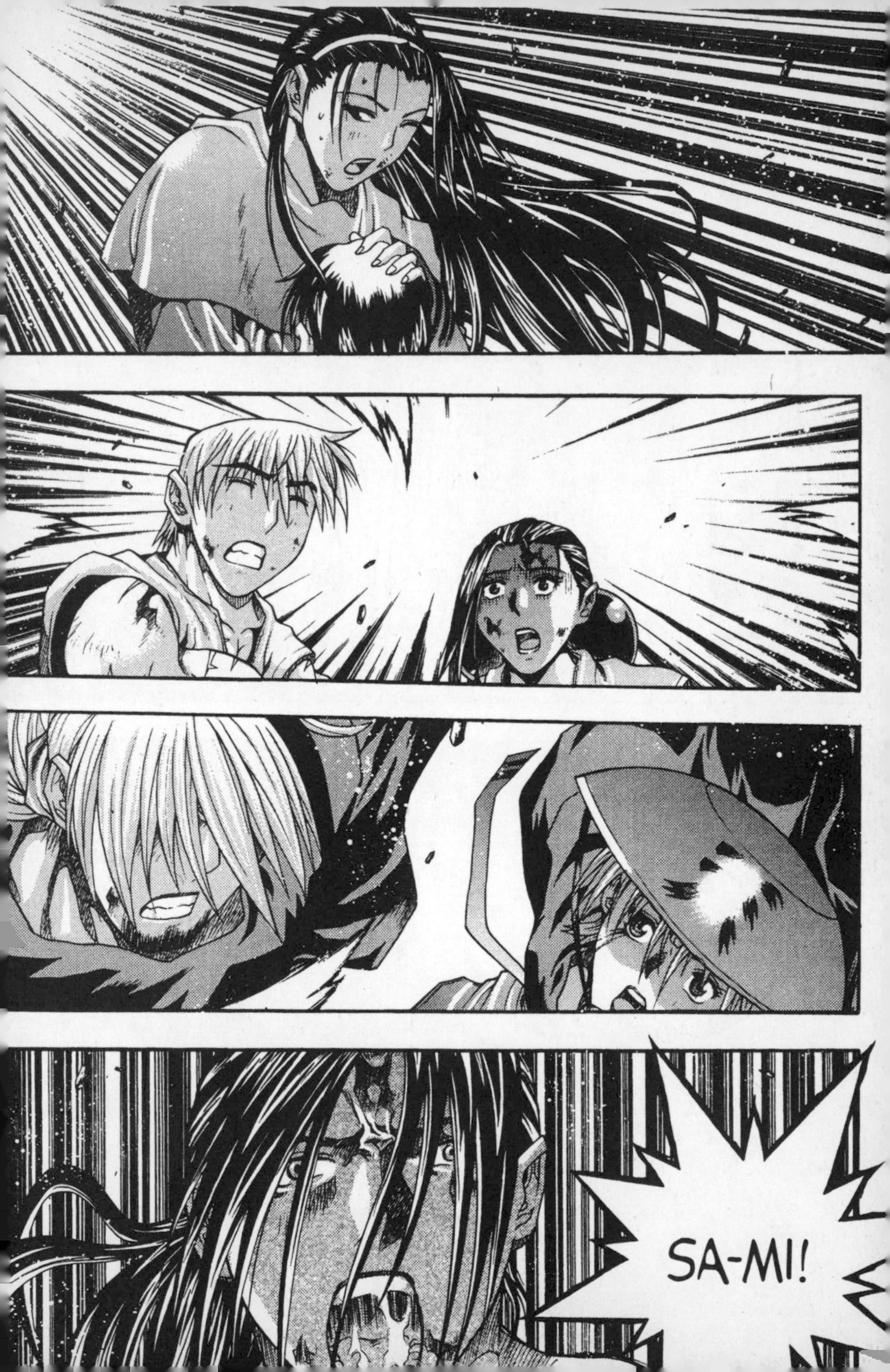
SA-MI!

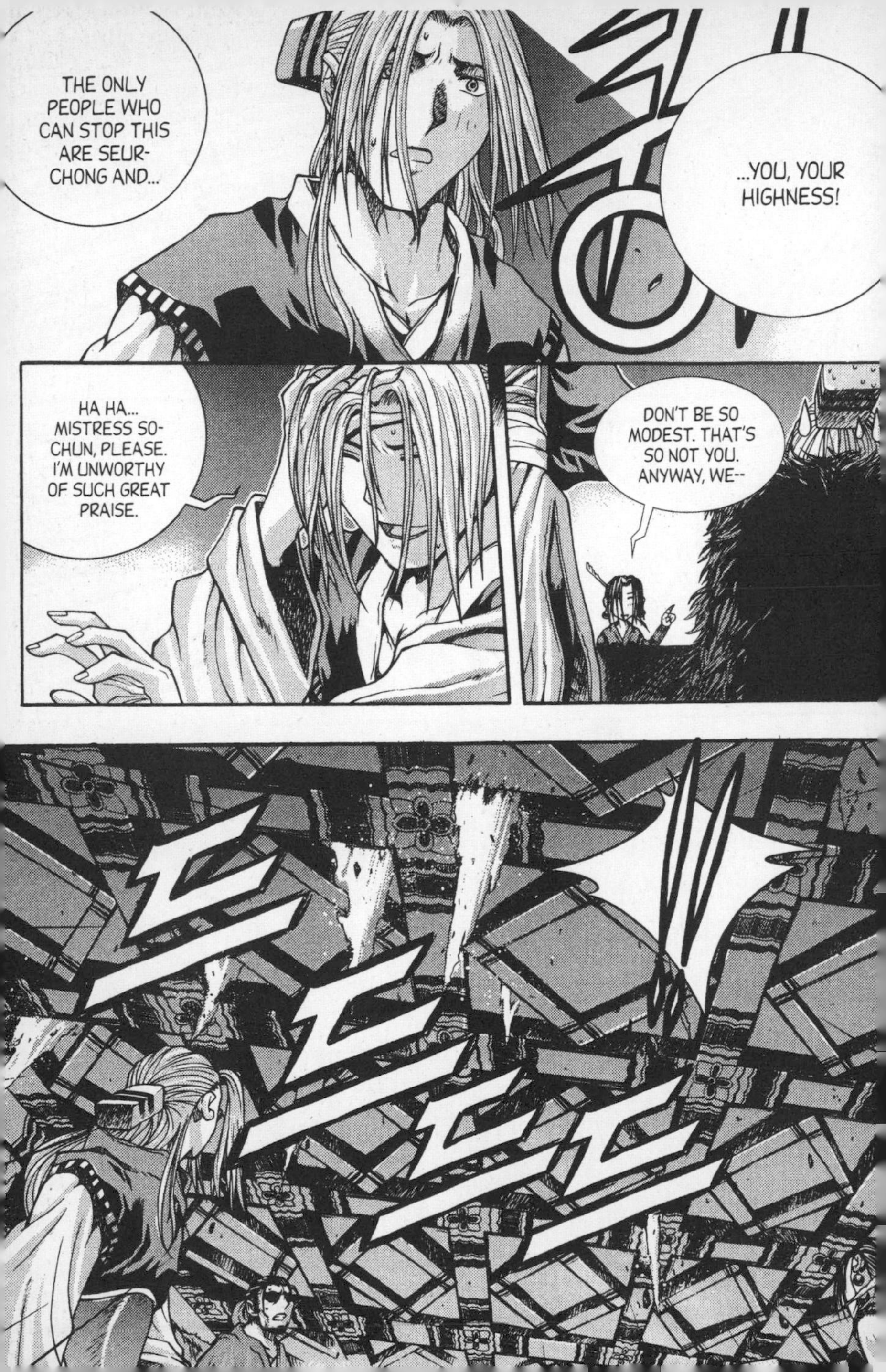
THE ONLY PEOPLE WHO CAN STOP THIS ARE SEUR-CHONG AND...
...YOU, YOUR HIGHNESS!
HA HA... MISTRESS SO-CHUN, PLEASE. I'M UNWORTHY OF SUCH GREAT PRAISE.
DON'T BE SO MODEST. THAT'S SO NOT YOU. ANYWAY, WE--

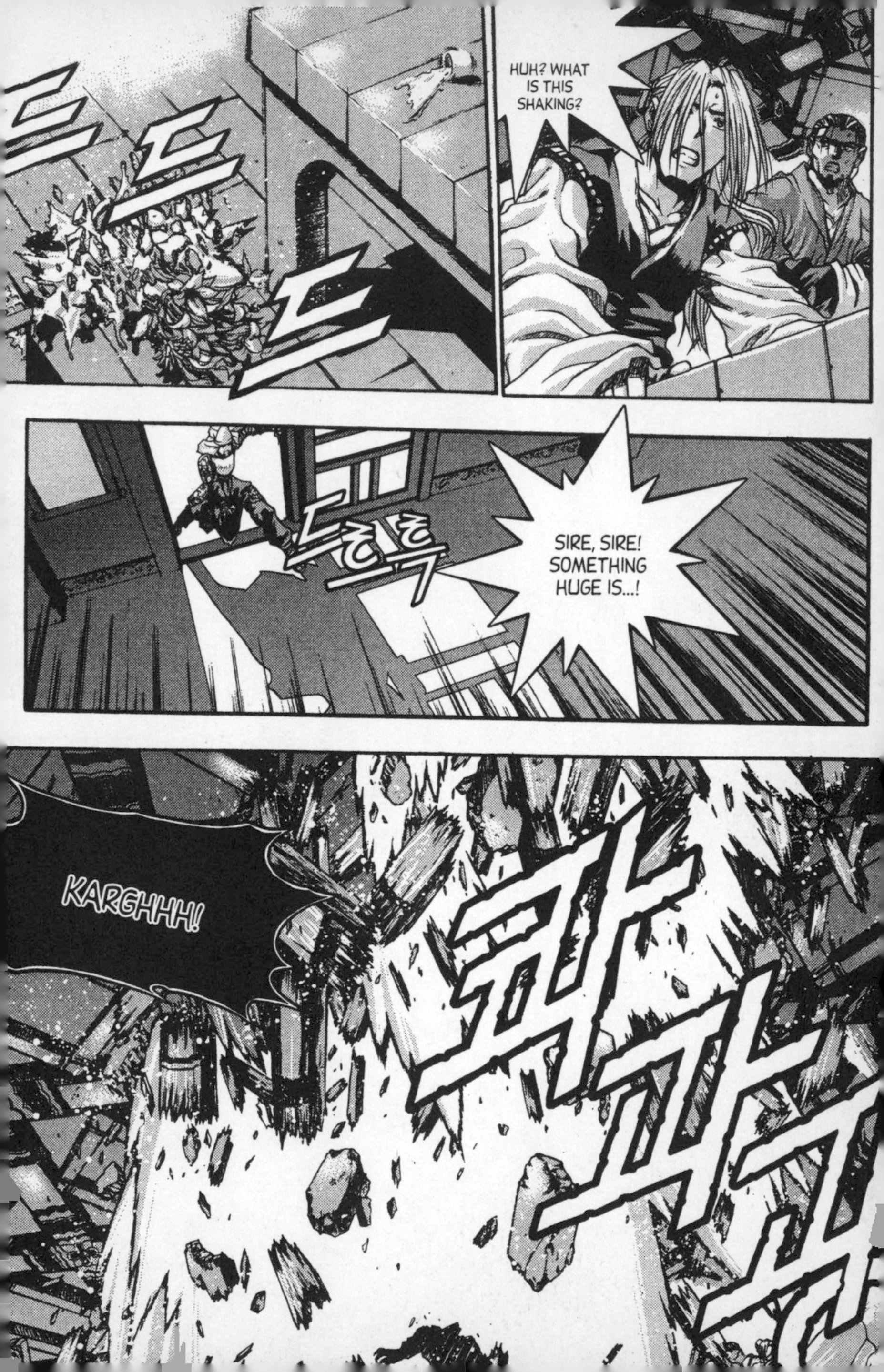
HUH? WHAT IS THIS SHAKING?
SIRE, SIRE! SOMETHING HUGE IS...!
KARGHHH!

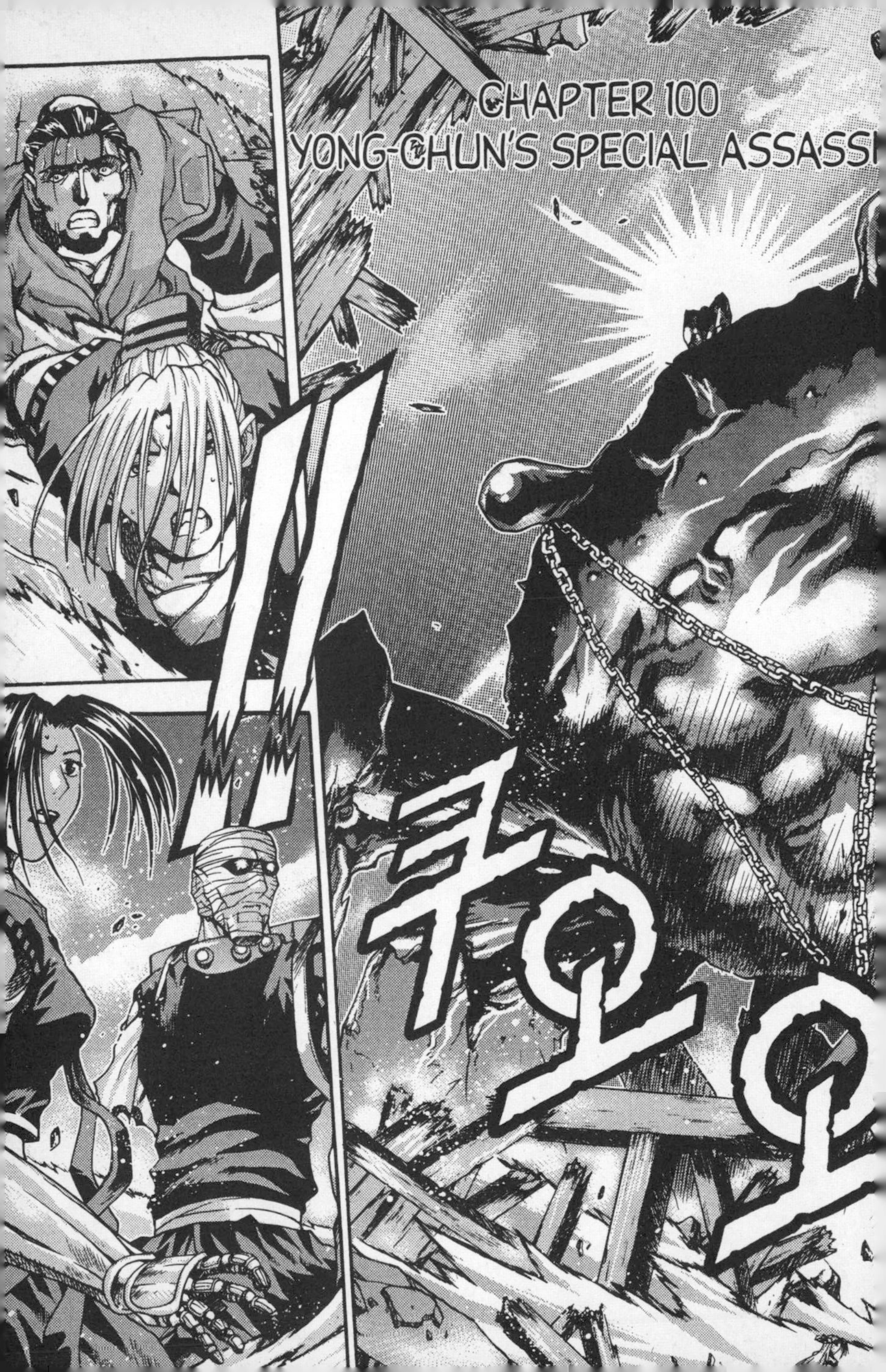
CHAPTER 100
YONG-CHUN'S SPECIAL ASSASSI

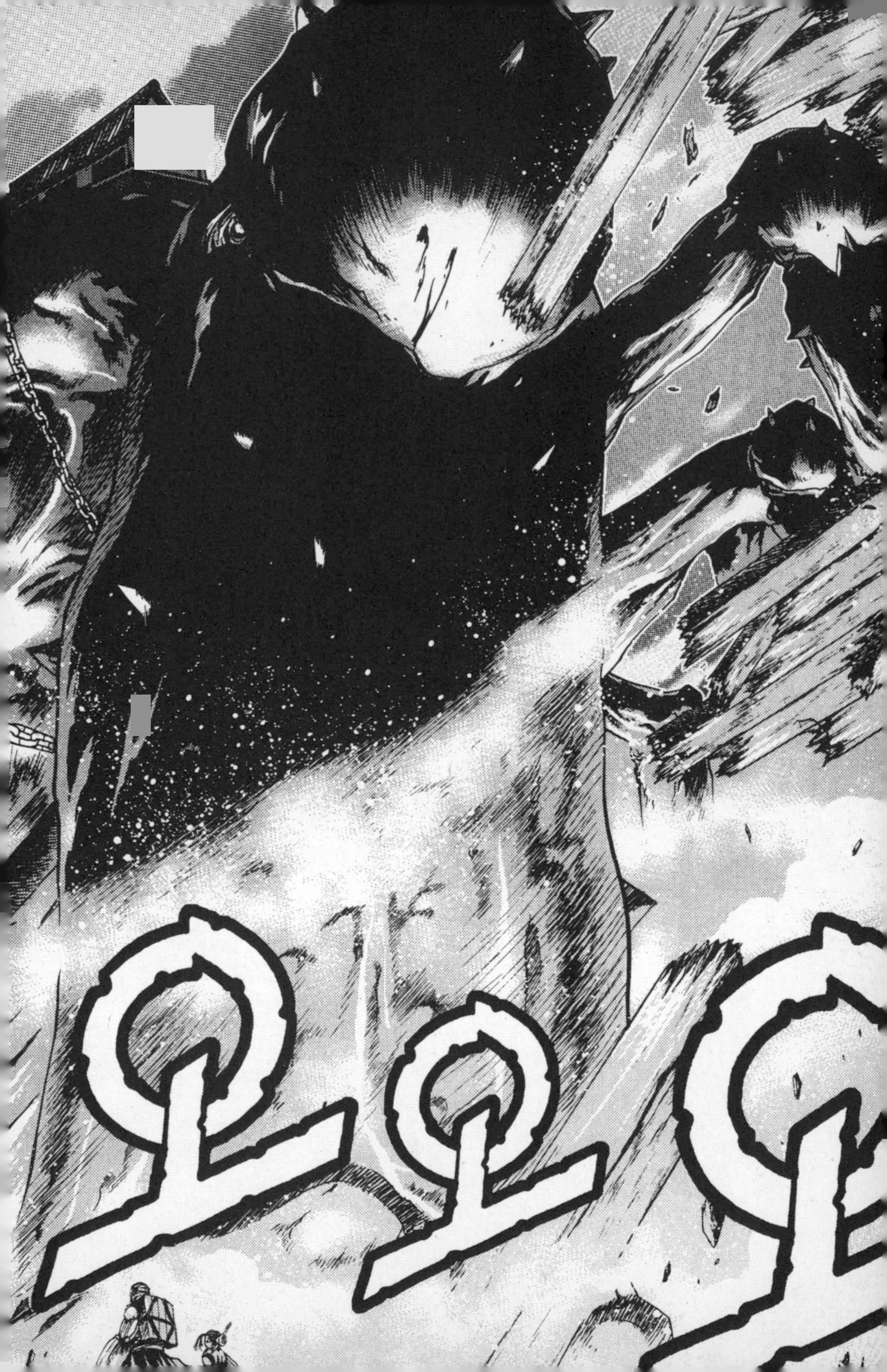

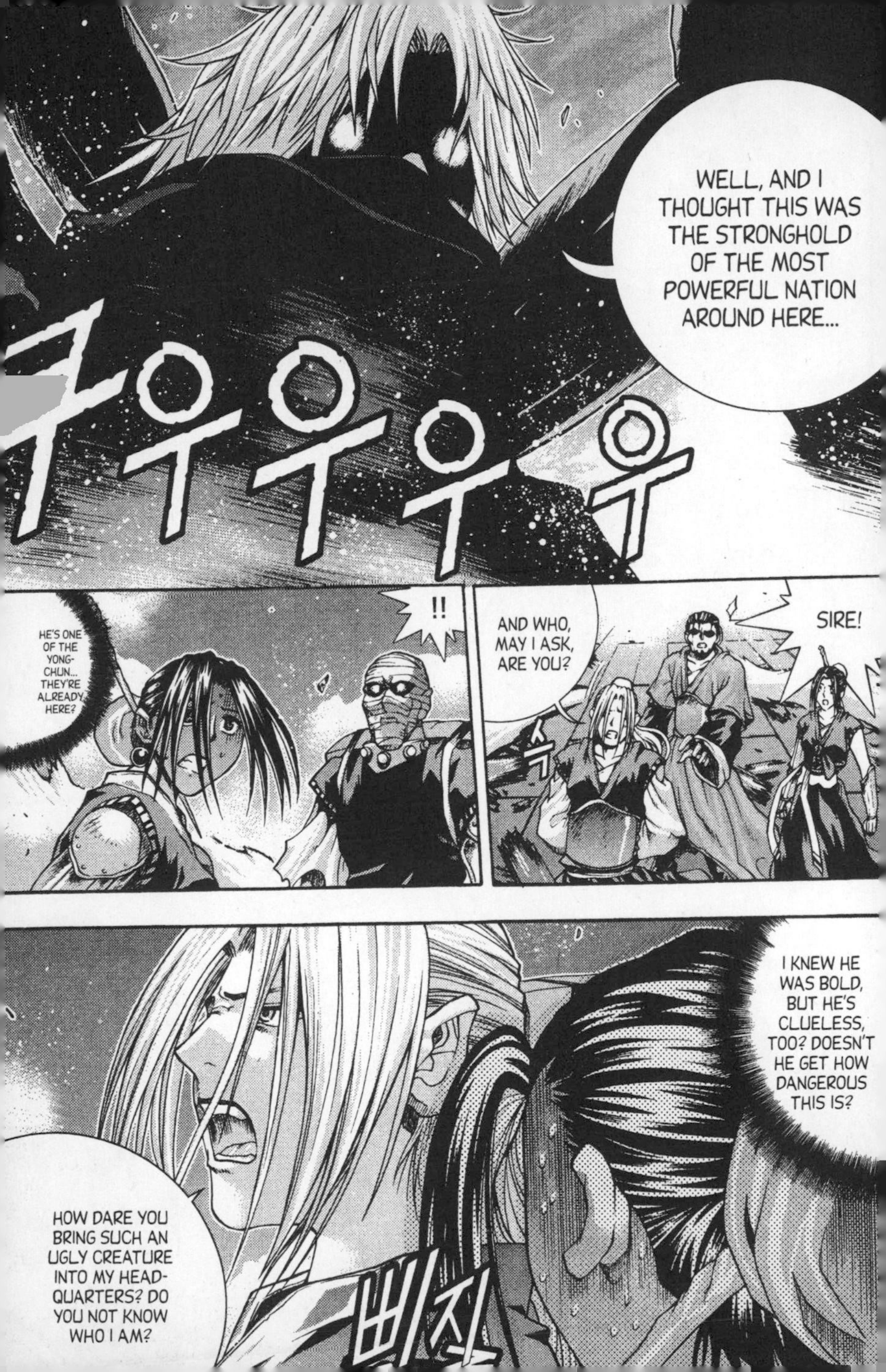

WELL, AND I THOUGHT THIS WAS THE STRONGHOLD OF THE MOST POWERFUL NATION AROUND HERE...
HE'S ONE OF THE YONG-CHUN... THEY'RE ALREADY HERE?
!!
AND WHO, MAY I ASK, ARE YOU?
SIRE!
HOW DARE YOU BRING SUCH AN UGLY CREATURE INTO MY HEAD-QUARTERS? DO YOU NOT KNOW WHO I AM?
I KNEW HE WAS BOLD, BUT HE'S CLUELESS, TOO? DOESN'T HE GET HOW DANGEROUS THIS IS?

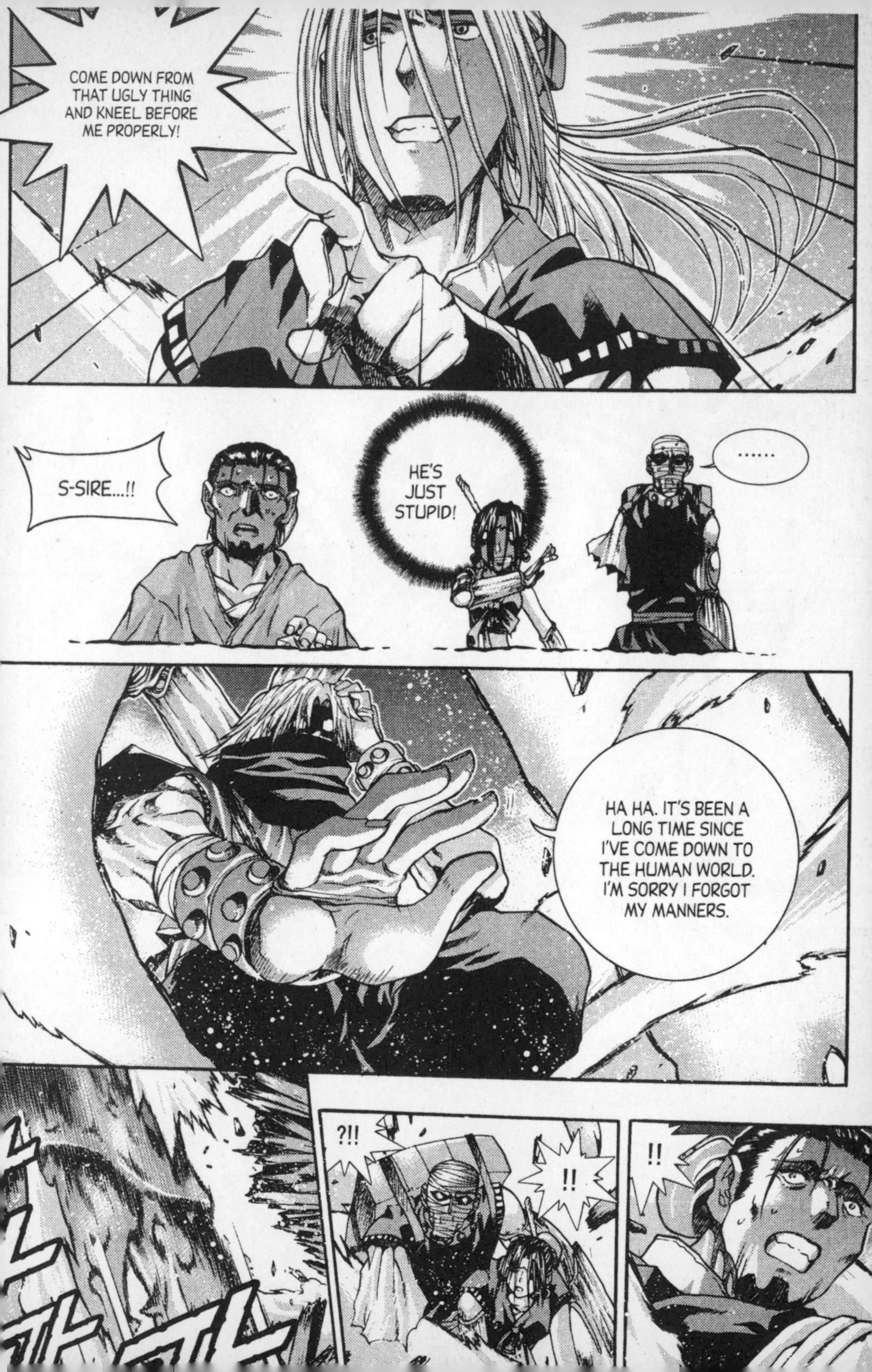
COME DOWN FROM THAT UGLY THING AND KNEEL BEFORE ME PROPERLY!
S-SIRE...!!
HE'S JUST STUPID!
......
HA HA. IT'S BEEN A LONG TIME SINCE I'VE COME DOWN TO THE HUMAN WORLD. I'M SORRY I FORGOT MY MANNERS.
?!!
!!
!!

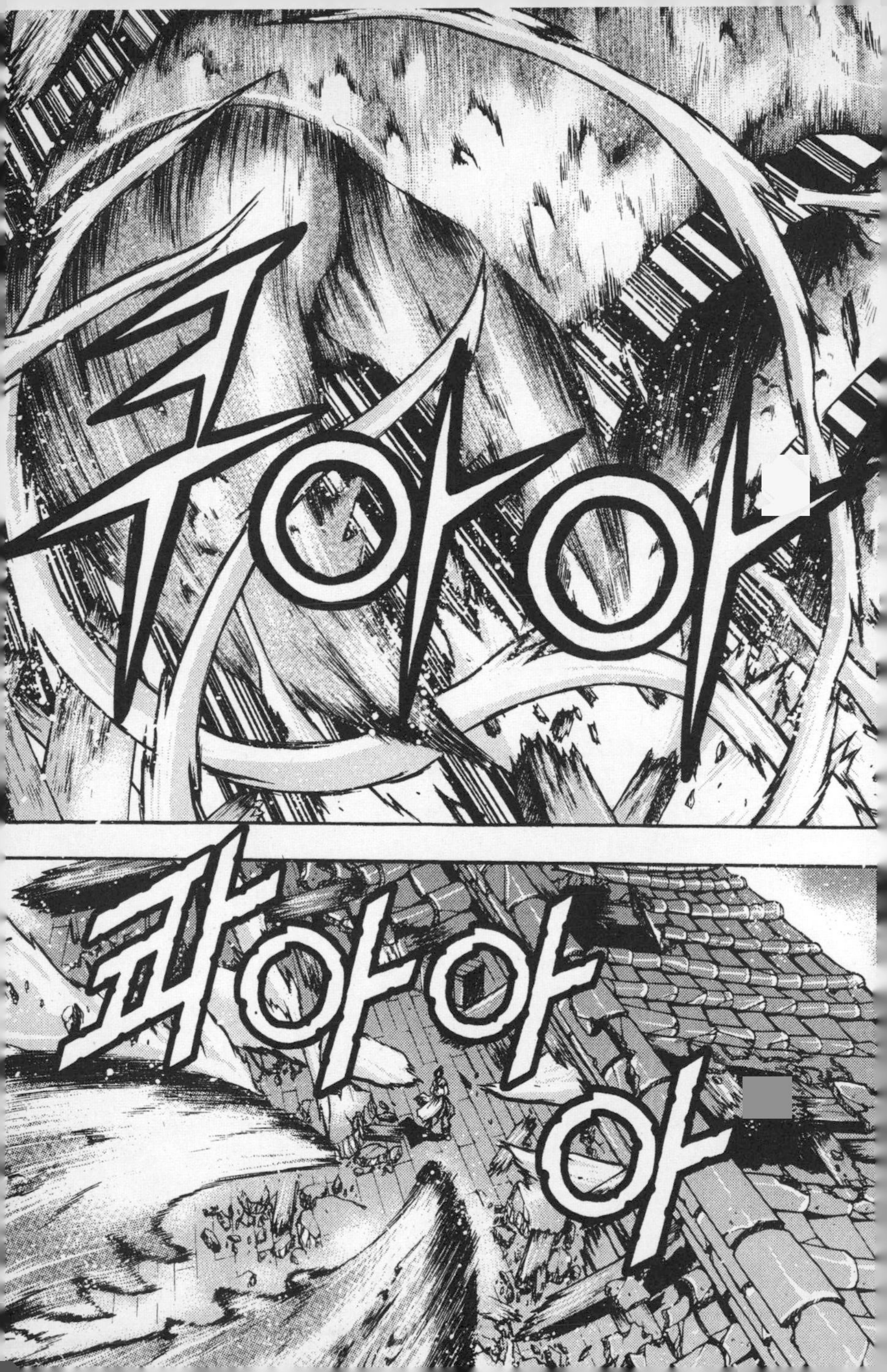
콰아아
파아아아

SALUTATIONS,
O GREAT ONE!

AAAAH!
WE MUST
GO!

SIRE!

MISTRESS!
WE HAVE TO
GET OUT!

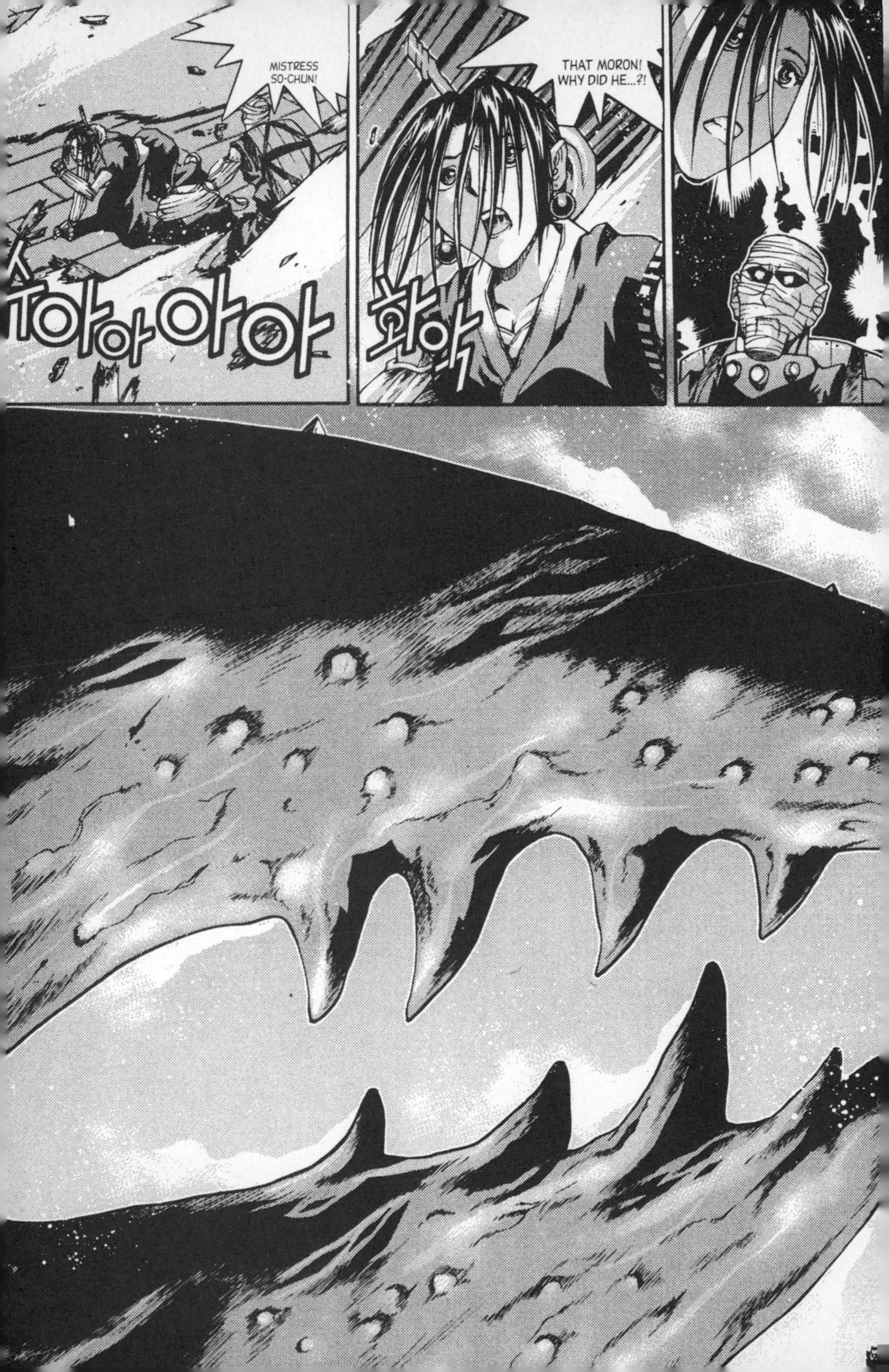
MISTRESS SO-CHUN!
스아아아아
THAT MORON! WHY DID HE...?!
화악

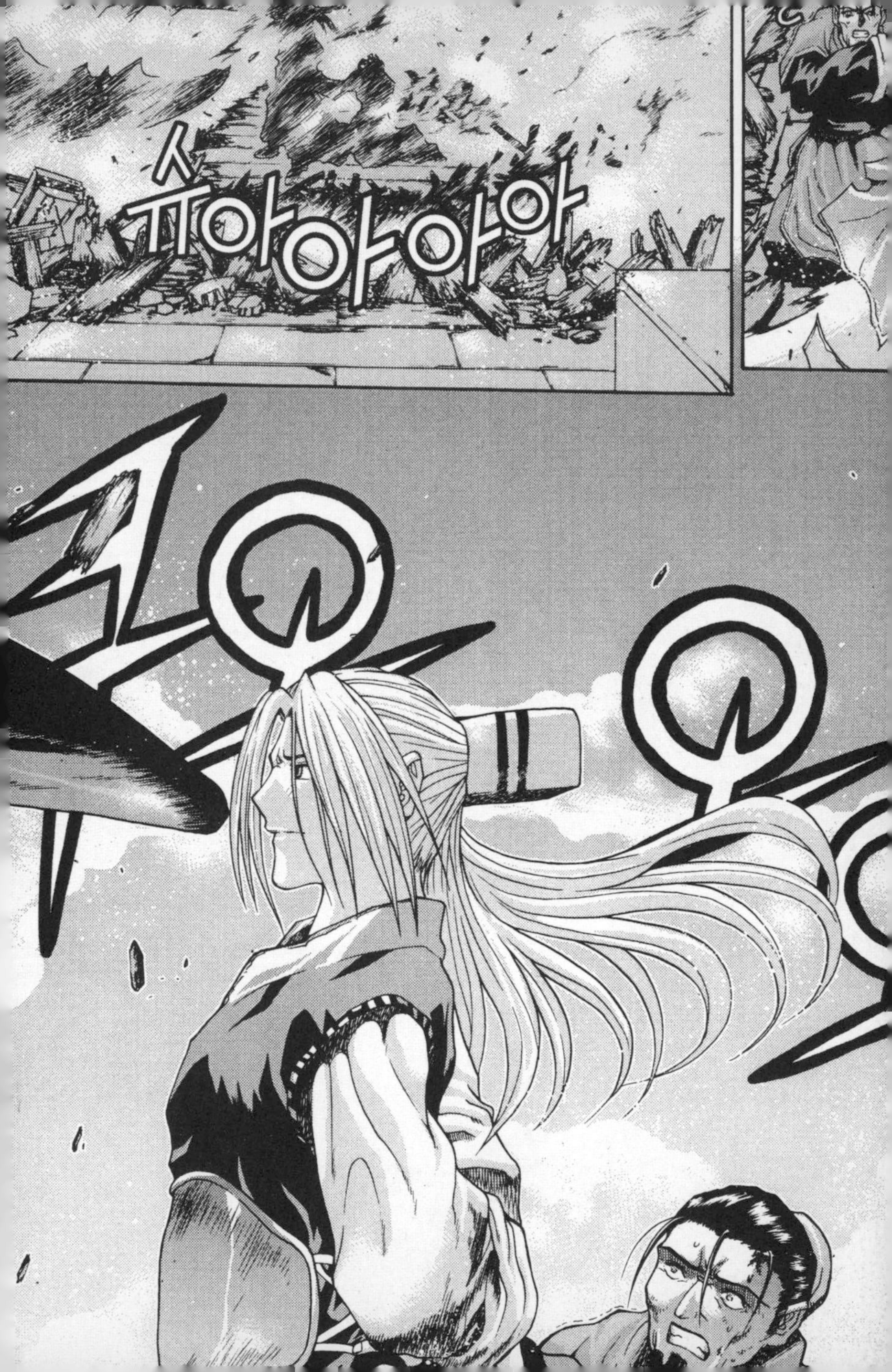
슈아아아아아
쿠오오오

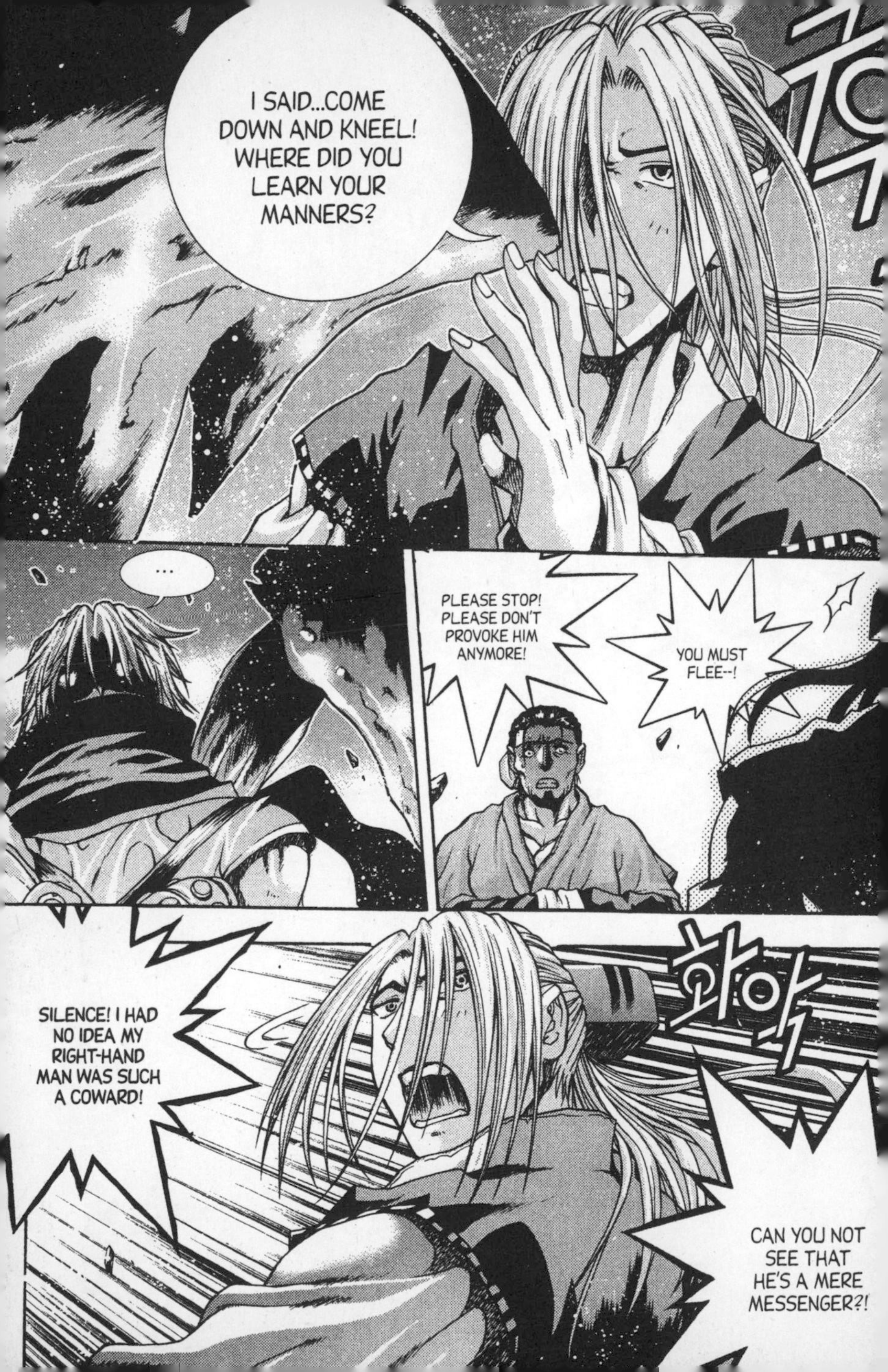
I SAID...COME DOWN AND KNEEL! WHERE DID YOU LEARN YOUR MANNERS?
...
PLEASE STOP! PLEASE DON'T PROVOKE HIM ANYMORE!
YOU MUST FLEE--!
SILENCE! I HAD NO IDEA MY RIGHT-HAND MAN WAS SUCH A COWARD!
화악
CAN YOU NOT SEE THAT HE'S A MERE MESSENGER?!

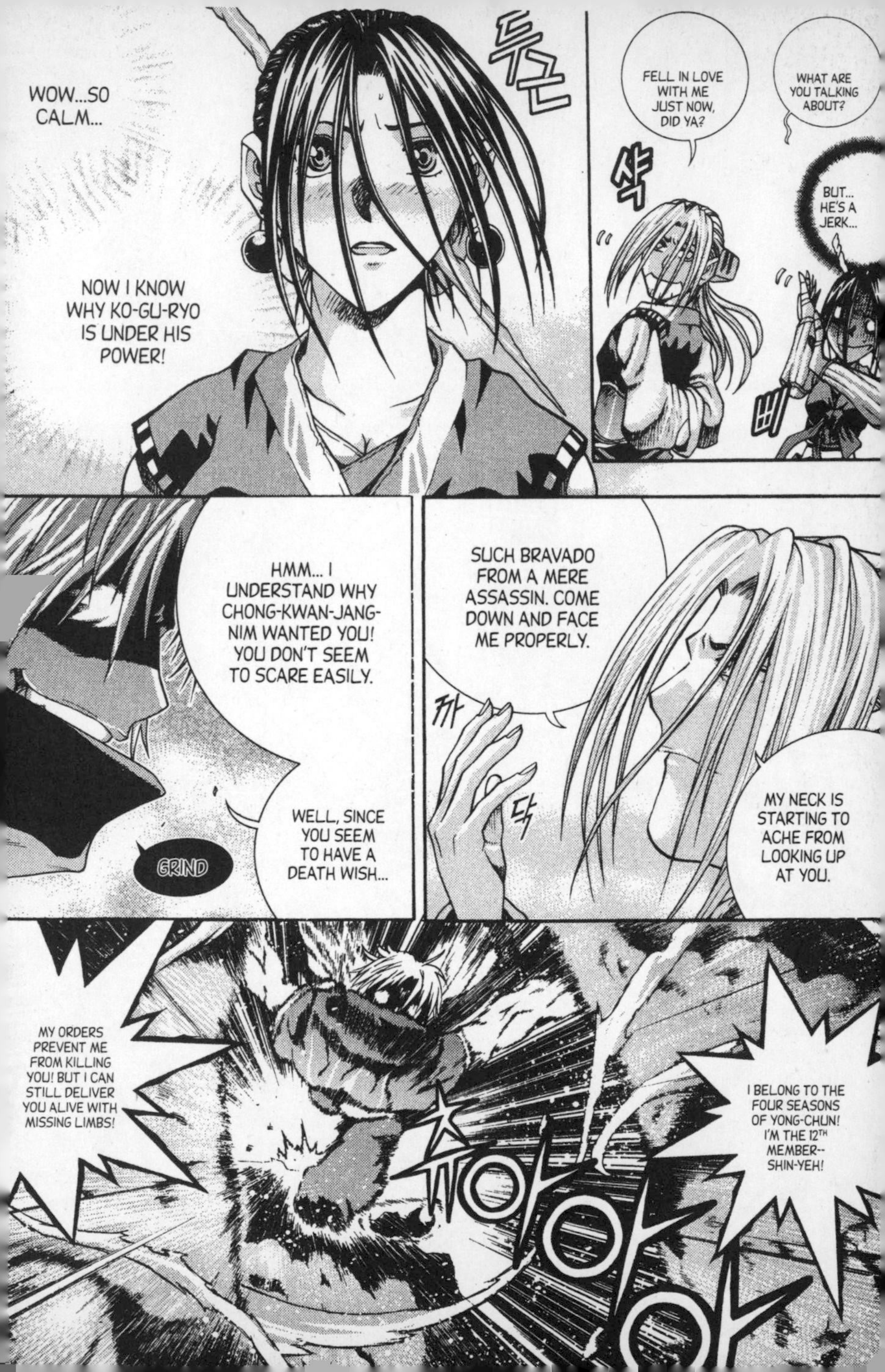
WOW...SO CALM...
NOW I KNOW WHY KO-GU-RYO IS UNDER HIS POWER!
FELL IN LOVE WITH ME JUST NOW, DID YA?
WHAT ARE YOU TALKING ABOUT?
BUT... HE'S A JERK...
HMM... I UNDERSTAND WHY CHONG-KWAN-JANG-NIM WANTED YOU! YOU DON'T SEEM TO SCARE EASILY.
GRIND
WELL, SINCE YOU SEEM TO HAVE A DEATH WISH...
SUCH BRAVADO FROM A MERE ASSASSIN. COME DOWN AND FACE ME PROPERLY.
MY NECK IS STARTING TO ACHE FROM LOOKING UP AT YOU.
MY ORDERS PREVENT ME FROM KILLING YOU! BUT I CAN STILL DELIVER YOU ALIVE WITH MISSING LIMBS!
I BELONG TO THE FOUR SEASONS OF YONG-CHUN! I'M THE 12TH MEMBER-- SHIN-YEH!

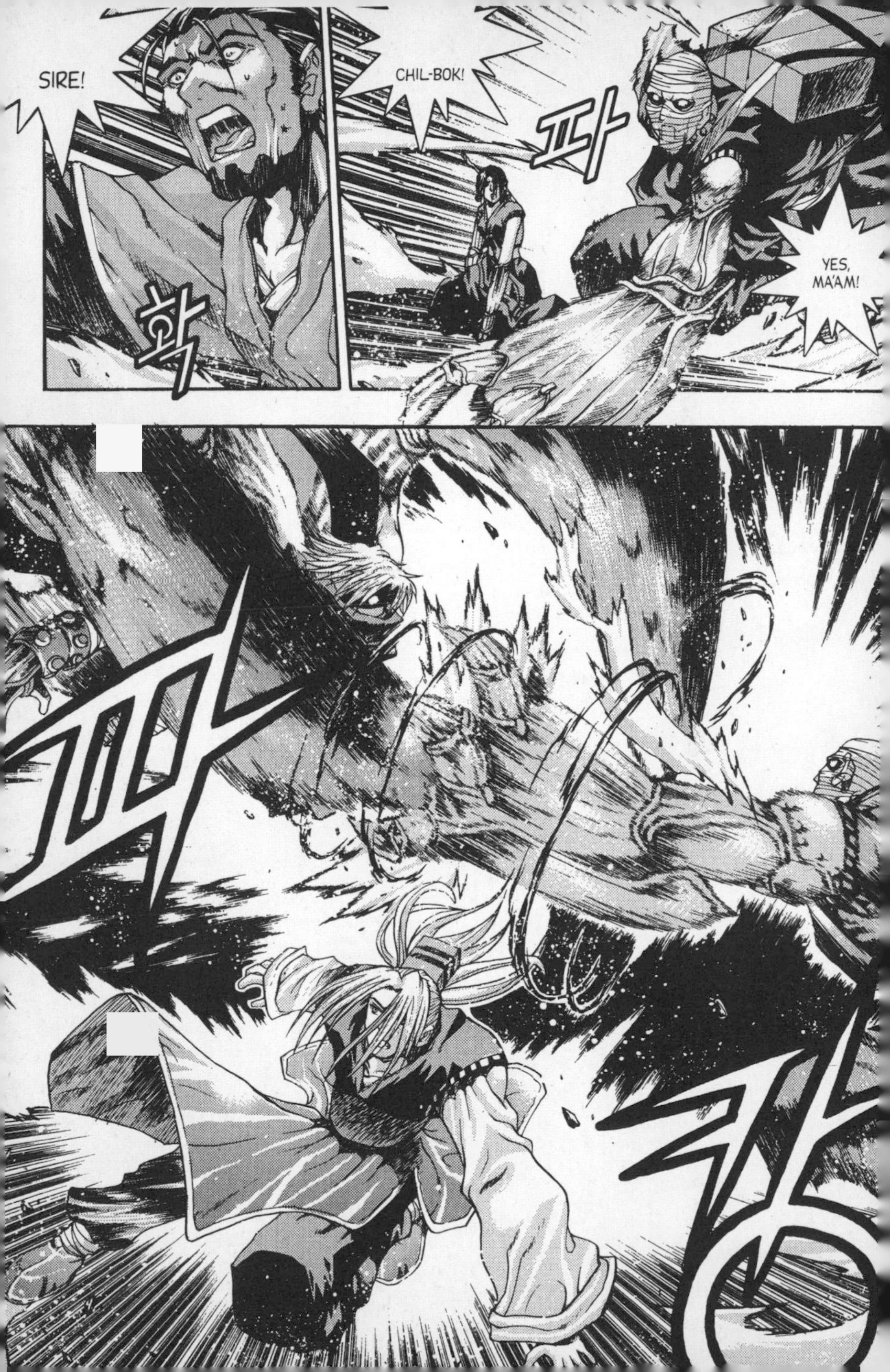
SIRE!
CHIL-BOK!
YES, MA'AM!

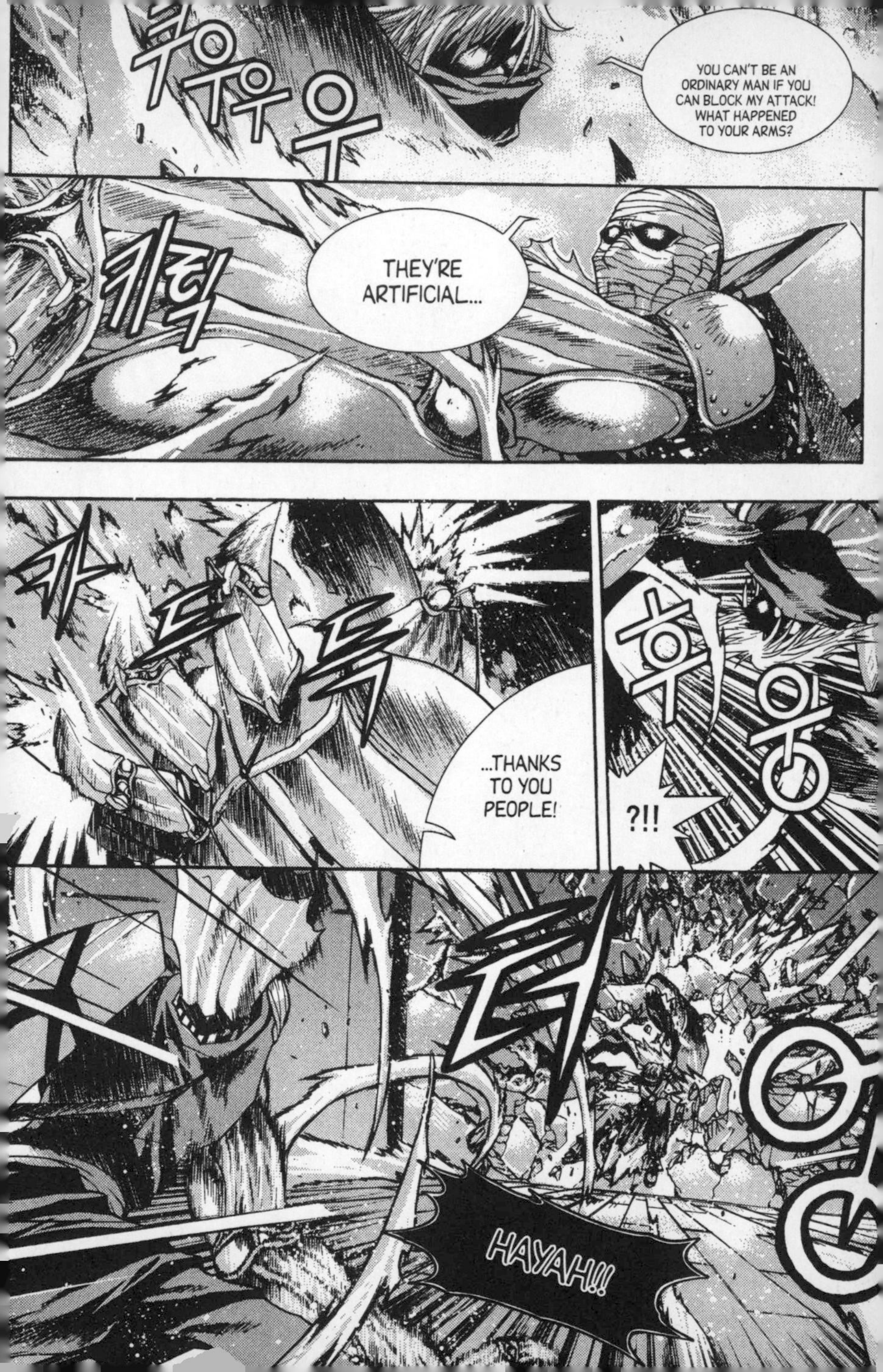
YOU CAN'T BE AN ORDINARY MAN IF YOU CAN BLOCK MY ATTACK! WHAT HAPPENED TO YOUR ARMS?
THEY'RE ARTIFICIAL...
...THANKS TO YOU PEOPLE!
?!!
HAYAH!!

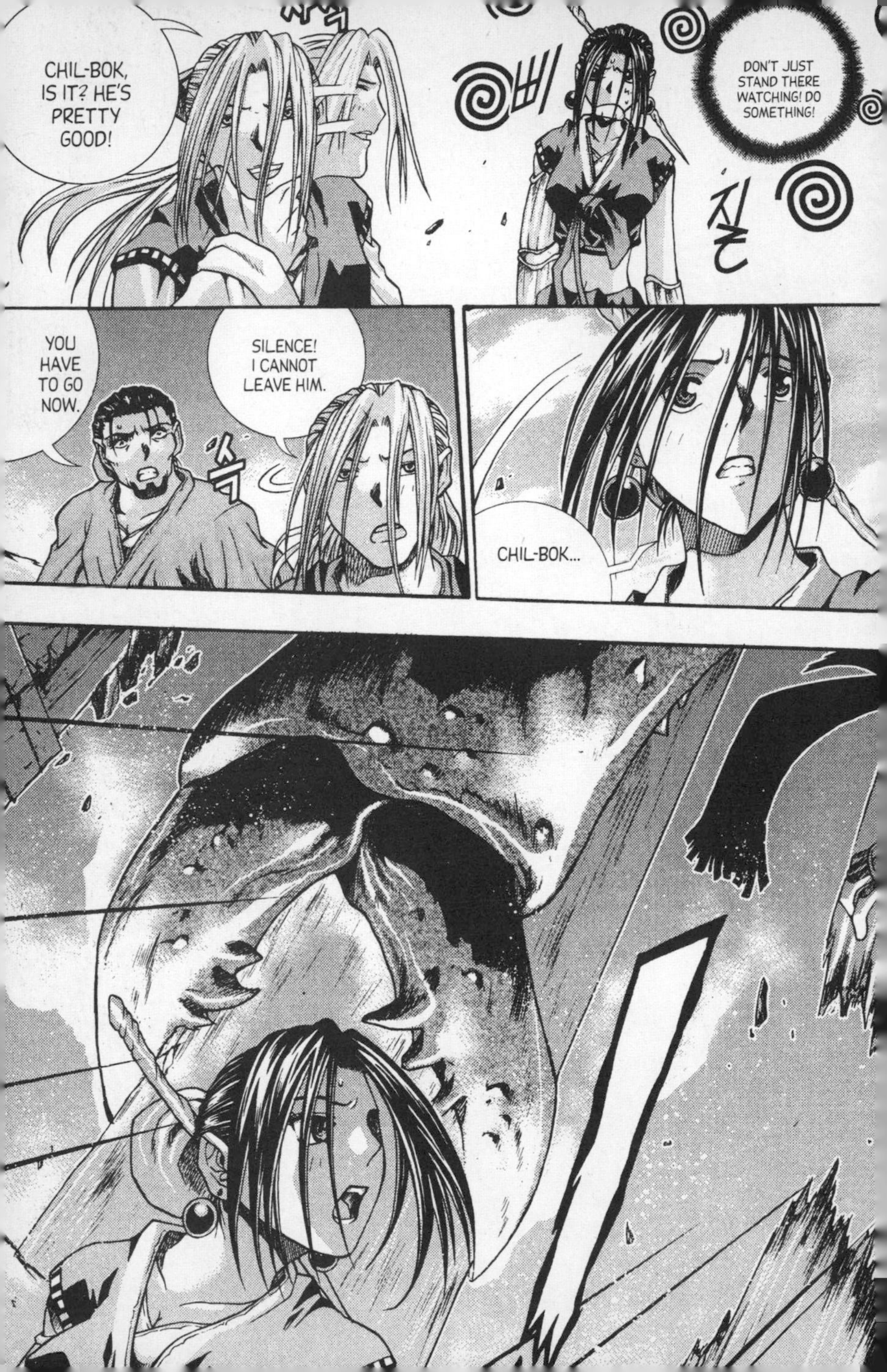
CHIL-BOK, IS IT? HE'S PRETTY GOOD!
DON'T JUST STAND THERE WATCHING! DO SOMETHING!
질끈
YOU HAVE TO GO NOW.
SILENCE! I CANNOT LEAVE HIM.
CHIL-BOK...

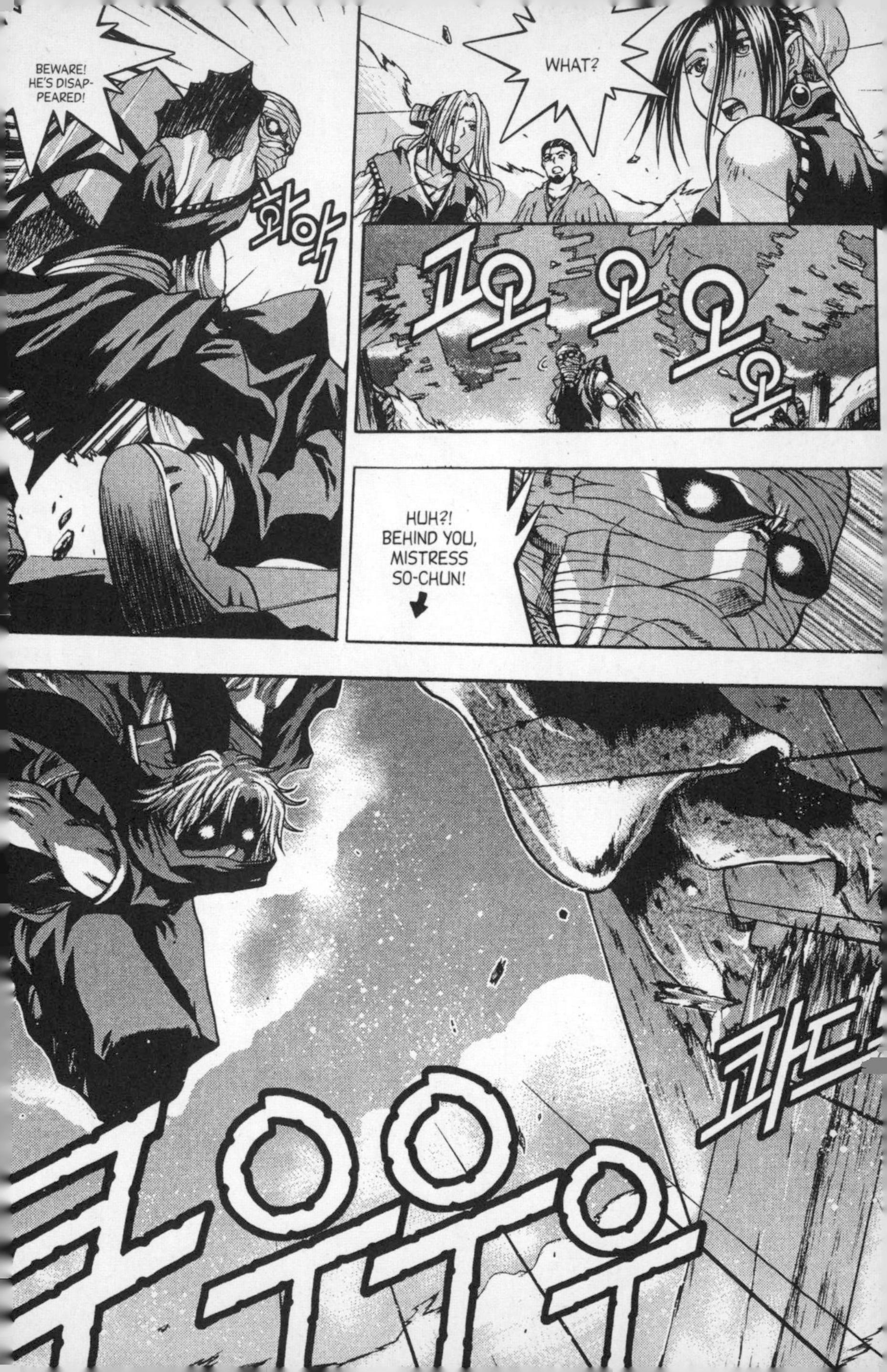
BEWARE! HE'S DISAP-PEARED!
화악
WHAT?
고오오오오
HUH?! BEHIND YOU, MISTRESS SO-CHUN!

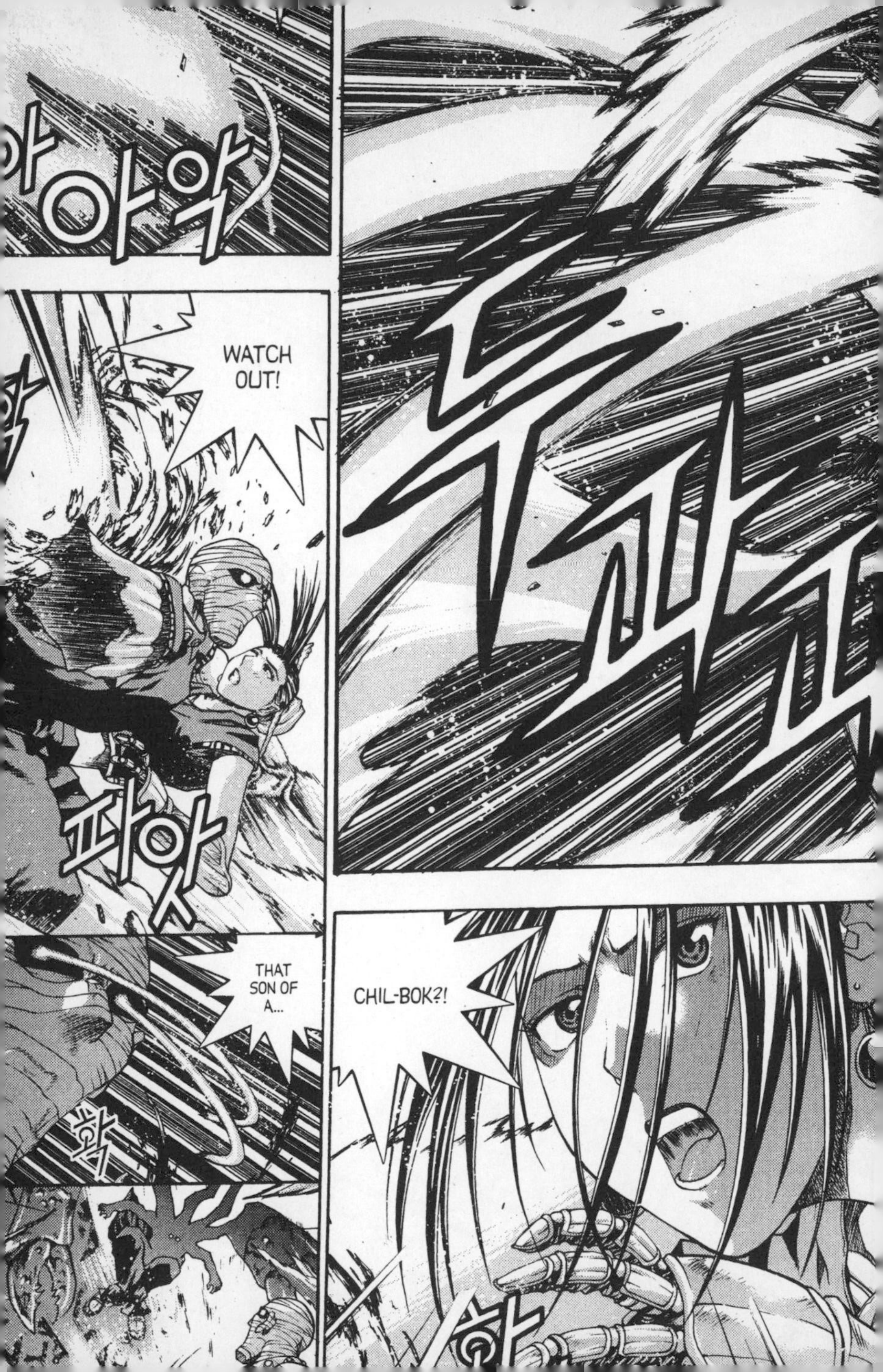
WATCH OUT!
THAT SON OF A...
CHIL-BOK?!

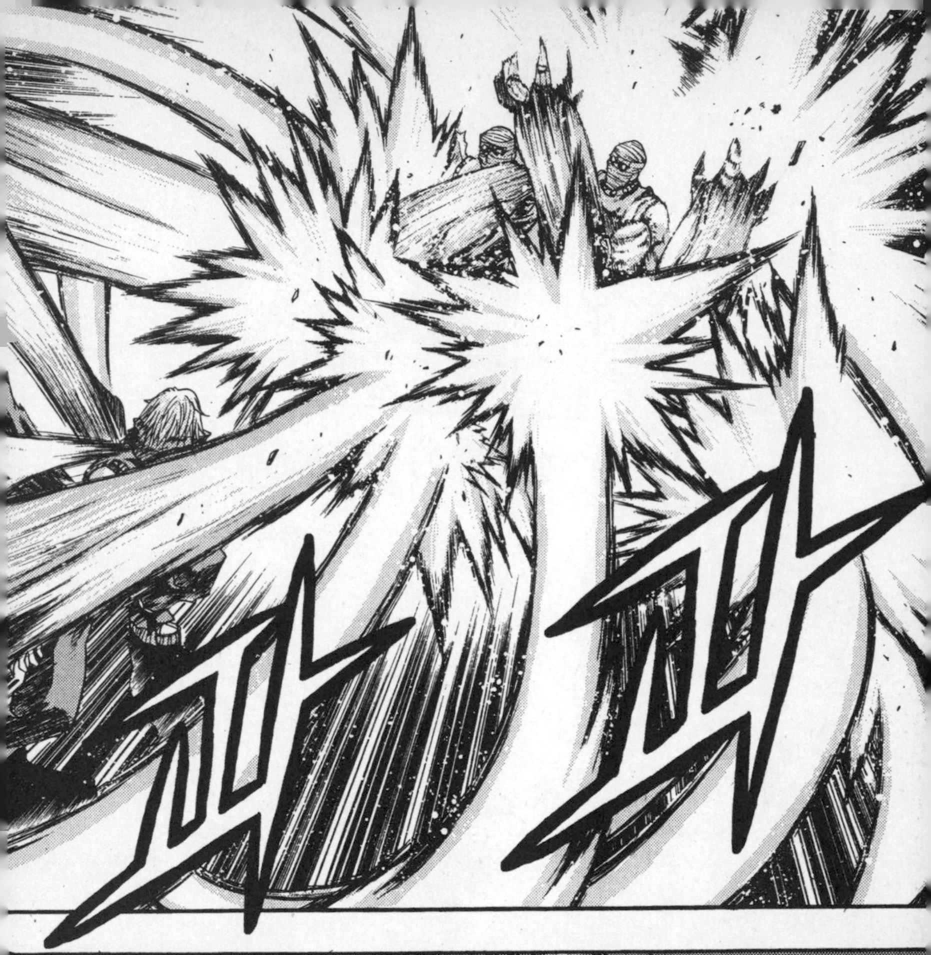
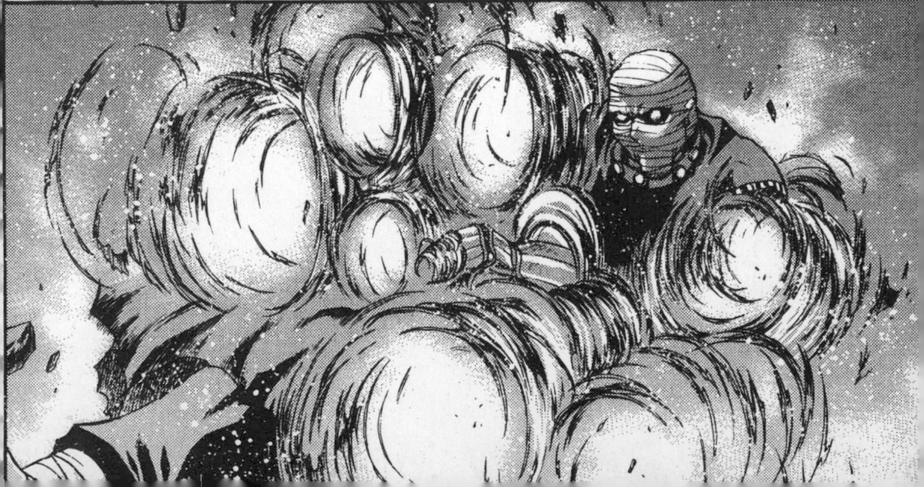

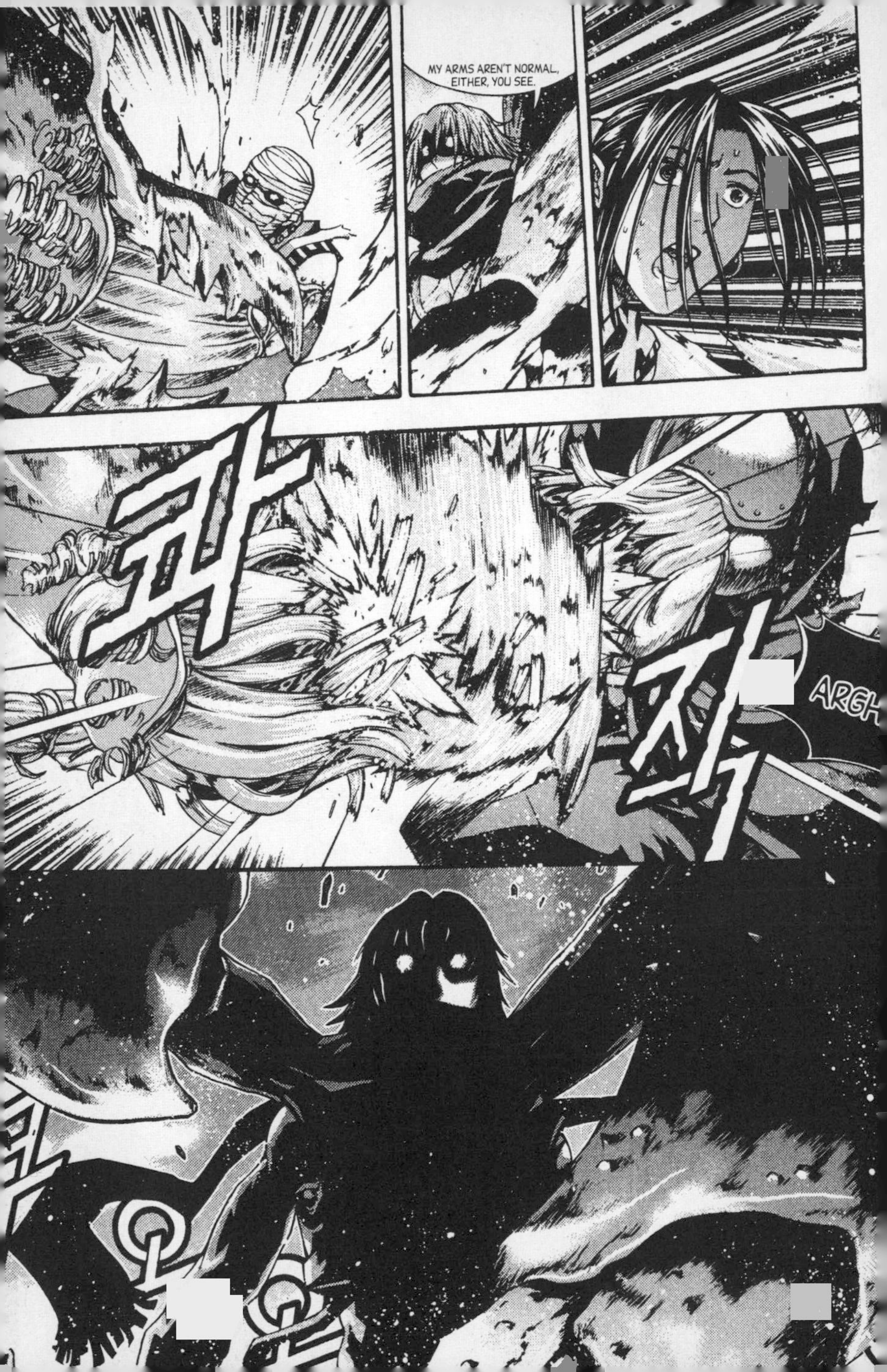
MY ARMS AREN'T NORMAL, EITHER, YOU SEE.
파
자
ARGH

CHAPTER 101
JUST TELL ME WHAT YOU WANT!

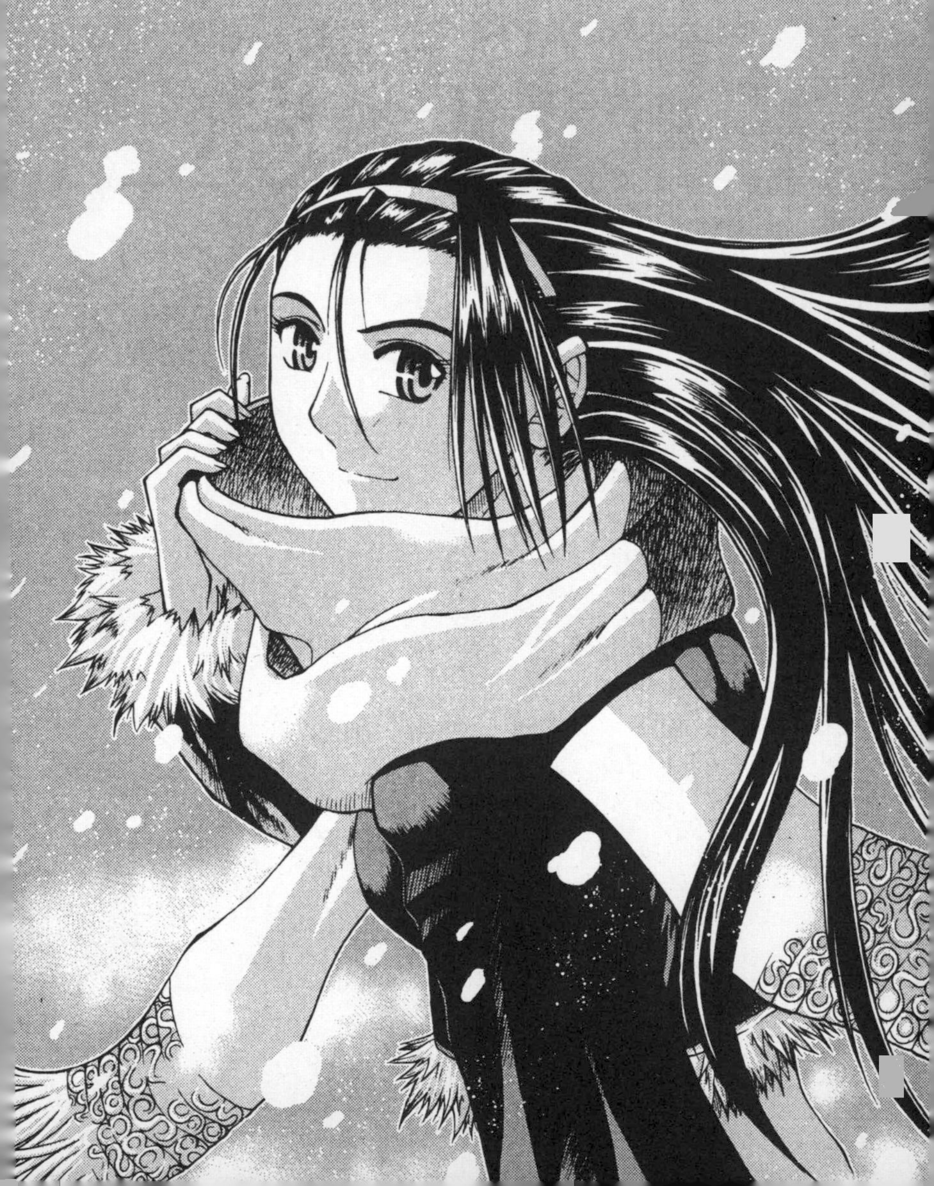

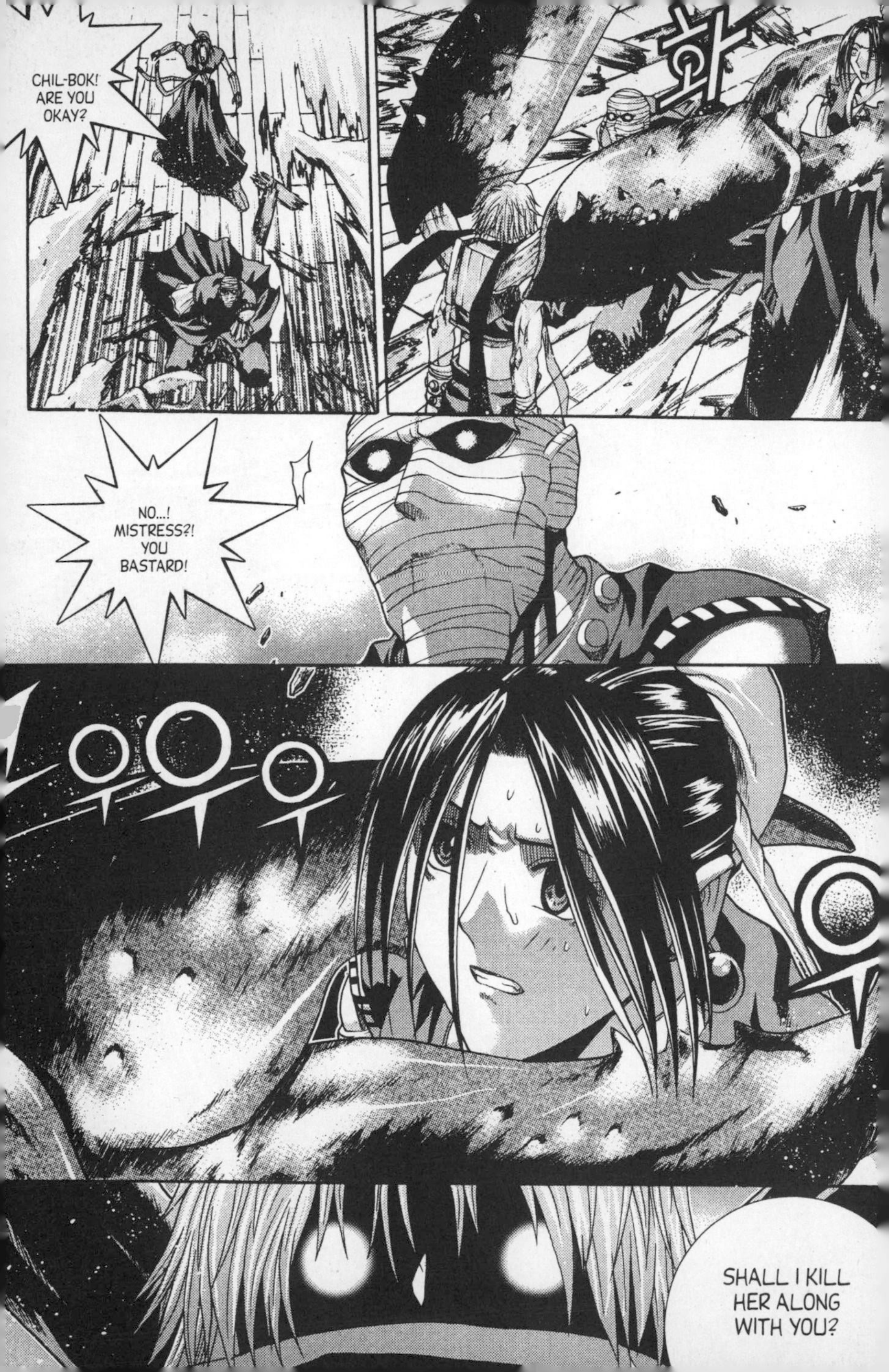

CHIL-BOK! ARE YOU OKAY?
NO...! MISTRESS?! YOU BASTARD!
SHALL I KILL HER ALONG WITH YOU?

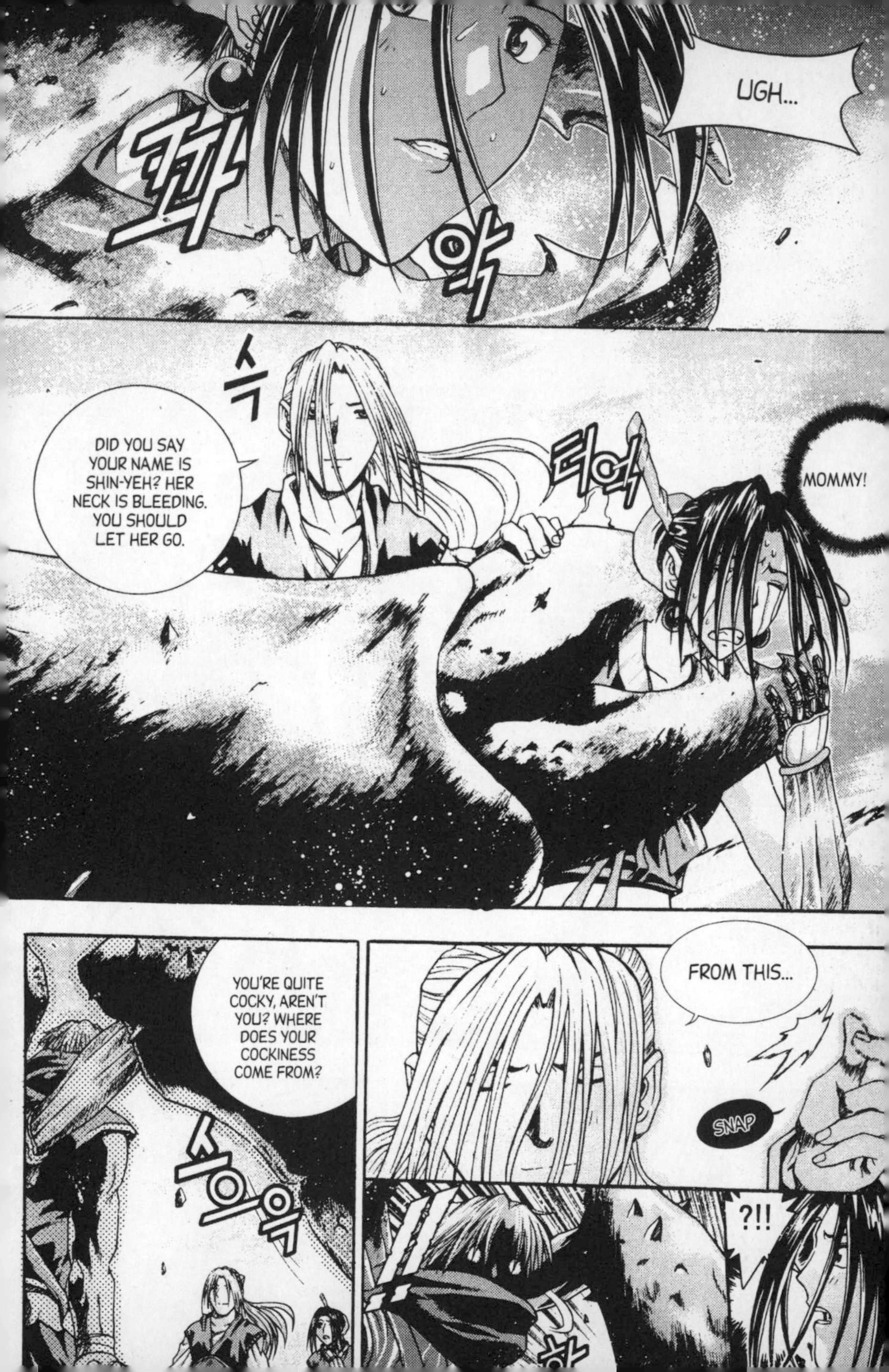
UGH...
DID YOU SAY YOUR NAME IS SHIN-YEH? HER NECK IS BLEEDING. YOU SHOULD LET HER GO.
MOMMY!
YOU'RE QUITE COCKY, AREN'T YOU? WHERE DOES YOUR COCKINESS COME FROM?
FROM THIS...
SNAP
?!!

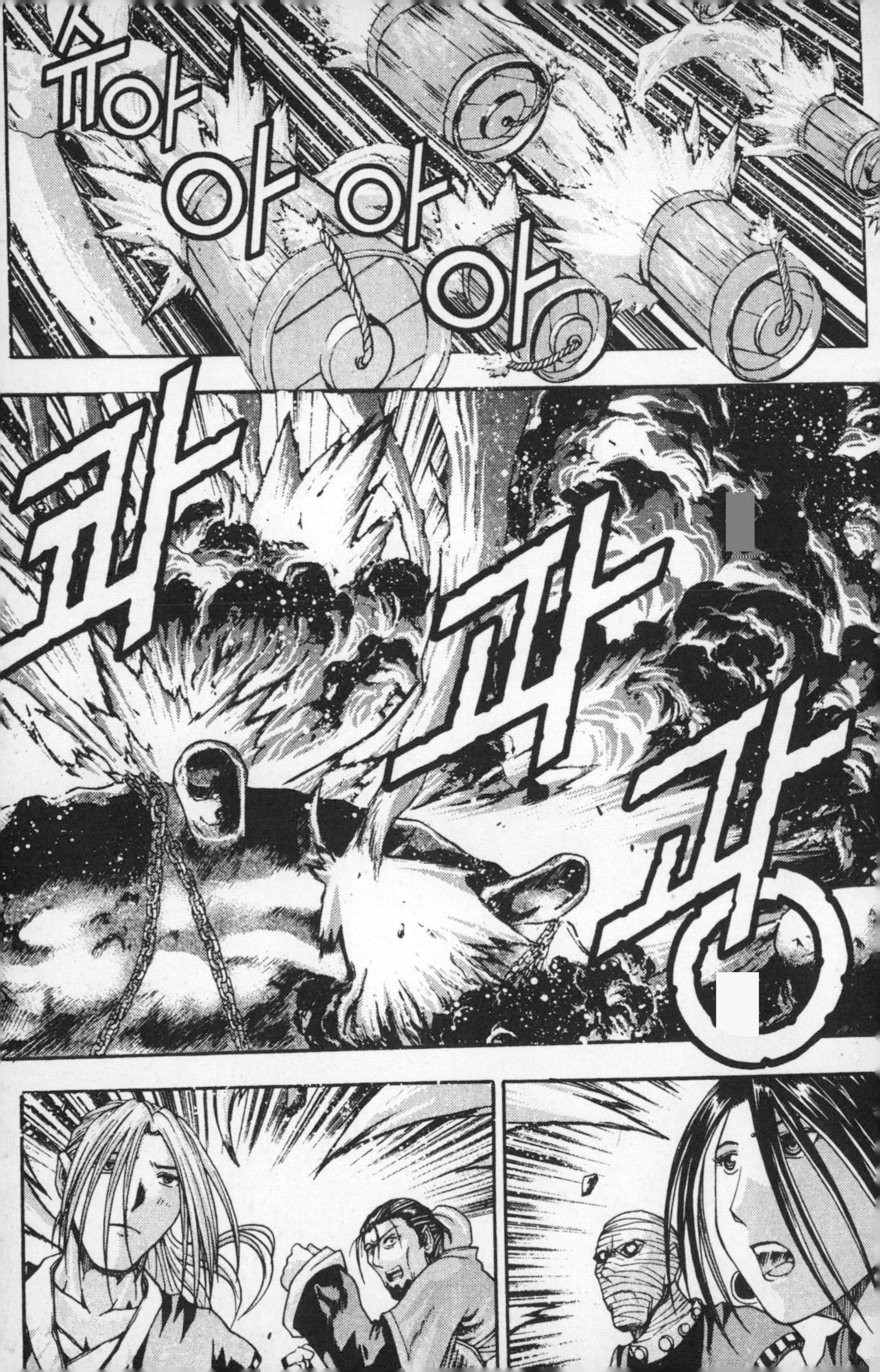

슈아아아아
콰과광

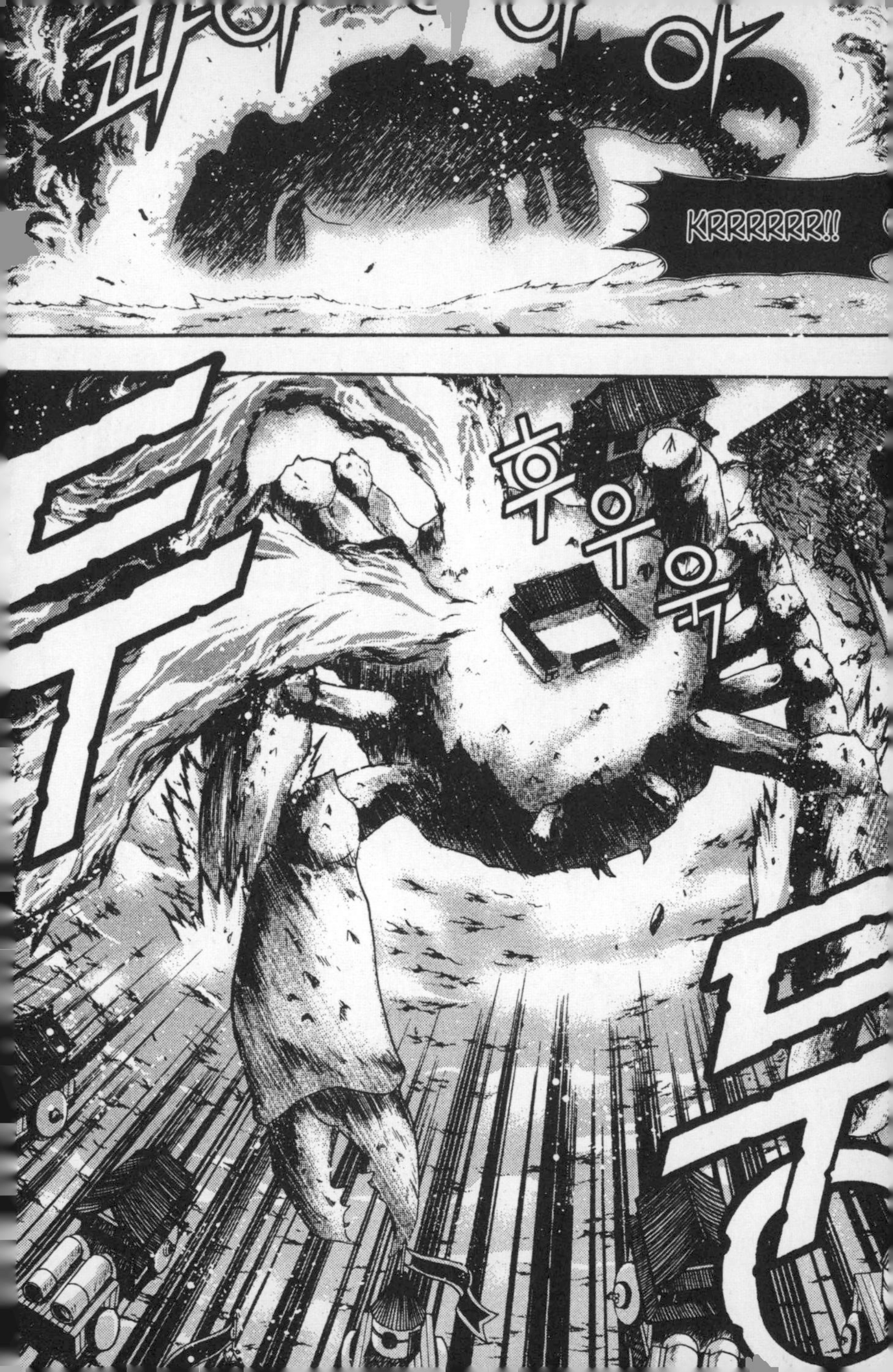
KRRRRRR!!
후우웅

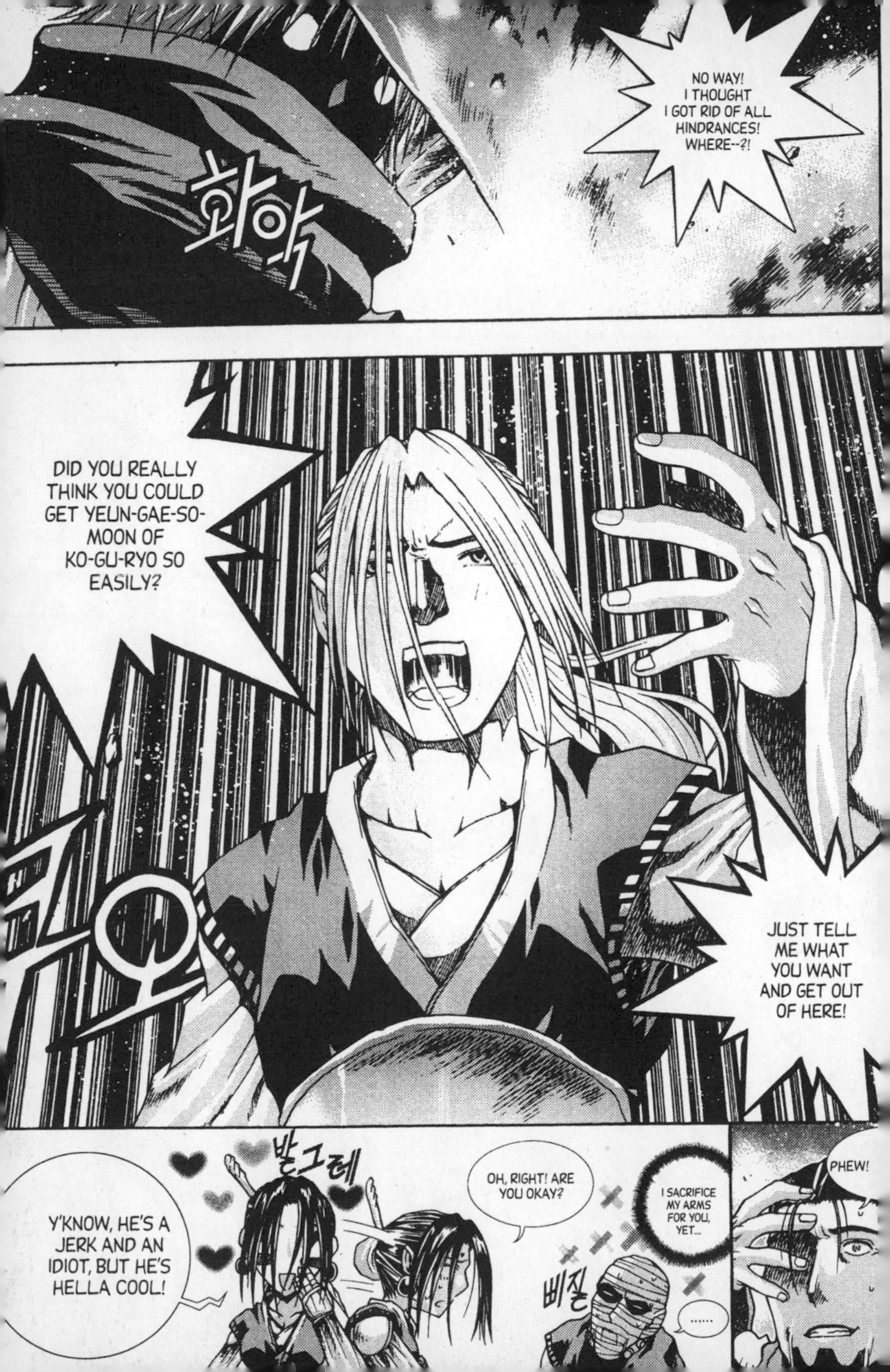
화악
NO WAY! I THOUGHT I GOT RID OF ALL HINDRANCES! WHERE--?!
DID YOU REALLY THINK YOU COULD GET YEUN-GAE-SO-MOON OF KO-GU-RYO SO EASILY?
JUST TELL ME WHAT YOU WANT AND GET OUT OF HERE!
Y'KNOW, HE'S A JERK AND AN IDIOT, BUT HE'S HELLA COOL!
발그레
OH, RIGHT! ARE YOU OKAY?
I SACRIFICE MY ARMS FOR YOU, YET...
삐질
......
PHEW!

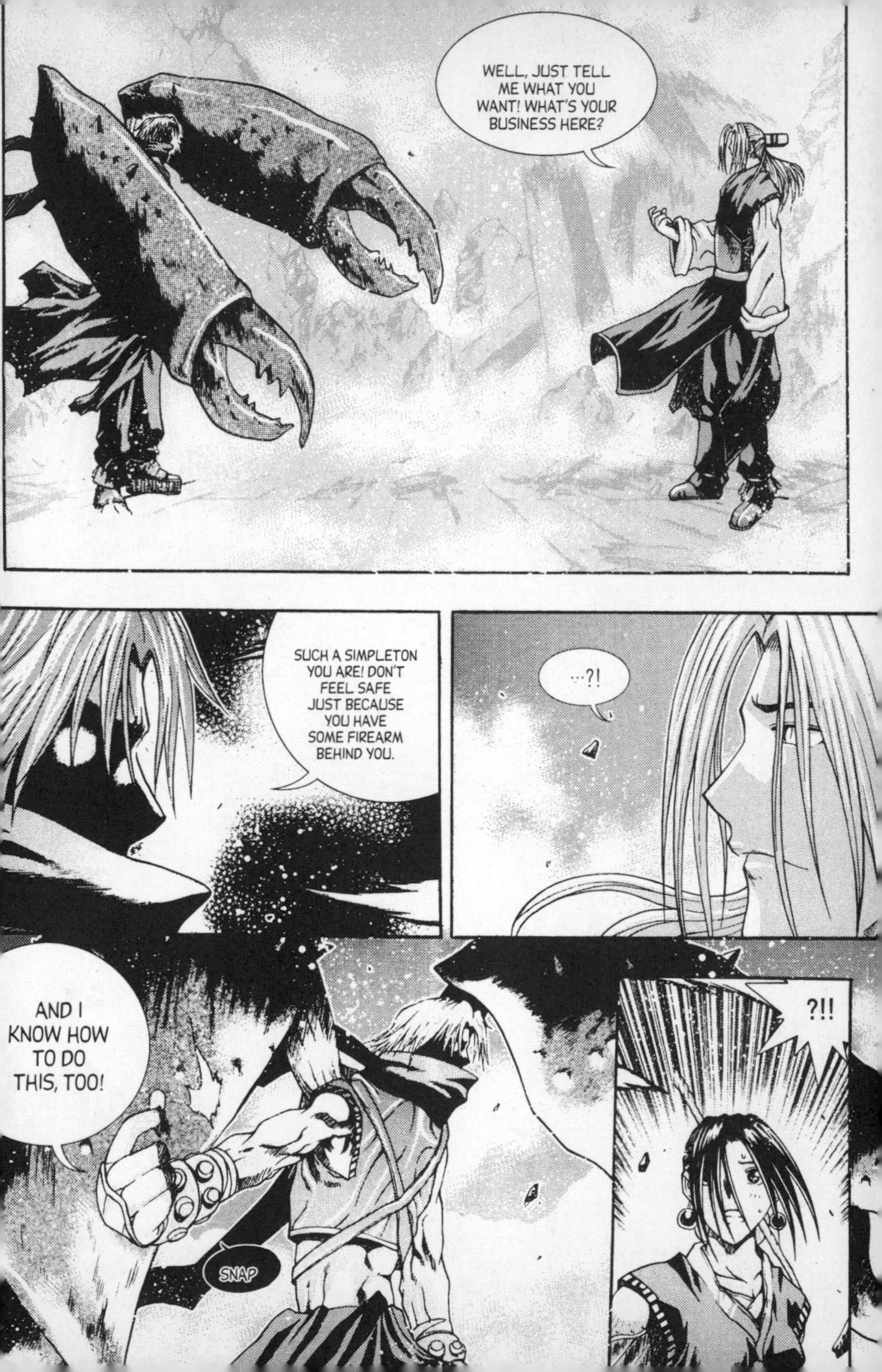
WELL, JUST TELL ME WHAT YOU WANT! WHAT'S YOUR BUSINESS HERE?
SUCH A SIMPLETON YOU ARE! DON'T FEEL SAFE JUST BECAUSE YOU HAVE SOME FIREARM BEHIND YOU.
...?!
AND I KNOW HOW TO DO THIS, TOO!
SNAP
?!!

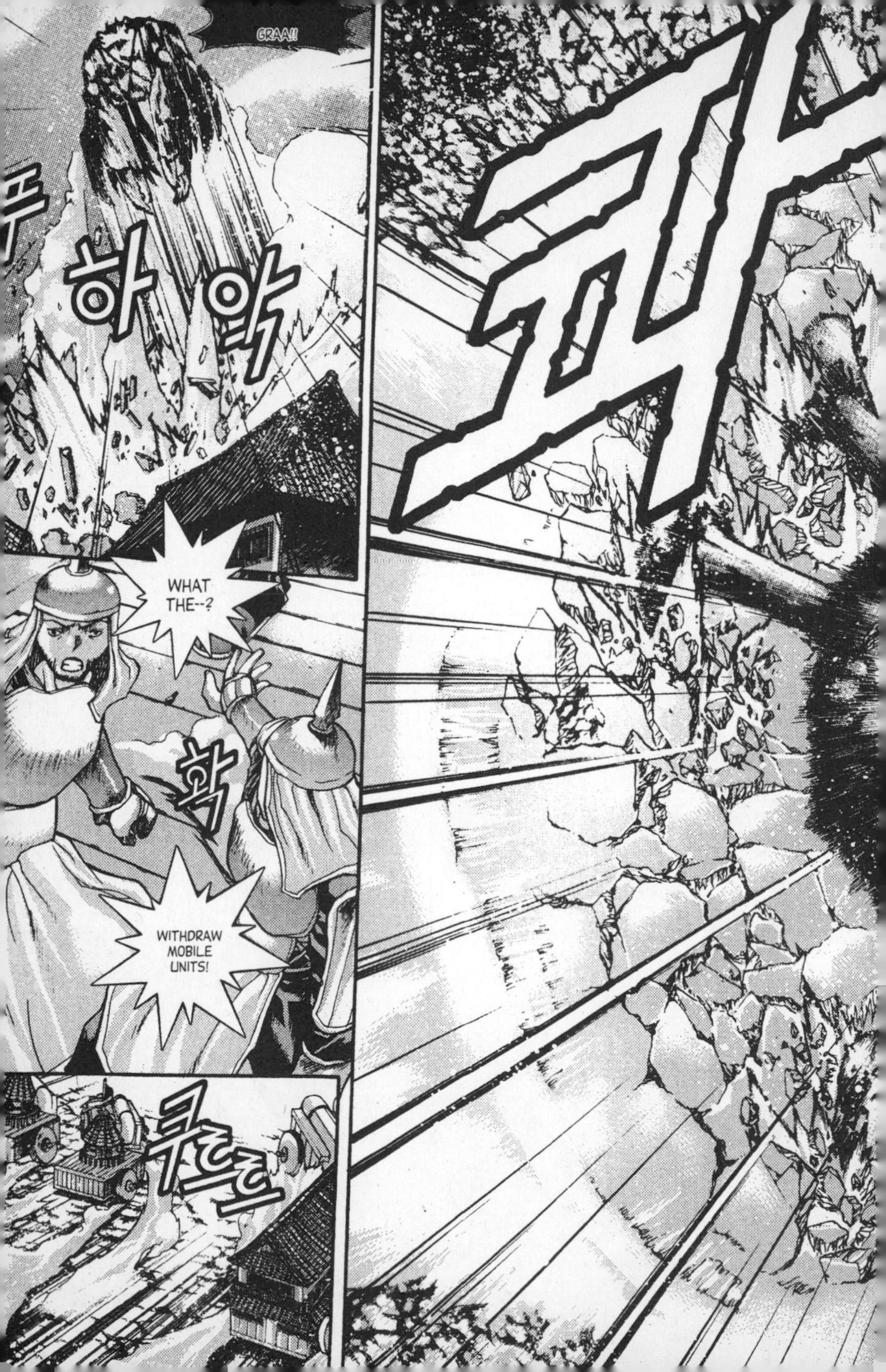
GRAA!!
WHAT THE--?
WITHDRAW MOBILE UNITS!

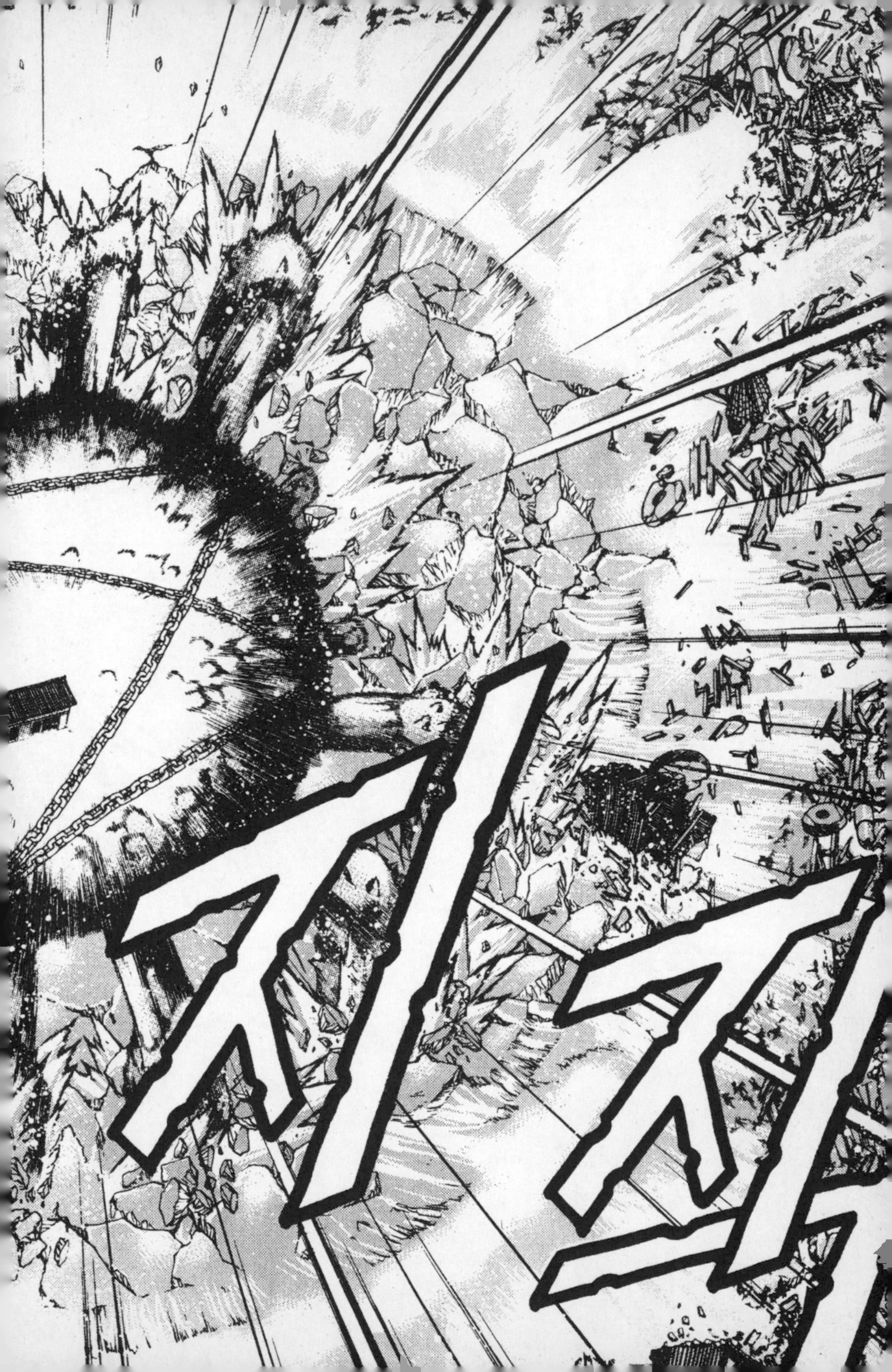

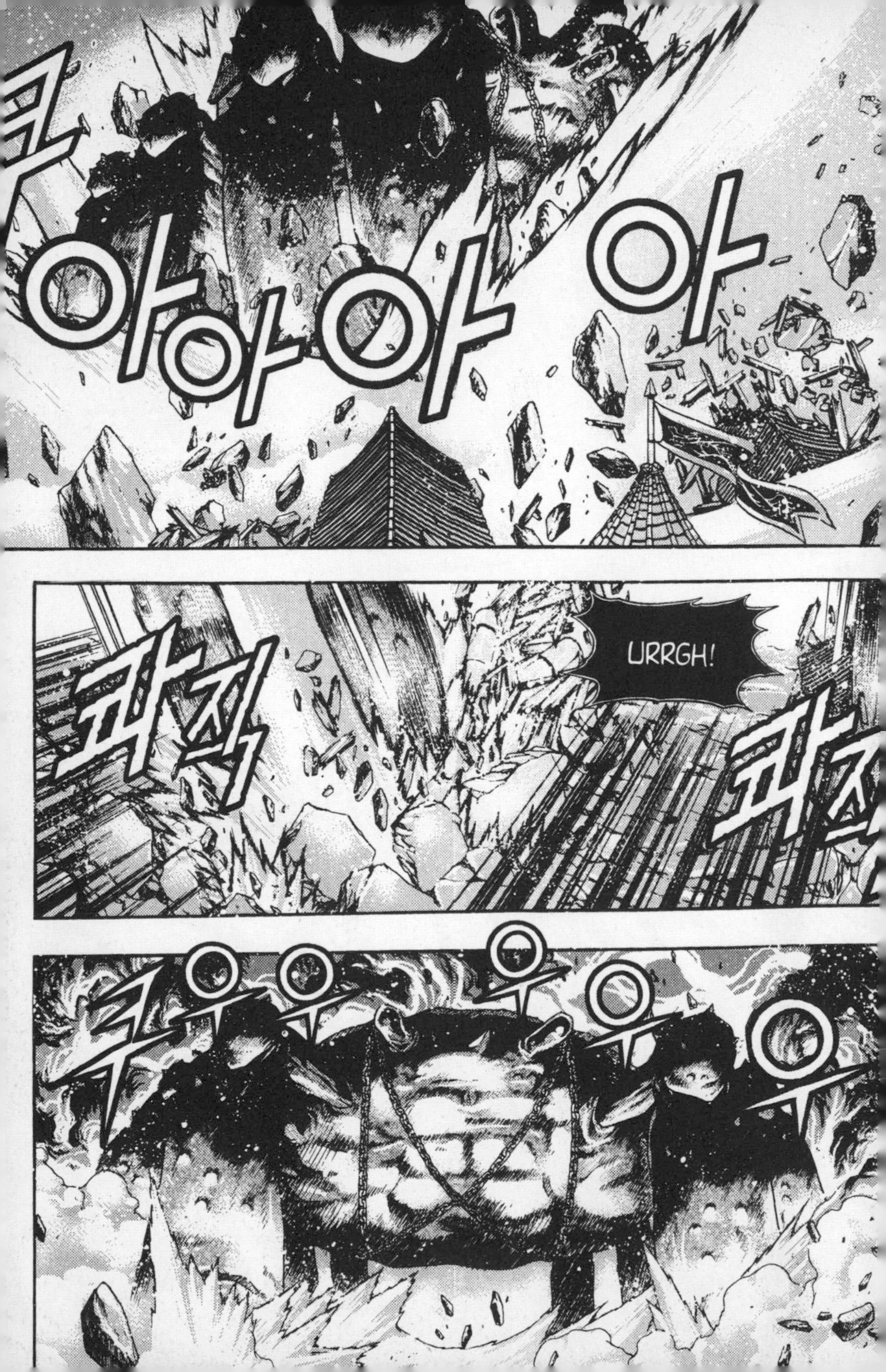
파직
URRGH!

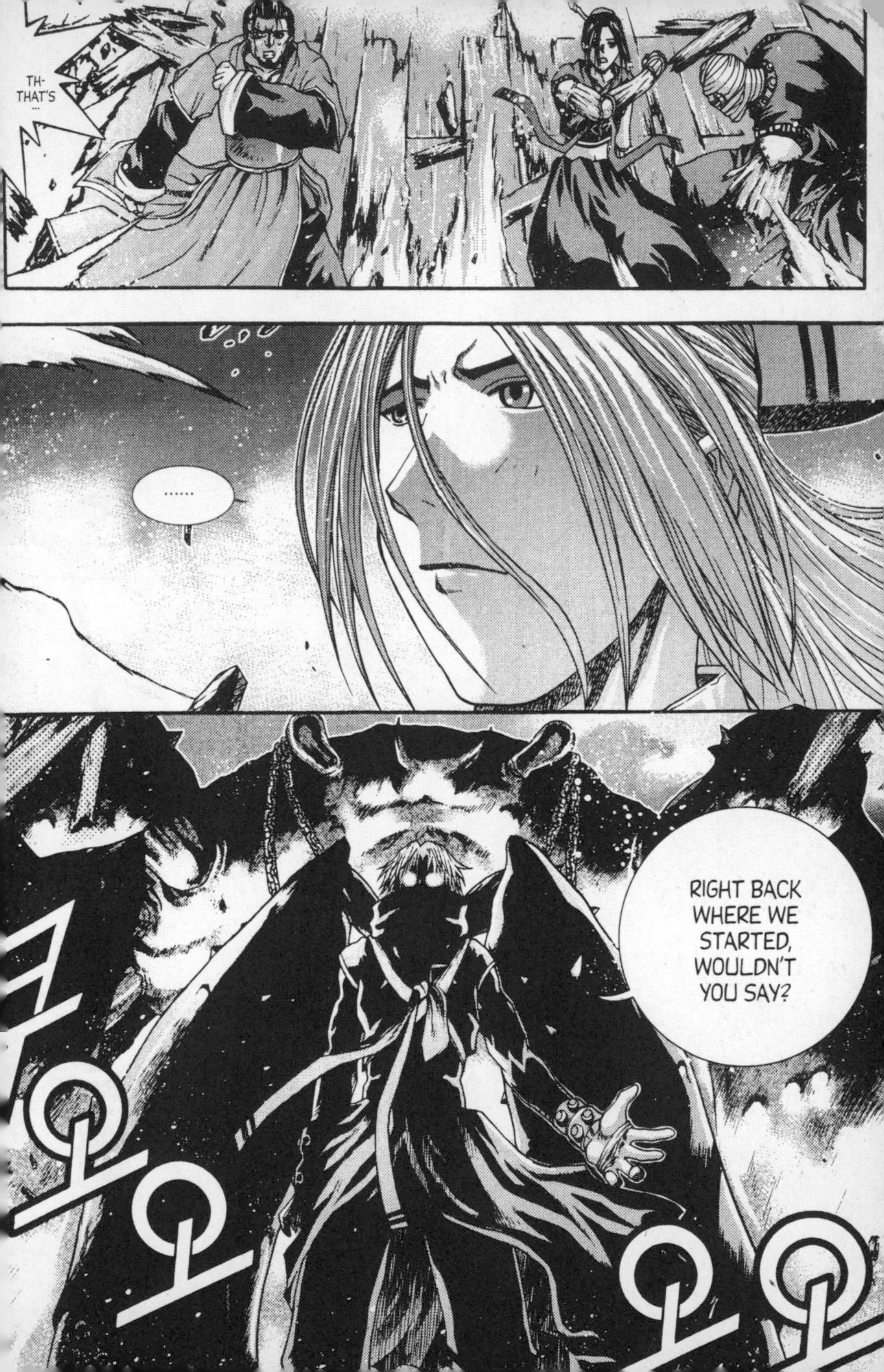
TH-
THAT'S
...
......
RIGHT BACK WHERE WE STARTED, WOULDN'T YOU SAY?

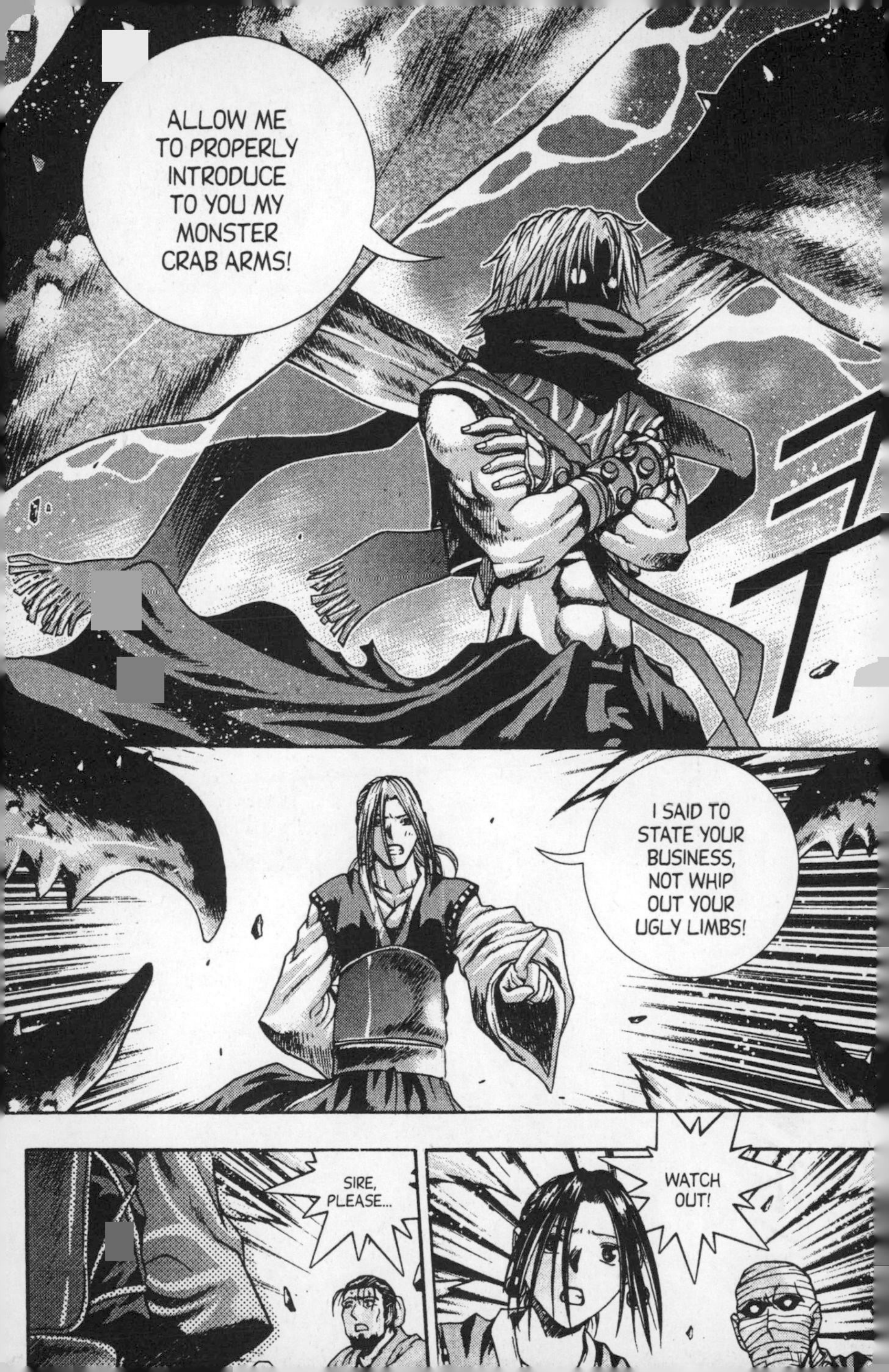
ALLOW ME TO PROPERLY INTRODUCE TO YOU MY MONSTER CRAB ARMS!
I SAID TO STATE YOUR BUSINESS, NOT WHIP OUT YOUR UGLY LIMBS!
SIRE, PLEASE...
WATCH OUT!

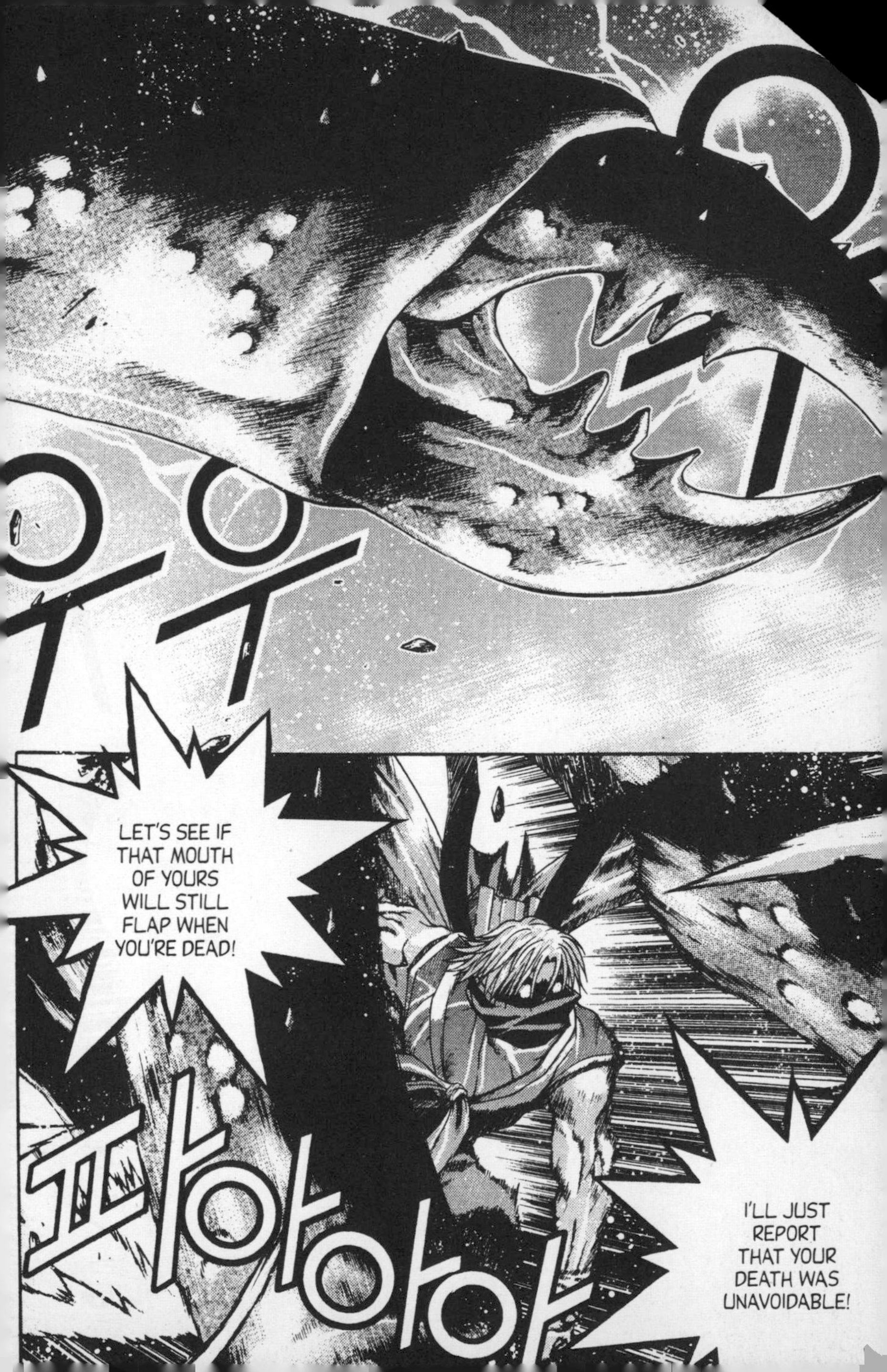
LET'S SEE IF THAT MOUTH OF YOURS WILL STILL FLAP WHEN YOU'RE DEAD!
I'LL JUST REPORT THAT YOUR DEATH WAS UNAVOIDABLE!

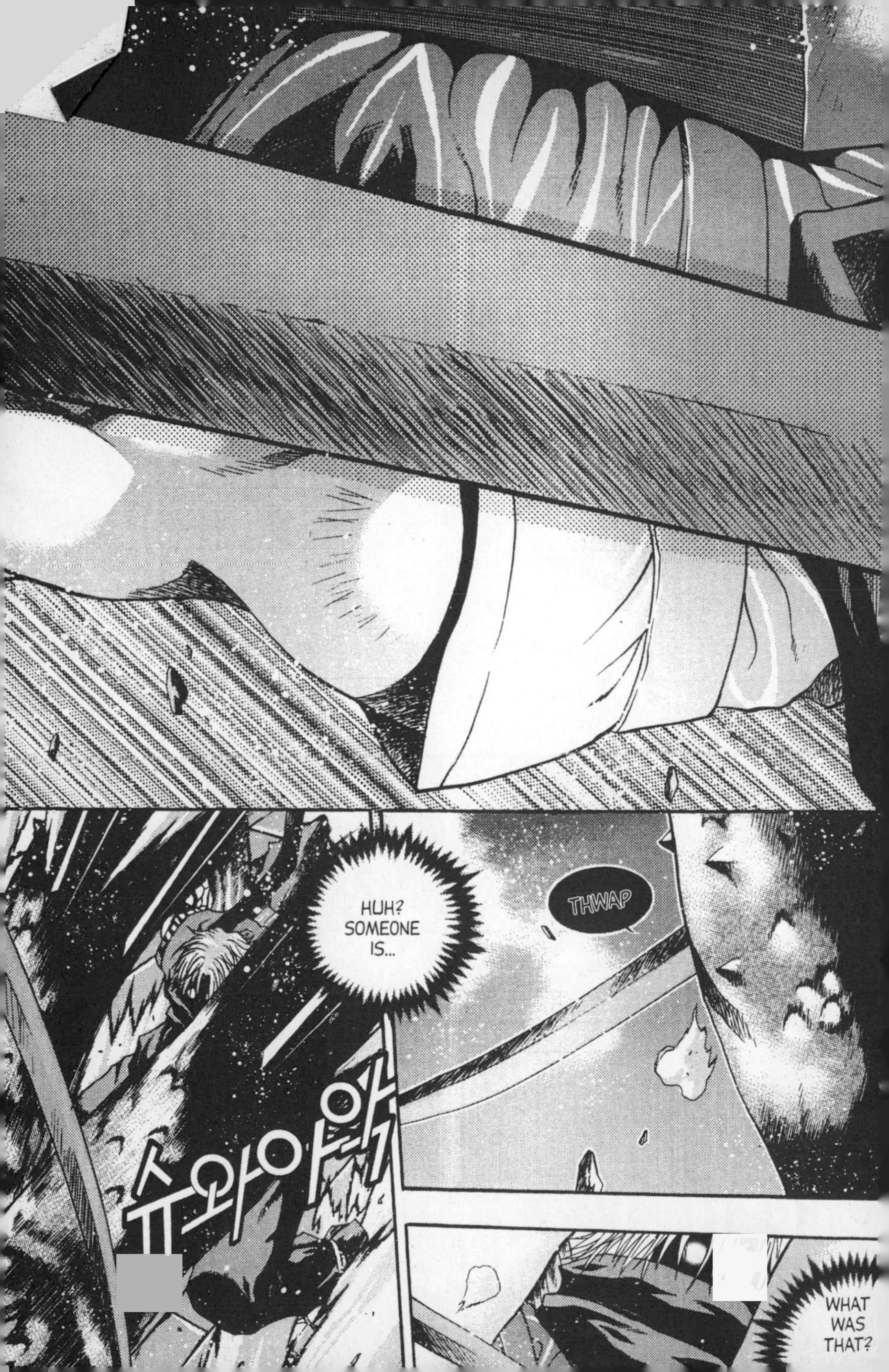
HUH? SOMEONE IS...
THWAP
WHAT WAS THAT?

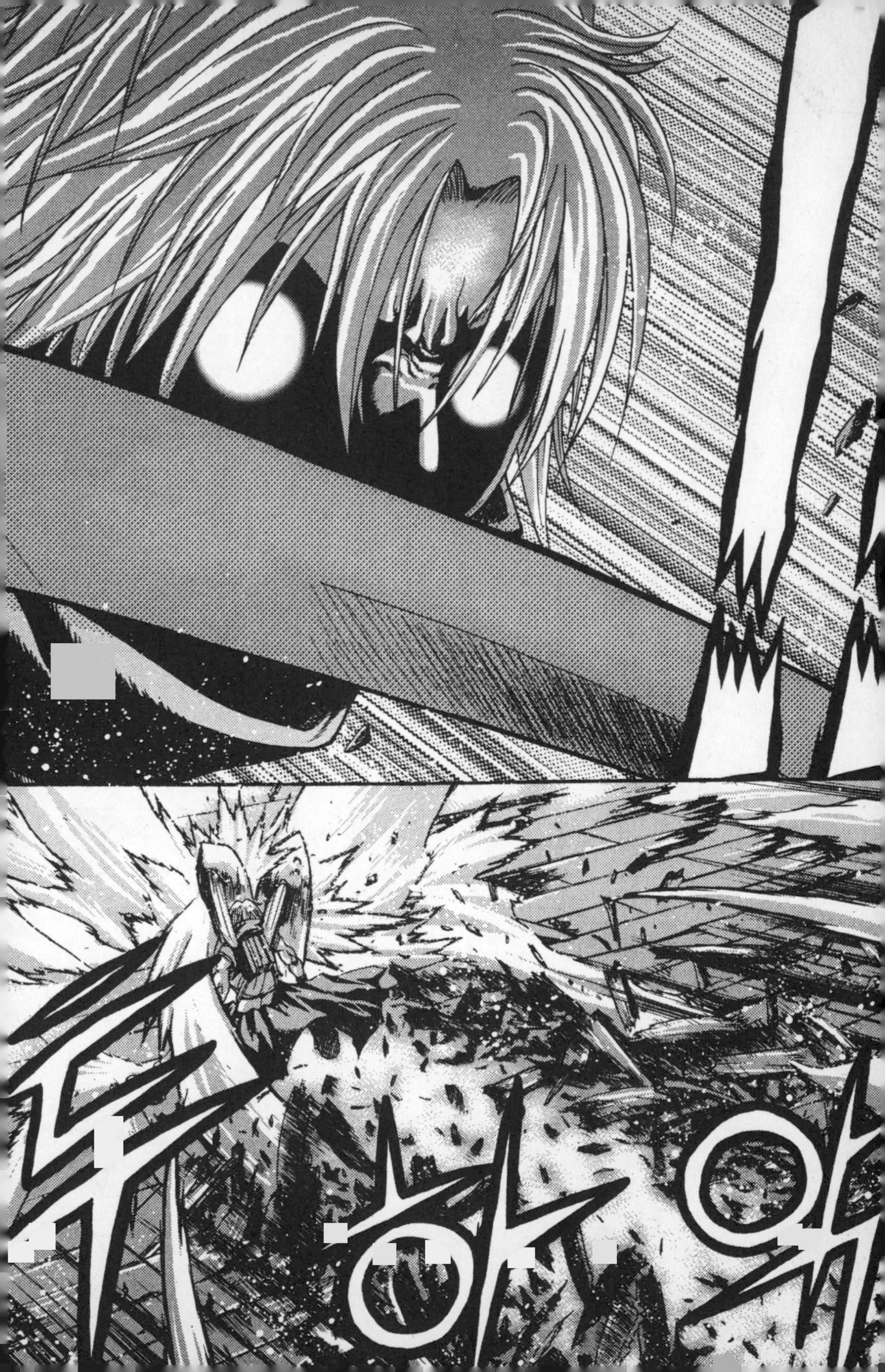

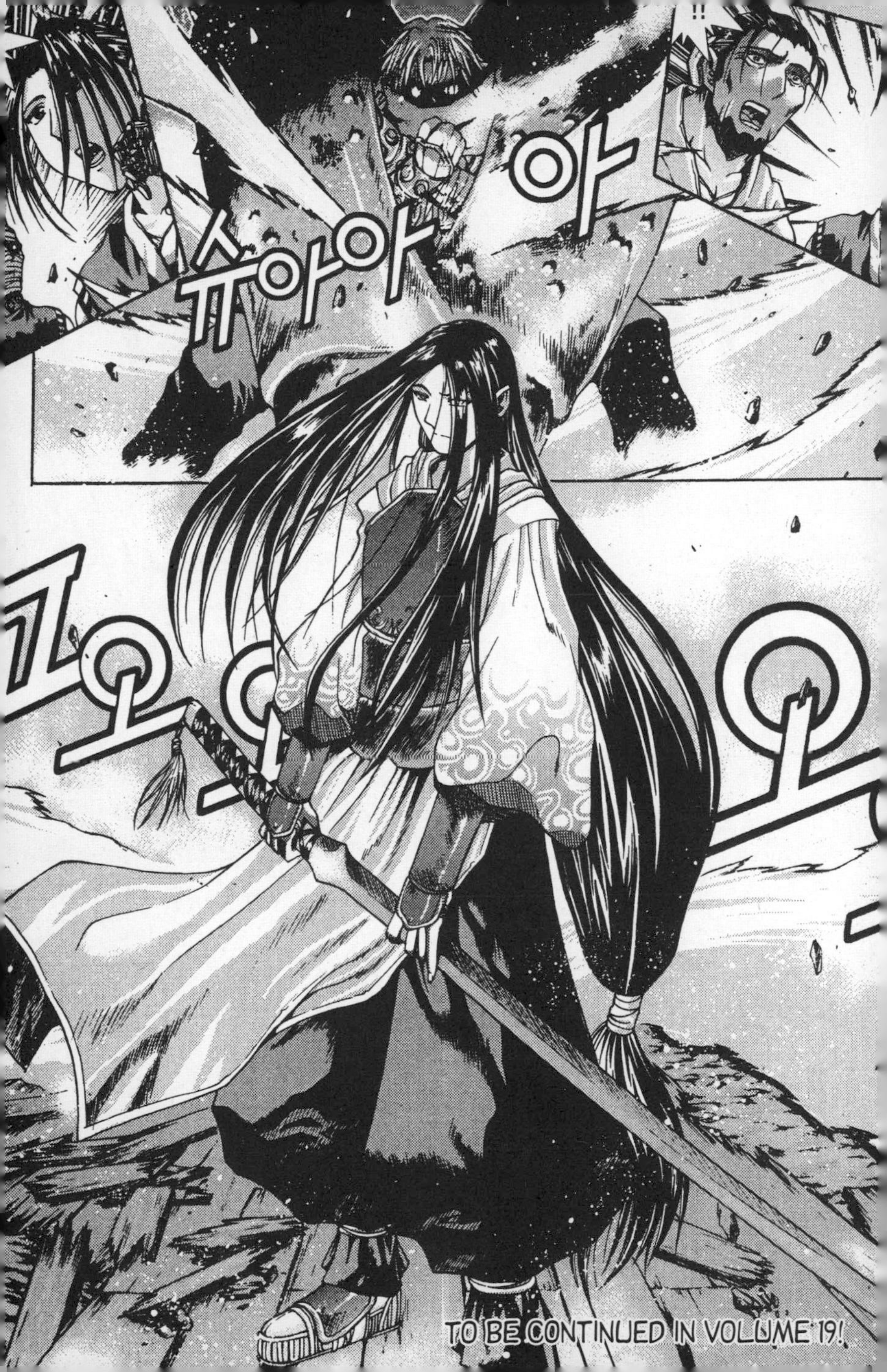
!!
고오오오
TO BE CONTINUED IN VOLUME 19!